MANAGERIAL ETHICS

*Managing the Psychology
of Morality*

MANAGERIAL ETHICS

ETHICS

Managing the Psychology of Morality

Edited by

Marshall Schminke

University of Central Florida,
Orlando, U.S.A.

Routledge
Taylor & Francis Group

NEW YORK AND LONDON

Routledge
Taylor & Francis Group
711 Third Avenue,
New York, NY 10017

Routledge
Taylor & Francis Group
27 Church Road
Hove, East Sussex BN3 2FA,UK

First issued in paperback 2014

Routledge is an imprint of the Taylor and Francis Group, an informa business

International Standard Book Number 13: 978-1-84872-833-2 (Hardcover)
International Standard Book Number 13: 978-0-415-65552-1 (Paperback)

Library of Congress Cataloging-in-Publication Data

Managerial ethics : managing the psychology of morality / editor, Marshall
Schminke.
    p. cm.
Includes bibliographical references and index.
ISBN 978-1-84872-833-2 (hardcover : alk. paper)
    1. Management--Moral and ethical aspects. 2. Business ethics. I. Schminke,
Marshall.

HF5387.M3345 2010
174'.4--dc22   2010010913

Visit the Taylor & Francis Web site at
http://www.taylorandfrancis.com

and the Psychology Press Web site at
http://www.psypress.com

To Maureen

Contents

Section III   New Theoretical Perspectives

Preface

Conversations about business often turn to business ethics. The first edition of *Managerial Ethics: Morally Managing People and Processes* was published by Lawrence Erlbaum Associates in 1998. It explored the ties between businesses and ethics, seeking to better understand the close—but at times uneasy—relationship between the two. The goal of this revision is to extend that investigation by offering updates of three works from the original volume (Chapters 1, 9, and 13), while adding several new authors and new topics to the mix. In particular, the revision broadens its scope by including the insights of several new authors as well as several established European scholars. It expands the scope of topics to include issues relevant to ethics at a more macro level than addressed in the first volume (e.g., ethical leadership, corporate character, and corporate social responsibility). Finally, it offers several scholars from the first edition the opportunity to speak to new issues and challenges they see in the field.

This book is intended to serve three purposes. First, it provides a basic reference volume for current business ethics researchers. Second, it seeks to stimulate new ways of thinking about, and creating interest in, links between management and ethics among those researchers. Third, it hopes to prompt leading management and ethics researchers, those who do not currently study business ethics problems, to consider the implications of each to their current interests. As such, the volume is appropriate for business ethics researchers, a broader audience of management scholars for whom ethics research is rapidly becoming more important, and ethics scholars with interests in management and organizations. In addition, the chapters reflect important practical problems. Therefore, the book is intended not only for students and scholars of business, management, strategy, organizational studies, and organizational psychology, but thoughtful managers as well.

In all, this volume seeks to initiate conversations among researchers with similar interests but different perspectives, thereby creating a symbiotic mix of ethics and management theory that will spark a higher level of sophistication and rigor from both perspectives. The level of work in the chapters is rigorous. However, the authors approach their subjects from a descriptive perspective, so no special mathematical, statistical, or methodological expertise is required.

Each chapter in the book considers an important practical topic in management research like moral leadership, ethical failure, punishment, and corporate social responsibility. Building from a foundation in state-of-the-science management theory, each set of authors considers the ethical issues and implications involved in that chapter's topic. Each essay thereby integrates these ethical issues with management research and practice in meaningful, theoretically grounded ways.

Following an introductory chapter by Schminke and Priesemuth (Chapter 1, "Management and Ethics: Revisiting Distant Neighbors") the book is organized into three sections. The first is titled "Ethics From the Top Down." This section examines broad-based influences on organizational ethics. It opens with a paper by Cropanzano and Walumbwa that provides a review of leadership styles relevant to organizational ethics and behavior (Chapter 2, "Moral Leadership: A Short Primer on Competing Perspectives"). Next, Chun explores the intergration of ethics and corporate social responsibility (CSR) (Chapter 3, "Organizational Virtue, CSR, and Performance"). Rupp, Williams, and Aguilera follow by exploring the psychology of firm CSR behavior (Chapter 4, "Increasing Corporate Social Responsibility Through Stakeholder Value Internalization (and the Catalyzing Effect of New Governance): An Application of Organizational Justice, Self-Determination, and Social Influence Theories." Finally, Mitchell and Palmer propose a new construct in the realm of ethics research, ethical efficacy (Chapter 5, "The Managerial Relevance of Ethical Efficacy").

The second section of the book is titled "Unethical Behavior: Causes, Consequences, and Comebacks." This section shifts the focus to ethics at the individual level. It opens with De Cremer's essay on preventing and dealing with ethical failures (Chapter 6, "On the Psychology of Preventing and Dealing With Ethical Failures: A Behavioral Ethics Approach"). Umphress, Campbell, and Bingham follow with a discussion of a different type of unethical act, that which is intended to benefit others rather than to harm them (Chapter 7, "Paved With Good Intentions: Unethical Behavior Conducted to Benefit the Organization, Coworkers, and Customers"). Next, Hess examines an ethical issue that reaches outside organizational boundaries, by exploring organizational service failures from the customer's perspective (Chapter 8, "Failures, Losses, and Fairness: The Customer's Perspective"). Treviño and Weaver then explore punishment in organizations (Chapter 9, "Advances in Research on Punishment in Organizations: Descriptive and Normative Perspectives"), an update of a chapter that appeared in the first volume.

The third and final part of the book, titled "New Theoretical Perspectives," presents a series of thought-provoking new directions in ethics research. Folger and Cropanzano open this section by examining moral emotions in the context of social hierarchies (Chapter 10, "Social Hierarchies and the Evolution of Moral Emotions"). In the following chapter, Price looks to the evolutionary psychology literature to address long-standing criticisms of a central tenet of justice research: equity theory (Chapter 11, "Free Riders as a Blind Spot of Equity Theory: An Evolutionary Correction"). Next, Mayer addresses the shortcomings of ethics research in terms of its nearly exclusive focus on proscriptions of unethical behavior (Chapter 12, "From Proscriptions to Prescriptions: A Call for Including Prosocial Behavior in Behavioral Ethics"). In the closing chapter of this section, also an update from the first volume, Schminke, Caldwell, and Vestal emphasize the importance of considering nonrational models of ethical decision making (Chapter 13, "A Review and Assessment of Ethical Decision Making Models: Is a Garbage Can Approach the Answer?").

In all, these chapters reflect a three-pronged approach to improving our understanding of business ethics. Three of the chapters (Chapters 1, 9, and 13) provide the opportunity for authors from the first edition to update and extend their thoughts on issues represented in that edition. Two of the chapters (Chapters 2 and 10) demonstrate the evolving interests of authors from the first edition, as they press into new areas of inquiry. The remaining chapters reflect the thoughts of a new set of geographically diverse scholars, many of whom were not yet engaged in managerial ethics research at the time the first edition appeared. In all, the collection represents an ideal melding of "cagey veterans" and younger scholars, as they explore both new venues and more established issues, seeking a better understanding of each.

One of the greatest strengths of business ethics research lies in the variety of backgrounds of those interested in knowing more about it. Where else could we find moral philosophers, industrial psychologists, political scientists, and organizational sociologists hard at work exploring the same issues? These scholars bring to the table an intriguing mix of skills and viewpoints, many of which may be quite different from—and complementary to—those trained in management. However, this diversity also creates a weakness. Researchers from such different backgrounds may either be unable or unwilling to talk to and work with each other in understanding more about the issues. There is a need to bridge that gap and to initiate conversations in which the theoretical and empirical approaches from all sides might be better integrated. This book attempts to do that.

Acknowledgments

Producing a volume like this truly "takes a village." I wish to thank each of the authors for their contributions, and the cheerful and timely manner in which they produced and revised them. I also thank Erin Flaherty and the other members of the Routledge/Psychology Press/Taylor & Francis editorial and production staff who had a hand in this effort. To a person, they were at all times professional, helpful, and in good spirits, all of which are needed throughout a process like this. I thank the early reviewers of the proposal for this project for their extremely helpful insights: Manuel London of the State University of New York at Stony Brook, Karl Aquino of the University of British Columbia, and Scott J. Reynolds of the University of Washington. Finally, I offer a very special thank-you to Anne Duffy, my senior editor on this and the previous edition of *Managerial Ethics*. She's the best.

About the Editor

Marshall Schminke is BB&T Professor of Business Ethics at the University of Central Florida. His research spans organizational ethics and justice, and focuses on the means by which organizational characteristics like structure and work climate influence individual ethics and justice outcomes. His work has appeared in *Academy of Management Journal, Journal of Applied Psychology, Organizational Behavior and Human Decision Processes, Business Ethics Quarterly, Research in Organizational Behavior,* and *Research in Personnel and Human Resources Management*. He has served as Associate Editor at the *Academy of Management Journal* and as a visiting scholar at Oxford University. He is currently an Associate Editor at *Business Ethics Quarterly*, an Academic Fellow of the Ethics Resource Center in Washington, D.C., and a member of the Society for Organizational Behavior. His previous edited volume, *Managerial Ethics: Moral Management of People and Processes*, was published by Lawrence Erlbaum Associates.

Contributors

Ruth V. Aguilera
Department of Business
　Administration
College of Business
University of Illinois at Urbana-
　Champaign

John B. Bingham
Department of Organizational
　Leadership and Strategy
Marriott School of Management
Brigham Young University

James L. Caldwell
Department of Management and
　Marketing
Harrison College of Business
Southeast Missouri State
　University

Joanna Tochman Campbell
Department of Management
Mays Business School
Texas A&M University

Rosa Chun
Marketing International Business
　and Strategy
Manchester Business School
University of Manchester

Russell Cropanzano
Department of Management and
　Organizations
Eller College of Management
University of Arizona

David De Cremer
Erasmus Centre of Behavioural
　Ethics
Rotterdam School of Management
Erasmus University and
　Organizational Behaviour
　Division
London Business School

Robert Folger
Department of Management
College of Business
　Administration
University of Central Florida

Ronald L. Hess, Jr.
Department of Marketing
Mason School of Business
　Administration
College of William & Mary

David M. Mayer
Department of Management and
　Organizations
Ross School of Business
University of Michigan

Marie S. Mitchell
Department of Management
Terry College of Business
University of Georgia

Noel F. Palmer
Leadership Institute
University of Nebraska

Michael E. Price
Department of Psychology
School of Social Sciences
Brunel University

Manuela Priesemuth
Department of Management
College of Business
    Administration
University of Central Florida

Deborah E. Rupp
Department of Psychology
School of Labor and Employment
    Relations
University of Illinois at Urbana-
    Champaign

Marshall Schminke
Department of Management
College of Business
    Administration
University of Central Florida

Linda Klebe Treviño
Department of Management and
    Organization
Smeal College of Business
The Pennsylvania State University

Elizabeth E. Umphress
Department of Management
Mays Business School
Texas A&M University

Alex Vestal
Department of Management
College of Business
    Administration
University of Central Florida

Fred O. Walumbwa
Department of Management
W. P. Carey School of Business
Arizona State University

Gary R. Weaver
Department of Business
    Administration
Alfred Lerner College of Business
    & Economics
University of Delaware

Cynthia A. Williams
Osgoode Hall Law School
York University

1

Management and Ethics: Revisiting Distant Neighbors

Marshall Schminke
Manuela Priesemuth
University of Central Florida

In the year 2000, Enron was firmly entrenched as one of the most admired firms in America. *Fortune* magazine had consistently named it the most innovative company in the U.S. as well as one of the 100 best companies to work for. Similarly impressive honors surrounded firms like WorldCom, Tyco, Arthur Andersen, Adelphia, and AIG as well. All were highly respected companies delivering quality, innovative products and services across a variety of markets. Ten short years later, the ethical, financial, and legal scandals that devastated these and other firms demonstrate that this has been perhaps the most turbulent decade for business ethics ever.

Shortly before this epidemic of ethical failure began, the first edition of *Managerial Ethics* went to press (Schminke, 1998). (Of course, we caution the reader to avoid the "post hoc ergo propter hoc" fallacy of false cause!) The goal of the first edition was to initiate conversations among researchers from a variety of backgrounds who shared an interest in business ethics. The authors who contributed to it addressed the theoretical, empirical, and practical implications of ethical issues including privacy, performance monitoring, selection, punishment, quality, politics, manipulation, technology, and decision making. In all, it was a very strong collection. Many of these authors, and the work they produced, laid the foundation for considerable improvements in our understanding of managerial ethics.

Now, just over a decade later, the need for continued attention to the challenges of business ethics remains clear. This second edition of *Managerial Ethics* derives from that need. Its goal is to press further into the theoretical and practical problems posed by modern business ethics. In doing so, this new edition reiterates and updates some of the foundational material provided in the first edition. However, it probes important new areas as well. It does so by blending the perspectives of authors from the previous edition with a set of new voices. The result is a compilation of theoretical, empirical, and practical insights that span a broad spectrum of ethical issues important to managers and researchers alike.

The relationship between business and ethics continues to be a stormy one, in both theory and practice. This opening chapter seeks to shed light on the core causes of that sometimes uneasy association. It aims to improve ties between the two by reiterating and then extending some of the basic themes presented in the opening chapter of the first edition.

We begin with a brief recap of the most fundamental challenges facing business ethics research. We then outline an agenda for overcoming these challenges. Finally, we provide brief overviews of the remaining chapters in the volume, each of which expands our thinking about business ethics research in a manner consistent with this agenda. In all, our objective is to set the stage for the terrific collection of thoughts about managerial ethics that follows.

Recurring Challenges in Business Ethics Research

Throughout its history, research in business ethics has faced a consistent set of challenges. Many of these emanate from the nature of relationships among business ethics issues and the scholars interested in those issues. Popper's (1972) observations on the structure of social systems provides some insight about the nature of these relationships.

Popper (1972) distinguished between social systems that are like clocks and those that are like clouds (Cropanzano & Schminke, 1997; Guzzo & Shea, 1990). Clocks are rational, orderly, machines. Their parts move in predictable ways and in predictable relationships to the other parts. Alternatively, clouds are neither predictable nor orderly. To the extent that they have "parts," they do not move in clearly defined or predictable ways in relation to the other parts. From a distance, they may appear to be substantial objects with clear boundaries. However, up close they are fuzzy, flexible, organic creations. This metaphor for social systems also describes research systems; some are like clocks and others are like clouds. Business ethics research is more cloudlike than clocklike. From a distance, it appears to be a singular, solid, substantial thing. But up close it is fuzzy, flexible, and organic.

One of the greatest strengths of business ethics research lies in the diversity of those interested in knowing more about it. Where else could we find moral philosophers, industrial psychologists, political scientists, management scholars, organizational sociologists, and behavioral economists, all exploring the same issues? Scholars from these and other disciplines bring to the table an intriguing mix of skills and perspectives. In doing so, they reflect a common interest in questions regarding business, ethics, and the relationship between the two. However, with this strength also comes a weakness. Researchers from such diverse backgrounds often find it difficult to communicate with one another in meaningful ways. Nowhere has this been truer than with business ethics.

Over the years, scholars have addressed the natural conflicts that arise between those with different perspectives on the field of business ethics. Much of this work echoes two central challenges facing business ethics scholars. First, how might we best integrate the two very different areas—business and ethics—that provide the scholarly foundation for the field? Second, how might we create closer ties between business ethics research and real business settings? Helping to overcome those challenges is the central agenda for this volume.

The First Challenge: Integrating Business and Ethics Scholarship

Business ethics research consists of two distinct subdisciplines. Scholarship in business, which is primarily descriptive and based in the social sciences, addresses the question of "what is." Scholarship in ethics, which is primarily normative or prescriptive and based in moral philosophy, addresses the question of "what ought to be." Historically, these two approaches represented distinct areas of inquiry, and the literature points to a number of issues that inhibit efforts to integrate them.

One roadblock to integration is fear. For example, Victor and Stephens (1994) note that historically, philosophy and social science have exhibited a sort of division of labor with respect to business ethics. Philosophers address normative issues and social scientists, descriptive ones. However, forces in each area impede attempts to integrate the two. For example, philosophers fear a creeping "naturalistic fallacy" in the face of advancing empiricism. That is, they fear that discoveries of "what is" may come to define our thinking of "what ought to be." Similarly, social scientists express concern over breaking ranks with a positivist tradition, which asserts that facts are distinct from values. If "truth" cannot carry with it any value judgments, how can empiricists consider addressing questions regarding "what ought to be?"

A second roadblock to integration is differences in purpose. For example, Fleming (1987) notes that there is "an almost complete lack of integration between normative and descriptive research efforts" (1987, p. 21) in business ethics. He predicts the two may eventually converge by developing distinctive contributions to practicing managers. That is, the normative

approach would evolve into an *instructive* tool, identifying what constitutes moral behavior, how it is learned, and how it may be converted into
business practices. The descriptive approach would develop *predictive*
competence, to be implemented into practical business decision making.

A third roadblock to integration lies in the background of scholars in
each area. For example, Treviño and Weaver (1994) distinguish between
business schools' concentration on the *business* perspective of business
ethics, and philosophy and theology departments' focus on the *ethics*
perspective. They point out that researchers from each area differ in a
number of important ways, including academic background, language,
and underlying assumptions, as well as how they use, apply, and evaluate
theory. Although Treviño and Weaver reiterate previous calls for unity,
they note that these calls for integration have, for the most part, failed to
provide clear guidance as to what an integrated field would look like or
how it might be accomplished.

The challenges presented by these roadblocks continue to play out in
business ethics research. Consider several recent attempts to understand
business ethics at a more global level via literature reviews. O'Fallon and
Butterfield's (2005) review of the ethical decision making literature, Treviño,
Weaver, and Reynolds' (2006) review of the behavioral ethics literature,
and McClaren's (2000) review of the sales management literature each represent well-crafted reviews of substantial bodies of work. However, each
embraces only the social science side of the mix. (For an exception, see Nill
and Shibrowski's (2007) review of the marketing ethics literature, which
includes both normative and positive aspects of the literature.)

Of course, decisions to limit reviews in this way are understandable.
Space limitations often require that attention be focused on specific sub-
sets of relevant literatures, and in this sense, business ethics research may
be a victim of its own success. An ABI/Inform database seach (limited
to scholarly journals in business and economics only) reveals more than
3500 articles in which the word "ethics" appears in the title, and this is for
work published just in the the past decade! Thus, creating a manageable
subset of the literature requires that authors make some coarse initial cuts
on that literature. For better or worse, that cut often entails separating
the philosophical or normative from the social science or descriptive and
addressing only one or the other. However, such decisions influence how
(and how often) business ethics scholars successfully integrate sound philosophy and social science in their work.

Toward a More Integrated Field

Kahn's (1990) essay on creating an agenda for business ethics research
may help to address the question of how to facilitate greater integration
in the business ethics literature. Like others, he distinguishes between

the normative (prescriptive) and contextual (descriptive) traditions in the field. He argues that at present the two areas resemble distinct circles in a Venn diagram that overlap little, if at all. Because the two areas rise from relatively distinct underlying disciplines, little shared ground exists between them. Further, individuals possess strong theoretical and methodological ties to their primary disciplines. As scholars attempt to reinforce their own areas, those areas may become even more impenetrable to others. Researchers continue to be inadequately grounded in at least one of the two disciplines, often differing significantly in how they identify ethical issues in business. Therefore, the shared ground is not likely to grow and may even shrink! He relates one author's comments regarding the dilemma facing business ethics researchers:

> [Researchers] in applied ethics are in the inherently comic position of carrying water from wells they haven't dug to fight fires they can't quite find. (1990, p. 313)

Kahn (1990) sketches four images—conversation, history, vision, and community—that he believes outline an ideal ethical system. Members of such a system would talk to each other. They would respect and understand each others' historical roots. They would provide clear and imaginative ideas. Finally, they would work within the larger community toward shared goals. These images provide a sound basis for integrating business ethics researchers. That is, they would be an interactive community of scholars, with diverse historical (academic) backgrounds and imaginative ideas, working toward a shared goal of understanding and creating more ethical organizations and business systems.

In all, most business ethics scholars agree that the question is not whether the two traditions represented by the philosophical and social science roots of business ethics should interact. They should. The more important question is what that integration should look like. That is, when the circles in the Venn diagram overlap, what should be going on in that shared territory? This is an important question for the development of the business ethics literature.

Parallel, Symbiotic, and Integrative Approaches

Weaver and Treviño (1994) propose three categories for thinking about the relationship between normative and empirical approaches in business ethics research: parallel, symbiotic, and integrative views. The three views represent a continuum of how tightly integrated normative and empirical approaches can be (or to take a more normative perspective, should be).

Parallelism suggests that normative and empirical approaches are, and should remain, distinctly separate paths to understanding business ethics issues. Both practical and conceptual conflicts drive this view (e.g., differences in training and methodology, and differences in whether "is" or "ought" represents the correct question to be asked). *Symbiosis* reflects a cooperative, collaborative relationship between normative and empirical approaches. Shared research agendas and theoretical foundations may guide and inform the progress for each path of inquiry. Finally, *integration* represents an even stronger melding of normative and empirical approaches. Moving beyond simply sharing theoretical or methodological models, the integrative view seeks to create a unified hybrid theory of business ethics by melding the theoretical foundations of each area.

In the end, Weaver and Treviño (1994) view symbiotic inquiry as the most promising, a position Donaldson (1994) echoes. Donaldson rejects parallelism, acknowledging that research in business ethics should include both normative and empirical insights. However, he also strongly rejects integration, stating that "the temptation to [fully] integrate must be boldy resisted" (p. 157). He argues that such a move to combine the fundamentally different normative and empirical approaches is akin to "combining triangularity and circularity" (p. 157). Further, he believes that such a combination would lead to confusion within and without the field and, eventually, irrelevance for the entire discipline. In the end, he supports a balanced, symbiotic approach.

In the main, business ethics scholars generally suggest that a symbiotic relationship between normative and empirical approaches is not only possible, but desirable. However, the real issue is broader than a simple debate between normative empirical foundations. Not all of philosophy is normative. Not all of social science is empirical. Therefore, integrating the two is more complicated than simply applying sound empirical research methods to test ethical theory. For a truly sustainable symbiosis to emerge, business ethics researchers need to think beyond how one perspective's research methodology or intellectual processes can inform the other's thinking. We need to rethink the relationships between our basic theoretical models.

A Meta-Business Ethics View

Meta-ethics concerns the development of ethical theories and the relationships between different theoretical systems and disciplines (Fleming, 1987). We propose that a *meta-business ethics* view of the field is an appropriate path for advancing our understanding of business ethics. That is, a theoretical symbiosis must precede any meaningful and enduring methodological and empirical symbiosis. Thus, business ethics researchers must first identify and map the relationships between ethical and social science theories in order to discover and capitalize on synergies between the two.

Striking examples of the efficacy of such an approach already exist in the literature. Perhaps the best known of these involves Kohlberg's (1984) work on moral development. Kohlberg wedded an array of ethical theoretic bases (egoism, utilitarianism, deontology) with Jean Piaget's emerging social science theories of cognition and developmental psychology. This and related work (e.g., Rest, 1986) has exerted a more profound impact on research on ethical decision making than perhaps any other. That is no accident. It demonstrates that well-crafted theory that first integrates ethics and social science at the theoretical level provides a foundation on which significant additional work may build. For example, Rest's Defining Issues Test, which draws heavily on Kohlberg's work, has itself spawned over 500 studies (Rest, 1994). Kohlberg's work has exhibited "legs" not in spite of its theoretical duality, but because of it.

We believe this symbiotic theoretical approach holds the greatest promise for researchers seeking to make meaningful, lasting, contributions. Davis (1971) notes that the most significant research, that which gets noticed and has a lasting impact is, at its core, interesting. And it is interesting because it violates some (but not all) key assumptions of its audience. Research that denies no assumptions may be disregarded as "ho hum," while research that denies all assumptions risks being dismissed as irrelevant (Campbell, Daft, & Hulin, 1982). Joint theoretical approaches to business ethics research are likely to reach that middle ground. On the one hand, research conceived, conducted, and distributed within either philosophy or social science is obviously more likely to conform to the theoretical and methodological assumptions of that field. It is therefore less likely to break with core assumptions of the field. On the other hand, research conceived and conducted within one field, but then distributed across the other, will likely violate so many basic assumptions of the target audience as to be dismissed out of hand. However, crafting symbiotic theoretical approaches may strike closer to Davis's notion of moderate assumption violation. Thus, each area maximizes its opportunities to create not only new, but meaningful, research contributions.

A number of promising joint theoretical approaches surfaced in the literature in the 1990s. For example, Donaldson and Dunfee (1994) united the organization studies constructs of bounded rationality and satisficing with the philosophical concepts of social contracts in creating their theory of integrative social contracts. Greenberg and Bies (1992) considered utilitarian, egoism, and Kantian approaches to ethics and their relationship to how we theorize about issues surrounding organizational fairness, rewards, and punishment. Ciulla (1995) melded normative theories of ethics with traditional models of leadership to shift the question from "what is leadership?" to "what is good leadership?" Others combined ethical theory with the economic concept of agency theory (Bowie & Freeman, 1992; Noe & Rebello, 1994), decision and attribution theory (Decker, 1994), business strategy (Singer, 1994) and social psychology theories of impression management and cognitive distortions (Payne & Giacalone, 1990). A reader familiar with the current business ethics literature will recognize many of these papers as the platform from which considerable additional work emerged over the past decade.

Fortunately, joint theoretical approaches continue to emerge in the literature. Research on moral identity (e.g., Shao, Aquino, & Freeman, 2008), ethical leadership (Brown, Treviño, & Harrison, 2005), and ethics education (Donaldson, 2008) have all benefitted from theoretical foundations based solidly in both philosophical and social science domains. Approaches like these provide the greatest chance of creating truly symbiotic partnerships between ethicists and social scientists in the quest to understand business ethics.

In all, business ethics research has suffered from a lack of common ground between the business and ethics scholars who seek to understand its intricacies. However, longstanding critiques in the literature appear to be having a positive impact on the development of the field. More scholars, and more areas of scholarship, are benefitting from genuinely symbiotic approaches to research. When theoretical foundations from ethics and business are successfully wedded, they create a groundwork upon which new, interesting, and important research streams may thrive. The chapters in this book provide additional examples of just this type of symbiotic, meta-business ethics theorizing.

The Second Challenge: Business Ethics in Real Business Settings

The second theme that emerges from an examination of the field of business ethics reflects a long-standing interest in forging closer ties with real business settings and issues (Jackson, 2006; McDonald, 2000; Shaupp & Lane, 1992). The chapters that follow address this concern as well. As such, it is useful to explore more deeply how we might define success on this front.

In an essay entitled "What's the Matter With Business Ethics?" Stark (1993) wondered why professions like law, medicine, and government have had much greater success than business in integrating ethical philosophy with practitioners' daily concerns. Most major corporations are active in integrating ethics into their organizations. However, many observers still lament what seems to be a misfit between the type of expertise and advice business ethics scholars bring to their organization and the organizations' needs.

Stark (1993) suggested that business ethicists must shoulder much of the blame. Historically, business ethics has tended to be too general, too theoretical, and too impractical to be of much use to practicing managers. It is perceived as too general, often attempting to address meta-issues like the moral justification for capitalism or broad corporate social responsibility issues, rather than the workaday concerns of organizational members. It is thought to be too theoretical in that it often couches ethical issues in lofty terms like formalism, and utilitarianism, teleology, and deontology. Managers are left to wonder how these relate to everyday work experiences. Finally, it is seen as too impractical in that it does not give very clear guidance to managers trying to behave morally in a complex world with often-conflicting business, personal, family, and moral pressures.

In response, Stark proposed a "new" business ethics. This approach may be more business friendly in that it allows for conflict to exist between individuals' ethics and their pursuit of personal and organizational interests. It seeks to guide managers as they try to behave ethically and socially responsibly, without jeopardizing their careers or companies. It calls "the creation of actionable strategies for the pragmatists" (1993, p. 48) the most critical task in business ethics.

In more recent years, others have made similar observations, questioning how researchers might contribute more to understanding what Treviño and Weaver (1994) refer to as morally significant business practices, with particular emphasis on *practices* (e.g., Jackson, 2006; McDonald, 2000). Still other scholars have taken the cause even a step further. Not content to simply call for a more practical study of business ethics, Kahn (1990) proposed a multidimensional research agenda for business ethics that integrates practice with theory. He suggested that researchers should pursue research questions that reflect philosophical ethical principles, organizational context, and a balance between philosophic ideals and pragmatic work demands. His model not only tolerates but embraces the potential conflict between ideal ethical settings and pragmatic workplace pressures. He noted that ethical principles and organizational contexts carry equal relevance to those struggling to live morally, and that meaningful ethical systems will be created where those forces intersect.

Perhaps the most direct call for a more applied approach to business ethics research was offered by Robertson (1993), who provided three directives that relate directly to this issue. The first is to provide an increased normative focus for ethics research. She noted investigators' common reluctance to address the "what ought to be" issue because of questions about what exactly constitutes ethical behavior. Yet she correctly noted that normative decisions have always played a role in descriptive research; experimental treatments often reflect implicit normative ethical positions. (For example, studies may assume that kickbacks, padding expense accounts, "churning" clients' investment portfolios, and so on, are unethical.) Even such basic decisions as what issues are worth studying carry normative overtones (Forsyth, 1980).

The second directive is to emphasize behavior as the key dependent variable. Robertson (1993) believes that since the purpose of business ethics research is to discover the meaning and causes of ethical behavior, then behavior should be the focus. Moral attitudes and moral reasoning may represent important determinants, but behavior is key. Because managers commonly seek assistance in understanding what to *do*, this suggestion addresses those concerns.

The third directive is to build links to managerial and public policy applications. Robertson (1993) contends that the ultimate purpose of business ethics research is to guide higher-quality ethical decision making. Therefore, researchers' focus must be on how to make research results useful to those in positions to influence policy, like providing assistance in creating corporate codes of ethics.

Over the past decade, researchers have been quite successful meeting the second of these challenges, an increased focus on behavior. Ten years ago the term *behavioral ethics* was not in common use in the literature. However, by 2005 sufficient research—and interest in that research—existed to motivate the editorial team of the *Journal of Management* to invite a review of the literature for their annual review issue. For many, the publication of the Treviño et al. (2006) review of behavioral ethics legitimized the area as a valid component of the business ethics literature. Several of the chapters that follow explicitly embrace a behavioral ethics label. We believe this focus on ethical behavior, its causes, and its consequences, cannot help but improve the picture in terms of the first and third issues as well: a more applied approach to business ethics research that will lead to improved managerial applications.

Of course, this issue of increased applicability of research goes beyond business ethics; it emerges in organizational studies in general. For example, Daft and Lewin (1990) stated that "organization studies have been a recurrent source of disappointment for practitioners" and "the body of knowledge published in academic journals has practically no audience in business or government" (p. 1). Campbell, Daft, and Hulin (1982) identified several characteristics of significant research in organizational studies. Three of these in particular provide sound guidance for business ethics researchers committed to exploring and understanding real business issues:

1. *Significant research is an outcome of investigator involvement in the physical and social world of organizations.* Investigators should go into organizations, talk to managers and practitioners, and use these contacts to inform their thinking about worthwhile research subjects.
2. *Significant research focuses on real problems.* Abstract academic notions are useful. They provide theoretic guidance and under-

standing. But research that addresses real problems of real people in real organizations carries the greatest chance of enduring.

3. *Significant research reaches into the uncertain world of organizations and returns with something clear, tangible, and well understood.* Investigators might view organizational actors and actions through lenses thick with theory and jargon. However, the final product should be precise and ordered and most importantly, usable.

In all, the business ethics literature has been both persistent and consistent in its assessment of the main challenges we face as we look to the future. For business ethics research to be useful, it must eventually touch business. But to do that in a sustainable way, it must be grounded in sound theory that integrates ethics and social science perspectives. The chapters that follow in this book attempt to do both.

Outline of the Book

As with the first edition, the purpose of this book is twofold. First, it seeks to initiate conversations among researchers with similar interests but different perspectives. By doing so, it aims to create a symbiotic mix of ethical and managerial theory, one that will allow us to take our research to a higher level of sophistication and rigor from both perspectives. Second, it attempts to focus those conversations on topics of interest to today's managers. The chapters cut across theoretical and practical arenas, and address individual as well as systemic issues. Some will be controversial. However, all address current, relevant issues that affect the people and processes that make up organizational life.

The book is organized into three sections. The first is titled "Ethics from the Top Down." This section examines broad-based influences on organizational ethics. It opens with a paper by Cropanzano and Walumbwa that provides a review of leadership styles relevant to organizational ethics and behavior (Chapter 2, "Moral Leadership: A Short Primer on Competing Perspectives"). This chapter demonstrates the power of managers in influencing ethical behavior in the workplace. The authors suggest that four leadership research paradigms—ethical leadership, servant leadership, spiritual leadership, and authentic leadership—share central concerns for moral issues. They provide overviews of each paradigm and explore how each of the four perspectives provides insight into the nature of moral management.

Next, Chun explores the integration of ethics and corporate social responsibility (CSR) (Chapter 3, "Organizational Virtue, CSR, and Performance").

She argues that the rationalist assumptions of Kantianism and utilitarianism have not been fully satisfying for understanding corporate social responsibility (CSR), and suggests that adding virtue ethics to the mix may provide significant additional clarity. She explores the link between organizational virtue and nonfinancial performance and presents a case study to illustrate the process by which this occurs.

Rupp, Williams, and Aguilera follow by exploring the psychology of firm CSR behavior (Chapter 4, "Increasing Corporate Social Responsibility Through Stakeholder Value Internalization [and the Catalyzing Effect of New Governance]: An Application of Organizational Justice, Self-Determination, and Social Influence Theories). The authors draw on justice theory to shed light on different motives of stakeholders that may hinder or facilitate CSR. In addition, self-determination theory provides insights on how autonomy or competence may increase CSR behavior of firms.

Finally, Mitchell and Palmer propose a new construct in the realm of ethics research, ethical efficacy (Chapter 5, "The Managerial Relevance of Ethical Efficacy"). Drawing on Bandura's concept of self-efficacy, the authors argue that whistleblowers, such as Sherron Watkins of Enron and Cynthia Cooper of Worldcom, possess a characteristic beyond good morals alone that drive them to ethical action, even when facing long odds. The chapter identifies antecedents, consequences, and cognitive processes related to ethical efficacy, and describes the broad-based managerial relevance of the construct.

The second section of the book is titled "Unethical Behavior: Causes, Consequences, and Comebacks." This section shifts the focus to ethics at the individual level. It opens with De Cremer's essay on preventing and dealing with ethical failures follows (Chapter 6, "On the Psychology of Preventing and Dealing With Ethical Failures: A Behavioral Ethics Approach"). This chapter provides insights about the shift in ethical research from a prescriptive approach, which deals with people upholding moral principles when faced with an ethical dilemma, to a descriptive approach, involving how people actually act when faced with an ethical dilemma. De Cremer uses these two perspectives to explain individuals' engagement in unethical behavior. In addition, the chapter seeks to understand the motives involved in unethical actions as well as how best to remedy these ethical failures.

Umphress, Campbell, and Bingham follow with a discussion of a different type of unethical act, that which is intended to benefit others rather than to harm them (Chapter 7, "Paved With Good Intentions: Unethical Behavior Conducted to Benefit the Organization, Coworkers, and Customers"). The authors explore antecedents and motivations for these "prosocial" unethical behaviors, including those based on social exchange, social identity, and mood perspectives. They conclude by outlining the theoretical and practical implications of this alternative type of unethical behavior at multiple levels of analysis.

Next, Hess examines an ethical issue that reaches outside organizationl boundaries, by exploring organizational service failures from the customer's perspective (Chapter 8, "Failures, Losses, and Fairness: The Customer's Perspective"). This chapter provides new insights for the service failure–recovery paradigm by offering an improved understanding of the inequity that is felt by customers after a service failure. It examines the variety of losses a customer can experience by introducing a multidimensional conceptualization of loss types. Furthermore, it proposes three theoretical models of recovery that may enhance an organization's ability to restore customers' perceptions of fairness, satisfaction, and loyalty.

Treviño and Weaver then explore punishment in organizations (Chapter 9, "Advances in Research on Punishment in Organizations: Descriptive and Normative Perspectives"). In this update of a chapter that appeared in the first volume of *Managerial Ethics*, the authors guide us from the conventional behaviorist view of punishment to recent research theories that focus on cognitive and affective states of observer and participant. Finally, the chapter provides a normative perspective on punishment in organizations based on philosophical and criminological writings about punishment in society.

The third and final part of the book, titled "New Theoretical Perspectives," presents a series of thought-provoking new directions in ethics research. Folger and Cropanzano open this section by examining moral emotions in the context of social hierarchies (Chapter 10, "Social Hierarchies and the Evolution of Moral Emotions"). By taking an evolutionary perspective on behavioral ethics, the authors seek to answer two questions. First, are humans by nature hierarchical or egalitarian? Second, why are some moral norms associated with emotions whereas others are not? The ethical perspective of deonance and social hierarchies are integrated to understand how emotions relate to moral dictates in society.

In the following chapter, Price looks to the evolutionary psychology literature to address long-standing criticisms of a central tenet of justice research: equity theory (Chapter 11, "Free Riders as a Blind Spot of Equity Theory: An Evolutionary Correction"). In particular, he develops evolutionary perspectives that address concerns about equity theory's inability to deal effectively with overreward situations. He argues that an evolutionary perspective may help to explain why free rider problems commonly occur at all organizational levels and how solving these problems may be a key to improving organizational productivity.

Next, Mayer addresses the shortcomings of ethics research in terms of its nearly exclusive focus on proscriptions of unethical behavior (Chapter 12, "From Proscriptions to Prescriptions: A Call for Including Prosocial Behavior in Behavioral Ethics"). Mayer argues that for the ethics domain to thrive and grow, scholars should turn their attention to prescriptions involving ethical and prosocial behavior as well. This chapter provides a set of guidelines for how ethics research might be more closely integrated with work on prosocial behavior, and outlines the practical and managerial implications of doing so.

In the closing chapter of this section, Schminke, Caldwell, and Vestal emphasize the importance of considering nonrational models of ethical decision making (Chapter 13, "A Review and Assessment of Ethical Decision Making Models: Is a Garbage Can Approach the Answer?"). This update of a chapter that appeared in the first edition of *Managerial Ethics* reviews recent models of ethical decision making, most of which rest on an assumption of linear, rational, decision making. It reiterates the potential value of considering nonrational models in general, and the "garbage can" approach in particular. Finally, it reviews briefly the broad range of domains in which the garbage can approach to decision making has been applied, and develops a model for its application to managerial ethics.

In all, these chapters reflect a three-pronged approach to improving our understanding of business ethics. Three of the chapters (Chapters 1, 9, and 13) provide the opportunity for authors from the first edition to update and extend their thoughts on issues represented in that edition. Two of the chapters (Chapters 2 and 10) demonstrate the evolving interests of authors from the first edition, as they press into new areas of inquiry. The remaining chapters reflect the thoughts of a new set of scholars, many of whom were not yet engaged in managerial ethics research at the time the first edition appeared. In all, the collection represents an ideal melding of "cagey veterans" and younger scholars, as they explore both new venues and more established issues, seeking a better understanding of each.

Closing

The central goal for this edition of *Managerial Ethics* is to continue where the first edition left off, by enacting a *reflect and connect* strategy for business ethics researchers. That is, the authors in this volume challenge readers to reflect on their own and others' approaches to exploring ethics issues, and to connect those pursuits with those other fields and, eventually, to the business world itself. Campbell, Daft, and Hulin (1982) are correct to remind us that true innovation rarely comes from inside one's own field (cf., Stein, 1974; 1975). Rather, the most effective strategies for discovering new and meaningful ideas come from both interaction with other disciplines and contacts with the "real" world. This book's purpose is not simply to encourage more research in business ethics; research not worth doing is not worth doing well. Rather, the goal is to unfreeze our thinking about our own and other theoretical bases and biases, to identify situations in which theory—ethical *and* managerial—may guide our thinking when exploring both what is and what ought to be, and to ground that work in real organizational settings. The result may be research that is important to academics *and* practitioners, shaping both theory and practice (Kahn, 1990).

The past decade has been a turbulent one indeed, for managers and managerial ethics. We hope this book will play a significant role in helping ethics scholars (both current and potential), ethics students, and ethics practitioners lead the way in thinking about these increasingly important issues.

References

Bowie, N. E., & Freeman, R. E. (Eds.). (1992). *Ethics and agency theory: An introduction*. Oxford: Oxford University Press.

Brown, M. E., Treviño, L. K., & Harrison, D. (2005). Ethical leadership: A social learning perspective for construct development and testing. *Organizational Behavior and Human Decision Processes, 97*, 117–134.

Campbell, J. P., Daft, R. L., & Hulin, C. L. (1982). *What to study: Generating and developing research questions*. Beverly Hills, CA: Sage.

Ciulla, J. B. (1995). Leadership ethics: Mapping the territory. *Business Ethics Quarterly, 5*, 5–28.

Cropanzano, R., & Schminke, M. (1997). Justice as the mortar of social cohesion. In M. Turner (Ed.), *Groups at work: Advances in theory and research*. Hillsdale, NJ: Lawrence Erlbaum & Associates.

Daft, R. L., & Lewin, A. Y. (1990). Can organization studies begin to break out of the normal science straightjacket? An editorial essay. *Organization Science, 1*, 1–9.

Davis, M. S. (1971). That's interesting! Toward a phenomenology of sociology and a sociology of phenomenology. *Philosophy of Social Science, 1*, 309–344.

Decker, W. H. (1994). Unethical decisions and attributions: Gains, losses, and concentration of effects. *Psychological Reports, 75*, 1207–1214.

Donaldson, L. (2008). Ethics problems and problems with ethics: Toward a promanagement theory. *Journal of Business Ethics, 78*, 299–311.

Donaldson, T. (1994). When integration fails: The logic of prescription and description in business ethics. *Business Ethics Quarterly, 4*, 157–169.

Donaldson, T., & Dunfee, T. W. (1994). Toward a unified conception of business ethics: Integrative social contracts theory. *Academy of Management Review, 19*, 252–284.

Fleming, J. (1987). A survey and critique of business ethics research, 1986. In W. Frederick (Ed.) *Research in corporate social performance and policy: Vol. 9* (pp. 1–24). Greenwich, CT: JAI Press.

Forsyth, D. R. (1980). A taxonomy of ethical ideologies. *Journal of Personality and Social Psychology, 39*, 175–184.

Guzzo, R. A., & Shea, G. P. (1990). Group performance and intergroup relations in organizations. In M. D. Dunnette & L. M. Hough (Eds.), *Handbook of industrial and organizational psychology* (pp. 269–313). Palo Alto, CA: Consulting Psychologists Press.

Greenberg, J., & Bies, R. J. (1992). Establishing the role of empirical studies of organizational justice in philisophical inquiries into business ethics. *Journal of Business Ethics, 11*, 433–444.

Jackson, K. T. (2006). Breaking down the barriers: Bringing initiatives and reality into business ethics education. *Journal of Management Education, 30*, 65–89.

Kahn, W. A. (1990). Toward an agenda for business ethics research. *Academy of Management Review, 15*, 311–328.

Kohlberg, L. (1984). *The psychology of moral development*. San Francisco: Harper & Row.

McClaren, N. (2000). Ethics in personal selling and sales management: A review of the literature focusing on empirical findings and conceptual foundations. *Journal of Business Ethics, 27*, 285–303.

McDonald, G. (2000). Business ethics: Practical proposals for organisations. *Journal of Business Ethics, 25*, 169–184.

Nill, A., & Shibrowski, J. A. (2007). Research on marketing ethics: A systematic review of the literature. *Journal of Macromarketing, 27*, 256–273.

Noe, T. H., & Rebello, M. J. (1994). They dynamics of business ethics and economic activity. *American Economic Review, 84*, 531–547.

O'Fallon, M. J., & Butterfield, K. D. 2005. A review of the empirical ethical decision-making literature: 1996–2003. *Journal of Business Ethics, 59*, 375–413.

Payne, S. L., & Giacalone, R. A. (1990). Social psychological approaches to the perception of ethical dilemmas. *Human Relations, 43*, 649–665.

Popper, K. R. (1972). *Objective knowledge*. London: Oxford University Press.

Rest, J. R. (1986). *Moral development: Advances in theory and research*. New York: Praeger.

Rest, J. R. (1994). Background: Theory and research. In J. R. Rest & D. Narvaez (Eds.), *Moral development in the professions* (pp. 1–26). Hillsdale, NJ: Lawrence Erlbaum Associates.

Robertson, D. (1993). Empiricism in business ethics: Suggested research directions. *Journal of Business Ethics, 12*, 585–599.

Schminke, M. (1998). *Managerial ethics: Moral management of people and processes*. New York: Psychology Press/Routledge.

Shao, R., Aquino, K., & Freeman, D. (2008). Beyond moral reasoning: A review of moral identity research and its implications for business ethics. *Business Ethics Quarterly, 18*, 513–540.

Shaupp, D., & Lane, M. S. (1992). Teaching business ethics: Bringing reality to the classroom. *Journal of Business Ethics, 11*, 225–229.

Singer, A. E. (1994). Strategy as moral philosophy. *Strategic Management Journal, 15*, 191–213.

Stark, A. (1993). What's the matter with business ethics? *Harvard Business Review, 71*, 38–48.

Stein, M. J. (1974). *Stimulating creativity* (Vol. 1). New York: Academic Press.

Stein, M. J. (1975). *Stimulating creativity* (Vol. 2). New York: Academic Press.

Treviño, L. K., & Weaver, G. R. (1994). Business ETHICS/BUSINESS ethics: One field or two? *Business Ethics Quarterly, 4*, 113–128.

Treviño, L. K., Weaver, G. R., & Reynolds, S. J. (2006). Behavioral ethics in organizations: A review. *Journal of Management, 32*, 951–990.

Victor, B., & Stephens, C. U. (1994). Business ethics: A synthesis of normative philosophy and empirical social science. *Business Ethics Quarterly, 4*, 145–155.

Weaver, G. R., & Treviño, L. K. (1994). Normative and empirical business ethics: Separation, marriage of convenience, or marriage of necessity? *Business Ethics Quarterly, 4*, 129–143.

Section I

Ethics From the Top Down

2

Moral Leadership: A Short Primer on Competing Perspectives

Russell Cropanzano
University of Arizona
Fred O. Walumbwa
Arizona State University

A Short Primer on Moral Leadership

Behavioral ethicists have long been concerned with why moral transgressions occur and how they can be prevented (Treviño, Weaver, & Reynolds, 2006). Frequently, this entails examining unethical behavior in one of two ways. In the first, and probably the most common instance, researchers have investigated the individual determinants of transgressions. For example, studies have examined moral development (e.g., Ashkanasy, Windsor, & Treviño, 2006; Reynolds, 2006; Reynolds & Ceranic, 2007; Schminke, Ambrose, & Newbaum, 2005) and assorted models of ethical decision making (e.g., Connolly & Hardman, 2009; Coughlan & Connolly, 2008; Krebs & Denton, 2005; Treviño, 1986; Treviño & Youngblood, 1990). A second research tradition emphasizes characteristics of organizations. For example, scholars have documented the important influence of ethical work climates (e.g., Arnaud & Schminke, 2007; Dickson, Smith, Grojean, & Ehrhart, 2001; Martin & Cullen, 2006; Schminke, Arnaud, & Kuenzi, 2007; Victor & Cullen, 1988), collective corruption (e.g., Ashforth & Anand, 2003; Brief, Bertram, & Dukerich, 2001; Palmer, 2008), and formal policies that could encourage or discourage unethical conduct (e.g., Robertson & Anderson, 1993; Smith, Simpson, & Huang, 2007; Treviño & Weaver, 2001). Speaking practically, it is the action of individuals, often managers, who span the chasm between individual integrity and into workplace action.

Moral leadership, broadly defined, is how managers use their character to shape ethical and effective work units. Stated simply, to be a moral leader, one has to actually *lead.* In a broad sense this implies urging other individuals into a purposeful and ethical direction (Sims, 2000; Thomas, Schermerhorn, & Dienhart, 2004).

Behavioral ethicists have not ignored this topic, and we will see that a good deal of promising research exists. Toward this end, we will provide an introductory review of the literature on moral leadership. In order to keep our task manageable, as well as to introduce the reader to an emerging literature, we have imposed strict inclusion requirements on ourselves. Among other things, we omit general theories of leadership even when these have ethical implications. For that reason we will not discuss such well-known topics as transformational leadership (e.g., Bass & Steidlmeier, 1999) and charismatic leadership (e.g., Conger & Kanungo, 1998; Howell & Avolio, 1992), except briefly as they pertain to the topic at hand. Second, we make no attempt to develop a comprehensive model of moral leadership. Rather, we explore four programs of study that have an explicitly moral focus—ethical leadership, spiritual leadership, servant leadership, and authentic leadership. As moral leadership is a relatively new area of inquiry, one or more of these research areas may not be familiar to the reader. Given all this, our chapter is intended to serve as a short primer on this topic. We review the four best known and most widely studied approaches to this phenomenon. Our goal is to treat these leadership paradigms separately, so as to highlight the unique strengths and weaknesses of each. For this reason, we pay special attention to conceptual definitions, construct explication, and operational measures.

Ethical Leadership

Among the theoretical perspectives reviewed in this chapter, research on ethical leadership has probably been the most influential (for reviews, see Brown & Treviño, 2006; Brown, Treviño, & Harrison, 2005; Treviño & Brown, 2004). Brown and his colleagues pose a formal definition: *"the demonstration of normatively appropriate conduct through personal actions and interpersonal relationships, and the promotion of such conduct to followers through two-way communication, reinforcement, and decision-making"* (p. 120, italics in original). As one can see, ethical leadership includes behavior that shows personal character and decency toward others. This is not a controversial point (for additional evidence, see Badaracco, 2006; Dickson, Smith, Grojean, & Ehrhart, 2001; Schminke, Ambrose, & Neubaum, 2005; Wright & Goodstein, 2007; Wright & Huang, 2008). Those who lack moral integrity but push it on others have been designated as "Hypocritical Leader[s]" by Treviño, Hartman, and Brown (2000, p. 137). However, Brown et al.'s definition goes further, making it clear that their personal ethics is not enough to make one a leader (see also Sims, 2000; Treviño & Brown, 2004).

The most effective moral leaders may certainly be moral persons, but they must take the additional steps of modeling appropriate conduct, communicating clear standards, and encouraging others to behave morally (Brown, 2007; Treviño & Brown, 2004; Treviño et al., 2000). In other words, ethical leaders must *do* something. This question brings us to the seminal question of ethical leadership: What must be done by those in charge so as to promote moral conduct within a work team or organization?

The Qualitative Tradition of Ethical Leadership

To answer this question, Treviño, Brown, and Hartman (2003) conducted a qualitative study. The authors conducted 40 interviews. Twenty of these were with ethical compliance officers, who would be expected to have knowledge of the subject; 20 others were with senior executives, who have had to make decisions with ethical implications. While there were some differences between these two groups, there were also important commonalities. To be sure, ethical leadership included having and exhibiting a people orientation and, as the authors put it, "visible ethical actions and traits" (p. 15). These include such virtues as behaving respectfully, being honest and forthright, and exhibiting willingness to "walk the talk" (p. 15). Still, though character was found to be important, there was more to the matter than this. Ethical leadership also included transactional or managerial attributes. Ethical leaders established moral norms through careful communication. They then set high expectations and enforced the rules, including the use of rewards and punishments.

In a follow-up study, Weaver, Treviño, and Agle (2005) interviewed 20 former MBA students who had experience working with an ethical role model (for a discussion of ethical role modeling, see Sims & Brinkmann, 2002). The goal was to examine ethical leadership from the perspective of the subordinate. As with earlier work, Weaver et al. found that the leader's personal character was important. Honesty trustworthiness, integrity, and other desirable qualities worked in the manager's favor. Also consistent with the earlier Treviño et al. (2003) study, Weaver and his colleagues found that people-oriented interpersonal behaviors were important as well (e.g., showing "Care, concern, and compassion," "Accepts others' failures," p. 316). Finally, Weaver et al. observed that sound transactional management practices made an individual an attractive role model. This included treating others fairly (e.g., "Resources distributed equitably," p. 316), and also establishing and enforcing ethical standards (e.g., "Communicates high ethical standards," "Holds others ethically accountable," p. 316).

The qualitative work of Treviño et al. (2003) and Weaver et al. (2005) paints an interesting picture of the ethical leader, and it does so from three important perspectives—the leader or executive, the compliance officer, and the subordinate seeking a role model. Consistent with other research, the personal character of the leader is important (Badaracco, 2006; Wright & Goodstein, 2007; Wright & Huang, 2008). Beyond this, though, the ethical leader must also act as a conscientious manager. He or she needs to clearly communicate moral standards and enforce them through the use of rewards and punishments (Treviño & Brown, 2004). Wise decision making is also important (Brown et al., 2005; Conger & Hooijberg, 2007). The picture that emerges is not of a supernatural being issuing lofty pronouncements from on high. Rather, the ethical leader is an active role model, promoting ethical conduct through the use of concrete and sound transactional behaviors (Badaracco, 2002; Sims, 2000). These insights provide a framework upon which scholars were able to build, as we shall see in our next section.

Operationalizing Ethical Leadership

Brown, Treviño, and Harrison (2005)

Based upon the earlier qualitative research, Brown, Treviño, and Harrison (2005) designed and validated a psychometrically sound measure of ethical leadership. In a series of seven studies, including diverse samples of MBA students, faculty members, and working individuals, Brown and his colleagues constructed the ten-item measure that is displayed in Table 2.1. Their initial studies established the item conduct and single-factor structure. Later studies went further, building ethical leadership's nomological network. For example, in their Study 4, Brown et al. found that, as anticipated, ethical leadership was positively related to affective organizational commitment and negatively related to abusive supervision.

Study 7 was the most comprehensive. Brown et al. (2005) set out to predict a composite variable called "supervisor effectiveness." Supervisor effectiveness consisted of four highly correlated indicators—a direct rating of effectiveness, satisfaction with the supervisor, willingness to exert extra effort, and the willingness to come forward with problems. There were two antecedent variables. The first was ethical leadership and, of course, the second was idealized influence. Idealized influence is a dimension of transformational leadership (for details, see Avolio, 1999; Bass, 1998; Bass & Steidlmeier, 1999). Overall, the results showed that ethical leadership predicted variance in supervisor effectiveness beyond idealized influence, but idealized influence did not predict beyond ethical leadership.

Brown et al.'s (2005, see Table 2.1 in this chapter) ten-item measure of ethical leadership has become by far the most widely used measure of

TABLE 2.1

Ethical Leadership Items

---

1. Conducts his/her personal life in an ethical manner
2. Defines success not just by results but also the way that they are obtained
3. Listens to what employees have to say
4. Disciplines employees who violate ethical standards
5. Makes fair and balanced decisions
6. Can be trusted
7. Discusses business ethics or values with employees
8. Sets an example of how to do things the right way in terms of ethics
9. Has the best interests of employees in mind
10. When making decisions, asks "what is the right thing to do?"

Note: From "Ethical Leadership: A Review and Future Directions," by M. E. Brown, and L. K. Treviño, 2006, *Leadership Quarterly, 17*, 595–916. All items used a seven-point Likert scale. Anchors ranged from 1 ("Strongly Disagree") to 5 ("Strongly Agree").

this construct (for empirical examples, see Mayer, Aquino, Greenbaum, & Kuenzi, 2008; Mayer, Kuenzi, Greenbaum, Bardes, & Salvador, 2009; Walumbwa & Schaubroeck, 2009). Even studies that do not use the full Brown et al. measure tend to employ very similar assessment devices (see Detert, Treviño, Burris, & Andiappan, 2007; Mayer, Schminke, Treviño, Shapiro, & Harned, 2008). Despite this general success, it is not the only tool available.

Resick, Hanges, Dickson, and Mitchelson (2006)

A somewhat different approach to assessment was taken by Resick, Hanges, Dickson, and Mitchelson (2006). Resick and his coauthors emphasized personal attributes of the leader, such as thoughts and actions. Drawing from measures available in the Project GLOBE database (cf. Avolio, Walumbwa, & Weber, 2009; House & Javidan, 2004), as well as on a detailed literature review, Resick et al. identified six conceptual dimensions that they viewed as critical for ethical leadership: (a) character and integrity, (b) community/people-orientation, (c) motivating, (d) encouraging/empowering, (e) ethical awareness, and (f) managing ethical accountability. The researchers were unable to address the latter two dimensions—ethical awareness and managing ethical accountability. However, they were able to construct a 23-item scale that measured the first four concepts. These four scale dimensions had slightly different names—character/integrity, altruism (for community/people-orientation), collective motivation (for motivating), and encouragement (for encouraging/empowering). This four-factor scale was administered to respondents in 62 nations, clustered into 10 cultural groups. Results suggested that each of the scales had a similar meaning across the different nations. Moreover, all cultures saw these attributes as important, though they varied as to how much this was so.

Comparing the Two Measures of Ethical Leadership

It is worthwhile to compare the Resick et al. (2006) measure to that of Brown et al. (2005). Though we have seen that their measures have some differences, we would also argue that there is an underlying similarity in their conceptual approaches. To illustrate, Table 2.2 contains our attempt to map the Brown et al. (2005) measure to the Resick et al. (2006) conceptual dimensions. For example:

- Brown et al. include two items that assess personal integrity: "Conducts his/her personal life in an ethical manner" and "Can be trusted."
- There are two other items that seem to pertain to community or people orientation: "Makes fair and balanced decisions" and "Has the best interests of employees in mind."
- Brown et al. have two items that would seem similar to ethical awareness: "Defines success not just by results but also the way that they are obtained" and "When making decisions, asks 'what is the right thing to do?'"

TABLE 2.2

Mapping the Brown et al. Items (2005) onto the Resick et al. (2006) Conceptual Dimensions

Resick et al. (2006) Dimensions	Items from Brown et al. (2005)
Character and integrity	Items 1, 6
Community/People-orientation	Items 5, 9
Motivating	Item 7
Encouraging and empowering	Item 3
Ethical awareness	Items 2, 10
Managing ethical accountability	Item 4

Note: From "Ethical Leadership: A Social Learning Perspective for Construct Development and Testing," by M. E. Brown, L. K. Treviño, and D. A. Harrison, 2005, *Organizational Behavior and Human Decision Processes, 97,* 126 and "A Cross-cultural Examination of the Endorsement of Ethical Leadership," by C. J. Resick, P. J. Hanges, M. W. Dickson, and J. K. Mitchelson, 2006, *Journal of Business Ethics, 63,* 350. Though ethical awareness and managing ethical accountability were seen as conceptually important, neither was assessed by the Resick et al. (2006) measure.

We concede that this is an unscientific analysis, and the astute reader could disagree with the particulars; our modest point is simply that the two scales overlap. While they certainly do not correspond perfectly, they possess some theoretical similarities. This suggests that Brown et al. (2005) and Resick et al. (2006) are assessing a common set of ideas, though future research is necessary to address this possibility with greater precision.

Evidence for Ethical Leadership

The qualitative research tradition of Treviño et al. (2003) and Weaver et al. (2005) suggests that the moral leader is a functioning business manager, with a sense of ethical awareness, who models appropriate conduct, communicates moral standards, and holds his or her subordinates accountable. This suggests that a primary mechanism for ethical leadership is modeling and reinforcement (Treviño et al., 2000). For this reason, scholars such as Detert, Treviño, Burris, and Andiappan (2007) and Mayer et al. (2009) have interpreted ethical leadership in terms of Bandura's social learning theory (Bandura, 1962, 1997; later designated, "social cognitive theory," Bandura, 1986, 2005).

There is something surprisingly prosaic about this. Can leader behaviors so straightforward and transactional actually work? As it happens, there is good reason to think so. In an interesting insight, Treviño and Brown (2004, p. 71) observe:

> [M]ost adults in industrialized societies are at the "conventional" level of cognitive moral development, and less than twenty percent are at the "principled" level where thinking is more autonomous and principle-based. In practice this means that most adults are looking outside themselves for guidance in ethical dilemma situations.

In other words, because many of us do not carry around an adequate "internal compass," the guidance of an ethical leader can be critical for promoting moral workplace behavior (Sims, 2000; Sims & Brinkmann, 2002).

Similar conclusions have been drawn by decision scientists, though they have typically done so without relying on stage models of moral reasoning (cf. Krebs & Denton, 2005). For example, a review by Connolly and Hardman (2009) demonstrates that ethical judgments are heavily influenced by the social and organizational setting. It may also be the case that people utilize heuristics rather than careful and logical deliberation. If this is so, then a gentle "push" from sound leadership can have a beneficial impact. Palmer (2008) makes this point explicitly. He observes that moral judgments are often "mindless," in the sense of being automatic and without effortful cognitive processing. Such judgments, therefore, can be buffeted in a more or less moral direction based upon the setting in which they are made. From this point of view, an ethical leader could well have substantial influence on the ethical behavior of employees by setting standards and encouraging appropriate conduct.

Ethical Leadership Among Managers

Detert, Treviño, Burris, and Andiappan (2007): Ethical leadership in the restaurant industry. In a seminal study, Detert and his colleagues (2007) explored counterproductive work behavior (CWB) in 265 branches of a restaurant chain. CWB was operationalized as food loss, a criterion variable that is very important in this industry. As additional outcome measures, Detert et al. also examined profitability and customer satisfaction. There were also three predictors: ethical leadership, abusive supervision, and managerial oversight (the ratio of shift managers to employees). All of these measures were unit-level measures, considered at the level of the individual store.

Detert and his fellow researchers (2007) were successful in predicting food loss (interpreted as CWB in this study). Even so, from the point of view of ethical leadership, their findings were not especially promising. The authors found that abusive supervision increased food loss, while heightened oversight decreased it. Food loss, in turn, led to dwindling restaurant profits and diminished customer satisfaction. Ethical leadership, unfortunately, was not significantly associated with any of the three criterion variables. Detert et al. were cautious, not ruling out the possibility that ethical leadership may be important in different settings. In restaurants, inventory shrinkage may involve unambiguous moral violations such as theft. In cases where the ethical norms are clear, individuals may be less influenced by the social setting (cf., Mayer, Aquino, et al., 2008; Palmer, 2008; Robertson & Anderson, 1993). Given this, we must turn our attention to ethical leadership in other settings.

Mayer, Aquino, et al. (2008): Ethical leadership and moral identity. Mayer, Aquino, and their colleagues (2008) sampled work units from a number of different industries. In their first study, Mayer, Aquino, et al. examined 137 departments, assessing ethical leadership with the Brown et al. (2005) measure, reviewed above. The researchers also measured unethical behavior and the amount of relationship conflict in each unit. As was true for Detert et al. (2007), each of these variables was aggregated to the level of the department. In support of their predictions, Mayer, Aquino, et al. (2008) found that increased amounts of ethical leadership reduced unethical behavior and alleviated relationship conflict. These findings are consistent with the qualitative (Treviño et al., 2003; Weaver et al., 2005) and quantitative (Brown et al., 2005) results that we discussed earlier.

There was another interesting aspect of Mayer, Aquino, et al.'s (2008) study. These scholars also investigated moral identity as an antecedent to ethical leadership. Moral identity has two dimensions (Aquino & Reed, 2002; Reed & Aquino, 2003). The first, *internalization,* is the extent to which ethical attributes are central to one's self-concept. The second, *symbolization,* is the extent to which these traits are manifested in one's behavior toward others. In other words, the former is private and the latter is public (Shao, Aquino, & Freeman, 2008). In Study 1, ethical leadership was predicted by identity symbolization, the public manifestation of morality, but not by internalization.

Mayer, Aquino, et al. (2008) obtained even stronger results in their second field study. This time analyzing data from 195 departments, representing a number of industries, the authors replicated the essential findings for ethical leadership. That is, more ethical leadership engenders less unit-level unethical behavior and less unit-level relationship conflict. In Study 2, unlike Study 1, both internalization and also symbolization predicted ethical leadership.

Walumbwa and Schaubroeck (2009): Ethical leadership and employee voice. Walumbwa and Schaubroeck explored ethical leadership in a large sample of 884 workers in a financial organization. Ethical leadership was rated by subordinates but then aggregated to the level of the work unit. The authors found that ethical leadership tended to build a psychologically safe work climate. When workers felt this safety they were more likely to exercise voice, speaking up and offering helpful suggestions. Interestingly, Walumbwa and Schaubroeck also examined personality traits as antecedents of ethical leadership. They found that ethical leaders tended to be more agreeable and conscientious than were their less ethical counterparts.

Ethical Leadership Among Senior Management

The evidence we have reviewed thus far is somewhat encouraging, at least at the unit or departmental level of analysis (e.g., Brown et al., 2006; Mayer, Aquino, et al., 2008). While promising, such evidence does not fully capture the richness of applied writings on ethical leadership. A number of authors (e.g., Sims, 2000; Sims & Brinkmann, 2002; Thomas et al., 2004) have argued that ethical leadership should begin at the top of the organization. High moral standards, in turn, can be passed down to junior or middle managers. It is these individuals who ultimately impact their work teams in their face-to-face interaction. Evidence of this process is difficult to obtain, but two studies are available with informative results.

Mayer et al. (2009): A "trickle-down" model of ethical leadership. Mayer and his colleagues surveyed 905 individuals working in 195 units from 160 different firms. Respondents rated the ethical leadership of top management, as well as the ethical leadership of their direct department head. As criterion measures, Mayer et al. considered both organizational deviance and organizational citizenship behaviors (OCB). Consistent with earlier work, data were aggregated to the unit level.

Supporting predictions, both top management ethical leadership and also supervisory ethical leadership predicted workplace deviance and OCB. These predictions held regardless of whether the criterion scores were obtained from the supervisor or from the subordinates. Likewise, supervisors showed levels of ethical leadership similar to that of senior managers ($r = .72$). Most critical for the cascading model, when supervisory ethical leadership was controlled, the upper management leadership had no effect on either deviance or OCB. In other words, supervisory leadership mediated the impact of executive leadership on the criterion variables. This suggests that ethical conduct trickles down from top management to the supervisors, and in this way impacts the behavior of workers.

Mayer, Schminke, et al. (2008): Moderator effects on ethical leadership. Building on the initial Mayer et al. (2008) study, Mayer, Schminke, and their colleagues took this line of conceptual thinking a step further. Using a sample of more than 33,000 participants, they found that when workers believed their upper management was ethical they also observed less immoral behavior among their peers and, in the event that something untoward were to occur, were more willing to report the infraction. What makes this study especially interesting, though, is the use of two additional predictors—supervisor ethical leadership and coworker ethical behavior. Mayer, Schminke, et al. (2008) referred to supervisor and peer behavior as "local influences" (e.g., on p. 26) because they took place in the employee's immediate work group. Both of these local influences were found to interact with upper management ethical leadership.

For observations of unethical behavior, the influence of upper management was *stronger* when either supervisor ethical leadership or peer ethical behavior was *low*. In other words, unethical behavior was most likely to transpire when both influences were *low*. If any of the three sources of influence was high—be that upper management, the supervisor, or other employees—then respondents were relatively unlikely to observe unethical conduct. The shape of the interaction was somewhat different for one's willingness to report wrongdoing. The effect of upper management ethical leadership on reporting was *stronger* when either of the local influences was *high*. In other words, reporting was most likely when an ethical upper management was accompanied by an ethical supervisor or else by ethical peers. Mayer, Schminke, et al.'s (2008) study is important. It suggests that influences matter at all levels of the organization—senior leadership, direct supervisor, and coworkers. However, these authors argue that ethics does not trickle down in a passive fashion. Rather, the impact of moral leadership at the top is shaped and qualified by one's boss and peers.

Closing Thoughts on Ethical Leadership

We have traced the origins of ethical leadership from its origins in qualitative research (Treviño et al., 2003; Weaver et al., 2005) and through initial efforts to operationalize it (Brown et al., 2005; Resick et al., 2006). Currently, effort is being devoted to understanding the antecedents and consequences of ethical leadership. Much of this work is promising (e.g., Mayer, Aquino, et al., 2008; Mayer et al., 2008; Mayer, Schminke, et al., 2009), though questions remain (Detert et al., 2007). Two features of this literature are striking. The first is its newness. The seminal investigations were conducted less than ten years ago, making this a novel area for organizational sciences. The second is the cumulative nature of the research, as it has moved from semistructured interviews to empirical investigations, with each study building on the ones that came earlier. This bodes well for the future.

A unique feature of ethical leadership is its quality of *moral management*. An ethical leader is a sound supervisor, who emphasizes transactional behaviors, standard setting, and the enforcement of moral norms. As important as this seems to be, it should be emphasized that effective management does not fully capture the domain of moral leadership. Other potentially valuable attributes, such as those pertaining to personal authenticity (Avolio & Walumbwa, 2006) have not yet been considered. In this regard, both Brown and Treviño (2006) and Fry (2003) observe that ethical leadership overlaps but is distinct from other leadership constructs, such as spiritual leadership and authentic leadership. Even though there is much to learn from the ethical leadership literature, we shall see that there is more to the story.

Spiritual Leadership

Precise definitions of spiritual leadership have proven elusive (Dent, Higgins, & Wharff, 2005), so it might be useful to begin with some general considerations. Fry (2003, p. 727) remarks that "The ultimate effect of spiritual leadership is to ... create a sense of fusion among the four fundamental forces of human existence (body, mind, heart, and spirit)." Speaking in a similar vein, Duchon and Plowman (2005, p. 811) add that "employees have spiritual needs (i.e., an inner life), just as they have physical, emotional, and cognitive needs." Summarizing some common themes, we can see that students of spiritual leadership see spirituality as a core aspect of human functioning. It is related to but distinguishable from more traditional psychological considerations, such as affect and cognition. Contemporary work organizations sometimes impinge on or ignore human spiritual needs. A spiritual leader, therefore, is one who addresses the spiritual needs of the worker. In the long run, this will benefit the organization as well as the worker (for additional reviews, see Fry, 2003; 2007; Fry & Slocum, 2007; Giacalone, Juriewicz, & Fry, 2005; Miller, 2000).

With these considerations in mind, we can now consider a formal definition of spiritual leadership. Based on the earlier work of Ashmos and Duchon (2000), Duchon and Plowman (2005, p. 811) define "spirituality" as *"the recognition that employees have an inner life that nourishes and is nourished by meaningful work that takes place in the content of community"* (italics in original). Notice that this characterization contains three important features of spiritual leadership—an emphasis on inner life, meaningful work, and community. Ideas such as these are broad ones, so it might also be helpful to put some boundaries on them.

Spiritual leadership is *not* intended to endorse any particular religious denomination or form of theology (Fry, 2003; Fry & Slocum, 2007; Reave, 2005). Spiritual leadership researchers have taken great care not to be advocates for one religion (or for any religion) at the expense of others. In one thoughtful passage, Fry (2007, p. 752) observes that:

> [R]eligion is concerned with faith in the claims of one faith tradition or another and connected with systems of belief, ritual prayer, and formalized practices and ideas. Spirituality, on the other hand, is concerned with qualities of the human spirit, including positive psychological concepts such as love and compassion, patience, tolerance, forgiveness, contentment, personal responsibility, and a sense of harmony with one's environment.

This sort of conceptualization makes spirituality a tractable topic for leadership researchers. For example, Reave (2005) examined a number of studies that considered what she termed "spiritual ideas, such as integrity, honesty, and humility" (p. 655). She finds that these ideals have tended to produce valuable outcomes for employees and organizations. It should be noted that the Reave review does not test a formal theory of spirituality. By focusing on the personal attributes of the leader, her paper is similar to research on workplace character (cf., Wright & Goodstein, 2007; Wright & Huang, 2008). Still, the conclusions are promising. Armed with a workable definition and some promising evidence, spiritual leadership researchers have conducted research studies (Ashmos & Duchon, 2000; Duchon & Plowman, 2005) and implemented workplace interventions (Delbecq, 2000; Fry et al., 2005). Nevertheless, definitional questions remain (Avolio et al., 2009). In the sections that follow we shall review the empirical evidence for spiritual leadership.

Fry's (2003, 2005, 2007) Theory of Spiritual Leadership

Perhaps the best articulated theory of spiritual leadership has been presented by Fry (2003) and Fry, Vitucci, and Cedillo (2005). Fry and his colleagues argue that an effective spiritual leader exhibits three critical dimensions:

- *Vision* articulates the firm's mission and why it is a valuable one. In so doing, vision provides employees with a sense of identity.

- *Hope/faith* provides an optimistic assurance that the vision will be achieved and that something worthwhile will result.

- *Altruistic love* is a genuine and sincere concern for the well-being of others in your work community. More generally, Fry et al. (2005, p. 844) view it as "a sense of wholeness, harmony, and well-being."

The items for these three dimensions are presented in Table 2.3. These measures illustrate how broadly the term *spiritual* can be understood, and this could pose a construct validity question. We shall return to this potential concern once we have reviewed the available evidence supporting the model.

Tests of the Causal Model

In Fry's (2003) framework there are three dimensions of spiritual leadership that address the spiritual needs of subordinates. These needs include a sense of meaning/calling and of membership. Meaning or calling refers to the belief that one is contributing to a positive mission. Membership is the belief that one is a valued part of a caring workplace community. The sense of meaning and the sense of membership are necessary for spiritual survival. This, in turn, should boost productivity, commitment, and worker health. There is evidence that favors the model. In one study, Fry and his colleagues (2005) surveyed soldiers who were part of a helicopter attack squadron. Most of the predictions were supported. Specifically, leader hope and faith seems to have improved leader vision and altruistic love. (Love, in turn, had a feedback loop back to hope/faith.) Vision, in turn, boosted the soldiers' sense of meaning, while altruistic love increased their sense of community membership. Finally, membership enhanced commitment and productivity, while meaning enhanced only productivity.

In a second study, Fry and Malone (2003) selected two public schools. One was treated as a control group, while the other underwent an intervention to improve its spiritual leadership. Results were mixed. At Time 2 commitment increased in the school that had undergone the intervention, but productivity did not. In the control school commitment and productivity actually dropped. Hence, it is possible that spiritual leadership training prevented a similar drop in the treatment school, but this cannot be established definitively.

TABLE 2.3

Spiritual Leadership Items

Vision

I understand and am committed to my organization's vision.

My workgroup has a vision statement that brings out the best in me.

My organization's vision inspires my best performance.

I have faith in my organization's vision for its employees.

My organization's vision is clear and compelling to me.

Hope/Faith

I have faith in my organization and am willing to "do whatever it takes" to insure that it accomplishes its mission.

I persevere and exert extra effort to help my organization succeed because I have faith in what it stands for.

I always do my best in my work because I have faith in my organization and its leaders.

I set challenging goals for my work because I have faith in my organization and want us to succeed.

I demonstrate my faith in my organization and its mission by doing everything I can to help us succeed.

Altruistic Love

My organization really cares about its people.

My organization is kind and considerate toward its workers, and when they are suffering, wants to do something about it.

The leaders in my organization "walk the walk" as well as "talk the talk."

My organization is trustworthy and loyal to its employees.

My organization does not punish honest mistakes.

The leaders in my organization are honest and without false pride.

The leaders in my organization have the courage to stand up for their people.

Note: From "Spiritual Leadership and Army Transformation: Theory, Measurement, and Establishing a Baseline," by L. W. Fry, S. Vitucci, and M. Cedillo, 2005, *Leadership Quarterly, 16,* 835–862. All items used a seven-point Likert scale. Anchors ranged from 1 ("Strongly Disagree") to 5 ("Strongly Agree").

How "Spiritual" is Spiritual Leadership?

Despite the supportive evidence presented by Fry et al. (2005) and Fry and Malone (2003), there is an operational concern. It can be questioned whether the spiritual leadership items presented in Table 2.3 are, strictly speaking, spiritual. Let us begin by examining more closely what is meant by the word *spiritual*; then we shall be in a better position to ascertain whether or not the construct is adequately assessed.

In their discussion, Ashmos and Duchon (2000, p. 135) include such exemplars as "personal transformation, rediscovering self, beginning a personal journey, having utopian visions, and experiencing renewal." Based on her review of the literature, Reave (2005, p. 656) argues that it could include such things as one's relationship to a supernatural being

(God), a transcendent experience, and a sense of interconnectedness to others and to the natural world. Likewise, Fry (2003, p. 702) speaks of spirit as "the vital principle or animating force traditionally believed to be the intangible, life affirming force in self and in all human beings." He adds, "It is a state of intimate relationship with the inner self of higher values and morality as well as recognition of the truth of the inner nature of people." These are fascinating ideas, but it is not clear that they are captured by the operational measure displayed in our third table. Arguably, there are few explicit references to spiritual practices, transcendent beliefs, truth, or even to higher purposes. To better illustrate this concern, let us look more closely at the three dimensions.

Consider first the concept of vision. Within the management literature, vision is not necessarily a spiritual ideal. To be sure, some authors have discussed vision in a manner that makes reference to transcendent missions and higher purposes (e.g., Collins & Porras, 1994; Kouzes & Posner, 1995), but others have focused more narrowly on business strategy (e.g., Crotts, Dickson, & Ford, 2005) or on writing mission statements (e.g., Pearce & David, 1987). The items in Table 2.3 simply ask about *vision*, and do not directly assess spiritual matters. Consequently, there is nothing to distinguish this spiritually based view of vision from less spiritual perspectives, such as those of Pearce and David (1987) or Crotts et al. (2005).

A related issue can be found in the hope/faith scale. Notice that in items 1, 3, 4, and 5 the "faith" refers directly to "faith in my organization." Only item 2 hints at more, when it refers to "faith in what it [the organization] stands for." There are few mentions of transcendent meaning, higher purpose (save perhaps item 2), and the panoply of ideas that are often associated with spirituality.

Similar concerns can be raised about the seven items assessing altruistic love. Neither altruism nor love is directly queried. Instead, the scale bears a superficial resemblance to organizational commitment or perhaps organizational support. Though we know of no available data assessing the association between support and altruistic love, Fry et al. (2003, p. 845) found that commitment and altruistic love were correlated at $r = .83$. When we corrected this association for attenuation due to measurement error, it was above .90. This suggests that the spiritual concept of altruistic love shares a good deal in common with the nonspiritual concept of organizational commitment. Matters such as this should be addressed in future research.

Duchon and Plowman (2005): Spirituality Among Health Care Professionals

Ashmos and Duchon (2000) constructed and validated a measure of work unit spirituality. Their measure was found to have three dimensions— meaning at work, community, and inner life. Meaning and community, of course, are similar to the concepts assessed by Fry et al. (2005). Inner life was a new dimension that was explicitly spiritual. It was assessed by such items as "I consider myself a spiritual person," "My spiritual values influence the choice I make," and "Prayer is an important part of my life" (Duchon & Plowman, 2005, p. 830).

In a later paper, Duchon and Plowman (2005) conducted some additional analyses of the data reported originally by Ashmos and Duchon (2000). They explored spirituality among a group of six units in a hospital. These three dimensions of spirituality were expected to cause unit performance, here operationalized as patient satisfaction. Even though it was the case that none of the relationships was significant at the conventional .01 or .05 probability levels, many of the observed correlations were sizable and promising (see Duchon & Plowman, 2005, Table 2 on p. 822).

For purposes of the present chapter, which is concerned with leadership, the data presented by Ashmos and Duchon (2000) and Duchon and Plowman (2005) are somewhat limited. This is because their studies tested the impact of work *unit* spirituality and did not empirically assess spiritual *leadership*, per se. Nevertheless, these authors do not neglect spiritual leadership, and view it as important for establishing spirituality among organizational groups. Duchon and Plowman (see their Figure 3 on p. 825) endorse the causal model suggested by Fry et al. (2005; Fry, 2003), arguing that spiritual leadership is built from the aforementioned troika of vision, hope/faith, and altruistic love.

Closing Thoughts on Spiritual Leadership

Spiritual leadership shares much in common with the ethical leadership that we have already discussed. Brown and Treviño (2006) observe that both concepts emphasize concern for others, the personal integrity of the leader, and the importance of role-modeling appropriate behavior. However, there are also differences. Ethical leadership, as we saw earlier, is concerned with moral management. The approach is transactional, dealing with such things as rewards and punishments. Spiritual leadership, as conceptualized by such scholars as Fry (2003, 2005, 2007) and Duchon and Plowman (2005), focuses more on such things as overall vision and the organization's sense of mission. In this regard, spiritual leadership is perhaps closest to servant leadership, a topic to which we shall now turn.

Servant Leadership

Among the four moral leadership paradigms discussed in this chapter, servant leadership would seem to be the best represented in the popular business press (e.g., Autry, 2004; Block, 1993; Hunter, 1998; 2004). Servant leadership also appears to be well known among writers with a religious, and particularly Christian, outlook (e.g., Blanchard & Hodges, 2008; Warneka, 2007). Despite all this attention, a precise definition of servant leadership has proven elusive.

In its original conceptualization, Greenleaf (1977) observed that servant leadership focuses on developing employees to their fullest potential in the areas of task effectiveness, community stewardship, self-motivation, and future leadership capabilities. This list was later expanded somewhat by Spears (2004), who identified ten characteristics that define a servant leader. These include awareness, building community, commitment, conceptualization, empathy, foresight, healing, listening, persuasion, and stewardship. Building on this, Hale and Fields (2007, p. 397) defined servant leadership as "an understanding and practice of leadership that places the good of those led over the self-interest of the leader, emphasizing leader behaviors that focus on follower development, and de-emphasizing glorification of the leader."

Despite the fact that these conceptualizations differ somewhat in their particulars, they share important commonalities. Servant leaders not only recognize their moral responsibility (personal integrity), such leaders also stress the importance of serving others, including employees, customers, and other organizational stakeholders (Ehrhart, 2004; Liden, Wayne, Zhao, & Henderson, 2008). In this regard, servant leaders are similar to the ethical leaders discussed by Brown and his colleagues (2005). Personal integrity is one important attribute, but successful servant and/or ethical leaders must go beyond their individual ethical beliefs. Servant leadership not only represents a model of leadership that is inspirational, it also contains the moral safeguards that are lacking from well-known leadership styles (Graham, 1991; Greenleaf, 1977). In the sections that follow we shall review the empirical evidence for servant leadership.

Servant Leadership, Transformational Leadership, and Leader–Member Exchange (LMX)

Servant leadership is a broad concept, and researchers have been concerned that might overlap substantially with other leadership paradigms. The two conceptualizations to which it is most often compared are transformational leadership (e.g., by Smith, Montagno, & Kuzmenko, 2004) and leader–member exchange (LMX) (e.g., by Ehrhart, 2004).

Transformational leadership is generally understood to have four dimensions (Avolio, 1999; Bass, 1998; Bass & Steidlmeicr, 1999).

- *Idealized influence:* Acting as a role model for important values and principles.

- *Inspirational motivation:* Inspirational leadership, much like charisma (Conger & Kanungo, 1998; Howell & Avolio, 1992), that inspires followers by providing a sense of meaning and purpose.
- *Intellectual stimulation:* Encouraging workers to question assumptions, thereby becoming more innovative and creative.
- *Individualized consideration:* Attending to the individual needs of each employee.

Leader–member exchange (LMX) refers to the different relationships supervisors have with their subordinates to achieve particular outcomes. These could be *economic exchange relationships,* which are transactional in nature and emphasize short-term interactions between supervisors and subordinates. Alternatively, they could be *social exchange relationships,* which are characterized by high levels of shared identity, loyalty, emotional connections, long duration, and mutual support (Bishop, Scott, & Burroughs, 2000). Importantly, according to LMX theory, when supervisors and subordinates are in a high-quality social exchange relationship, subordinates tend to go beyond formal duty (e.g., helping others or putting extra effort at work). In this respect, LMX appears to share some conceptual space with servant leadership (Graen & Uhl-Bien, 1995). For example, both theories focus on dyadic relationships and account for individualized consideration. However, LMX does not enumerate an idealized notion of leadership nor does LMX circumscribe leaders' behavioral motivation as in the case of servant and transformational leadership theories.

As one can see from even this brief description, servant leadership shares much with both transformational leadership and LMX, though most scholars seem to agree that these conceptualizations, while overlapping somewhat, also make distinct contributions.

To illustrate we shall first consider the theoretical distinctions. As we shall see, these have focused on direct comparisons of servant and transformational leadership. We shall turn our attention to the empirical evidence. Empirical studies have tended to compare all three types of leadership simultaneously.

Theoretical Differences Between Servant Leadership and Transformational Leadership

According to Smith et al. (2004) servant and transformational leadership have a number of important differences. They suggested that servant leaders may be more genuinely concerned about their followers' well-being than transformational leaders, even though transformational leaders have been shown to express such concern through the individualized consideration component of that style of leadership. They also suggested that while transformational leaders inspire and engage followers as the means to attain mission-focused ends, servant leaders focus on their followers' individual growth and development as the ends versus the means. In other words, transformational leaders were seen as more mission based in terms of motivating followers. Servant leaders, on the other hand, used different motivational approaches.

Interestingly, Smith et al. (2004) suggest that the organizational setting might determine whether transformational leadership or servant leadership is most effective. Some environments could favor the former, though others might favor the latter. Specifically, they considered the extent to which the firm was dynamic and rapidly changing. These authors argued that transformational leadership, with its focus on the mission and on organizational change, may be more appropriate in a dynamically changing context. On the other hand, as servant leadership, with its focus on stewardship and attending to the needs of workers, may function more effectively in less dynamic or more stable contexts.

While agreeing that servant leadership can be meaningfully distinguished from transformational leadership, Graham (1991) took a somewhat different approach than that of Smith and his colleagues. He suggested that servant leadership differs from transformational leadership because servant leadership includes an explicit moral component, is responsive to all organizational stakeholders, and engages in self-reflection to attenuate the leader's hubris. Transformational leaders, on the other hand, emphasize symbolic leader behaviors, visionary, inspirational messages, emotional feelings, ideological values, individualized attention and intellectual stimulation (Bass, 1985). As we summarize below, these theoretical distinctions have received some empirical support.

Empirical Comparisons of Servant Leadership to Transformational Leadership and LMX

Among the earliest studies to directly compare servant leadership to other paradigms is the work of Ehrhart (2004). Specifically, Ehrhart explored servant leadership, transformational leadership, and LMX. He provided empirical evidence indicating that servant leadership significantly predicted an additional 5% of the variance in employee commitment, 7% in satisfaction with supervisor, 4% in perceived supervisor support, and 8% in procedural justice above and beyond that of both LMX and transformational leadership.

In later study, Barbuto and Wheeler (2006) attempted to develop a new measure of servant leadership. This new scale was related to transformational leadership and LMX, as one might expect, but it also predicted variance in several outcome variables including extra effort, satisfaction, and organizational effectiveness. In this study however, the authors did not test whether servant leadership explained variance beyond that of LMX or transformational leadership. Accordingly, Barbuto and Wheeler's study attests to the importaof servant leadership, but it does not establish that servant leadership differentially predicts beyond other leadership constructs.

A more direct test was provided by Liden et al. (2008), who examined the same three styles of leadership in terms of their ability to explain citizenship behavior and in-role performance. Consistent with the earlier work of Ehrhart (2004), servant leadership predicted variance in these variables beyond that of transformational leadership and LMX. Taken together, theory and empirical data to date seem to suggest that although servant leadership is positively related other existing leadership theories (as it should for convergent validity purposes), the construct also appears to be distinct and unique in its own right.

Evidence for Servant Leadership

Thus far we have discussed the conceptual definitions of servant leadership, as well as reviewed evidence that it is distinguishable from transformational leadership and LMX. In the course of doing this, we have seen that servant leadership is related to more positive worker attitudes and more effective job behaviors (Barbuto & Wheeler, 2006; Ehrhart, 2004; Liden et al., 2008). Other studies have also linked servant leadership to leader trust (e.g., Joseph & Winston, 2005) and leaders' values of empathy, integrity, and competence (e.g., Washington, Sutton, & Field, 2006).

Recent work by Mayer, Bardes, and Piccolo (2008) empirically examined the relationship between servant leadership and job satisfaction. These authors also investigated the mechanisms through which servant leadership is related to job satisfaction. They found that servant leadership was positively related to job satisfaction, and that this relationship was mediated by organizational justice and need satisfaction. Likewise, Walumbwa, Hartnell, and Oke (2009), using data from Kenya, investigated the multi-level effects of servant leadership. Results from a sample of 815 employees and 123 immediate supervisors revealed that at the individual level of analysis, commitment to the supervisor and self-efficacy partially mediated the relationship between servant leadership and citizenship behavior beneficial to individuals. At the group level of analysis, Walumbwa et al. (2009) reported that procedural justice climate and climate for service fully mediated the relationship between servant leadership and citizenship behavior beneficial to the work group. They also investigated the cross-level effects and found that procedural justice climate and individual-level servant leadership interacted to influence employee commitment to the supervisor and self-efficacy.

Closing Thoughts on Servant Leadership

Although both theory and limited research to date suggest that servant leadership is indeed a unique leadership theory, there are questions that need further research attention. Future research may also focus on examining the perceptions of servant leadership across different levels within as well as across a broader range of organizations, because a great deal of the empirical research on servant leadership has been conducted in public and not-for-profit organizations such as churches and schools (for exceptions, see Ehrhart, 2004; Walumbwa et al., 2009). Finally, future research on servant leadership will need to address much of the same criticisms of other leadership research including the inherent problems associated with using single source/single method cross-sectional designs. Moreover, future research needs to consider including the most appropriate performance measures for testing how a servant leader who expresses a great deal of caring for others should impact performance, as well as to extend the testing of this theoretical framework across different cultures. In this regard, the Walumbwa and colleagues' (2009) study is a step in the right direction.

Authentic Leadership

Authentic leadership developed out of the research on transformational leadership that we discussed earlier. In an influential paper, Bass and Steidlmeier (1999) revisited the original theory of transformational leadership proposed by Bass (1985, 1998). Bass and Steidlmeier were interested in understanding how seemingly charismatic leaders, such as Hitler, could impel people to do horrific things. They argued by making a distinction between authentic transformational leadership and pseudotransformational leadership. The authentic transformational leadership was primarily distinguished from pseudo based on the moral and ethical component related to all aspects of transformational leadership described in more detail below. From a behavioral perspective, the pseudotransformational leader may have superficially "looked" exactly like an authentic transformational leader, but underlying their decisions and actions was the absence of high moral conduct and values.

Bass and Steidlmeier's (1999) distinction led to the emergence of authentic leadership theory, which has attempted to articulate *more clearly* the components of transformational leadership that distinguish it from being authentic versus pseudo in nature. To date, the theory of authentic leadership has received considerable intuitive and theoretical attention (see Avolio, Gardner, Walumbwa, Luthans, & May, 2004; Gardner, Avolio,

Luthans, May, & Walumbwa, 2005; George, 2003; Harter, 2002; Ilies, Morgeson, & Nahrgang, 2005, among others). Although there are several reasons for this appeal, perhaps one of the most important is practical. It seems to be the case that the characteristics associated with authentic leaders may be crucial to creating and sustaining healthy work environments (George & Sims, 2007; George, Sims, McLean, & Mayer, 2007; Macik-Frey, Quick, & Cooper, 2009; Shirey, 2006) and that authentic leadership may be positively related to employee attitudes and behaviors, including performance (Avolio et al., 2004; Gardner et al., 2005; George, 2003; Ilies et al., 2005).

Ilies et al. (2005) suggested that authentic leaders are likely to have a positive influence on followers' behaviors because authentic leaders provide support for followers' self-determination. In support, Kernis (2003) and Kernis and Goldman (2005) found higher levels of self-reported authenticity to be related to higher levels of student engagement in goal pursuits and determination. Similarly, Walumbwa, Wang, Wang, Schaubroeck, and Avolio (in press) have argued that leaders who are perceived to be more authentic play a central role in facilitating employee helping behavior by making employees more aware of the importance of helping one another and demonstrating the value and safety of openly sharing information. In summarizing the importance of authentic leadership Bill George, in an article entitled *"Seven Lessons for Leading in Crisis,"* featured in *The Wall Street Journal* (March 19, 2009) said:

> Virtually every American institution is facing major crises these days, from declining businesses to evaporating financial portfolios. To get out of these crises, authentic leaders must step forward and lead their organizations through them. The current crisis was not caused by subprime mortgages, credit default swaps, or failed economic policies. The root cause is failed leadership ... They can only be solved by new leaders with the wisdom and skill to put their organizations on the right long-term course.

Definition and Conceptualization

To be authentic as a leader means that leaders are comfortable with demonstrating both their strengths and weaknesses (Luthans & Avolio, 2003; May, Chan, Hodges, & Avolio, 2003). Avolio et al. (2004) argued that a higher level of authenticity enables leaders to express their true capabilities, motivation, and emotions to their followers. Similarly, Luthans and Avolio (2003) suggested that authentic leaders have a deep sense of self; they know where they stand on important issues, values, and beliefs. With this base, they stay their course and convey to others, oftentimes through actions, not just words, what they desire to represent in terms of principles, values, and ethics. Reaffirming these positions, Walumbwa, Avolio,

Gardner, Wernsing, and Peterson (2008, p. 94) defined authentic leadership as "a pattern of leader behavior that draws upon and promotes both positive psychological capacities and a positive ethical climate, to foster greater self-awareness, an internalized moral perspective, balanced processing of information, and relational transparency on the part of leaders working with followers, fostering positive self-development." At the group level of analysis, authentic leadership operates like a shared leadership, wherein all group members, "including the authentic leader, view *authentic leadership* similarly and as a shared responsibility of all members" (Yammarino, Dionne, Schriesheim, & Dansereau, 2008, p. 8).

According to theory (e.g., Gardner et al., 2005; Ilies et al., 2005), authentic leaders display four types of theoretically distinct but related substantive behaviors: self-awareness, relational transparency, internalized moral perspective, and balanced processing.

- *Self-awareness* refers to the extent to which a leader appears to understand her own strengths, weaknesses, and motives as well as how others view her. Leaders who are self-aware also show an understanding of their strengths and weaknesses, and are cognizant of their impact on other people (Kernis, 2003).

- *Relational transparency* involves promoting trust through disclosures that include openly sharing information and expressions of a leader's true thoughts and feelings, while simultaneously trying to minimize displays of inappropriate emotions.

- *Internalized moral perspective* refers to leader behaviors that are guided by internal moral standards and values as opposed to being based on external pressure such as peers, organizational and societal pressures, and which results in decision making and behavior that is consistent with these internalized values (Avolio et al., 2004; Gardner et al., 2005).

- *Balanced processing* involves objectively analyzing all relevant information before making a decision. Leaders who are perceived as exhibiting very balanced processing solicit views from others that challenge their deeply held positions.

These four components of authentic leadership distinguish it from other frameworks (for detailed comparisons, see Brown & Treviño, 2006; Walumbwa et al., 2008). Each of the four attributes appears in transformational leadership, though this latter (and older) framework places less emphasis on relational transparency and balanced processing than does authentic leadership. Likewise, while ethical leadership pays close attention to the leader's internalized moral perspective, it does not explicitly include the other three dimensions.

Empirically, Walumbwa et al. (2008), using five separate samples obtained from China, Kenya, and the United States, provided initial evidence of both convergent and discriminant validity for authentic leadership with respect to transformational and ethical leadership. Walumbwa et al. also reported that the core factor of authentic leadership was a significant positive predictor of organizational commitment, satisfaction with supervision and self-reported organizational citizenship behavior controlling for ethical and transformational leadership behaviors, as well as job satisfaction and supervisor-rated job performance controlling for organization climate.

Evidence for Authentic Leadership

Although research has progressed remarkably well on the theoretical end, empirical research linking authentic leadership to important organizational outcomes still lags behind. There are, however, a few important exceptions. Sosik, Jung, and Dinger (2009) examined whether managers' values intensities and self-concept salience influence supportive leadership behavior and performance. Although they did not directly test authentic leadership per se, using multisource data from 935 subordinates and their 218 superiors, Sosik et al. found that subordinates' ratings of managers' authentic behavior also predicted superiors' ratings of managerial performance. They also found that managers' self-monitoring moderated the relationships between self-construals, supportive behavior, and performance.

In another study involving two telecom firms (a state-owned firm and a jointly owned firm) from China, Walumbwa, Wang et al. (in press) examined the direct and indirect effects of authentic leadership behavior on the organizational citizenship behavior and work engagement of followers. Using a sample of 387 employees and their 129 immediate supervisors, Walumbwa, Wang et al. found that authentic leadership behavior was positively related to supervisor-rated organizational citizenship behavior and work engagement, controlling for ideal power distance, company type, and followers' demographics such as age and sex. They also reported that the effect of authentic leadership on employee citizenship behavior and work engagement was realized through the followers' level of identification with the supervisor and their feelings of empowerment.

Research on authentic leadership has also begun at the group level of analysis. Walumbwa, Luthans, Avey, and Oke (in press) investigated the role that group psychological capital and trust may play in explaining the effect of authentic leadership on group-level organizational citizenship behavior and job performance. Utilizing 146 intact groups from a large financial institution and controlling for the effect of transformational leadership, Walumbwa, Luthans et al. found that authentic leadership was significantly related to both group-level citizenship behaviors and job performance. Results also showed that the effect of group-level authentic leadership on group-level citizenship behavior and performance was jointly mediated by group-level psychological capital and trust.

Closing Thoughts on Authentic Leadership

Although empirical evidence linking authentic leadership to important individual, group, and organizational outcomes is just beginning to emerge, the limited research available to date appears to confirm the earlier conceptual predictions. However, more research is still needed before any definitive generalizations regarding the effect of authentic leadership can be made. In addition to providing further evidence for construct validity of authentic leadership, there is also a need to articulate the theoretical rationale for expecting authentic leadership to relate to important individual, group, and organizational outcomes. Such studies are needed to determine whether authentic leadership really adds something new to the leadership literature.

Finally, given the importance of authentic leadership to organizations (George, 2009), research focusing on the antecedents of authentic leadership and conditions under which authentic leaders are more (or less) effective are obviously needed to understand how such leadership may be developed in organizations. Such research may focus on the role of followers, leaders' biographies, demographics such as age, ethnicity and sex, personal characteristics such as personality, or the role of organizational context, and/or cultural differences.

Conclusions

In the past few years moral and ethical considerations have become major societal concerns (Schminke et al., 2007). How can organizations foster ethical actions and decisions in the face of considerable corruption in government and business? One answer has been that they could provide moral leadership (Sims, 2000; Sims & Brinkmann, 2002). Organizational scientists, mindful of the need for precise conceptual models and empirical evidence, have responded with four research paradigms—ethical leadership, spiritual leadership, servant leadership, and authentic leadership. All of these approaches share an explicit concern with moral issues and maintain that effective leadership is grounded in the personal integrity of the leader. However, the four frameworks further argue that individual morality is insufficient, and to be a moral leader one engages in additional activities that build an ethical work climate.

Despite these commonalities and a good deal of overlap, each of these four perspectives also provides unique theoretical insights into the nature of moral management. For example, ethical leadership, unlike the other three approaches reviewed here, places more emphasis on the managerial or transactional side of morality (Brown & Treviño, 2006). In this regard, the ethical leadership literature provides concrete steps that one can take to promote moral work behavior, such as setting standards and rewarding proper conduct. The spiritual leadership literature, as the name implies, is more focused on employees' spiritual life (Fry, 2003). This research tradition places special emphasis on personal calling and the sense of transcendent purpose. Servant leadership is the most explicitly employee centered of the four perspectives (Hunter, 1998, 2004). This is somewhat different than other frameworks, such as ethical leadership, which we might loosely categorize as *standard centered*. That is, the ethical leader, in Brown et al.'s (2005) sense, is expected to communicate and enforce rules of proper conduct. The servant leader, on the other hand, is expected to subordinate his or her own interests to those of the workforce. Finally, authentic leadership devotes considerable attention to the personal attributes of the moral leader, emphasizing such things as leader self-awareness and balanced processing (Avolio & Walumbwa, 2006). As we can see, there is something to learn from each of these models.

Perhaps the most striking characteristic of this literature is its youth. Most of the research we have discussed is under ten years old, rending our present paper as little more than a snapshot of an emerging literature. Still, it is an important one. Research on moral leadership studies the active agency of people of high integrity who are working to create more ethical organizations. Few topics have more self-evident value.

References

Aquino, K., & Reed, A., II. (2002). The self-importance of moral identity. *Journal of Personality and Social Psychology, 83*, 1423–1440.

Arnaud, A., & Schminke, M. (2007). Ethical work climate: A weather report and forecast. In S. W. Gilliland, & D. D. Steiner, & D. P. Skarlicki (Eds.), *Managing social and ethical issues in organizations* (pp. 181–227). Greenwich, CT: Information Age Publishing.

Ashforth, B. E., & Anand, V. (2003). The normalization of corruption in organizations. In R. M. Kramer & B. M. Staw (Eds.), *Research in organizational behavior* (Vol. 25, pp. 1–52). Amsterdam, The Netherlands: Elsevier Ltd.

Ashkanasky, N. M., Windsor, C. A., & Treviño, L. K. (2006). Bad apples in bad barrels revisited: Cognitive moral development, just world beliefs, rewards, and ethical decision-making. *Business Ethics Quarterly, 16*, 449–473.

Ashmos, D. & Duchon, D. (2000). Spirituality at work: A conceptualization and a measure. *Journal of Management Inquiry, 9,* 132–145.

Autry, J. A. (2004). *The servant leader: How to build a creative team, develop great morale, and improve bottom-line performance.* New York: Three Rivers Press.

Avolio, B. J. (1999). *Full leadership development: Building the vital forces in organizations.* Thousand Oaks, CA: Sage.

Avolio, B. J., Gardner, W. L., Walumbwa, F. O., Luthans, F., & May, D. R. (2004). Unlocking the mask: A look at the process by which authentic leaders impact follower attitudes and behaviors. *Leadership Quarterly, 15,* 801–823.

Avolio, B. J., & Walumbwa, F. O. (2006). Authentic leadership: Moving HR leaders to a higher level. In J. J. Martocchio (Ed.), *Research in personnel and human resources management* (Vol. 25, pp. 273–304). Amsterdam: Elsevier.

Avolio, B. J., Walumbwa, F. O., & Weber, T. J. (2009). Leadership: Current theories, research, and future directions. In S. T. Fiske, D. L. Schacter, & C. Zahn-Waxler (Eds.), *Annual review of psychology* (Vol. 60, pp. 421–449). Palo Alto, CA: Annual Reviews, Inc.

Badaracco, J. L., Jr. (2002). *Leading quietly: An unorthodox guide to doing the right thing.* Cambridge, MA: Harvard Business School Press.

Badaracco, J. L., Jr. (2006). *Questions of character: Illuminating the heart of leadership through literature.* Cambridge, MA: Harvard Business School Press.

Bandura, A. (1962). Social learning through imitation. In Mr. Jones (Ed.), *Nebraska symposium on motivation* (Vol. 10, pp. 211–274). Lincoln, NB: University of Nebraska Press.

Bandura, A. (1986). *Social foundations of thought and action: A social cognitive theory.* Englewood Cliffs, NJ: Prentice Hall.

Bandura, A. (1997). *Self-efficacy: The exercise of control.* New York: Freeman.

Bandura, A. (2005). The evolution of social cognitive theory. In K. G. Smith & M. A. Hitt (Eds.), *Great minds in management: The process of theory development* (pp. 9–35). New York: Oxford University Press.

Barbuto, J. E., Jr., & Wheeler, D. W. (2006). Scale development and construct clarification of servant leadership. *Group and Organization Management, 31,* 300–326.

Bass, B. M. (1985). *Leadership and performance beyond expectations.* New York: Free Press.

Bass, B. M. (1998). *Transformational leadership: Industrial, military, and educational impact.* Mahwah, NJ: Erlbaum.

Bass, B. M., & Steidlmeir, P. (1999). Ethics, character, and authentic transformational leadership. *Leadership Quarterly, 10,* 181–217.

Bishop, J. W., Scott, K. D., & Burroughs, S. M. (2000). Support, commitment, and employee outcomes in a team environment. *Journal of Management, 26,* 1113–1132.

Blanchard, K., & Hodges, P. (2008). *Leader like Jesus: Lessons from the greatest leadership role model of all time.* Nashville, TN: Thomas Nelson.

Block, P. (1993). *Stewardship: Choosing service over self interest.* San Francisco, CA: Berrett-Koehler Publishers.

Brief, A. P., Buttram, R. T., & Dukerich, J. M. (2001). Collective corruption in the corporate world: Toward a process model. In M. E. Turner (Eds.), *Groups at work: Theory and research* (pp. 471–499). Mahwah, NJ: Erlbaum.

Brown, M. E. (2007). Misconceptions of ethical leadership: How to avoid pitfalls. *Organizational Dynamics, 36,* 140–155.

Brown, M. E., & Treviño, L. K. (2006). Ethical leadership: A review and future directions. *Leadership Quarterly, 17,* 595–916.

Brown, M. E., Treviño, L. K., & Harrison, D. A. (2005). Ethical leadership: A social learning perspective for construct development and testing. *Organizational Behavior and Human Decision Processes, 97,* 117–134.

Collins, J. C., & Porras, J. I. (1994). *Built to last: Successful habits of visionary companies.* New York: HarperBusiness.

Conger, J., & Hooijberg, R. (2007). Acting wisely when facing ethical dilemmas in leadership. In E. H. Kessler & J. R. Bailey (Eds.), *Handbook of organizational and managerial wisdom* (pp. 133–150). Los Angeles, CA: Sage.

Conger, J. A., & Kanungo, R. N. (1998). *Charismatic leadership in organizations.* Thousand Oaks, CA: Sage.

Connolly, T., & Hardman, D. (2009). "Fools frush in": A JDM perspective on the role of emotions in decisions, moral and otherwise. In D. M. Bartels, C. W. Bauman, L. J. Skitka, & D. L. Medin (Eds.), *The psychology of learning and motivation* (Vol. 50, pp. 275–306). Burlington, VT: Academic Press.

Coughlan, R., & Connolly, T. (2008). Investigating unethical decisions at work: Justification and emotion in dilemma resolution. *Journal of Managerial Issues, 20,* 348–365.

Crotts, J. C., Dickson, D. R., & Ford, R. C. (2005). Aligning organizational processes with mission: The case of service excellence. *Academy of Management Executive, 19,* 54–68.

Delbecq, A. L. (2000). Spirituality for business leadership: Reporting on a pilot course of MBAs and CEOs. *Journal of Management Inquiry, 9,* 117–128.

Dent, E. B., Higgins, A. E., & Wharff, D. M. (2005). Spirituality and leadership: An empirical review of the definitions, distinctions, and embedded assumptions. *Leadership Quarterly, 14,* 729–768.

Detert, J. R., Treviño, L. K., Burris, E. R., & Andiappan, M. (2007). Managerial modes of influence and counterproductivity in organizations: A longitudinal business-unit-level investigation. *Journal of Applied Psychology, 92,* 993–1005.

Dickson, M. W., Smith, D. B., Grojean, M. W., & Ehrhart, M. (2001). An organizational climate regarding ethics: The outcome of leader values and the practices that reflect them. *Leadership Quarterly, 12,* 197–217.

Duchon, D., & Plowman, D. A. (2005). Nurturing the spirit at work: Impact on work unit performance. *Leadership Quarterly, 16,* 807–833.

Ehrhart, M. G. (2004). Leadership and procedural justice climate as antecedents of unit-level organizational citizenship behavior. *Personnel Psychology, 57,* 61–94.

Fry, L. W. (2003). Toward a theory of spiritual leadership. *Leadership Quarterly, 14,* 693–727.

Fry, L. W. (2007). Spirituality and leadership at work. In S. G. Rogelberg (Ed.), *Encyclopedia of industrial and organizational psychology* (Vol. 2, pp. 751–754). Thousand Oaks, CA: Sage.

Fry, L. W., & Malone, P. N. (August, 2003). *Organizational transformation through spiritual leadership: A field experiment.* Paper presented at the annual meeting of the Academy of Management. Seattle, WA.

Fry, L. W., & Slocum, J. W. (2007). Maximizing the triple bottom line through spiritual leadership. *Organizational Dynamics, 37*, 86–96.

Fry, L. W., Vitucci, S., & Cedillo, M. (2005). Spiritual leadership and army transformation: Theory, measurement, and establishing a baseline. *Leadership Quarterly, 16*, 835–862.

Gardner, W. L., Avolio, B. J., Luthans, F., May, D. R., & Walumbwa, F. O. (2005). "Can you see the real me?" A self-based model of authentic leader and follower development. *Leadership Quarterly, 16*, 343–372.

George, W. (2003). *Authentic leadership: Rediscovering the secrets to creating lasting value.* San Francisco: Jossey-Bass.

George, W. (March, 19, 2009). Seven lessons for leading in crisis. *Wall Street Journal.*

George, B., & Sims, P. (2007). *True north: Discover your authentic leadership.* Jossey-Bass.

George, B., Sims, P., McLean, A. N., & Meyer, D. (February 2007). Discovering your authentic leadership. *Harvard Business Review, 85*, 129–138.

Giacalone, R. A., Jurkiewich, C. L., & Fry, L. W. (2005). From advocacy to science: The next steps in workplace spirituality research. In R. F. Paloutzian & C. L. Park (Eds.), *Handbook of psychology and religion* (pp. 515–528). Thousand Oaks, CA: Sage.

Graen, G. B., & Uhl-Bien, M. (1995). Relationship-based approach to leadership: Development of leader-member exchange (LMX) theory of leadership over 25 years: Applying a multi-level multi-domain perspective. *Leadership Quarterly, 6*, 219–247.

Graham, J. W. (1991). Servant-leadership in organizations: inspirational and moral. *Leadership Quarterly, 2*, 105–119.

Greenleaf, R. K. (1977). *Servant leadership.* New York: Paulist Press.

Hale, J. R., & Fields, D. L. (2007). Exploring servant leadership across cultures: A study of followers in Ghana and the USA. *Leadership, 3*, 397–417.

Harter, S. (2002). Authenticity. In C. R. Snyder & S. J. Lopez (Eds.), *Handbook of positive psychology* (pp. 382–394). London, U.K.: Oxford University Press.

House, R. J., & Javidan, M. (2004). Overview of GLOBE. In R. J. House, P. J. Hanges, M. Javidan, P. W. Dorfman, & V. Gupta (Eds.). *Culture, leadership and organizations: The GLOBE study of 62 societies* (pp. 9–26). Thousand Oaks, CA: Sage.

Howell, J. M., & Avolio, B. J. (1992). The ethics of charismatic leadership: Submission or liberation? *Academy of Management Executive, 6*, 43–54.

Hunter, J. C. (1998). *The servant: A simple story about the true essence of leadership.* New York: Prima.

Hunter, J. C. (2004). *The world's most powerful leadership principle: How to become a servant leader.* Colorado Springs, CA: WaterBrook Press.

Ilies, R., Morgeson, F. P., & Nahrgang, J. D. (2005). Authentic leadership and eudaemonic well-being: Understanding leader-follower outcomes. *Leadership Quarterly, 16*, 373–394.

Joseph, E. E., & Winston, B. E. (2005). A correlation of servant leadership, leader trust, and organizational trust. *Leadership & Organization Development Journal, 26*, 6–22.

Kernis, M. H. (2003). Toward a conceptualization of optimal self-esteem. *Psychological Inquiry, 14*, 1–26.

Kernis, M. H., & Goldman, B. M. (2005). From thought and experience to behavior and interpersonal relationships: A multicomponent conceptualization of authenticity. In A. Tesser, J. V. Wood & D. Stapel (Eds.), *On building, defending and regulating the self: A psychological perspective* (pp. 31–52). New York: Psychology Press.

Kouzes, J. M., & Posner, B. Z. (1995). *The leadership challenge: How to keep getting extraordinary things done in organizations.* San Francisco, CA: Jossey-Bass.

Krebs, D. L., & Denton, K. (2005). Toward a more pragmatic approach to morality: A critical evaluation of Kohlberg's model. *Psychological Review, 112,* 629–649.

Liden, R. C., Wayne, S. J., Zhao, H., & Henderson, D. (2008). Servant leadership: Development of a multidimensional measure and multi-level assessment. *Leadership Quarterly, 19,* 161–177.

Luthans, F., & Avolio, B. J. (2003). Authentic leadership development. In K. S. Cameron, J. E. Dutton, & R. E. Quinn (Eds.), *Positive organizational scholarship* (pp. 241–261). San Francisco: Barrett-Koehler.

Macik-Frey, M., Quick, J. C., & Cooper, C. L. (2009). Authentic leadership as a pathway to positive health. *Journal of Organizational Behavior, 30,* 453–458.

Martin, K. D., & Cullen, J. B. (2006). Continuities and extensions of ethical climate theory: A meta-analytic review. *Journal of Business Ethics, 69,* 175–194.

May, D. R., Chan, A., Hodges, T., & Avolio, B. J. (2003). Developing the moral component of authentic leadership. *Organizational Dynamics, 32,* 247–260.

Mayer, D. M., Aquino, K., Greenbaum, R. L., & Kuenzi, M. (2008). *Who displays ethical leadership and why does it matter? An examination of antecedents and consequences of ethical leadership.* Unpublished manuscript.

Mayer, D. M., Bardes, M., & Piccolo, R. F. (2008). Do servant-leaders help satisfy follower needs? An organizational justice perspective. *European Journal of Work and Organizational Psychology, 17,* 180–197.

Mayer, D. M., Kuenzi, M., Greenbaum, R., Bardes, M., & Salvador, R. (2009). How low does ethical leadership flow? Test of a trickle-down model. *Organizational Behavior and Human Decision Processes, 108,* 1–13.

Mayer, D. M., Schminke, M., Treviño, L. K., Shapiro, D. L., & Harned, P. J. (2008). *Tuning in or toning down: How supervisors and coworkers can enhance or detract from ethical "tone at the top."* Unpublished manuscript.

Miller, B. (2000). Spirituality for business leadership. *Journal of Management Inquiry, 9,* 132–133.

Palmer, D. (2008). Extending the process model of collective corruption. In B. Staw (Ed.), *Research in organizational behavior* (Vol. 28, pp. 107–135). Greenwich, CT: JAI Press.

Pearce, J. A., II., & David, F. (1987). Corporate mission statements: The bottom line. *Academy of Management Executive, 1,* 109–116.

Reave, L. (2005). Spiritual values and practices related to leadership effectiveness. *Leadership Quarterly, 16,* 655–687.

Reed, A., II., & Aquino, K. F. (2003). Moral identity and the expanding circle of moral regard toward out-group members. *Journal of Personality and Social Psychology, 84,* 1270–1286.

Resick, C. J., Hanges, P. J., Dickson, M. W., & Mitchelson, J. K. (2006). A cross-cultural examination of the endorsement of ethical leadership. *Journal of Business Ethics, 63,* 345–359.

Reynolds, S. J. (2006). A neurocognitive model of the ethical decision-making process: Implications for study and practice. *Journal of Applied Psychology, 91*, 737–748.

Reynolds, S. J., & Ceranic, T. L. (2007). The effects of moral judgment and moral identity on moral behavior: An empirical examination of the moral individual. *Journal of Applied Psychology, 92*, 1610–1624.

Robertson, D. C., & Anderson, E. (1993). Control systems and task environment effects on ethical judgment: An exploratory study of industrial salespeople. *Organization Science, 4*, 617–644.

Schminke, M., Ambrose, M. L., & Neubaum, D. O. (2005). The effect of leader development on ethical climate and employee attitudes. *Organizational Behavior and Human Decision Processes, 97*, 135–151.

Schminke, M., Arnaud, A., & Kuenzi, M. (2007). The power of ethical work climates. *Organizational Dynamics, 36*, 171–186.

Shao, R., Aquino, K., & Freeman, D. (2008). Beyond moral reasoning: A review of moral identity research and its implications for business ethics. *Business Ethics Quarterly, 18*, 513–540.

Shirey, M. R. (2006). Authentic leaders creating healthy work environments for nursing practice. *American Journal of Critical Care, 15*(3), 256–268.

Sims, R. R. (2000). Changing an organization's culture under new leadership. *Journal of Business Ethics, 25*, 65–78.

Sims, R. R., & Brinkmann, J. (2002). Leaders as moral role models: The case of John Gutfreund at Salmon Brothers. *Journal of Business Ethics, 35*, 327–339.

Smith, N. C., Simpson, S. S., & Huang, C. Y. (2007). Why managers fail to do the right thing. *Business Ethics Quarterly, 17*, 633–667.

Smith, B. N., Montagno, R. V., & Kuzmenko, T. N. (2004). Transformational and servant leadership: Content and contextual comparisons. *Journal of Leadership and Organizational Studies, 10*, 80–92.

Sosik, J. J., Jung, D., & Dinger, S. L. (2009). Values in authentic action: Examining the roots and rewards of altruistic leadership. *Group and Organization Management, 34*, 395–431.

Spears, L. C. (2004). The understanding and practice of servant leadership. In L. C. Spears, & M. Lawrence (Eds.), *Practicing servant-leadership: Succeeding through trust, bravery, and forgiveness* (pp. 9–24). San Francisco, CA: Jossey-Bass.

Thomas, T., Schermerhorn, J. R., Jr., & Dienhart, J. W. (2004). Strategic leadership of ethical behavior in business. *Academy of Management Executive, 18*, 56–66.

Treviño, L. K. (1986). Ethical decision making in organizations: A person situation interactionist model. *Academy of Management Review, 11*, 601–617.

Treviño, L. K., & Brown, M. E. (2004). Managing to be ethical: Debunking five business ethics myths. *Academy of Management Executive, 18*, 69–204.

Treviño, L. K., Brown, M. E., & Hartman, L. P. (2003). A qualitative investigation of perceived executive ethical leadership: Perceptions from inside and outside the executive suite. *Human Relations, 56*, 5–37.

Treviño, L. K., Hartman, L. P., & Brown, M. (2000). Moral person and moral manager: How executives develop a reputation for ethical leadership. *California Management Review, 42*, 128–142.

Treviño, L., K., & Weaver, G. R. (2001). Organizational justice and ethics program "follow-through": Influences on employees' harmful and helpful behavior. *Business Ethics Quarterly, 11,* 651–671.

Treviño, L. K., Weaver, G. R., & Reynolds, S. J. (2006). Behavioral ethics in organizations: A review. *Journal of Management, 32,* 951–990.

Treviño, L. K., & Youngblood, S. A. (1990). Bad apples in bad barrels: A causal analysis of ethical decision-making behavior. *Journal of Applied Psychology, 75,* 378–385.

Victor, B., & Cullen, J. B. (1988). The organizational bases of ethical work climates. *Administrative Science Quarterly, 33,* 101–125.

Walumbwa, F. O., Avolio, B. J., Gardner, W. L., Wernsing, T. S., & Peterson, S. J. (2008). Authentic leadership: Development and validation of a theory-based measure. *Journal of Management, 34,* 89–126.

Walumbwa, F.O., Hartnell, C. A., & Oke, A. (August, 2009). Servant leadership, justice and service climates, and work-related outcomes: A multilevel framework. Paper to be presented at the annual meeting of the Academy of Management. Chicago, IL.

Walumbwa, F.O., Luthans, F., Avey, J., & Oke, A. (in press). Authentically leading groups: The mediating roles of psychological capital and trust. *Journal of Organizational Behavior.*

Walumbwa, F. O., & Schaubroeck, J. (2009). Leader personality traits and employee voice behavior: Mediating roles of ethical leadership and workgroup psychological safety. *Journal of Applied Psychology, 94,* 1275–1286.

Walumbwa, F.O., Wang, P., Wang, H., Schaubroeck, J., & Avolio, B.J. (in press). Psychological processes linking authentic leadership to employee citizenship behaviors and work engagement. *Leadership Quarterly.*

Warneka, T. H. (2007). *Black belt leader, peaceful leader: An introduction to Catholic servant leadership.* Cleveland, OH: Asogomi.

Washington, R. R., Sutton, C. D., & Field, H. S. (2006). Individual differences in servant leadership: The roles of values and personality. *Leadership and Organization Development Journal, 27,* 700–716.

Weaver, G. R., Treviño, L. K., & Agle, B. (2005). "Somebody to look up to": Ethical role models in organizations. *Organizational Dynamics, 34,* 313–330.

Wright, T. A., & Goodstein, J. (2007). Character is not "dead" in management research: A review of individual character and organizational-level virtue. *Journal of Management, 33,* 928–958.

Wright, T. A., & Huang, C-C. (2008). Character in organizational research: Past directions and future prospects. *Journal of Organizational Behavior, 29,* 981–987.

Yammarino, F. J., Dionne, S. D., Schriesheim, C. A., & Dansereau, F. (2008). Authentic leadership and positive organizational behavior: A meso, multilevel perspective. *Leadership Quarterly, 19,* 693–707.

3

Organizational Virtue, CSR, and Performance

Rosa Chun
Manchester Business School

The study of corporate social responsibility (CSR) of an organization has predominantly focused on rationalist assumptions (Kantian or utilitarian approaches) and external ethical image (e.g., marketing). This chapter first aims to integrate the emotional aspect of virtue ethics into existing CSR themes such as the three-dimensional model (e.g., Carroll, 1979), stakeholder theory, and ethical theory. It also explores the antecedents and consequences of virtue at the organizational level, by linking customer perceptions of the ethical character of The Body Shop to organizational outcomes such as emotional attachment and satisfaction.

Concept and Theory: The Integration of CSR

Conceptual Development

The purpose of this section is to provide an overview the conceptual development of CSR and introduce virtue ethics as a way of assessing CSR and nonfinancial performance. In the early days, the primary responsibility of the corporation was to produce profit (Frederick, 1960). Concerning the fact that responsibility reflects obligational rather than motivational issues, the late 1970s saw the emergence of the concept of *responsiveness*. Some preferred to replace responsibility with responsiveness (Ackerman & Bauer, 1976), while others added responsibility between obligation and responsiveness. Sethi (1975) suggests a three-state schema of social performance as including social obligation, social responsibility, and social responsiveness. In this schema, social obligation involves corporate behavior in response to market forces or legal constraints, and social responsibility implies elevating corporate behavior to a level where it is congruent with

TABLE 3.1

Three Way Integration of CSR Theories

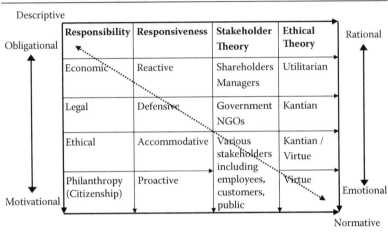

Descriptive						Rational
Obligational	**Responsibility**	**Responsiveness**	**Stakeholder Theory**	**Ethical Theory**		
	Economic	Reactive	Shareholders Managers	Utilitarian		
	Legal	Defensive	Government NGOs	Kantian		
	Ethical	Accommodative	Various stakeholders including	Kantian / Virtue		
Motivational	Philanthropy (Citizenship)	Proactive	employees, customers, public	Virtue		Emotional
						Normative

prevailing social norms, values, and expectations. Social responsiveness, on the other hand, is not concerned with how corporations should respond to social pressures, but with what should be anticipatory and preventive in their long-run role in a dynamic social system.

The three-state schema became the basis of the well-quoted three-dimensional model of Carroll (1979). The model integrated social responsibility (economic, legal, ethical, and discretionary) into responsiveness and social issues. Steiner's "voluntary" category is analogous to Carroll's "discretionary responsibility" (Carroll, 1979), which later was reoriented to become voluntary (Carroll, 1983) and philanthropy or citizenship (Carroll, 1999).

In addition to responsibility and responsiveness, in the last decade CSR has embraced other alternative concepts such as stakeholder theory and business ethics theory (Carroll, 1999; Clarkson, 1995; Swanson, 1995). With the emergence of stakeholder theory, the management of noninvestor stakeholders' satisfaction, perceptions, and emotions has become important. No one simple model can integrate every aspect of CSR but Table 3.1 attempts to integrate its common characteristics across four complementing CSR themes—responsibility, responsiveness, stakeholder theory, and ethical theory, which have evolved over time, and suggests a possible way of theory integration.

The Emergence of Virtue Ethics

The profit maximizing models in CSR mainly concern economic responsibility for shareholders and align with the spirit of utilitarianism, one of the two leading ethical theories (together with the Kantian approach) until the 1990s. The models based on the utilitarian approach in CSR are usually descriptive, and empirically testable with respect to what the firm *is* and what it *does*, therefore, allowing managers to access its strategic implication. From this utilitarian perspective, linking corporate social responsibility and financial performance has been popular, but results are rather contentious. The mixed findings include no relationship (McWilliams & Siegel, 2000), a positive relationship (Waddock & Graves, 1997), and a negative relationship (Wright & Farris, 1997) between CSR and performance. These inconsistent results are mainly due to the variety of measures employed for assessing corporate social responsibility and performance (Griffin & Mahon, 1997). The mixed result is, however, likely to send confusing messages to managers, and leaves the fundamental question as to how one measures the harm or benefit of an ethical action unanswered (Solomon, 1992).

The Kantian approach shares rationalization with utilitarianism but puts an emphasis on fulfilling duties and universal ethical principles such as "don't lie" or "don't cheat." As a result of focusing on the utilitarian and Kantian views, CSR is often conceived as a set of impositions on business behavior (Donaldson & Dunfee, 1994), leaving one important question open: "Why should a firm be ethical?" Aligned with the spirit of virtue ethics, what became known more widely as corporate social responsibility seems to emphasize ethical and philanthropic responsibility embracing the notion of proactive responsiveness to meet various stakeholders' interests as presented in the bottom half of Table 3.1.

Developing the ethical character of an organization is the core theme in virtue ethics theory. Virtue ethics theory denies that making moral decisions is a matter of calculation or principle-based duties (Hartman, 1998; Stark, 1993). Instead, it focuses on aspirational values through the ongoing development of ethical character. Despite the increasing popularity in the last decade of applying the virtue ethics perspective to business ethics, the managerial implications of organizational-level virtue have not been well transmitted, mainly because existing studies within virtue ethics have tended to focus on a person's moral character, not on the organization as a whole (Solomon, 1999). The strength of organizational virtue ethics is its focus on stakeholder emotion and satisfaction through the development of organizational ethical character, factors that are known to influence the satisfaction of both internal and external stakeholders. More recently, scholars have turned their attention to the organizational level of virtue: the author's own work has produced a scale where respondents are invited to imagine that an organization has "come to life" as a person and to assess his/her character, which then allows empirical testing of the link between organizational virtue and stakeholder satisfaction (Chun, 2005). The validated scale (Virtue Ethical Character Scale, or VECS) has six dimensions of organizational virtue: empathy, warmth, integrity, conscientiousness, courage, and zeal (Figure 3.1).

FIGURE 3.1
Virtue Ethical Character Scale. From "Ethical Character and Virtues: An Empirical Assessment and Strategic Implications," by Rosa Chun, 2005, *Journal of Business Ethics*, 57(3), 269–284. Reprinted with permission of the author.

Empathy in a firm's character strengthens bonds with stakeholders. When there is a delegation of responsibilities conveyed to others in an empathetic manner it creates more *confident, supportive,* and *caring* relationships (Burke, 1999). Integrity in an organization implies acting on a personal commitment to *honesty, openness,* and *fairness*—living by and for our standards (Becker, 1998; Ventrella, 2001). Integrity is defined as a reputation for *trustfulness* and *honesty* of the trusted person (Butler & Cantrell, 1984). Warmth (friendly, open, pleasant, and straightforward) is important in promoting customer satisfaction with a services business. Zeal differentiates virtue ethics from the Kantian approach by focusing on nonobligational virtues such as being exciting, innovative, and spirited.

Conscientiousness refers to the traits of being *dependable* and *hardworking,* reflecting one of the Big Five human personality factors (Barrick & Mount, 1991; Becker, 1998). Some ethical dimensions may be more important than others, depending on the stakeholder group, company, and industry. For example, job applicants' perceptions of a firm's fairness during the application process is based on criteria such as *consistency, honesty, sympathy, trustworthiness, warmth,* and *respect* (Gilliland, 1993).

Antecedents and Consequences of Organizational Virtue

A company has responsibilities to various stakeholders. In particular, how the company is seen by their customers has a direct impact on the company's performance because customers have the purchasing power. The increasing pressure for companies to fulfill their social obligations naturally leads managers to focus on creating an ethical image of the brand (Bauer & Fenn, 1973) because they believe a positive customer evaluation of a company has positive and direct impact on financial performance. On the other hand, customers' negative perceptions of the company, or worse, boycotting activities when customers feel the company does not live up to their responsibility expected by the society, can have detrimental effects on the financial performance of the company. There are a number of antecedents and consequences to a positive organizational virtue character as perceived by customers. The relational and moral motives of customers play a great role in their desire to get involved with companies with high ethical identity and reputation (Aguilera, Rupp, Williams, & Ganapathi, 2007). One desirable outcome for company efforts in developing a favorable reputation would be a positive consumer evaluation of the brand expressed as loyalty and satisfaction, which will lead to repeated purchase and therefore profitability.

Brand Reputation and Ethical Character

The customer's favorable evaluation of the brand can be projected into the market place largely through three factors: the perception and feelings customers hold of the ethical character of the brand, how similar the brand's perceived ethical character is to their own, and how closely customers feel emotionally attached to the brand. One of the factors leading to the financial success of a brand is customer satisfaction and loyalty. Managers believe that the customer's perception of a brand's ethical character influences their purchase decision. Cause-related marketing is one example where companies believe that their engagement with a good cause, such as a charity, can potentially result in customer loyalty and therefore growing market share (Mullen, 1997). Many companies promote their ethical character through advertising, social audit, and various CSR programs, while some companies go further by setting up a company purely based on ethical ideology.

Similarity of Ethical Character: The Customer Self and the Brand

There are an increasing number of brands whose founding ideology has an ethical stance. One of the leaders in this league is the cooperative group in Britain. In 1844 the Rochdale Pioneers developed the first successful retail cooperative; at its core was a belief that business should involve concern for human rights and social justice as well as profit. In more recent times, many other brands such as The Body Shop and Ben & Jerry's have followed suit. One of the common goals of using an ethical platform for firms is to differentiate themselves from their competitors in a similar line of business. Although they gained respect for pioneering an ethical stance in business, they were often criticized as being *green capitalists*, in other words using an ethical positioning more to gain commercial benefit than to fulfill a social role. The good intentions of these companies can often contrast with a less positive reality, for example, Ben & Jerry's problems related to outsourcing and salary inequalities with respect to their Rainforest Crunch ice cream (Dreifus, 1994), and The Body Shop's issues with animal testing and fair trade (Entine, 1994).

According to the marketing literature, companies promote a favorable, perhaps ethical and distinctive image for their brands by emphasizing similarity between the consumers and the brand. An ethical brand would position itself toward customers who see themselves as ethical, or those who would like to see themselves so. Such thinking is largely based on brand personality congruence theory, which states that a brand preference is influenced by one's perception of how similar the personality of brand is to one's own (Kassarjian, 1971). When a consumer buys a product, he or she buys not only functional benefits but also reputation, prestige, symbols, and social meanings associated with the image of the brand. Customers make purchase decisions on a product's symbolic meaning and images, which can be used to maintain or enhance self-image (Levy, 1959). For example, a man who considers himself rugged and masculine should prefer Marlboro cigarettes, whereas a woman who considers herself attractive, modern, and liberated should prefer Virginia Slims cigarettes. Marketers have capitalized on this desire by creating distinctive product images that will fit different customers' self-images and no less so in the ethical arena.

Emotional Attachment

The role of stakeholder emotion—for example, how employees or customers feel about the company or the brand—has been often overlooked in the search for links between CSR and financial performance from Kantian or utilitarian approaches. Building norms or values does not only come from a clear mission or affluent resources, but from managing group levels of emotion and their interaction (Druskat & Wolff, 2001). What matters is how management can promote positive feelings within their firm so that any ethical decision process is made by members who sense the state of the ethical character of their firm (Gaudine & Throne, 2001). The following case study demonstrates how the level of emotional attachment consumers have with a brand is expected to play an important role in creating positive brand evaluation and likely to be influenced by the level of customers' self–brand image congruence.

Case Study: The Body Shop

To explore the antecedents and consequences of a virtue character, we have chosen The Body Shop International, a natural cosmetics and toiletries company founded in 1976 in Brighton, United Kingdom by Anita Roddick. The company is well known for its distinctive identity as being an ethical cosmetics company with values inherited from Roddick as founder, who had been the cochairperson until 2002, and later a nonexecutive director until she died in 2007. The company was acquired by French luxury goods manufacturer L'Oréal for £652 million in March 2006. This case study utilizes two sources of data: two recent *The Body Shop Values Reports* published biannually; one was published in 2005 (*The Body Shop Values Report 2005*) and the other in 2007 after the acquisition (*The Body Shop Values Report 2007*). The second source of the data is a 317-questionnaire survey involving The Body Shop customers. Some offered to provide more insights into their experience with the brand through in-depth interviews.

In this research, customer respondents to a survey were asked to rate their own ethical character traits and those of The Body Shop using a five-point Likert scale ranging from 1 (strongly disagree) to 5 (strongly agree), with 3 being neutral. The research was conducted just before the merger with L'Oréal was announced and before the death of the founder Anita Roddick, so there was no bias in consumer evaluation due to such a major organizational change. Figure 3.2 shows the results for three dimensions (integrity, courage, and empathy) of the Virtue Ethical Character Scale, as these are the dimensions that are most emphasized in the values of The Body Shop and most relevant to the analysis that follows.

Although customers rated the ethical character of The Body Shop reasonably highly, they rated their own personality higher still (Figure 3.2). This is surprising given that, logically there should have been little or no gap if shoppers seek a store whose values are congruent with those they hold themselves. Secondly, one might have expected The Body Shop's values to be higher, not lower than those of its customers. After all it is supposed to be a campaigning brand, one capable of leading customer opinion, not following it. Some insights into the reasons for such gaps between self and company ratings are explored next.

Integrity

By analyzing The Body Shop value reports, the most prominent values appear as those associated with the integrity, empathy, and courage virtue character dimensions. The 2005 report emphasizes values with a specific focus on integrity and empathy. On the other hand, the 2007 report

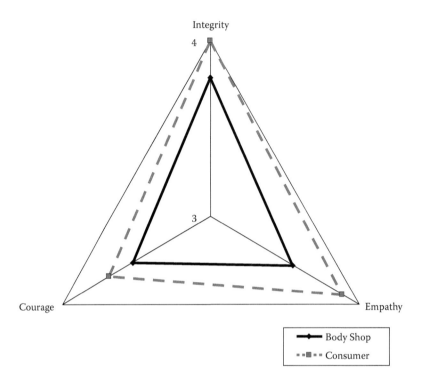

FIGURE 3.2
The ethical character of The Body Shop. Figures represented are the mean scores for each group in a 5-point Likert scale.

emphasizes values rather generally but also more specifically on the courage virtue.

> Earning the Trust—Walking the talk, running our business with integrity and delivering against our promises are key to maintaining the trust of all our stakeholders. (CEO statement, *The Body Shop Values Report*, 2005)

Despite the emphasis on its social mission, The Body Shop received a number of challenges on their integrity from the media. Its key ethical slogan of selling products derived from natural ingredients that are neither tested on animals nor extracted in a way that is environmentally harmful, nor manufactured by means of exploitive employment practices was found to be exaggerated (McNeish, 1999). In effect, the company's values, or rather their presentation to the public, were toned down. Some might have been disappointed to see The Body Shop forced to acknowledge that their self-promotion had not survived media and legal scrutiny.

Empathy

Empathy is one's capability to share and understand another's feelings and is therefore a character trait of being concerned, reassuring, and sympathetic. The Body Shop promotes the empathy virtue through various media including their own value report:

> Listening to stakeholders—Our engagement with stakeholders provides us with valuable ideas for improvements and on-the-ground knowledge of emerging issues. We listen to Non Governmental Organizations, business networks, franchisees, employees, communities, suppliers and investors to understand where we can help make a difference. (CEO statement, *The Body Shop Values Report*, 2005)

The Body Shop's focus on creating its image as a "caring" company with "natural," high-quality products also appeared in its advertising. While projecting a caring brand image, the company apparently pays their store workers minimum wages that are well below the official European "decency threshold" for pay, and is opposed to trade unions.[1] However, empathy plays a greater role in stakeholders' loyalty and emotional attachment with the company. The merger of The Body Shop with L'Oréal is perceived by their core customers as being less than empathetic. On the day of the announcement, shares in The Body Shop surged more than 10%, but consumers' satisfaction rating, measured by BrandIndex,[2] dropped by 11 points to 14, the brand's "trendiness" fell by 10 points to −4.[3] and the ethical rating measured by Ethiscore[4] immediately plunged from 11 out of 20 to just 2.5. The magazine *Ethical Consumer* urged a boycott of Body Shop products in protest, not only of the French cosmetics group's ownership, but also its links with allegedly the most boycotted company in Britain, Nestlé, which owns 26% of L'Oréal (*The Guardian*, 2006). The media were busy creating headlines containing negative phrases such as "The Brand Reputation Was in Risk," and "Body Shop's Popularity Plunges after L'Oréal Sale" (*The Independent*, 2006); "Anita Sells Her Body" (*The Sun*, 2006); and "Roddick Sold Out Body Shop to L'Oréal, the Sort of Company That People Went to Body Shop to Avoid" (*The Times*, 2006). Customers and the media could well remember Roddick's strident condemnation of the typical large cosmetics business, which she once described as "tacky," one of her more printable labels. Now she had literally sold out to one of the same businesses she once condemned. The fact that she intended to use her profits to pursue her charitable work was ignored; the symbolism of L'Oréal owning The Body Shop was the issue, not that charities would benefit.

The negative reaction by the media and consumers appears to came from consumers' emotional attachment to the ethical values that The Body Shop had promoted as being their raison d'étre over the last 30 years, which were perceived as being threatened by the takeover. This problem, of other brands repositioning themselves toward The Body Shop, diluted The Body Shop's appeal. At the same time, the company had to fight off increasing media scrutiny of their ethical platform. The Body Shop regularly threatened journalists and hired private detectives to stalk editors to try to suppress the story of how it stole its name, product ideas, store and bottle design from another company, and then exaggerated its image as a "caring" company with "natural," high-quality products (Entine, 1996) The company was in danger of being seen as having *feet of clay*—much admired but perhaps fatally flawed.

Courage

The courage virtue dimension (ambitious, achievement oriented, and competent) emphasizes commercial success of an organization. But focusing on the courage virtue through ambitious expansion programs didn't give The Body Shop the same competitive advantage as the integrity and empathy virtues did. The company lost ground in the late 1990s as mainstream competitors also began to sell natural, herbal-based products, cutting into The Body Shop sales. The problems were accelerated after an ambitious program of international expansion failed to pay off (Anonymous, 2004) and the brand was eventually sold to L'Oréal in 2006. One noticeable change in the chairman and CEO's statement from *The Body Shop Value Report* (2007) is in the emphasis on financial success, that is the virtue of courage, but less emphasis on integrity and empathy, which were emphasized in its previous value report.

> Everyone on the Executive is passionate about delivering a commercially successful company that has values. (CEO statement, *The Body Shop Value* Report, 2007).

Given that the 2007 report this is the first report since the merger with L'Oréal, the emphasis on the courage virtue is perhaps not surprising. However, the contrast between the two values reports does imply a change in direction, precisely what the ethical customer would not want to hear.

Consumer Self-Brand Similarity

For CSR-led cosmetic brands, their target consumers are supposedly those who share similar ethical values and personality with the brand. During the interviews for The Body Shop study, respondents were asked to describe the typical kind of person that would shop at The Body Shop, and if they saw themselves as being a socially responsible person. According to the interviews, The Body Shop customers can be grouped largely into three groups. The first group includes consumers who seek value for money.

Most Body Shop consumers we interviewed took a surprisingly utilitarian approach to their brand choice. The *integrity* of the Body Shop only played a significant role in customer loyalty when customers held ethical beliefs themselves. The following are some representative comments:

> When it comes to a typical Body Shop customer, I think of someone who is price conscious, quite simplistic, and uncomplicated.
>
> Obviously it is nice when a company that you buy things from acts ethically, but other things like price and reliability come into it as well.
>
> However, it has been a debate whether they test on animals because it's "too good to be true" to be a successful and profitable company as well as socially responsible and ethical. It's very difficult to combine both sides although they are trying to.
>
> Yes, I'd like to think myself as a socially responsible person. I get the odd fair trade coffee here and there … obviously that's a bit lame but I do try when I can.

A brand can show *empathy* for its customers in many ways, but in the case of The Body Shop it is particularly important to acknowledge the ethical views of customers. We came across many examples:

> Well, because I am a scientist, I would appreciate using organic brands and products. I think Body Shop is the brand that makes sense for me because I believe in the power of nature. I also think there is more goodness on natural ingredients than in chemical derivatives.
>
> Yes I do. I do care a lot about animals. I donate monthly to RSPCA. I am volunteering in the dog shelter here in Manchester. So I do contribute.
>
> Because of the quality and the natural basis of their product it is good value for money. It is also an affordable price to pay and if you would do something good for your health for that kind of price, then that's good too.
>
> As a PhD student, I am a researcher and very busy and sometimes work very long hours. I really try to find some time to relax and indulge myself. As for my personality, I think I am open, cheerful, self-confident, expressive and sometime emotional and exuberant. I am not really bothered what people see about me and I am what I am. That's why I shop here.

Interestingly given the refocusing of the brand on *courage* after its acquisition by L'Oréal, we found few examples in our survey. Some even mentioned the lack of innovation, which is part of the *zeal* character dimension. For example:

I think that their products aren't as innovative. They emphasize too much on the brand and their values but don't say much about their products. I think that some of the stuff is just the same. They need to be more up to date.

Practical Implications and Discussion

One of the difficulties in managing corporate ethics as an ongoing process is the need to elevate ethical character in people's thinking and behavior (Aguilar, 1994). The last decade saw an increasing number of marriages between companies who need more resources and large multinational companies whose poor reputation needed a makeover. For example, Pret a Manger, Britain's organic sandwiches maker, sold a third of its business to McDonald's; Pepsi acquired P&J Smoothies; Cadbury Schweppes bought Green & Black's organic chocolate; and Go Organic and Ben & Jerry's are now owned by Unilever. Both Coca Cola and McDonald's have been criticized for providing unhealthy food that is too high in fat or sugar and bad for health as sugar rots your teeth, caffeine is an artificial stimulant, and a high-fat diet leads to obesity. McDonald's has been nominated as the least ethical company (*The Observer*, 2006). Cadbury Schweppes has also received poor press recently with a series of product recalls and was charged due to health and safety issues over salmonella contamination (Manning, 2007).

In April, 2009, Innocent, another organic smoothie maker, set up with a strong ethical ethos, sold a 20% stake to Coca Cola. The sale came after seeing its annual sales fall for the first time since its foundation in 1999 due to the competition from two rival products, Pepsico's Tropicana and Nestlé's Boost. News headlines presented the deal as a Faustian pact and as making Innocent just 20% less innocent, according to *The Guardian*.[5] After having been under the ownership of Unilever for 5 years, Ben & Jerry launched an advertising campaign that focuses on social issues, not their ice cream, in an effort to return the brand to its roots. Ben & Jerry's CEO Walt Freese admitted that Ben & Jerry's has been soft in recent years on continuing its founders' (Ben Cohen and Jerry Greenfield) tradition of social consciousness.[6]

In its heyday, The Body Shop was the darling of the London stock market. It was seen as unique and tapping into a growth in consumer demand for more ethical and socially responsible products. The problem with mixing capitalism with ethics is that the latter is clearly no guarantee of long-term financial success. When the big cosmetics companies woke up to the need to add an ethical dimension to their offerings, The Body Shop, from a commercial perspective, needed to move on to different causes from animal testing and natural ingredients, especially as their own claims were being challenged.

The case emphasizes how difficult it is to generalize on the links between CSR and financial performance. The links are as yet unproven and probably never will be if ethics is viewed from a Kantian perspective. That is not how commerce functions. Utilitarianism offers even less of a way forward as it focuses on outcome, and for corporations, the most ethical thing you can do is make a good return for your shareholders. All else is pure fluff.

Perhaps virtue ethics offers a new, if conditional, approach for managers. What matters is that your company has virtues that come from its inner values. Those virtues may not always accord with what the majority regard as ethical, but often there will be an overlap. Such virtues will create associations with your brands and appeal to those who wish similar virtues. Understanding what your real corporate values and virtues are is then central to the approach. Virtue is not invented at a corporate retreat. It is not akin to deciding which charity has an image most congruent with our brand's new positioning. Most organizations have virtue, otherwise few employees would want to work for them or deal with them. If these are distinctive, then they offer the marketer a way of making a brand more distinctive and relevant to their desirable identity. However, from the many examples of the acquisition of a virtuous brand by a company perhaps less virtuous, it appears that virtue cannot be bought and sold.

Virtue is moral excellence; its antonym is vice. They cannot be cosmetic (no pun intended in the context of The Body Shop), grafted onto a product in an advertising campaign. They have to stem from the beliefs of the company as to what is ethical. To link their beliefs in CSR to commercial performance, the company should engage their core customers—those who share similar values and beliefs on the social cause, have significant emotional attachment to the brand, and will ultimately be loyal to the brand.

Endnotes

1. "What's wrong with The Body Shop," www.McSpotlight.org/beyond/companies/bodyshop.html, Accessed December 2009.
2. YouGov's BrandIndex is a daily measure of public perception of more than 1,100 consumer brands across 32 sectors, gleaned from 2,000 interviews from its 130,000-person panel.

3. From"Body Shop Brand Reputation Is Battered by Sale to L'Oreal," by Suzanne Bidlake, Brand Republic, March 29, 2006. Retrieved May 17, 2006 from http://www.brandrepublic.com/bulletins/br/article/549982/body-shop-brand-reputation-battered-sale-loreal/.

4. *Ethical Consumer* magazine runs an online shoppers guide, available at http://www.ethiscore.org/, that rates companies and their products on their ethical credentials.

5. From *The Guardian*, "Smoothie Operators Innocent Tread Familiar Path to Lucrative Deal," April 7 2009. Retrieved April 10, 2009 from http://www.guardian.co.uk/business/2009/apr/07/innocent-smoothies-coca-cola.

6. From *USA Today*, "Ben & Jerry's Returns to Social Issues, October 16, 2005. Retrieved April 5, 2009 from http://www.usatoday.com/money/advertising/2005-10-16-ben-jerry-usat_x.htm.

References

Ackerman, R.W., & Bauer, Raymond A. (1976). *Corporate social responsiveness.* Reston, VA: Reston.

Aguilar, Francis J. (1994). Elevating the ethical character of the firm. In *Managing Corporate Ethics* (pp. 119–143). New York: Oxford University Press.

Aguilera, R.V., Rupp, D. E. Williams, C., & Ganapathi, J. (2007). Putting the S back in corporate social responsibility: A multi-level theory of social change in organizations. *Academy of Management Review 32*(3), 836–863.

Ahearne, Michael, Bhattacharya, C. B., & Gruen, Thomas (2005). Antecedents and consequences of customer-company identification: Expanding the role of relationship marketing. *Journal of Applied Psychology, 90*(3), 574–585.

Anonymous (2004). Best of brands. *Marketing Management, 13*(2), 7–8.

Barrick, M. R., & Mount, M. K. (1991). The big five personality dimensions and job performance: A meta-analysis. *Personnel Psychology, 44*, 1–26.

Bauer, Raymond A., & Fenn, Dan H., Jr. (1973, January–February). What is a corporate social audit? *Harvard Business Review.*

Becker, Thomas E. (1998). Integrity in organizations: Beyond honesty and conscientiousness. *Academy of Management Review, 23*(1), 154–161.

Bhattacharya, C. B., and Sen, Sankar. (2003). Consumer-company identification: A framework for understanding consumers' relationships with companies. *Journal of Marketing, 67*(2), 76–88.

Body Shop, The. (2005), *The Body Shop Values Report*. Retrieved April 2009 from *http://valuesreport.thebodyshop.net/pdfs/bodyshop_valuesreport_2005.pdf.*

Body Shop. The. (2007). *The Body Shop Values Report*. Retrieved April 2009 from *http://valuesreport.thebodyshop.net.*

Burke, Frances. (1999). Ethical decision-making: Global concerns, frameworks, and approaches. *Public Personnel Management, 28*(4), 529–540.

Butler, J. K., & Cantrell, R. S. (1984). A behavioral decision theory approach to modeling dyadic trust in superiors and subordinates. *Psychological Reports, 55*, 19–28.

Carroll, Archie B. (1979). A three-dimensional conceptual model of corporate performance. *Academy of Management Review, 4*(4), 497–505.

Carroll, Archie B. (1983). Corporate social responsibility: Will industry respond to cutbacks in social program funding? *Vital Speeches of the Day, 49*, 604–608.

Carroll, Archie B. (1999). Corporate social responsibility: Evolution of definitional construc. *Business and Society, 38*(3), 268–295.

Chun, Rosa. (2005). Ethical character and virtues: An empirical assessment and strategic implications. *Journal of Business Ethics 57*(3), 269–284.

Clarkson, Max B. (1995). A stakeholder framework for analyzing and evaluating corporate social performance. *Academy of Management Review, 20*(1), 92–117.

Donaldson, Thomas, & Dunfee, Thomas. (1994). Toward a unified conception of business ethics: Integrative social contracts theory. *Academy of Management Review, 19*(2), 252–284.

Dreifus, Claudia. (1994, December 18). Passing the scoop: Ben & Jerry. *New York Times Magazine,* pp. 38–41.

Druskat, Vanessa Urch, & Wolff, Steven B. (2001). Building the emotional intelligence of group. *Harvard Business Review*, 81–90.

Entine, Jon. (1994, September/October). Shattered image. *Business Ethics*, 23–28.

Entine, Jon. (1995). When rainforest ice cream melts: The messy reality of "socially responsible business. *Electronic Journal of Radical Organizational Theory, 1*(1). http://www.mngt.waikato.ac.nz/research/ejrot/Vol1_1/Dialogue/Entine.asp.

Entine, Jon. (1996, June 20). Blowing the whistle on meaningless "good indentions." *Chicago Tribune.* Retrieved June 2009 from http://www.jonentine.com/reviews/blowing_the_whistle.htm.

Fournier, Susan. (1998). Consumers and their brands: Developing relationship theory in consumer research. *Journal of Consumer Research, 24*(4), 343–373.

Frederick, W. C. (1960). The growing concern over business responsibility. *California Management Review, 2*, 54–61.

Gaudine, Alice, & Throne, Linda. (2001). Emotion and ethical decision-making in organizations. *Journal of Business Ethics, 31*, 175–187.

Gilliland, Stephen W. (1993). The perceived fairness of selection systems: An organizational justice perspective. *Academy of Management Review, 18*, 694–734.

Griffin, Jennifer J., & Mahon, John F. (1997, March). The corporate social performance and corporate financial performance debate: Twenty-five years of incomparable research. *Business & Society*, 5–31.

Guardian, The. (2006, June 8). When big business bites. Retrieved August 10, 2006 from http://business.guardian.co.uk/story/0,,1792511,00.html#article_continue.

Hartman, Edwin M. (1998). The role of character in business ethics. *Business Ethics Quarterly, 8*(3), 547–559.

Independent, The. (2006, April 10). Body Shop's popularity plunges after L'Oréal sale.

Kassarjian, Harold H. (1971, November). Personality and consumer behavior: A review. *Journal of Marketing Research, 8*, 409–418.

Levy, Sidney J. (1959). Symbols by which we buy. In Lynn H. Stockman (Ed.), *Advancing Marketing Efficiency* (pp. 409–416). Chicago. American Marketing Association.

Manning, Louise. (2007). Food safety and brand equity. *British Food Journal, 109*(7), 496–510.

McNeish, Jim. (1999). HRD in a values-driven business: The Body Shop International Plc. *Human Resource Development, 2*(3), 283–287.

McWilliams, Abagail, and Siegel, Donald. (2000). Corporate social responsibility and financial performance: Correlations or misspecification? *Strategic Management Journal, 21*, 603–609.

Mullen, J. (1997). Performance-based corporate philanthropy: How "giving smart" can further corporate goals. *Public Relations Quarterly, 42*(2), 42–48.

Observer, The. (2006, April 16). Big Mac tops "unethical" poll. Retrieved June 2009 from http://www.guardian.co.uk/business/2006/apr/16/theobserver.observerbusiness1.

Sethi, S. Prakash. (1975). Dimensions of corporate social responsibility. *California Management Review, 17*(3), 58–64.

Solomon, Robert C. (1992). *Ethics and excellence: Cooperation and integrity in business.* New York: Oxford University Press.

Stark, Andrew. (1993, May/June). What is the matter with business ethics? *Harvard Business Review*, 38–48.

Swanson, D. L. (1995). Addressing a theoretical problem by reorienting the corporate social performance model. *Academy of Management Review, 20*, 43–64.

Sun, The. (2006, March 18). Anita sells her body.

Times, The. (2006, April 11). L'Oréal & Body Shop: Business commentary.

Ventrella, Scott W. (2001). Intentional integrity. *Executive excellence, 18*(5), 9–10.

Waddock, S., & Graves, S. (1997). The corporate social performance–financial performance link. *Strategic Management Journal, 18*, 303–319.

Wright, P., & Farris, S. (1997). Agency conflict and corporate strategy: The effect of divestment on corporate value. *Strategic Management Journal, 18*, 77–83.

4

Increasing Corporate Social Responsibility Through Stakeholder Value Internalization (and the Catalyzing Effect of New Governance): An Application of Organizational Justice, Self-Determination, and Social Influence Theories

Deborah E. Rupp
Cynthia A. Williams
Ruth V. Aguilera
University of Illinois at Urbana-Champaign

> Societies and organizations are not persons, but function through the agency of their individual members—present and past—and the social norms and cultural products they create. (Kelman, 2006, p. 19)
>
> [B]y failing to provide supports for competence, autonomy, and relatedness of employees, socializing agents and organizations contribute to alienation and ill-being. (Ryan & Deci, 2000, p. 74)
>
> The operation of rules, roles, and values in socialization and social control is illustrated in an analysis of people's emotional reactions when they find themselves deviating from societal standards in the domain of responsibility or propriety. (Kelman, 2006, pp. 12–13)

This chapter is about the *psychology* of corporate social responsibility (CSR). CSR (more recently given the broader term *organizational responsibility*), refers to "context-specific organizational actions and policies that take into account stakeholders' expectations and the triple bottom line of economic, social, and environmental performance" (Aguinis, in press; see also Bowen, 1953; Caroll, 1979; Waddock, 2004). CSR as an area of inquiry has served to shift the view of the firm as existing for the purpose of shareholder profit maximization to a view of the firm as a global citizen whose actions should be accountable to many stakeholder groups (e.g., local communities, the environment, employees, consumers, etc., in addition to stakeholders). As such, organizations are being held accountable as conduits of social justice more than ever before (Fortanier & Kolk, 2007).

This trend has led sociologists, anthropologists, and law scholars to uncover a dizzying array of issues that speak to the complexity of corporate social responsibility as a potential catalyst for positive social change. In the organizational behavior literature, a great deal of research has focused on the seemingly incongruent goals of wealth maximization and social responsibility. This research has suggested that these goals are not necessarily incompatible and that CSR may actually be leveraged to serve a strategic advantage. That is, empirical research has sought to determine if there is a significant link between corporate social performance and corporate financial performance. The first of these studies was conducted by Bragdon and Marlin (1972) who found a positive relationship between these two variables. Thirty-five years and over 200 studies later, we still do not seem to have a clear answer.

For example, a meta-analysis by Orlitsky, Schmidt, and Rynes (2003) considered 52 studies comprising over 30,000 observations and concluded that there seems to be a relationship between social performance and firm performance, although it really depends on how both are operationalized and measured. Their moderator analysis showed that effects are more likely to be observed when social performance is measured via reputation as compared to other indicators, and when firm performance is measured via accounting-based indicators as opposed to market-based indicators. Mackey, Mackey, and Barney (2007) have shown mathematically that CSR initiatives might be funded in publically traded firms that, although not maximizing the present value of the firms' future cash flows, might still maximize the market value of the firm. In the most recent meta-analysis of the social performance–firm performance link, Margolis, Elfenbein, and Walsh (2009) show, using a sample of 251 studies, that the overall CSR effect on firm performance is positive, yet small (mean $r = .13$, median $r = .09$, weighted $r = .11$). Further, they were unable to show that any of the moderators explored in past research made a notable difference on this effect (with the exception of the effect of revealed misdeeds on financial performance). These authors conclude that firms should be engaging in CSR for the sole purpose of enhancing social performance itself and avoiding harm, and that a continued search for a *business case* for CSR is futile.

In the legal literature, there has been a focus on the effects of "new governance" or "soft law" structures on corporate social responsibility (Williams, 2004). New governance refers to a shift from governments requiring compliance to various regulatory standards, to one where stakeholder pressure leads to the formation and adoption of voluntary, transnational standards for conducting business. Thus, we see organizations complying with evolving standards of social responsibility, not because they are legally required to do so, but because of social pressures imposed on them by consumers, industrial associations, intergovernmental entities, corporate interest groups, some kinds of institutional investors, and nongovernmental organizations (Conley & Williams, 2005).

It has recently been pointed out that organizational and social psychology is a discipline that might have much to contribute to the CSR discourse, but it has been slow to take up that challenge (Aguinis, in press; Rupp & Aquino, 2009). Whereas law, strategy, and organizational behavior have been instrumental in defining the domain of CSR and uncovering its placement within broader business practices and global governance frameworks, there is still much uncharted territory in areas where a more psychological perspective could be fruitful. Such a perspective would seek to uncover the phenomenological processes that explain *why* various stakeholders care about CSR, the *motivational* structures that lead to the engagement of socially responsible or irresponsible behaviors by organizations, and the *internalization* processes by which CSR stops being a set of practices organizations feel pressured by external groups to carry out and starts becoming a set of practices that represent a manifestation of the organization's and stakeholders' shared values.

These are the phenomena on which we will focus in this paper. We will begin with an account of why CSR is important to stakeholders. For this discussion, we will pull from the organizational justice literature, specifically, the multiple needs theory of organizational justice (Cropanzano, Byrne, Bobocel, & Rupp, 2001), as well as our previous work, which has applied this model to CSR (Aguilera, Rupp, Williams, & Ganapathi, 2007). Second, we consider the contextual factors that lead CSR to be valued by stakeholders. For this, we apply self-determination theory (Ryan & Deci, 2000) to show how structures that increase feelings of competence, relatededness, and autonomy lead to CSR being internalized and integrated into stakeholders' value frameworks and sense of self. Third, we consider the contagion properties of CSR—looking specifically at how CSR values might be internalized at the institutional level, and spread to other practices internal and external to the organization.

The final section of our paper describes a case through which we hope to illustrate the propositions made in the first three sections. Here we describe how global banks have become global sustainability regulators through their commitment to the Equator Principles, a voluntary set of standards that global financial institutions have developed for evaluating and managing social and environmental risk in privately financed development projects. We hope to show, as both an illustration and as a stimulus for future empirical research, how the motivational and social influence processes described in the paper have led to the reconfiguration of transnational governance in this instance.

Third-Party Justice and the Motives of Stakeholders

Our foray into the psychology of CSR begins with the identification of stakeholders, and in particular, what motives they might have for putting pressure on firms to be more socially responsible. Corporate social responsibility is often viewed as an organizational-level construct. Scholars write about the socially responsible or irresponsible acts of the *firm*, metrics of social impact and sustainability involve audits of organizational *practices*, and empirical analyses of the relationship between social and financial performance place the organization as the unit of analysis. Our work, however, has argued that although CSR generally refers to the social and environment consciousness of the firm, it is individuals who ultimately make decisions on behalf of the organization, and individuals who evaluate and respond to organizational decisions (see also Kelman, 2006). For this reason, it behooves the organizational sciences to consider research relevant to individual perception formation and decision making to fully understand how and why socially responsible and irresponsible decisions are made, and how and why they are perceived of as such and reacted to by those witnessing their effects.

As previous research has argued, a particularly well-suited literature in organizational psychology that would allow for such an investigation is that of organizational justice (Aguilera et al., 2007; Rupp, Ganapathi, Aguilera, & Williams, 2006). Research in this area has shown very certainly that individuals care about fairness. It is an evolutionarily-based response to react with emotion when treated unfairly and to seek justice when mistreated. Thus, it is not surprising that meta-analytic evidence indicates that individuals' perceptions of how fairly they are treated significantly predicts a wide variety of attitudinal and behavioral outcomes such as job performance, citizenship behavior, organizational commitment, and the like (Cohen-Charash & Spector, 2001; Colquitt, Conlon, Wesson, Porter, & Ng, 2001). It seems that individuals care about fairness both because it serves a self-protective or outcome maximization function (Adams, 1965), and because being treated fairly gives individuals certainty regarding their status and standing in groups (Tyler & Lind, 1992).

The story doesn't end there, however. More recent research has shown justice is about more than the self, and that people (and some animals) have visceral reactions not only when they themselves are treated unfairly, but also when they witness others being treated unfairly (Folger, 1998). Indeed, both laboratory experiments and field studies have shown that individuals show a willingness to sacrifice their own resources to punish a party who has victimized another in some way—and individuals need not identify with the victims in any way to show such tendencies. The research evidence to date suggests that in addition to being a means to an instrumental and relational end, justice is also an end in itself—that people care about justice for justice's sake, and will go to great lengths to uphold it (Kahneman, Knetsch, & Thaler, 1986; O'Reilly, Aquino, & Skorlicki, 2010; Rupp & Bell, 2010; Turillo, Folger, Lavelle, Umphress, & Gee, 2002).

It is the fact that individuals react strongly to how *others* are treated (also known as third-party justice; DeCremer & Van Hiel, 2006; Ellard & Skarlicki, 2002; Skarlicki & Kulik, 2005) that is essential to understanding the psychology of corporate social responsibility. In fact, CSR can be conceptualized as multistakeholder third-party justice. In other words, a large number of parties may judge the actions of the firm and subsequently retaliate (or support) perceived acts of social irresponsibility (or responsibility). This observation pushes the scope of organizational accountability beyond its current conceptualization in the organizational behavior literature. It suggests that organizations are not only being judged by stakeholder groups regarding practices that support or threaten the best interest of the group that is making the judgment, but that each stakeholder group also has concern for the greater good and also reacts to how they perceive the firm is treating each other stakeholder group.

As theorized by Aguilera et al. (2007), each stakeholder group (e.g., employees, consumers, shareholders, top management, nongovernmental organizations (NGOs), governments, local communities) has instrumental, relational, and ethics-based motives for caring about CSR and will evaluate the actions of the firm through the lens of their unique motive structures. Further, they will apply this lens when evaluating not only the actions that affect them, but also the actions that affect other stakeholders. Thus, a complex web of judgments is created, which influences a complex web of behaviors (that can be very broadly categorized into commitments and retaliations), which collectively have the potential to affect *both* the financial and social performance of the firm. This increases the complexity of CSR phenomena beyond current treatments, and might explain many of the inconsistent findings in the social performance–firm performance literature. Future research is certainly needed to test these propositions.

Contextual Influences on CSR: Competence, Relatedness, and Autonomy

Just as it is important to consider the perceptual processes of stakeholder groups who evaluate and react to an organization's CSR-related decisions, it is also important to understand more fully the psychology behind those decisions themselves. That is, what leads organizations to engage in socially responsible behaviors? The field of social psychology is especially relevant here in that it is rich with theories about how the social context affects decisional processes. Particularly germane for the current investigation is that of self-determination theory (Deci & Ryan, 1985, 1991; Ryan, 1995; Ryan & Deci, 2000).

Self-determination theory (SDT), considered among the most influential theories of human motivation, shows that humans, at their psychological best, are motivated and responsible. However, given certain conditions, "the human spirit can be diminished or crushed [leading] individuals [to] sometimes reject growth and responsibility" (Ryan & Deci, 2000, p. 68). SDT scholars have equated irresponsible behavior with nonoptimal human functioning and noted the abundance of such tendencies in modern society. They argue that the decisions of individuals to be either constructive or irresponsible reflect more than personality or genetic differences—that irresponsible behavior may certainly be construed as a reaction to elements of the social environment. Thus, in essence, self-determination theory is a theory about the conditions that either foster or undermine positive human potential. We feel such a theory, and the tomes of empirical evidence supporting it, are quite illuminating in understanding socially responsible decisions in organizations.

At the foundation of self-determination theory are three psychological needs, namely, *autonomy, competence*, and *relatedness*. The meeting of these needs has been shown to be essential for facilitating growth and constructive social development. Although the term *constructive social development* is generally used in psychology to refer to the social development of a person, this theory lends itself nicely to considering social development at the level of the organization or society. Said differently, we are proposing that the level of social responsibility inherent in the decisions made and policies set by organizational actors will be influenced by the extent to which the decisions are self-determined; that is, that the acts are seen as either externally valuable or intrinsically rewarding—which is determined by the extent to which the organizational context meets the competence, relatedness, and autonomy needs of the actors.

Thus, the questions become: (a) What would the optimal context be that would motivate socially responsible decisions among organizational leaders? and (b) What structural variables, within the domain of ethics and social responsibility, would not only give leaders a sense of competence, relatedness, and autonomy, but would also motivate them to promote social responsibility throughout the organization (which we will see in the next section has the power to catalyze value internalization and integration)?

Applying self-determination to this context would suggest, first, that more CSR is likely when decision makers have discretion over the ethicality of their judgments. Although this may at first sound counterintuitive, it suggests that more "good" is possible if decision makers feel they are doing good because they want to, not because they have to (i.e., increased *autonomy*). Thus, whereas required compliance (e.g., environmental protection laws) may be necessary to ensure a certain level of responsibility by organizations, allowing autonomy in policy making may have the potential to catalyze more transformative CSR than a strict, legalist framework may be capable of accomplishing.

Second, more CSR is likely when decision makers receive feedback, communication, and rewards (as well as freedom from demeaning evaluations) that induce feelings of *competence*. Decision makers will show more motivation for engaging in CSR when they feel empowered, competent, and efficacious in creating policies, and can see that the success of their decisions is due to their competence rather than external factors. In psychology, this is known as *perceived locus of causality*. When leaders see a positive social effect resulting from their CSR-directed behaviors, and similarly when other stakeholder groups see the positive social effects resulting from organizational decisions and policies, this should have a motivating effect that should not only increase social performance, but also aid in the internalization and integration of CSR values among various stakeholder groups—a process that we will discuss in more depth later in this chapter. We propose that it is via transparent management, coupled with voluntary social auditing and reporting, that such effects can be revealed.

Finally, the organizational context can influence CSR motivation to the extent that it meets *relatedness* needs. Psychological research has found that the motivational effects of relatedness are evident even in infancy, with intrinsic motivation higher among babies with secure attachments to a parent (Bowlby, 1980). In adults, a great deal of research has shown that the social (in our case organizational) environment can facilitate or forestall motivation. Thus, we propose that CSR motives will be stronger for decision makers who feel secure in their attachment and identification with the organization. Again drawing upon the social psychology literature, characteristics of such a relationship would include feelings of emotional closeness, comfort with mutual dependence, and feelings of acceptance by the organization (Fraley & Shaver, 2000). Research would suggest that securely attached leaders would have positive views of both themselves and the people with whom they work, and feel satisfaction from their relationship with the organization.

In organizational psychology, we would describe this set of characteristics as representative of a positive social exchange relationship between employees and employers (Blau, 1964), and the contextual element shown most likely to produce relatedness is a climate for justice (Cropanzano & Rupp, 2008). Thus, our analysis has led to a conclusion that a key to motivating corporate social responsibility (a macro-operationalization of justice) is organizational fairness (a micro-operationalization of justice).

If our propositions are correct, it would suggest that justice begets justice. Such a statement implies multilevel justice/CSR as having contagion properties (e.g., Degoey, 2000; Masterson, 2001), which is relevant to our next set of propositions.

Stakeholder Internalization and Integration of CSR Values

Motivation is not only about the choice to engage in a set of behaviors (in our case socially responsible behaviors on the part of organizational decision makers), but it also involves persistence with and commitment to a chosen goal over time (Kanfer, 1990; Latham & Locke, 2007). Further, implied in our discussion above was that the *goal* that is pursued in the quest for corporate social responsibility is commitment to a set of values that influences major organizational decisions. Thus, given our multi-level and multistakeholder perspective of CSR, our next set of challenges becomes one of understanding both the creation and spreading of CSR value commitment among all stakeholders who have influence over the creation, regulation, and implementation of CSR policies.

Self-Determination Theory Revisited

SDT provides an initial set of insights on this matter. That is, SDT research has shown that motivation toward a particular goal (e.g., social responsibility in decision making) can range from a motivation or unwillingness, to passive compliance, to active personal commitment (Ryan & Deci, 2000). The theory has introduced the concepts of *internalization*, which refers to "taking in" a value, and *integration*, which refers to the transformation of the value such that its embodiment emanates directly from one's sense of self. In other words, individuals with integrated CSR values will not promote corporate social responsibility because they feel pressured to do so, or because they are mandated to abide by a set of standards. Instead they will act to embody CSR values because the values have been internalized and integrated into their self-concept. In this way, goal-consistent behaviors come more automatically without a great deal of processing on the part of the decision maker.

What is especially important here is that research has shown that when behavior is regulated through these sorts of processes (i.e., identified, integrated, and intrinsic motivation), effort, quality of decisions/outcomes, volitional persistence, social assimilation, and well-being are increased (Miserandino, 1996; Ryan, Kuhl, & Deci, 1997). Consequently, a key to increased and lasting CSR in organizations lies in the motivational structures of individuals. Organizational contexts that allow for autonomy, competence, and relatedness needs to be met can lead to the internalization and integration of CSR values, which can lead to heightened levels of ethical decision making and social performance in organizations (e.g., see Green-Demers, Pelletier, & Menard, 1997). On the flip side, when behavior is externally regulated, the internalization of CSR values is less likely and individuals would be expected to respond with alienation and low goal commitment because the values are not necessarily accepted as one's own (i.e., they are not assimilated into the self and do not allow for the experience of autonomy in action).

Kelman's Three-Process Model of Social Influence

A second major theory within social psychology that is highly relevant to our consideration of what might lead to the creation of authentic CSR values among stakeholder groups is Kelman's theory of social influence (1958; 2006). This theory is especially well-suited, and a nice next step beyond SDT, because it allows us to look more specifically at what can move individuals and groups of individuals from public conformity to CSR policies to internal acceptance and commitment to CSR (which SDT suggests is essential for optimal social performance). Further, the model has been shown to be valid both at the level of the individual, as well as the level of the organization and nation/society (Kelman, 1968). In fact, Kelman is well-known for his application of the theory to the promotion of social responsibility in the social sciences as well as international conflict resolution (e.g., the Israeli–Palestinian conflict, 1979).

Kelman's "three-process model" argues that behavior is significantly affected by social influences. As such, the behaviors of individuals, groups, organizations, and societies are influenced through three major processes. *Compliance* occurs when an individual or group seeks to attain a favorable reaction from an influencing party. This typically involves pursuit of some type of reward or the avoidance of some type of punishment that is controlled by the influencing party. *Identification* occurs when an individual or group accepts the influence of another party in order to establish or maintain a self-defining relationship with them. *Internalization* occurs when an individual or group accepts the influence of another party because the values of the two parties are congruent, and as a result, accepting the influence attempt allows the individual or group to both maintain consistency and reinforce the alignment between beliefs and actions.

Research has shown that the social context (e.g., an organization's structure, its history and culture, its formal policies) can have a strong impact on how influence is wielded. These structural variables create a context that leads to the formation of *system orientations*, which essentially shape motive structures of system actors. In other words, the context shapes how, when, and why individuals will be motivated to act in various ways. In the words of Kelman and Hamilton (1989, p. 87), "Many social influence situations are ... thoroughly embedded in the organizational or societal context. ... They represent ... part of the process whereby the society or organization ... socializes and controls its members and carries out its daily business, and whereby the members advocate policies, protest against existing practices, or seek to advance their personal or subgroup interests." So just as SDT allowed us to map the contextual elements of autonomy, relatedness, and competence onto the internalization and integration of motives, Kelman's model shows us what types of influence structures are most effective within varying system orientations and why (Kelman, 1974).

Compliance (interest) orientations are created and reinforced through the enforcement of formal rules and norms, and are empowered via social fear and the threat of embarrassment. Identification (relationship) orientations are created and reinforced not through behavioral requirements, but through the creation of role systems and are empowered via the avoidance of guilt and shame (or the promotion of pride and affiliation). Internalization (identity) orientations are created and reinforced through shared social values and are empowered via the avoidance of regret and self-disappointment (or the promotion of self-integrity and the adherence to personal standards). Kelman explains that these three orientations serve as both "the process and criteria by which perceived legitimacy is generated, assessed, and maintained" (2006, p. 15). In other words, influence attempts based on threats and bribes are likely only to induce change at the level of compliance. Attempts based on maintaining relationships between parties are likely to only induce change at the level of identification. Stable, enduring changes at the level of internalization are only likely when influence attempts are targeted at transformative change, creating a state of shared values and mutual problem solving among parties (Kelman 1996, 1997, 2006).

Putting the Pieces Together and the Illustrative Case of New Governance and Equator Principles

To recapitulate, we have presented three theoretical perspectives with which to encourage further thinking about the psychology of corporate social responsibility. First we discussed organizational justice theory to argue that stakeholders not only react to how they see the firm treating *them*, but also hold organizations accountable for the treatment of other stakeholder groups. We highlighted that individuals and groups, both

TABLE 4.1

Psychological Processes Influencing the Internalization of CSR: Insights from Theories of Multiple Needs, Social Influence, and Self-Determination

Active Motives	System Orientation	Method of Influence	Emotional Mechanisms	Psychological Needs
Self-interest	Compliance/ interest	Rules (e.g., government regulation)	Fear/threat	Competency/ control
Social relations	Identification/ relationships	Roles (e.g., professional standards)	Guilt/shame/ pride/affiliation	Relatedness/ belongingness
Ethics/values/ moral obligations	Internalization/ identities	Values (e.g., social policy)	Self-integrity/ regret/self- disappointment	Autonomy/ meaningful existence

internal and external to the organization, have instrumental, relational, and ethical reasons for pushing for CSR, and that research has barely begun to understand how this complex web of motives facilitates or hinders social change. Second, we used self-determination theory to explicate the contextual factors that might maximize socially responsible decisions in organizations. We proposed that decisional contexts that promote competence, relatedness, and autonomy may encourage more responsible actions than will strict regulatory structures that squelch the self-determining potential of socially responsible behaviors. Finally, we described further tenets of SDT as well as Kelman's theory of social influence to more concretely link the social context within which "responsibilization" occurs (Shamir, 2008) through the internalization of values, a process we feel is critical to the authentic and long-term practice of corporate social responsibility.

Table 4.1 lists the major components of the three psychological perspectives we have presented in this paper. In this section, we present a case with which to partially illustrate the phenomena we have described above. It involves an unintended positive consequence of deregulation and privatization within the banking industry.

The Privatization of Public Infrastructure

Prior to the 1980s, large public infrastructure projects such as oil and gas pipelines, hydroelectric dams, mines, and telecommunication facilities were funded primarily by multilateral public development banks. However, this practice changed in the 1980s and 1990s due to structural adjustments by the World Bank and International Monetary Fund coupled with effective activism by NGOs concerning controversial projects with significant environmental and human rights issues associated with them (e.g., the Three Gorges Dam project in China and the Narmada Valley projects in India). The result was significantly increased privatization of public and state-owned services such as energy, water, resource extraction, and basic industries, and a partial withdrawal of the public development banks from these projects (Williams & Conley, 2009). Thus, private Wall Street and City of London banks became much more involved with large-scale infrastructure development than they had been previously.

At first blush, this shift was viewed with great dismay by the NGOs, which had been fighting for at least a decade for increased environmental and social standards to be incorporated into public-sector infrastructure development. Now, with the privatization of the industry, the public-regarding standards developed by the World Bank and its private-investment subsidiary, the International Finance Corporation (IFC), seemed irrelevant. What has unfolded since that time is quite surprising, however, private banks have fully embraced the IFC's Social and Environmental Performance Standards, and indeed global banks have begun to act as quasi-regulators of social and environmental standards across the entire range of transnational development activities.

From Rules to Standards

This has come about through the development of the Equator Principles (EPs), a voluntary set of standards that global financial institutions have developed, which rely upon the IFC's standards for evaluating and managing social and environmental risk in privately financed development projects valued at more than $10 million (www.equator-pinciples.com). The Principles include rigorous requirements for incorporating environmental and human rights protections into management systems and loan covenants, and for incorporating community consultations and dispute resolution systems into project management.

As a first step in highlighting the psychological processes described in our paper, we will begin by pointing out that the initial development and adoption of the Equator Principles was instrumentally motivated. The method for providing private capital for large, privately sponsored infrastructure projects is nonrecourse *project finance*. Since this is nonrecourse lending, the bank providing the loan is only repaid through revenues generated upon project completion. Thus, even if the borrower is a powerful corporation such as Exxon Mobil, if the project is halted in any way, the bank must absorb the loss. Consequently, stakeholder issues such as those involving human rights, labor, the environment, and political unrest can be viewed as potential risks for project derailment and loan default. The development of the Equator Principles did not therefore evolve from ethical or moral concerns on the part of the banks, but out of the instrumental motive to reduce risk and to create a level playing field among competitors within the project finance industry (Lawrence & Thomas, 2004). Yet the establishment of the Equator Principles is changing the social context in which banks that participate in the project finance market operate, leading to the possibility that this social context could start to have a more transformative effect upon both the attitudes and behaviors of a number of stakeholder groups.

The Equator Principles are voluntary, and there are no agreed-upon methods for certifying that a project meets the EP standards, thereby requiring self-enforcement on the part of the banks. The banks that adopt the EPs commit to put in place internal policies that require all firms involved with the project (note that large-scale infrastructure projects often require the collaboration of many firms) to comply with the standards. The bank requires an environmental and social impact assessment of each project involved. Some projects in Organization for Economic Cooperation and Development (OECD) countries may have already had such an assessment conducted by law. However, projects proposed in developing countries may only be involved in such an assessment because the EP-committed banks require it as a prerequisite for project funding. When a project is identified as medium or high risk, EP-committed banks must require the project sponsor to develop a management plan to mitigate the risk, as well as loan covenants that require compliance to that management plan.

The Equator Principles were first drafted in 2003 and had 41 adopters (e.g., Barclays, Citibank, Credit Suisse, HSBC, ING, JP Morgan Chase, and Wells Fargo). A revision to the EPs was drafted in 2006, after the IFC had revised and strengthened their standards. As such, the revised EPs similarly included even stricter standards for issues such as labor, community health, safety, security, and public reporting. As of early 2009, there are 56 global banks and other financial institutions (e.g., export-import credit agencies) signed on to the EPs and it has been estimated that 75% of global project finance is carried out by EP-adopting banks. As a result, the international banking industry has emerged as a "global regulator" for corporate social responsibility and sustainability in project finance. Whereas the EPs are completely voluntary, and the standards do not have the force of law, we see examples of EP enforcement influencing how business is conducted in developed nations, and in emerging economies, importing rule of law and the development of business norms (Williams & Conley, 2009).

From Standards to Values

What we find especially interesting about this case, given our interest in the internalization and institutionalization of CSR motives within and between stakeholder groups, is the effect EP adoption has had on other aspects of banks' operations among some of the adopting firms. The EPs only apply to project finance, and project finance typically only makes up

5% of a financial institution's total business. However, research has shown a marked "CSR contagion" effect in some of the banks that have adopted the EPs, with adoption seeming to catalyze cultural change throughout the firm. Indeed, since signing on to the EPs, banks such as HSBC, Barclays, and JP Morgan Chase have used the Equator Principles as benchmark standards for setting up similar standards for social and environmental responsibility throughout the firm's practices (e.g., underwriting, commercial lending, retail banking, etc.). Further, we see the EPs used as an industry standard in other types of syndicated lending arrangements (e.g., joint ventures, high-value commercial loans, stock and bond underwriting), even when EP banks are not the lead lenders. In the words of Williams and Conley (2009, p. 6), "what began as a change in lending procedures by a number of global banks in an important but limited arena is spreading throughout the industry, and in some cases is starting to transform the values and business practices of the banks across a wide spectrum of lending and underwriting activities."

The Role of Competency, Relatedness, and Autonomy in the Internalization and Contagion of CSR

Thus, "new governance" mechanisms have the potential to create a context in which stakeholders push for CSR, not entirely out of self-interest, but also due to internalized ethical standards, which might catalyze CSR motives to trickle down, up, and across within a firm and between firms. This is a marked extension of traditional theories of both law compliance and the psychology of justice, which have historically been based on models of self-interest and utility maximization. We propose that the reason new governance mechanisms might have unique power in changing firms' actions and culture lies in the psychological processes we have described above.

As our case described, the impetus for the development of the Equator Principles was instrumental. The nonrecourse nature of project finance loans represents financial risk for the banks, and so requiring borrowers to comply with social and environmental standards assists the banks in mitigating such risks. Although self-interest is considered a lower-order motive in the Cropanzano et al. (2001) framework, and a lower-order system orientation in the Kelman (1974) framework, the privatization of public infrastructure and the development/adoption of the Equator Principles changed the social context. That is, the social influence structure in place to constrain banks' activities shifted from an inherently rules-based system of laws and government regulation regarding a wide range of individual transactions to a looser system based on voluntary standards that the banks themselves initiated.

It could be argued, and the three-process model would suggest, that this process led to a shift from an interest orientation to a relationship orientation within those banks with serious engagement with the Equator Principles, where interconnectedness and stakeholder relations became a more dominant motivator. For example, it has been observed that banks that have signed on to the Equator Principles more recently include institutions that are not nearly as exposed to reputational risk as the early-adopting institutions (Williams & Conley, 2009). It seems that the motives for signing on shifted from self-protection to relational normative pressures within the industry.

Finally, the "spreading" of the EP-based standards from project finance to other aspects of banks' business might be evidence of an internalization process, where the values of corporate social responsibly have become something that organizational actors identify with and feel are important to carry out, not just to mitigate risk and comply with industry norms, but because CSR is seen as the right thing to do, and acting in accordance to the EPs fulfills individual needs for meaningful existence (Cropanzano et al., 2001). In the word of Williams and Conley (2009, p.23), "it could be the case that the moral and ethical sensibilities of employers and managers are becoming involved."

Why might this have occurred? Self-determination theory would argue that the changes in the social context may have created an increased opportunity for organizational actors to experience autonomy, relatedness, and competence, which past research predicts would lead to an increased motivation for pushing for CSR. Take HSBC, which was awarded the *Financial Times'* first Sustainable Banking award in 2006, as an example. After issuing its first set of environmental risk standards in 2002, it made a decision not to rely on local laws and industry standards in determining risk, but to be "judged on higher global standards." HSBC employees were involved in the drafting of the Equator Principles, and their sustainable banking department has grown from three to 300 employees since 2003 (including prominent climate change economist Lord Nicholas Stern). In addition, HSBC has seen a spreading of EP-level social and environmental standards from project finance to a large number of additional product groups, and shows an *affirmative preference* for doing business with clients that show a commitment to strict CSR standards. We propose that (and invite empirical testing of whether) HSBC emerging as a de facto regulator of corporate social responsibly has come about due to changes in the three pillars of self-determination theory: (1) the *autonomy* employees and other stakeholders experienced during the shift from government regulation to voluntary standards, (2) the *competence* they experienced through participation in the drafting of the Equator Principles, and (3) the *relatedness* experienced through the EP's bringing together banking industry executives in a proactive, socially directed enterprise.

Conclusion

We have made many propositions in this paper, and have offered an illustrative case to more concretely articulate our theoretical ideas. Of course, all of our ideas should be viewed as tentative and subjected to critical empirical testing. We should also note that some have questioned the positive social impact that the Equator Principles have had. The purpose of this paper is not to make solid conclusions about the psychology of corporate social responsibility, but rather to introduce some potentially applicable psychological theories that might lead to greater understanding of the phenomena that leads individuals, groups, and organizations to push for positive social change through corporate responsibility initiatives.

A theoretical perspective from social psychology that might be considered in future research seeking to further integrate the ideas we have presented in this paper is goal systems theory (Kruglanski, Shah, Fishbach, Friedman, Chun, & Sleeth-Keppler, 2002). Goal systems theory argues that motivation is not separate from cognition, and as such, goals and means interact, compete for resources, and combine in complex ways in influencing behavior. Research in this area has shown that multiple goal systems can be activated simultaneously (e.g., financial, reputational, ethical), and that such goal systems can be influenced by environmental primes (e.g., rules, roles, values; Bargh & Barndollar, 1996), which can include structural elements of the environment, as well as social influence by other parties (e.g., the influence of other stakeholder groups; Kruglanski, 1989; Elis & Kruglanski, 1992). Research suggests that goal pursuit is resource dependent and that active goals can pull resources from the attainment of other goals (Kruglanski et al., 2000). This work has also observed that the emotions elicited during goal attainment have the power to shift a *means* to an *end*, such that activities that were initially in play in order to achieve a goal become rewarding in and of themselves, rendering the behavior intrinsically motivating (e.g., self-determined; Kruglanski et al., 2002). Finally, goal-system research has shown behavior to possess the property of multifinality—with desired actions being most likely when they are linked to multiple, dissimilar goals.

As the examples in the above paragraph imply, a goal-systems approach would easily lend itself to the integration of the competing motives presented by Cropanzano et al. (2001), the system orientations and contextual influences presented by Kelman (1974) and the precursors of intrinsic motivation outlined in self-determination theory (Ryan & Deci, 2000). It might also provide insights as to how we might empirically assess the evolution and spreading of CSR motives in organizations over time. Indeed, the methodologies common in social psychology and social cognition might also provide innovative ways to test the phenomena inherent in CSR not previously envisioned. We feel such research is greatly needed and look forward to its unfolding.

Acknowledgments

The authors would like to thank Robert Folger, C.Y. Chiu, Russell Cropanzano, Layne Paddock, Karl Aquino, and Marshall Schminke for insights and feedback during the writing of this chapter. This research was supported by grant number 864-2007-0265 from the Social Science and Humanities Research Council of Canada.

References

Adams, J. S. (1965). Inequity in social exchange. *Advances in Experimental Social Psychology, 2*, 267–299.

Aguilera, R. A., Rupp, D. E., Williams, C. A., & Ganapathi, J. (2007). Putting the S back in corporate social responsibility: A multilevel theory of social change in organizations. *Academy of Management Review, 32*, 836–863.

Aguinis, H. (in press). Organizational responsibility: Doing good and doing well. In S. Zedeck (Ed.), *APA handbook of industrial and organizational psychology.* Washington, DC: American Psychological Association.

Bargh, J. A., & Barndollar, K. (1996). Automaticity in action: The unconscious as repository of chronic goals and motives. In P. M. Gollwitzer & J. A. Bargh (Eds.), *The psychology of action* (pp. 457–481). New York: Guilford.

Blau, P. M. (1964). *Exchange and power in social life.* New York: John Wiley & Sons.

Bowen, H. R. (1953). *Social responsibilities of the businessman.* New York: Harper & Row.

Bowlby, J. (1980). *Attachment and loss.* New York: Basic Books.

Bragdon, J. H., & Marlin J. A. T. (1972). Is pollution profitable? *Risk Management,* **19**(4), 9–18.

Carroll, A. (1979). A three-dimensional conceptual model of corporate performance. *Academy of Management Review, 4*, 497–505.

Cohen-Charash, Y., & Spector, P. (2001). The role of justice in organizations: A meta-analysis. *Organizational Behavior and Human Decision Processes, 86*, 278–321.

Colquitt, J. A., Conlon, D. E., Wesson, M. J., Porter, C. O. L. H., & Ng, K. Y. (2001). Justice at the millennium: A meta-analytic review of 25 years of organizational justice research. *Journal of Applied Psychology, 86*, 425–445.

Conley, John M., & Williams, C.A. (2005). Engage, embed, and embellish: Theory versus practice in the corporate social responsibility movement. *Journal of Corporation Law, 31*(2), 1–38.

Cropanzano, R., Byrne, Z. S., Bobocel, D. R., & Rupp, D. E. (2001). Moral virtues, fairness heuristics, social entities, and other denizens of organizational justice. *Journal of Vocational Behavior, 58*, 164–209.

Cropanzano, R., & Rupp, D. E. (2008). Social exchange theory and organizational justice: Job performance, citizenship behaviors, multiple foci, and a historical integration of two literatures. In S. W. Gilliland, D. P. Skarlicki, & D. D. Steiner (Eds.), *Research in social issues in management: Justice, morality, and social responsibility* (pp. 63–99). Greenwich CT: Information Age Publishing.

Deci, E. L., & Ryan, R. M. (1985). *Intrinsic motivation and self-determination in human behavior*. New York: Plenum.

Deci, E. L., & Ryan, R. M. (1991). A motivational approach to self: Integration in personality. In R. Dienstbier (Ed.), *Nebraska Symposium on Motivation: Vol. 38. Perspectives on motivation* (pp. 237–288). Lincoln: University of Nebraska Press.

De Cremer, D., & Van Hiel, A. (2006). Effects of another person's fair treatment on one's own emotions and behaviors: The moderating role of how much other cares for you. *Organizational Behavior and Human Decision Processes, 100*, 231–249.

Degoey, P. (2000). Contagious justice: Exploring the social construction of justice in organizations. *Research in Organizational Behavior, 22*, 51–102.

Elis, S., & Kruglanski, A. W. (1992). Self as epistemic authority: Effects on experiential and instructional learning. *Social Cognition, 10*, 357–375.

Ellard, J. H., & Skarlicki, D. P. (2002). A third-party observer's reactions to employee mistreatment. In S. W. Gilliland, D. D. Steiner, & D. P. Skarlicki (Eds.), *Emerging perspectives on managing organizational justice* (pp. 133–158). Greenwich, CT: IAP.

Folger, R. (1998). Fairness as a moral virtue. In M. Schminke (Ed.), *Managerial ethics: Moral management of people and processes* (pp. 13–34). Mahwah, NJ: Erlbaum.

Fortanier, F., & Kolk, A. (2007). On the economic dimensions of corporate social responsibility: Exploring *Fortune* global 250 reports. *Business & Society 46*, 457–478.

Fraley, R.C., & Shaver, P.R. (2000). Adult romantic attachment: Theoretical developments, emerging controversies, and unanswered questions. *Review of General Psychology, 4*, 132–54.

Green-Demers, I., Pelletier, L. G., & Menard, S. (1997). The impact of behavioural difficulty on the saliency of the association between self-determined motivation and environmental behaviours. *Canadian Journal of Behavioural Sciences, 29*, 157–166.

Kanfer, R. (1990). Motivation theory and industrial/organizational psychology. In M. D. Dunnette and L. Hough (Eds.), *Handbook of industrial and organizational psychology. Volume 1. Theory in industrial and organizational psychology* (pp. 75–170). Palo Alto, CA: Consulting Psychologists Press.

Kahneman, D., Knetsch, J. L., & Thaler, R. H. (1986). Fairness and the assumption of economics. *Journal of Business, 59*, S285–S300.

Kelman, H. C. (1958). Compliance, identification, and internalization: Three processes of attitude change. *Journal of Conflict Resolution, 2*, 51–60.

Kelman, H. C. (1968). Education for the concept of a global society. *Social Education, 32*, 661–666.

Kelman, H. C. (1974). Social influence and linkages between the individual and the social system: Further thoughts on the processes of compliance, identification, and internalization. In J. Tedeschi (Ed.), *Perspectives on Social Power* (pp. 125–171). Chicago: Aldine.

Kelman, H. C. (1996). Negotiation as interactive problem solving. *International Negotiation, 1,* 99–123.

Kelman, H. C. (1997). Social-psychological dimensions of international conflict. In I. W. Zartman, & J. L. Rasmussen (Eds.), *Peace-making in international conflict: Methods and techniques* (pp. 191–237). Washington, DC: U.S. Institute of Peace.

Kelman, H. C. (2006). Interests, relationships, identities: Three central issues for individuals and groups in negotiating their social environment. *Annual Review of Psychology, 57,* 1–26.

Kelman, H. C., & Hamilton, V. L. (1989). *Crimes of obedience: Toward a social psychology of authority and responsibility.* New Haven, CT: Yale University Press.

Kruglanski, A. W. (1989). *Lay epistemics and human knowledge: Cognitive and motivational bases.* New York: Plenum.

Kruglanski, A. W., Shah, J. Y., Fishbach, A., Friedman, R., Chun, W. Y., & Sleeth-Keppler, D. (2002). A theory of goal systems. In M. P. Zanna (Ed.), *Advances in experimental social psychology* (Vol. 34). San Diego, CA: Academic Press.

Kruglanski, A. W., Thompson, E. P., Higgins, E. T., Atash N. N., Pierro, A., Shah, J. Y., & Spiegel, S. (2000). To "do the right thing" or to "just do it": Locomotion and assessment as distinct self-regulatory imperatives. *Journal of Personality and Social Psychology, 79,* 793–815.

Latham, G. P., & Locke, E. A. (2007). New developments in and directions for goal setting. *European Psychologist, 12,* 290–300.

Lawrence, R. F., & Thomas, W. L. (2004). The Equator Principles and project finance: Sustainability in practice? *Natural Resources and the Environment 19,* 20–34.

Mackey, A., Mackey, T. B., & Barney, J. B. (2007). Corporate social responsibility and firm performance: Investor preferences and corporate strategies. *Academy of Management Review, 32,* 817–835.

Margolis, J., Elfenbein, H. A., & Walsh, J. (2009). *Does It pay to be good … and does it matter? A meta-analysis of the relationship between corporate social and financial performance.* Unpublished manuscript.

Masterson, S. S. (2001). A trickle-down model of organizational justice: Relating employees' and customers' perceptions of and reactions to fairness. *Journal of Applied Psychology, 86,* 594–604.

Miserandino, M. (1996). Children who do well in school: Individual differences in perceived competence and autonomy in above-average children. *Journal of Educational Psychology, 88,* 203–214.

O'Reilly, Aquino, & Skarlicki (2010). *The lives of others: The role of moral identity in third parties' emotional, cognitive, and behavioral reactions to injustice.* Unpublished manuscript.

Orlizlky, M., Schmidt, F. L., & Rynes, S. L. (2003). Corporate social and financial performance: A meta-analysis. *Organization Studies, 24,* 403–441.

Rupp, D. E., & Aquino, K. (2009). Nothing so practical as a good justice theory. *Industrial and Organizational Psychology, 2,* 205–210.

Rupp, D. E., Bell, C. M. (2010). Extending the deontic model of justice: Moral self-regulation in third-party responses to injustice. *Business Ethics Quarterly, 20,* 89–106.

Rupp, D. E., & Cropanzano, R. (2002). Multifoci justice and social exchange relationships. *Organizational Behavior and Human Decision Processes, 89,* 925–946.

Rupp, D. E., Ganapathi, J., Aguilera, R. V., & Williams, C. A. (2006). Employee reactions to corporate social responsibility: An organizational justice framework. *Journal of Organizational Behavior, 27,* 537–543.

Ryan, R. M. (1995). Psychological needs and the facilitation of integrative processes. *Journal of Personality, 63,* 397–427.

Ryan R. M., & Deci, E. L. (2000). Self-determination theory and the facilitation of intrinsic motivation, social development, and well-being. *American Psychologist, 55,* 68–78.

Ryan, R. M., Kuhl, J., & Deci, E. L. (1997). Nature and autonomy: Organizational view of social and neurobiological aspects of self-regulation in behavior and development. *Development and Psychopathology, 9,* 701–728.

Shamir, R. (2008). Corporate social responsibility: Towards a new market-embedded morality? *Theoretical Inquiries in Law, 9*(2), Article 3.

Skarlicki, D. P., & Kulik, C. (2005). Third party reactions to employee (mis)treatment: A justice perspective. In B. Staw & R. Kramer (Eds.) *Research in organizational behavior* (Vol. 26, pp. 183–230). Greenwich, CT: JAI Press.

Turillo, C. J., Folger, R., Lavelle, J. J., Umphress, E. E., & Gee, J. O. (2002). Is virtue its own reward? Self-sacrificial decisions for the sake of fairness. *Organizational Behavior and Human Decision Processes, 89,* 839–865.

Tyler, T. R., & Lind, E. A. (1992). A relational model of authority in groups. In M. Zanna (Ed.), *Advances in experimental social psychology* (Vol. 25, pp. 115–191). San Diego, CA: Academic Press.

Waddock, S. A. (2004). Parallel universes: Companies, academics, and the progress of corporate citizenship. *Business and Society Review, 10,* 758–769.

Williams, C. A. (2004). Civil society initiatives and "soft law" in the oil and gas industry. *New York University Journal of Law and Politics, 36,* 457–502.

Williams, C. A., & Conley, J. M. (2009). *Global banks as global sustainability regulators: The equator principles.* Unpublished manuscript.

5

The Managerial Relevance of Ethical Efficacy

Marie S. Mitchell
University of Georgia
Noel F. Palmer
University of Nebraska

> When I discovered the problems ... my first reaction was to leave Enron as fast as I could. ... I was extremely disappointed about the events of that fall ... there was just an overwhelming feeling that justice would prevail, that the people responsible would have less chance to get away with it once my memos came to light.
>
> **—Sherron Watkins, Enron whistleblower (Watkins, 2003, pp. 8–9).**

> Most people are honorable and want to do the right thing. But sometimes it's tough, even when the line between right and wrong is clear ... The foundation of our character is laid brick by brick, decision by decision, in how we choose to live our lives.
>
> **—Cynthia Cooper, WorldCom whistleblower (Cooper, 2008, pp. 363–364)**

Being ethical is argued to be paramount for effective organizational functioning (Altman, 2005). Lately, however, it seems lost in a sea of corporate scandals and unethical business practices (e.g., WorldCom, Enron, Fannie Mae). Conventional economic wisdom suggests that being ethical produces too great of a burden on organizational agents because individuals are motivated by self-interest and swayed by market forces and competitive pressures (cf. Altman, 2005). In a context where innovation, risk-taking, and motivation for personal economic gain are the coinage of successful free enterprise, ethical considerations take a backseat. Consistent with this view, recent research suggests shady business practices have been downgraded to "efficient corruption" and justified by bottom-line tactics (Argandoña, 2005; Fisman & Svensson, 2007; Mobley & Humphreys, 2006).

Indeed, many organizations send an implicit message to employees to get the job done, regardless of legal or ethical concerns (Yeager, 1986), and, by and large, employees are rewarded for doing so (Bakan, 2004). In all, it appears individual integrity and moral fiber are irrelevant or somehow marginalized to fit corporate and individual interests (Jackall, 1988). The benefits of looking the other way or being unethical seem to outweigh the cost of doing what is right.

Sherron Watkins and Cynthia Cooper (quoted above) disagree. Watkins and Cooper exposed fraudulent and corrupt business practices and did so knowing the consequences of their actions (Amer, 2005; Watkins, 2003). Watkins warned Enron's CEO, Ken Lay, of the fraudulent accounting practices that ultimately destroyed the company. Cooper's internal audits unveiled illegal bookkeeping practices at WorldCom. Both Watkins and Cooper contend that bringing these corporate failures to light damaged their credibility among industry peers, making them unemployable in their fields. Yet both also emphasize that acting morally was an imperative. Watkins and Cooper knew they had to do the right thing, not for personal gain but to rectify severe wrongs (The interview, 2002). In our view, Watkins and Cooper demonstrated strong *ethical efficacy* beliefs—confidence in their ability to behave ethically when faced with a moral challenge. We argue ethical efficacy influences ethical behavior. Given the pressures to be unethical in today's business climate, strong ethical efficacy beliefs are greatly needed.

Research and the popular press highlight a variety of work pressures that compel employees to conform to actions that deviate from moral standards (Gellerman, 1986; Posner & Schmidt, 1987; Wahn, 1993). Further, the waning economy adds to these pressures, heightening self-interest. In a recent study of 1,200 American workers, 28% of the respondents said they would act unethically (i.e., lie, backstab, cheat) to save their jobs (Park, 2009). Overall, this research suggests individuals lack the motivation to do what is right. Organizational members who engage in unethical behavior or allow it to occur may simply lack the confidence to behave morally when challenged and pressured. In order to overcome these pressures, organizations must stress the importance of being ethical and a first critical step is developing ethical organizational members (Andrews, 1989; Thomas, Schermerhorn, & Dienhart, 2004).

The focus of this chapter is to build on these ideas and discuss the managerial relevance of ethical efficacy. We first discuss how individuals cognitively process (un)ethical events, which thereby influence behavior. We then outline the influence of ethical efficacy in this decision-making process. Drawing from principles of social cognitive theory of moral thought and action (Bandura, 1991), self-regulation (Bandura, 1986; Baumeister, 2005), and script theory (Gioia & Poole, 1984), we suggest that ethical efficacy enhances one's motivation to behave ethically. Ethical efficacy does so by instilling one's confidence in their ability to carry out ethical behavior. Lastly, we outline how ethical efficacy beliefs develop and can be strengthened, and more importantly, how organizations can influence individuals' ethical efficacy beliefs. Our goal is to show that individuals can be motivated to engage in ethical behavior by building their confidence to act ethically, regardless of pressures to do otherwise.

The Cognitive Process of Ethical Decisions and Behavior

Much of the behavioral ethics and management literatures embrace a four-step process of ethical decision making and behavior, proposed by Rest (1986): (1) moral awareness, (2) moral judgment, (3) moral motivation, and (4) moral conduct. Accordingly, individuals must first acknowledge or be aware that the situation contains a moral issue. A *moral*[1] issue is one that involves harm or benefit of others (Jones, 1991). From there, individuals evaluate the situation to determine what the possible courses of action are for the given ethical situation. Cognitive moral development theory (Kohlberg, 1969) suggests that individuals who hold higher moral reasoning abilities judge the situation in terms of normative ethical standards of what is just and right, whereas those with the lowest reasoning abilities judge the situation based on self-interest or fear of punishment.

Research investigating the influence of judgment on moral conduct suggests the correlation between the two is fairly small (see Blasi, 1980 for a review). Thus, just because individuals judge a situation as unethical and understand what should be done does not necessarily mean they will do what is right. This highlights the importance of the next stage of ethical decision making: moral motivation. Once the situation is assessed, individuals decide how they intend to behave, and research shows one's moral motivation (what one plans to do) more directly influences moral conduct than judgments (what one ought to do; Weber & Gillespie, 1998). Moral conduct is defined as behavior that abides by laws and/or is considered morally appropriate by larger society (Jones, 1991). Moral motivation forms the basis of behavior because it taps into how committed an individual is to engaging in moral behavior (Rest, Narvaez, Bebeau, & Thoma, 1999).

In our view, understanding factors that influence moral motivation is important for building an ethical workplace. If judgment alone does not strongly predict behavior, then understanding how to motivate ethical behavior is necessary. Yet little research or theory has been given to explain why individuals become more strongly motivated to engage in ethical behavior (see Treviño, Weaver, & Reynolds, 2006 for a review). In this chapter, we discuss how beliefs can enhance individuals' motivation to act ethically. In particular, we argue ethical efficacy beliefs strengthen moral motivation and, therefore, influence moral conduct.

The Role of Ethical Efficacy in Motivating Ethical Behavior

According to Bandura (1986), people are active *agents*—they intentionally seek change in their environment and do so through self-organizing, pro-active, and self-reflective efforts. Because of this, Bandura argues that how people behave is better predicted by their beliefs about their capabilities (called *efficacy beliefs*) rather than their actual capabilities (Bandura, 1997). General efficacy encompasses individuals' beliefs about the level of task difficulty (how difficult is it to engage a desired behavior?), strength of certainty (how certain am I that I have the ability to engage a desired behavior?), and generality about one's abilities (can I engage in the desired behavior over different tasks and situations?) (Bandura, 1986, 1997). Bandura (1991) also argues that efficacy beliefs are applicable to ethical situations, suggesting that individuals can maintain a level of confidence to engage in ethical behavior. We call this type of efficacy *ethical efficacy*.

We define ethical efficacy as individuals' beliefs in their ability to mobilize the motivation, cognitive resources, and courses of action necessary to execute ethical behavior. Ethical efficacy beliefs are a specific type of efficacy—a domain-specific form of efficacy. All individuals hold general self-efficacy beliefs, which involve their general confidence in their ability to master any task or successfully perform any behavior across differing situations (Bandura, 1977). Domain-specific forms of efficacy, however, are individuals' confidence in their abilities within a specific *domain* of behavior (Perrewé & Spector, 2002). General efficacy beliefs are more trait-like and distally influence behavior; domain-specific forms of efficacy are more statelike and produce confidence in one's abilities within a specific context (Kanfer, 1990, 1992). We argue that ethical efficacy is a domain-specific form because these beliefs extend across different tasks (like general efficacy) but are limited to situations involving a moral issue. In short, ethical efficacy beliefs involve a person's confidence in their ability to engage in ethical behavior when confronted with an ethical challenge or issue.

Theorists contend beliefs and intentions strongly predict behavior (Ajzen, 1985). Beliefs about one's confidence to behave ethically motivate individuals to follow through with what they believe is moral conduct (Youssef & Luthans, 2005). Consistent with this view, Bandura (1991) pro-posed a social cognitive theory of moral thought and action. Accordingly, individuals are guided by personal standards of ethics and they try to control their behavior to meet these standards. However, the capacity to maintain control (called *self-regulatory abilities*) is dependent on individuals' confidence in their ability to do what is right. Efficacy beliefs enhance one's motivation to control their behavior by instilling confidence in these abilities (Bandura, Caprara, Barbaranelli, Pastorelli, & Regalia, 2001; Bandura & Locke, 2003). Thus, the stronger the ethical efficacy beliefs, the more certain individuals are to behave ethically, which thereby motivates ethical behavior.

In short, ethical efficacy influences moral motivation and conduct because it instills the confidence needed to engage in ethical behavior and, accordingly, helps individuals control their actions to meet moral standards. When individuals control their behavior to meet social standards, self-regulatory abilities are maintained; when they do not, and instead engage in socially inappropriate behavior, self-regulatory abilities fail (Baumeister, 2005). Thus, ethical efficacy acts as a reinforcer of self-regulatory abilities, controlling behavior even in the face of situations that challenge moral standards.

Research provides some support for these ideas. Mitchell, Palmer, and Schminke (2008) presented their work on the first series of studies examining ethical efficacy. The results of three of their studies provided evidence of the construct validity of their new measure. Their fourth study examines whether ethical efficacy strengthens self-regulatory abilities. Mitchell et al. argued that when individuals face work situations that breach moral standards (specifically, unethical/abusive leaders and coworkers who violated ethics policies), they would be less likely to engage in ethical work behaviors (specifically, helping coworkers and engaging in behaviors to enhance the work environment, called *individual initiative behaviors*). They further argued that strong ethical efficacy beliefs would mitigate these effects, strengthening the likelihood of ethical behaviors. The results show individuals who held strong ethical efficacy beliefs were more likely to help coworkers and engage in individual initiative behavior when faced with an unethical and abusive supervisor. Further, those with strong ethical efficacy beliefs were more likely to engage in individual initiative behaviors when they perceived coworkers violated ethics policies, but they were not more likely to help coworkers. According to Mitchell et al., these results suggest that those with strong ethical efficacy beliefs did not see value in helping unethical coworkers, but nevertheless tried to change the overall work group environment (via individual initiative behaviors). In all, the results of their study provide evidence that ethical efficacy beliefs strengthen self-regulatory abilities by instilling confidence to maintain ethical behavior in the face of morally ambiguous situations.

Thus, theory and research suggests ethical efficacy beliefs play an important role in motivating moral conduct. When individuals hold strong ethical efficacy beliefs, they have the confidence to sustain behavior to meet moral standards and resist pressures to behave unethically (Bandura, 1986, 1991). But, how do ethical efficacy beliefs develop? How do they evolve? And can they be strengthened? We believe a review of how ethical efficacy beliefs develop will shed light on how such beliefs can be strengthened.

The Development of Ethical Efficacy Beliefs

According to Bandura (1991), two main factors influence ethical efficacy beliefs: personal factors and social factors. We discuss each in more detail below.

Personal Factors

Although there are a myriad of personality traits that may influence one's confidence to behave ethically (see Treviño et al., 2006 for a review), Bandura argues that two personal factors of the self primarily strengthen one's confidence to behave ethically: self-monitoring and successful ethical experiences. Self-monitoring involves recognizing whether one's behavior is consistent with personal standards. When individuals act in ways that violate personal standards, they are subject to self-condemnation. Self-monitoring helps to prevent self-condemnation because it highlights a level of self-awareness of one's moral standards. Therefore, self-monitoring acts as an audit of one's behaviors, comparing those behaviors to one's personal standards.

Of course, a key ingredient here is actually having moral standards by which to scrutinize one's behavior. Social learning theory (Bandura, 1977) suggests individuals learn standards of behavior—to include moral standards—vicariously (by watching others) and directly, through experiences. Experiences are particularly important in the development of ethical efficacy beliefs. As individuals face ethical challenges and respond appropriately, these experiences instill confidence.

Script theory (Gioia & Poole, 1984) makes similar predictions. According to this theory, individuals develop "scripts" of appropriate behavior. Scripts provide cognitive schema for how individuals should respond in a given situation. Thus, scripts provide individuals with appropriate prototypic responses to ethical challenges. Gioia and Poole (1984) argue there are two ways scripts develop. The first is through direct experience or direct interactions with people, events, and situations. When individuals first encounter a unique situation, this starts the script development process. As they repeat the event or engage in similar situations, the script becomes more in-depth and internalized.[2] The second way scripts develop is indirectly, such as through communication, media, or through modeling behavior observed in the environment. Stated differently, individuals can be *taught* how to behave ethically. Considerable research suggests individuals can learn moral standards and ethical behavior (see Bandura, 1991 and Rest, 1986 for reviews).

Social Factors

Social factors also play a critical role in developing and strengthening ethical efficacy beliefs (Bandura, 1991). Individuals compare their own personal standards to environmental circumstances. Yet ethical situations vary in intensity (Jones, 1991), and this affects the strength of ethical efficacy. One's confidence in their ability to engage in ethical behavior, therefore, depends in part on the situation itself. Social situations that promote ethical values are inherently less difficult than unethical situations. In such cases, behavioral standards would be more consistent with personal moral standards, making it easier to do what is right and engage in ethical behavior. In short, the social environment provides support for what the individual already understands to be morally appropriate and it is understood that unethical behavior within that context is not status quo—there is no tension pulling at one's moral core.

Consistent with these arguments, Maddux (2002) demonstrated the importance of collective confidence in building individuals' efficacy beliefs. Collective efficacy motivates individuals to act similarly to achieve a common goal. In short, social environments that promote ethics strengthen individuals' ethical efficacy beliefs and make ethical behavior more likely (Youssef & Luthans, 2005).

Further, based on principles of social learning theory (Bandura, 1977) and script theory (Gioia & Poole, 1984), we understand the importance of role models in establishing behavioral standards. Essentially, individuals learn standards by watching what people do. Significant and credible role models (e.g., parents, teachers) are a primary source of vicarious learning as we develop personal standards for ethical behavior. These are individuals who are required to set the tone of the environment, and in doing so, convey moral rules of behavior and communicate what is ethical in a particular context. Role models play a primary role in building the social environment. Those who act in such a way and communicate that moral standards are valued lay a foundation for individuals to act similarly and be committed to those same standards (Bandura, 1986, 1991). We argue that role models who express moral values and display ethical conduct can potentially influence and strengthen others' ethical efficacy.

Research by Eden and colleagues (Eden & Aviram, 1993; Eden & Kinnar, 1991) provides some support for the influence of significant role models (leaders) on efficacy beliefs. These authors tested and demonstrated evidence of the *Galatea effect* on statelike and general efficacy beliefs. The Galatea effect suggests performance can be increased by raising expectations through positive verbal persuasion (i.e., by telling individuals they can accomplish and perform at high levels). Their research suggests credible sources of feedback (i.e., role models) can raise efficacy beliefs and subsequently strengthen positive behavioral reactions. Given this research, we believe it is possible for ethical efficacy beliefs to be strengthened by significant role models.

In summary, the social environment can provide support needed for individuals to adhere to moral standards and engage in behavior that meets those standards. Significant role models set the tone of the social environment and communicate a baseline of what is considered appropriate within that context. Individuals understand what is appropriate based on which behavior is incentivized and sanctioned versus which is condemned and not reinforced. Environments that stress moral standards build individuals' confidence to act similarly.

How Organizations Can Strengthen Employees' Ethical Efficacy Beliefs

Understanding the factors that influence ethical efficacy development provides a foundation for how these principles can be applied in an organizational setting. We outline below how organizations can influence the *personal factors* that develop ethical efficacy beliefs. Specifically, we suggest that ethical efficacy is analogous to a muscle. In order to strengthen it, ethical efficacy beliefs need exercise or practice. Further, we discuss the relevance of the overall social context of organizations and describe how organizations can influence employees' ethical efficacy beliefs through different aspects of the organization's social environment.

Strengthening Ethical Efficacy "Muscle"

We outlined above that ethical efficacy strengthens as individuals respond to ethical experiences successfully and thereby develop scripts of appropriate behavior. These scripts serve as a reference of past successful behavior and instill confidence in one's ability to handle similar ethical dilemmas in the future. Successful experiences reinforce individuals' ethical confidence to maintain their behavior to meet moral standards. In this way, successful experiences assist in maintaining self-regulatory abilities. Baumeister and colleagues (e.g., Baumeister, Gailliot, DeWall, & Oaten, 2006; Muraven & Baumeister, 2000) argue that this is because self-regulation is like a muscle. Similar to a muscle, once individuals experience a self-regulatory activity, they become tired (Muraven & Baumeister, 2000). However, repeated activities over time (like exercise) improve self-regulatory abilities and individuals' ability to control their behavior to meet social standards (Gailliot, Plant, Butz, & Baumeister, 2007; Muravan, Baumeister, & Tice, 1999; Oaten & Cheng, 2006). Thus, individuals who experience repeated self-regulation activities "exercise" their self-regulatory muscle, strengthening it.

Similarly, we believe ethical efficacy can be strengthened through exercise. The more individuals experience ethical events and react appropriately, the more they develop confidence to control behavior to meet moral standards. Thus, ethical efficacy is a consequence of exercised moral control (i.e., self-regulatory abilities). The more individuals practice self-control, the stronger their confidence will be in doing the same in the future. Repeated successful ethical performances only strengthen these effects further.

We believe organizations can assist in this process by creating ethics programs designed to enhance the awareness of moral issues and appropriate responses to moral dilemmas (building scripts). However, one-shot training exercises are not good enough. If we consider ethical efficacy as akin to a muscle, one-time training efforts only exhaust the muscle and do not build strength. It is like working out once in the gym and hoping to see results. For ethical efficacy beliefs to strengthen, repeated ethics activities are needed to strengthen self-regulatory muscle. Research shows employees who are provided ethics training engage in more ethically oriented behaviors than those who were not provided with training, even when challenged to do otherwise (Ethics Resource Center, 2005; Greenberg, 2002). Thus, we believe ethics training and programs are one means of strengthening employee ethical efficacy beliefs.

Creating a Social Environment that Enhances Ethical Efficacy Beliefs

As emphasized before, the social environment influences ethical efficacy beliefs. This implies that work environments that stress the importance of moral values and principles make it easier on employees to engage in ethical behavior, thereby strengthening their confidence to behave appropriately. Within a work environment, there are a variety of ways organizations can influence moral standards. Based on ethics theory and research, we highlight the influence of the work environment on employees' ethical efficacy beliefs. In particular, we discuss the relevance of organizational role models (leaders), organizational ethical control systems, and organizational ethical context. Because research suggests these social factors influence moral conduct, we believe they will also influence employees' ethical efficacy beliefs. Each is discussed in more detail below.

Organizational social role models: Leaders. Literature on ethical leadership and ethical culture in organizations often cites social learning theory (Bandura, 1977) to explain the impact of leaders and supervisors as role models for ethical behavior (Brown & Treviño, 2006a; Treviño, Butterfield, & McCabe, 1998). Parents and teachers play an important role in the development of personal standards (Bandura, 1986). Within a work environment, organizational leaders and supervisors are relevant models of behavior. Organizational leaders are primarily responsible for the overall goals of the organization and the strategies for attaining those goals in the future. Because leaders make decisions that influence organizational members, employees look to them for direction.

In order for leaders to influence employees' ethical efficacy beliefs effectively, they must first be considered credible role models (Bandura, 1991). That is, employees must believe that they can rely on their leader for guidance (Treviño, 1986). The position of power provides the leader some credence, but the heart of moral credibility involves whether leaders are trustworthy, whether they make fair and principled decisions, and whether they can increase employees' ethical behaviors and decrease employees' unethical behaviors (Treviño, Brown, & Hartman, 2003; Treviño, Hartman, & Brown, 2000).

Mayer, Davis, and Schoorman (1995) suggest leader trustworthiness is comprised of three factors: ability, benevolence, and integrity. Ability is seen when leaders demonstrate the requisite skills, competencies, and characteristics needed to perform and influence their work domain. Leaders display benevolence when employees believe the leader cares about the employees' interests, rather than being motivated by self-interest. Lastly, leaders display integrity when they act in accordance with the moral values (Do they "walk the talk" and "practice what they preach"?). Research suggests that employees who perceive their leaders as trustworthy are more likely to engage in ethical and productive work behavior and less likely to engage in unethical work behavior (Colquitt, Scott, & LePine, 2007; Mayer & Gavin, 2005). We argue that leaders who are trustworthy make employees more confident to follow their lead, and when faced with an ethical challenge, they will be more willing to talk through the issues with their leaders and follow their guidance.

It is also important to emphasize how leaders influence employees' behavior. Organizational rewards and punishments are a primary form of influence; both direct and reinforce the types of behaviors desired by leaders (Luthans & Stajkovic, 1999). Rewards suggest what leaders' value and, therefore, motivate employees to act in ways to achieve them. Punishments communicate what is not valued and motivate employees to not engage in behaviors that will be disciplined. Leaders who focus on bottom-line tactics at the expense of legal or ethical standards promote unethical behavior (Yeager, 1986), particularly when they reward employees for doing so (Bakan, 2004). Whether intended or otherwise, these practices incentivize and reinforce unethical conduct. Further, we believe such practices deflate ethical efficacy beliefs because they pressure employees to be unethical and act in violation of their moral standards. Leaders who use these tactics are not credible, ethical role models. The irresponsibility is clear. Thus, ethical leaders must set high ethical standards and use rewards and punishments as indicators of whether those standards are being met (Brown & Treviño, 2006a). Leaders who incentivize ethical behavior instill more confidence in employees to engage in ethical behavior, strengthening ethical efficacy beliefs.

Thus, credible, ethical leaders demonstrate "normatively appropriate conduct through personal actions and interpersonal relationships, and the promotion of such conduct to followers through two-way communication, reinforcement, and decision-making" (Brown, Treviño, & Harrison, 2005, p. 120). When leaders set workplace standards in accordance with moral values and principles, employees are not pressured to engage in unethical behaviors. Research provides support for these ideas. Employees conform to the ethical values of their leaders (Schminke, Wells, Peyrefitte, & Sebora, 2002), and when employees' values are in congruence with their leaders' ethical values, they are less likely to engage in destructive and unethical work behavior (Brown & Treviño, 2006b). Ethical leadership also promotes a trickle-down effect of morality (Mayer, Kuenzi, Greenbaum, Bardes, & Salvador, 2009). When leaders are ethical, ethical behavior spills over into the work environment and provides a path for all employees to follow. Consequently, ethical leadership positively influences ethical behavior and negatively influences unethical behavior throughout the organization.

In this way, ethical leaders promote the effective functioning of their organizations and ultimately influence its overall culture (Dickson, Smith, Grojean, & Ehrhart, 2001). Research supports these arguments. For example, Schminke, Ambrose and Neubaum (2005) found leaders' ethics positively influenced the ethical climate of organizations. They found that leaders' moral values shape the overall value structure of the organization. Thus, beyond the vicarious learning experiences provided by leaders as role models, ethical leaders shape the context of an organization and dictate standards of moral appropriateness.

Because leaders play a primary role in setting the ethical tone of organizations, we believe leaders exert a strong influence on employees' ethical efficacy beliefs. Leaders can provide for a great source of support or pressure in terms of ethical and unethical behaviors. Ethical leaders engender trust among their followers (Treviño, Brown, & Hartman, 2003; Treviño, Hartman, & Brown, 2000), and in doing so model appropriate behaviors and strengthen employees' confidence to behave similarly (Mayer et al., 2009). Further, ethical leaders shape the overall social environment in the organization toward moral principles (Schminke et al., 2005). In contrast, leaders who engage in unethical behaviors strengthen the likelihood that employees will engage in similar and destructive behaviors because employees believe these are appropriate work behaviors (Detert, Treviño, Burris, & Andiappan, 2007; Mitchell, 2008). We argue that unethical leaders weaken ethical efficacy beliefs because employees will feel greater pressure to violate their moral standards to be consistent with organizational demands.

Organizational ethics control systems. Organizational ethics programs are considered a form of behavioral control. The primary goal of ethics controls is to maintain ethical conduct and legal compliance of organizational members (Weaver, Treviño, & Cochran, 1999b). The relevance of ethical efficacy is not a cure-all for ethics issues in organizations. Individuals' ethical endeavors are influenced by the extent to which ethical behavior is important to them (Bandura, 1986). If an individual desires to behave unethically, no amount of confidence in their ability to do the right thing matters. Thus, ethics controls are necessary to prevent employees from acting on self-interested gains at the cost of others and maintaining behavior to meet ethical and legal mandates. Yet, how organizations set up their controls can foster ethical efficacy and thereby promote ethical behavior and reduce unethical behavior.

Ethics programs can include many elements (e.g., codes of ethics, evaluation systems, communication systems) (Weaver, Treviño, & Cochran, 1999a). Researchers identified two primary types of ethics control orientations: compliance-oriented and values-oriented programs. These approaches are not mutually exclusive, and research shows that when either is present the incidence of unethical conduct is lower (Treviño, Weaver, Gibson, & Toffler, 1999). Both types of programs build awareness about ethical and legal issues and enhance employee commitment to ethical behavior; however, values-oriented controls are shown to be more impactful in terms of positive ethics outcomes (Treviño et al., 1999). Further, the use of both types of controls promotes even greater benefits (Treviño et al., 1999).

We argue that an organization's control orientation can influence ethical efficacy beliefs. Not all wrongdoing stems from individuals who desire to behave unethically. To the extent that controls are compliance oriented—focusing on punishment, monitoring, and other situational constraints—the control system works to diminish individual confidence in achieving unethical successes. Although it is important for organizations to make unethical behavior more difficult, it is also important to make ethical behavior easier. The more employees perceive resistance to ethical conduct, the less confident they will be in their ability to follow through with a moral course of action. This helps us understand why values-oriented controls are more successful.

Organizations can influence ethical efficacy by also integrating a values-oriented approach to ethics compliance. Values-oriented systems are those that "emphasize support for employees' ethical aspirations and the development of shared values" (Weaver et al., 1999b, p. 42). Values-oriented controls provide a foundation on which ethical efficacy beliefs can be strengthened and reinforced. Employees will be very aware of the organization's emphasis on moral behavior and will try to attain ethical goals for themselves and their organization. In short, values-oriented programs support moral principles, which decrease the likelihood of unethical pressures and questionable work practices. Thus, values-oriented programs innately set up employees to achieve ethics successes, strengthening ethical efficacy beliefs.

We believe organizations that emphasize both forms of ethics controls—compliance oriented and values oriented—provide the structural support for ethical behaviors. Employees become very aware of which behaviors do not meet the organization's ethical standards and violate moral principles. Compliance-oriented controls monitor employees and keep them in line with ethical and legal standards. Further, values-oriented controls highlight the importance of moral principles, by establishing ethical goals for the organization and supporting employees' commitment to ethical character.

Ethical organizational context. Within the business ethics literature, an organization's ethical context is fundamentally shaped by its ethical climate (Victor & Cullen, 1988) and culture (Treviño, 1990). Both ethical climate and culture embrace the internal social-psychological environment of an organization and involve organizational members' shared perceptions about the extent to which the organization emphasizes ethical values (Denison, 1996). Even though some researchers treat these concepts separately, by and large, research has shown that both capture the same perceptions: employees' perceptions of the values, beliefs, and assumptions about what constitutes ethical work behavior within the organization at large (Treviño, Butterfield, & McCabe, 1998). These perceptions are based on formal processes (e.g., programs, rules) and informal processes (e.g., peer discussions, observing others). Research suggests that ethical context influences employees' attitudes and behaviors. For example, ethical context positively influences employees' commitment to the organization, and negatively influences unethical behavior (Treviño et al., 1998).

Work contexts that emphasize unethical standards of behavior promote unethical behavior (O'Leary-Kelly, Griffin, & Glew, 1996). Consistent with social learning theory (Bandura, 1977), employees look to others in their work environment to see what is considered appropriate work conduct. Social information processing theory (Salancik & Pfeffer, 1978) makes similar arguments. According to this theory, individuals learn more about what is appropriate work behavior by watching coworkers and peers than by formal rules and procedures. When organizational members act immorally, employees believe these behaviors are appropriate and behave similarly. Research demonstrates these effects. For example, a study by Clinard (1983) of retired middle managers from *Fortune* 500 companies suggests the primary reason for unethical acts that had transpired in their tenure was due to the "ethical tone" of the organization. Further, Robinson and O'Leary-Kelly (1998) found that organizational newcomers who perceived coworkers acted unethically began to act similarly. They call this a "monkey see, monkey do" effect. Subsequent research reports similar findings in terms of workplace aggression and antisocial behavior (Aquino & Douglas, 2003; Glomb & Liao, 2003).

As we described previously, research suggests ethical leaders and control systems play an important role in the ethicality of organizational context (Treviño et al., 1999). These sources are, however, most meaningful when they contribute to a shared belief within organizations of moral principles. Leaders and control systems should enhance the ethics environment (the climate) and the overall assumptions, values, and belief systems of how things are done within the organization (the culture).

The presence of these shared beliefs and the means by which behavior is influenced parallels work on collective efficacy beliefs (Chen al., 2002). Collective efficacy is defined as a "group's shared belief in its conjoint capabilities to organize and execute the courses of action required to produce given levels of attainments" (Bandura, 1997, p. 477). Collective efficacy beliefs become homogenous as a result of common social interactions and shared experiences (Zaccaro, Blair, Peterson, & Zazanis, 1995). These principles align with findings from social information processing theory (Salancik & Pfeffer, 1978). Research suggests collective efficacy influences collective performance over and above individual performance (Durham, Knight, & Locke, 1997). An important implication from this research is that organizations that harness and strengthen individual employees' ethical efficacy beliefs may create collective ethical efficacy within organizational units. Collective ethical efficacy may then influence mass employees' behaviors and, in particular, positively influence ethical behavior and negatively influence unethical behavior.

In sum, we believe organizations can enhance ethical efficacy beliefs by creating a social environment that promotes moral values and behaviors. The context then must be a shared perception, wherein all employees understand that the organization expects and values ethical behavior. Again, leaders set the tone of what is valued; structural processes reinforce these values (i.e., ethics controls). Context defines the mental models that guide all employees' understanding. Ethical organizational contexts provide paradigms for problem solving. Context provides employees with the common assumptions of automatic patterns of how to deal with ethical dilemmas, challenges, and pressures (Schein, 1990). Because context guides how people think and respond to ethical situations, we believe it will influence employees' ethical efficacy beliefs.

Conclusion

Ethical efficacy instills employees' with the confidence to behave ethically and in doing so, shows promise in helping individuals act in accordance with moral standards. Because ethical efficacy influences individuals' intentions about their moral conduct, we argue that it enhances motivation and subsequent behavior. Individuals who hold strong ethical efficacy beliefs are better equipped to deal with ethical challenges because they are able to control their behavior, particularly when challenged to behave otherwise. Thus, it is greatly needed. Employees in today's business climate face many pressures and challenges to be competitive and productive for organizations. Consequently, they have been compelled to engage in behavior that they believe meets organizational expectations and rewards (Yeager, 1986). In short, organizations are acting quite irresponsibly by emphasizing short-term gains and constrain employees' ability to act morally (Mitchell, 2001).

Driven by the desire for success, business leaders have set a tone in organizations of getting the job done at whatever the cost. The downsides to these practices are great. Unethical behavior puts organizations at risk of declining market share and lower profits, and increased government regulation (Gagne, Gavin, & Tully, 2005). Not only do these practices negatively influence internal organizational functioning, but they cascade to society through costs associated with government oversight and regulation (Thomas et al., 2004). Though some argue that being ethical is difficult in today's work world, the benefits of unethical acts do not outweigh the costs (Jackall, 1988). Further, some argue that unethical behavior tears at the social fabric of society (Thomas et al., 2004).

Because of this, organizations and government officials are under pressure to control unethical behavior and heighten moral standards in business practices. We argue that enabling ethical behavior within organizations first starts with organizational members and, specifically, their ethical efficacy beliefs. Employees with strong ethical efficacy beliefs will be confident and motivated to abide by moral convictions. They will be better able to persevere against morally questionable work practices and be resilient to pressures to engage in unethical behavior and self-interested gains at the cost of others. We understand that developing employees' ethical efficacy beliefs will take effort and investment by organizations. However, research suggests that leaders who invest in ethics programs and enhance moral standards within their organizations find them beneficial to the overall performance and effectiveness of the organization (Wagner & Dittmar, 2006). In the end, such efforts should prove to be a worthwhile investment.

Endnotes

1. The terms *ethical* and *moral* are used synonymously.
2. These concepts also align with core theories of moral development (Kohlberg, 1969; Piaget, 1977). Accordingly, cognitive moral development theory suggests individuals develop higher levels of moral reasoning in time and after experiencing moral situations. More contemporary theory suggests that scripts provide a basis of intuitive reactions to ethical situations (Reynolds, 2006).

References

Ajzen, I. (1985). From intentions to actions: A theory of planned behavior. In J. Kuhland & J. Beckman (Eds.), *Action-control: From cognitions to behavior* (pp. 11–39). Heidelberg: Springer.

Altman, M. (2005). The ethical economy and competitive markets: Reconciling altruistic, moralistic, and ethical behavior with the rational economic agent and competitive markets. *Journal of Economic Psychology, 26*, 732–757.

Amer, S. (2005). Do the right thing. *Successful Meetings, 54*, 72.

Andrews, K. R. (1989). Ethics in practice. *Harvard Business Review, 67*, 99–104.

Aquino, K., & Douglas, S. (2003). Identity threat and antisocial behavior in organizations: The moderating effects of individual differences, aggressive modeling, and hierarchical status. *Organizational Behavior and Human Decision Processes, 90*, 195–208.

Argandoña, A. (2005). Corruption and companies: The use of facilitating payments. *Journal of Business Ethics, 60*, 251–264.

Bakan, J. (2004). *The corporation: The pathological pursuit of profit and power*. New York: Free Press.

Bandura, A. (1997). Self-efficacy: The exercise of control. New York: Freeman.

Bandura, A. (1991). Social cognitive theory of moral thought and action. In W. M. Kurtines & J. L. Gewirtz (Eds.), *Handbook of moral behavior and development*. Hillsdale, NJ: LEA.

Bandura, A. (1986). *Social foundations of thought and action: A social cognitive theory*. Englewood Cliffs, NJ: Prentice-Hall.

Bandura, A. (1977). Self-efficacy: Toward a unifying theory of behavioral change. *Psychological Review, 84*, 191–215.

Bandura, A., Caprara, G. V., Barbaranelli, C., Pastorelli, C., & Regalia, C. (2001). Socio-cognitive self-regulatory mechanisms governing transgressive behavior. *Journal of Personality and Social Psychology, 80*, 125–135.

Bandura, A., & Locke, E. (2003). Negative self-efficacy and goal effects revisited. *Journal of Applied Psychology, 88*, 87–99.

Baumeister, R. F. (2005). *The cultural animal: Human nature, meaning, and social life.* New York: Oxford University Press.

Baumeister, R. F., Gailliot, M., C. N. DeWall, & Oaten, M. (2006). Self-regulation and personality: How interventions increase regulatory success, and how depletion moderates the effects of traits on behavior. *Journal of Personality, 74*, 1773–1801.

Blasi, A. (1980). Bridging moral cognition and moral action: A critical review of the literature. *Psychological Bulletin, 88*, 1–45.

Brown, M. E., & Treviño, L. K. (2006a). Ethical leadership: A review and future directions. *Leadership Quarterly, 17*, 595–616.

Brown, M. E., & Treviño, L. K. (2006b). Socialized charismatic leadership, values congruence, and deviance in work groups. *Journal of Applied Psychology, 91*, 954–962.

Brown, M. E., Treviño, L. K., & Harrison, D. A. (2005). Ethical leadership: A social learning perspective for construct development and testing. *Organizational Behavior and Human Decision Processes, 97*, 117–134.

Chen, G., Webber, S. S., Bliese, P. D., Mathieu, J. E., Payne, S. C., Born, D. H., & Zaccaro, S. J. (2002). Simultaneous examination of the antecedents and consequences of efficacy beliefs at multiple levels of analysis. *Human Performance, 15*(4), 381–409.

Clinard, M. B. (1983). *Corporate ethics and crime: The role of middle management.* Beverly Hills, CA: Sage.

Colquitt, J. A., Scott, B. A., & LePine, J. A. (2007). Trust, trustworthiness, and trust propensity: A meta-analytic test of their unique relationships with risk taking and job performance. *Journal of Applied Psychology, 92*, 909–927.

Cooper, C. (2008). *Extraordinary circumstances: The journey of a corporate whistleblower.* Hoboken, NJ: John Wiley & Sons, Inc.

Denison, D. (1996). What is the difference between organizational culture and organizational climate? A native's point of view on a decade of paradigm wars. *Academy of Management Review, 21*, 619–654.

Detert, J. R., Treviño, L. K., Burris, E. R., & Andiappan, M. (2007). Managerial modes of influence and counterproductivity in organizations: A longitudinal business-unit-level investigation. *Journal of Applied Psychology, 92*, 993–1005.

Dickson, M. W., Smith, D. B., Grojean, M. W., & Ehrhart, M. (2001). An organizational climate regarding ethics: The outcome of leader values and the practices that reflect them. *Leadership Quarterly, 12*, 197–217.

Durham, C. C., Knight, D., & Locke, E. A. (1997). Effects of leader role, team-set goal difficulty, efficacy, and tactics on team effectiveness. *Organizational Behavior and Human Decision Processes, 72*, 203–231.

Eden, D., & Aviram, A. (1993). Self-efficacy training to speed reemployment: Helping people to help themselves. *Journal of Applied Psychology, 78*, 352–360.

Eden, D., & Kinnar, J. (1991). Modeling Galatea: Boosting self-efficacy to increase volunteering. *Journal of Applied Psychology, 76*, 770–780.

Ethics Resource Center. (2005). *National business ethics survey*. Washington, DC: Ethics Resource Center.

Fisman, R., & Svensson, J. (2007). Are corruption and taxation really harmful to growth? Firm-level evidence. *Journal of Development Economics, 83,* 63–75.

Gagne, M. L., Gavin, J. H., & Tully, G. J. (2005). Assessing the costs and benefits of ethics: Exploring a framework. *Business and Society Review, 110,* 181–190.

Gailliot, M. T., Plant, E. A., Butz, D. A., & Baumeister, R. F. (2007). Increasing self-regulatory strength can reduce the depleting effects of suppressing stereotypes. *Personality and Social Psychology Bulletin, 33,* 281–294.

Gellerman, S. W. (1986). Why "good" managers make bad ethical choices. *Harvard Business Review, 64,* 85–90.

Gioia, D. A., & Poole, P. P. (1984). Scripts in organizational behavior. *Academy of Management Review, 9,* 449–459.

Glomb, T. M., & Liao, H. (2003). Interpersonal aggression in work groups: Social influence, reciprocal, and individual effects. *Academy of Management Journal, 46,* 486–496.

Greenberg, J. (2002). Who stole the money and when? Individuals and situational determinants of employee theft. *Organizational Behavior and Human Decision Processes, 89,* 985–1003.

Jackall, R. (1988). *Moral mazes: The world of corporate managers.* New York: Oxford University Press.

Jones, T. M. (1991). Ethical decision making by individuals in organizations: An issue-contingent model. *Academy of Management Review, 16,* 366–395.

Kanfer, R. (1990). Motivation theory and industrial and organizational psychology. In M. D. Dunnette & L. M. Hough (Eds.), *Handbook of industrial and organizational psychology* (2nd Ed.) (Vol. 1, pp. 75–170). Chicago, IL: Rand McNally.

Kanfer, R. (1992). Work motivation: New directions in theory and research. In C. L. Cooper & I. T. Robertson (Eds.), *International review of industrial and organizational psychology,* (Vol. 7, pp. 1–53). New York: Wiley.

Kohlberg, L. (1969). Stage and sequence: The cognitive developmental approach to socialization. In D. A. Goslin (Ed.), *Handbook of socialization theory* (pp. 347–480). Chicago, IL: Rand McNally.

Luthans, F., & Stajkovic, A. D. (1999). Reinforce for performance: The need to go beyond pay and even rewards. *Academy of Management Executive, 13,* 49–57.

Maddux, J. E. (2002). Self-efficacy: The power of believing you can. In C. Snyder & S. Lopez (Eds.), *Handbook of positive psychology* (pp. 257–276). Oxford: Oxford University Press.

Mayer, D. M., Kuenzi, M., Greenbaum, R., Bardes, M., & Salvador, R. (2009). How low does ethical leadership flow? Test of a trickle-down model. *Organizational Behavior and Human Decision Processes, 108,* 1–13.

Mayer, R. C., Davis, J. H., & Schoorman, F. D. (1995). An integrative model of organizational trust. *Academy of Management Review, 20,* 709–734.

Mayer, R. C., & Gavin, M. (2005). Trust in management and performance: Who minds the shop while the employees watch the boss? *Academy of Management Journal, 48,* 874–888.

Mitchell, L. E. (2001). *Corporate irresponsibility.* New Haven, London: Yale University Press.

Mitchell, M. S. (2008). *Employees' reactions to supervisor aggression: An examination of situational and individual factors.* Paper presented at the Academy of Management annual meeting, Anaheim, CA. Unpublished manuscript.

Mitchell, M. S., Palmer, N. F., & Schminke, M. (2008). *Understanding the influence of ethical efficacy.* Paper presented at the Academy of Management annual conference, Anaheim, CA. Unpublished manuscript.

Mobley, M., & Humphreys, J. (2006). How low will you go? *Harvard Business Review, 84,* 33–44.

Muraven, M., Baumeister, R. F. (2000). Self-regulation and depletion of limited resources: Does self-control resemble a muscle? *Psychological Bulletin, 126,* 247–259.

Muraven, M., Baumeister, R. F., & Tice, D. M. (1999). Longitudinal improvement of self-regulation through practice: Building self-control strength through repeated exercise. *Journal of Social Psychology, 139,* 446–457.

Oaten, M., & Cheng, K. (2006). Longitudinal gains in self-regulation from regular physical exercise. *British Journal of Health Psychology, 11,* 717–733.

O'Leary-Kelly, A. M., Griffin, R. W., & Glew, D. J. (1996). Organization-motivated aggression: A research framework. *Academy of Management Review, 21,* 225–253.

Park, A. (2009). Lie, cheat, flirt: What people will do to keep a job. *Time,* www.time.com/time/health/article/0,8599,1884573,00.html. Retrieved March 14, 2009.

Perrewé, P. L., & Spector, P. E. (2002). Personality research in the organizational sciences. In Ferris, G. R., & Martocchio, J. J. (Ed.), *Research in personnel and human resource management* (pp. 1–63). Oxford: JAI Press, Elsevier Science, Inc.

Piaget, J. (1977). *Moral judgment of the child.* Middlesex, England: Penguin Books.

Posner, B. Z., & Schmidt, W. H. (1987). Ethics in American companies: A managerial perspective. *Journal of Business Ethics, 6,* 383–391.

Rest, J. R. (1986). *Moral development: Advances in research and theory.* New York: Praeger.

Rest, J. R., Narvaez, D., Bebeau, M. J., & Thoma, S. J. (1999). *Postconventional moral thinking: A neo-Kohlbergian approach.* Mahwah, NJ: LEA.

Reynolds, S. J. (2006). A neurocognitive model of the ethical decision-making process: Implications for study and practice. *Journal of Applied Psychology, 91,* 737–748.

Robinson, S., & O'Leary-Kelly, A. (1998). Monkey see, monkey do: The influence of work groups on antisocial behavior of employees. *Academy of Management Journal, 41,* 658–672.

Salancik, G. J., & Pfeffer, J. (1978). A social information processing approach to job attitudes and task design. *Administrative Science Quarterly, 23,* 224–253.

Schien, E. H. (1990). Organizational culture. *American Psychologist, 45,* 109–119.

Schminke, M., Ambrose, M. L., & Neubaum, D. O. (2005). The effect of leader moral development on ethical climate and employee attitudes. *Organizational Behavior and Human Decision Processes, 97,* 135–151.

Schminke, M., Wells, D., Peyreffite, J., & Sebora, T. C. (2002). Leadership and ethics in work groups: A longitudinal assessment. *Group and Organization Management, 27,* 272–293.

The interview. (2002). *Time, 160,* 58–60.

Thomas, T., Schermerhorn, J. R., & Dienhart, J. W. (2004). *Academy of Management Executive, 18,* 56–66.

Treviño, L. K. (1990). A cultural perspective on changing and developing organizational ethics. *Research in Organizational Change and Development, 4,* 195–230.

Treviño, L. K. (1986). Ethical decision making in organizations: A person-situation interactionist model. *Academy of Management Review, 11,* 501–517.

Treviño, L. K., Brown, M., & Hartman, L. P. (2003). A qualitative investigation of perceived executive ethical leadership: Perceptions from inside and outside the executive suite. *Human Relations, 55,* 5–37.

Treviño, L. K., Butterfield, K. D., & McCabe, D. L. (1998). The ethical context in organizations: Influences on employee attitudes and behaviors. *Behavioral Ethics Quarterly, 8,* 447–476.

Treviño, L. K., Hartman, L. P., & Brown, M. (2000). Moral person and moral manager: How executives develop a reputation for ethical leadership. *California Management Review, 42,* 128–142.

Treviño, L. K., Weaver, G. R., Gibson, D. G., & Toffler, B. L. (1999). Managing ethics and legal compliance: What works and what hurts. *California Management Review, 41,* 131–151.

Treviño, L. K., Weaver, G. R., & Reynolds, S. J. (2006). Behavioral ethics in organizations: A review. *Journal of Management, 32,* 951–990.

Victor, B., & Cullen, J. B. (1988). The organizational bases of ethical work climates. *Administrative Science Quarterly, 33,* 101–125.

Wagner, S., & Dittmar, L. (2006). The unexpected benefits of Sarbanes-Oxley. *Harvard Business Review, 84,* 133.

Wahn, J. (1993). Organizational dependence and the likelihood of complying with organizational pressures to behave unethically. *Journal of Business Ethics, 12,* 245–251.

Watkins, S. (2003). Ethical conflicts at Enron: Moral responsibility in corporate capitalism. *California Management Review, 45,* 6–19.

Weaver, G. R., Treviño, L. K., & Cochran, P. L. (1999a). Corporate ethics practices in the mid-1990s: An empirical study of the *Fortune* 1000. *Journal of Business Ethics, 18,* 283–294.

Weaver, G. R., Treviño, L. K., & Cochran, P. L. (1999b). Corporate ethics programs as control systems: Influences of executive commitment and environmental factors. *Academy of Management Journal, 42,* 41–57.

Weber, J., & Gillespie, J. (1998). Differences in ethical beliefs, intentions, and behaviors. *Business & Society, 37,* 447–467.

Yeager, P. C. (1986). Analyzing corporate offenses: Progress and prospects. *Research in Corporate Social Performance and Policy, 8,* 93–120.

Youssef, C. M., & Luthans, F. (2005). A positive organizational behavior approach to ethical performance. In R. A. Giacalone, C. L. Jurkiewicz, & C. Dunn (Eds.), *Positive psychology in business ethics and corporate responsibility* (pp. 1–22). Greenwich, CT: Information Age.

Zaccaro, S. J., Blair, V., Peterson, C., & Zazanis, M. (1995). Collective efficacy. In J. E. Maddux (Ed.), *Self-efficacy, adaptation, and adjustment: Theory, research, and application* (pp. 305–328). New York: Plenum.

Section II

Unethical Behavior

Causes, Consequences, and Comebacks

6

On the Psychology of Preventing and Dealing With Ethical Failures: A Behavioral Ethics Approach

David De Cremer
Erasmus University

Introduction

The last two decades have witnessed an onslaught of media reports on issues of fraud, corporate scandals, and other types of unethical behavior. Indeed, the numerous scandals in organizations such as Enron and WorldCom made all of us concerned about the emergence of unethical and immoral behavior in organizations. More recently, this concern has become even stronger due to the worldwide financial crisis in which it became explicitly clear that the irresponsible (and unethical) behavior of managers and organizations inflicts pain on society and its members.

One specific type of unethical situation that is frequently observed (and which is also examined in the studies reported in this chapter) involves the allocation of resources among different (interdependent) parties in unfair and morally unacceptable ways. For example, governments sometimes misrepresent the actual value of resources they allocate to health care and services. Departments within organizations compete for scarce resources and in this process use strategies of deception that reveal final unfair outcomes to other departments. Finally, auditing companies report income in benefiting ways that violate the fairness standards used by society at large. The consequence of these types of ethical failures is that the unfair behavior of one party influences the outcomes and welfare of other parties. As such, this type of unfair behavior can be regarded as unethical in that it violates the rules, values, and standards that our community employs to coordinate and cooperate, and therefore cannot be accepted by society at large (Tenbrunsel & Smith-Crowe, 2008).

Ethics in Organizations and Management: Prescriptive and Descriptive Approaches

Historically, the field of business ethics has adopted a *prescriptive* approach in addressing issues related to morality and ethics in group, organizational, and societal settings (Treviño & Weaver, 1994). Such an approach uses insights from important philosophical traditions to describe how moral and ethical people should behave. Under such an approach, the central focus has been on addressing "questions about whether specific business practices are acceptable" (Ferrell, Fraedrich, & Ferrell, 2008, p. 5). To define properly which practices are acceptable, research has been influenced primarily by notions taken from philosophy and morality, which stress the idea that we are motivated to act morally because we feel that we should or ought to respect other people and their interests. Thus, morality is an innate human value. Such an idea aligns well with Kant and his categorical imperative (Hill, 2000, p. 39), which holds that moral behavior is an end in itself because of "a rational moral requirement for everyone that is not based or conditional on its serving one's contingent personal ends." This influence of moral philosophy is also recognized in more recent theoretical approaches in the fields of justice and ethics, such as the deontic justice model (Folger, 2001; Folger & Salvador, 2008), fairness motivation (Lerner, 2003), and the integrated theory of moral convictions (Skitka, Bauman, & Mullen, in press). These justice theories advocate the idea that people value justice in society and business as an end in itself and therefore are convinced that just and fair interaction is a principle of moral duty.

However, it has been recently argued that such a view is too narrow in scope (Bazerman & Banaji, 2004; De Cremer, 2009; Treviño, Weaver, & Reynolds, 2006). Rather than the source of unethical behavior being a lack of information or misapplication of ethical principles, it has been argued that many ethical failures can be explained by a lack of awareness that one is even facing an ethical problem. This view helps to explain why we see many unethical failures, and yet still have many managers believing correctly that they are ethical people (De Cremer & van Dijk, 2005, 2008). In line with this perspective, a common understanding has emerged that, in addition to a prescriptive approach in which a moral principle is communicated and evaluated, we also need a behavioral approach that examines how individuals make actual decisions and engage in real actions when faced with ethical dilemmas. As such, a *descriptive* approach (what are people really doing) seems needed to get a better understanding of how and why individuals display unethical behavior. This realization has come to life in the new field of behavioral ethics, which "refers to individual behavior that is subject to or judged according to generally accepted moral norms of behavior" (Treviño, Weaver, & Reynolds, 2006, p. 952). Because of its focus on the actual behavior of the individual, research in behavioral ethics largely draws from work in psychology, which is the scientific study of human behavior and thought processes. As noted by Bazerman and Banaji (2004, p. 1150) "efforts to improve ethical decision making are better aimed at understanding our psychological tendencies."

The Relevance of Behavioral Ethics

It thus stands to reason that a behavioral ethics approach is well suited to investigate how one can arrive at an understanding of how to promote ethical behavior in organizations and management. That is, an approach focusing on the psychology of normative behavior may help to see the real drives underlying people's ethical versus unethical behavior. Although the prescriptive approach is without a doubt of value to define and interpret what is right and what is wrong (which leads to the implementation of codes of conduct), it becomes less impactful to promote confidently our knowledge as to whether positive and moral behavior can be promoted in companies by, for example, clearly dictating the rules of what should be done (as codes of conduct are supposed to do). One can imagine that if no severe ethical failures or transgressions emerge during a period of time, the conclusion can be quickly drawn that the code of conduct works. However, although a life without transgressions is noble and praiseworthy, it is not particularly noteworthy and thus reveals little insight into whether organizations are doing well with respect to managing the moral behavior of their members. In other words, ethical transgressions may teach us the most about the true motives of people and provide insights that can help to further promote the effectiveness of management. As such, a problem is that behavior that is consistent with the code of conduct provides no diagnostic evidence about an individual's underlying motives (Jones & Davis, 1965), that is, whether he or she is truly motivated to be an ethical individual. Thus, to be effective in motivating people to display ethical behavior, we also need to better understand the motives underlying people's actual decisions.

In a behavioral ethics approach, this would imply that we are looking for a response to the question of whether people are in general most strongly motivated to display positive behaviors (which are beneficial to the collective) or negative behaviors (which are hurtful to the collective). One way to examine this is to see whether individuals are more likely to model (reciprocate) positive and ethical behavior or more likely to model the negative and unethical behavior of their leaders and managers. Recent research by De Cremer and Aquino (2009) did exactly this. These authors investigated whether both positive and negative reciprocity emerge in equal ways in bargaining settings or whether one principle of reciprocity looms larger than the other. In bargaining games where resources are allocated, negative reciprocity refers to reciprocating unfavorable offers that are less than an equal division, whereas positive reciprocity refers to reciprocating favorable offers that are more than an equal share. Building on recent insights that negative information (bad) is assigned more weight than positive information (good; see Baumeister et al., 2001), De Cremer and Aquino argued that negative reciprocity will be more easily displayed than positive reciprocity.

To examine this question, the ultimatum bargaining game paradigm was used (Güth, Schmittberger, & Schwarze, 1982), in which two parties have to allocate a valued resource between them. One party takes the role of allocator and the other party the role of recipient. In the Güth et al. (1982) study, participants in the first phase of the experiment were named the recipient and they all received a very unfavorable offer (i.e., 100 chips were divided in such a way that the allocator kept 70 chips and gave 30 chips to the participant) or favorable offer (i.e., the participant received 70 chips and the allocator kept 30 chips). In this setting, the recipient was not able to reject the offer (i.e., dictator game; Forsyth, Horowitz, Savin, & Sefton, 1994; Kahneman, Knetsch & Thaler, 1986). In the second session, the participant became the allocator and the allocator of the first session became the recipient. The dependent variable of interest was how much the participant (who was recipient in the first round) gave to the other party (who was allocator in the dictator game in the first round).

The results showed that participants adhered very strongly to the principle of negative reciprocity (i.e., reciprocating with an offer that is lower than an equal share), and this tendency was enhanced when the participant had more power in the bargaining situation (i.e., more power meant that the participant has less to fear that the recipient would reject his/her offer). Participants, however, did not adhere to the positive reciprocity principle (i.e., reciprocating with an offer that is more than an equal share). Regardless of their power in the bargaining they made offers that were close to a 50-50 split. These results suggest that people are strongly motivated to model or reciprocate negative and unfair behavior, but that the motivation to model the same degree of positive and sacrificing behavior is not really present. Thus, negative reciprocity seems to loom larger than positive reciprocity when it comes down to making allocation decisions. At a more general level, these findings would suggest that as managers and leaders we need to be aware that our negative and unethical behaviors are more easily and quickly reciprocated than our positive and ethical behaviors.

On Preventing Unethical Behavior: The Fear of Things Going Wrong

The results of De Cremer and Aquino (2009) align well with the contemporary belief that organizations and society at large should devote more attention to identifying possible ethical pitfalls and thus to preventing the emergence of unethical behavior and decision making (see also De Cremer, 2009). Moreover, because people apparently seem motivated the most by the pursuit of self-interest (see Folger & Salvador, 2008, for an alternative perspective), the issue of monitoring and the application of sanctions (i.e., punishment of inappropriate and irresponsible behavior) is a primary focus in many organizations and political arenas. Indeed, by installing sanctioning systems, organizations aim to signal to employees that irresponsible behavior is not tolerated. Thus, sanctioning systems are considered to influence the interpretations of employees on what is right and what is wrong behavior. This way, sanctions should be able to eliminate self-interested behaviors (i.e., only pursuing one's own welfare) among employees.

Research has focused on the message that sanctions provide a signal with respect to the reasons that unethical behavior is punished. Generally, two reasons are identified for punishing unethical behavior (Carlsmith, 2006). A first reason concerns the idea of *retribution*, in which punishment is seen as an end in itself. The second reason concerns the idea of *utility*, in which punishment is used to limit future transgressions. The idea is that the costs of the punishment should negatively impact on how attractive a rational transgressor evaluates his or her future unethical behavior. This idea of utility has been demonstrated to be an important heuristic used by people when being confronted with conflicts of interest (e.g., own versus collective welfare). For example, research by Treviño and Ball (1992) showed that observers consider punishment of individuals acting unethically more fair when the punishment is more severe. In other words, the more unethical a person is perceived to be, the more people wish this person to be punished harshly. Interestingly, punishment does not always represent a formal organizational procedure that may carry financial costs with it, but can also be delivered in informal ways. For example, those acting unethically can also be ostracized by their peers, and as such be denied belongingness to the group or organization.

Taken together, the idea of preventing unethical behavior by means of monitoring and sanctioning is quite dominating in our business experiences. Such means of prevention are useful to limit the impact of self-interested motives, but I hasten to add that behavioral ethics research also needs to focus more closely on the issue of whether monitoring and sanctioning systems shape people's moral concerns at the same time (De Cremer & van Dijk, 2009). Indeed, if the current prevention approach is solely based on the idea of utility (i.e., making sure that the option of unethical behavior becomes less attractive by punishing it) and thus limits the impact of self-interest, ethical behavior will not become intrinsic and voluntarily (Mulder et al., 2006). That is, if employees only show ethical behavior because they want to avoid being punished (and thus incur costs), then possible ethical behavior on their behalf is largely externally determined. Therefore, if we wish to employ sanctioning systems as viable and effective tools of ethical behavior regulation in organizations, more research is needed to investigate how the presence of sanctions can also shape people's intrinsic moral motives (see e.g., Mulder, Verboon, & De Cremer, 2009).

So far, both the prescriptive and descriptive approach in the field of business ethics has revealed insights into what should be considered right and wrong and which motives people most strongly pursue. However, as one can easily imagine, it is an impossible task to prevent all unethical behavior. Consequently, unethical decisions will be made nevertheless and then it becomes important to understand how to remedy these emerging ethical failures. That is, rather than only devoting attention to the question of understanding the emergence and prevention of unethical behavior, we also have to realize that attention needs to be paid to the issue of how to deal with things when they have gone wrong. Indeed, if ethical awareness is lacking in groups and organizations, people are less likely to be willing to cooperate and to rely on the goodwill of others (Mayer, Davis, & Schoorman, 1995). As a result, the emergence of unethical behavior undermines significantly people's willingness to trust each other. Given the fact that "a more elusive benefit of ethics in organizations is trust" (Treviño, 2007, p. 49), it is necessary that we understand how trust can be repaired when ethical transgressions emerge. Although this conclusion seems obvious it is nevertheless also fair to note that behavioral business ethics has devoted little attention to this issue (De Cremer, Mayer, & Schminke, 2010).

On Doing Things Right: The Issue of Restoring Trust

It is an understatement that we should be concerned about the question of how to manage trust when ethical failures take place. In fact, when ethical failures emerge, it is communicated that integrity is suffering and that acting out of goodwill is a problem. For this reason, a lack of ethics may erode trust. In circumstances of ethical failures, the stakes are thus high because trust is an important antecedent of organizational performance (De Cremer et al., 2001). Companies that manage ethical failures well tend to preserve or even promote a good reputation (Pillutla, Murnighan, & De Cremer, 2009). Those companies that take a long time to respond to an ethical crisis may be permanently hurt in terms of their reputation. But what do we know as yet about the practice of restoring trust?

The issue of trust has been on the forefront of research agendas across a variety of subdisciplines in the social sciences including psychology, management, organizational behavior, economics, and law among others (Kramer, 1999; Rousseau, Sitkin, Burt, & Camerer, 1998; Tyler & Huo, 2002). Across these disciplines a wide range of definitions of trust exist, but recently the vast number of studies on trust rely on the perspective that trust is a psychological state based upon positive expectations of the intentions or behavior of another (Rousseau, Sitkin, Burt, & Camerer, 1998). A common theme of many trust studies is that they primarily focus on understanding what happens when trust is present and alive. At the same time it is noteworthy that only a small number of studies focus on understanding what happens when trust is reduced (i.e., distrust). This perspective in the trust literature is most likely affected by the notion that trust is easier to destroy than to create (Meyerson, Weick, & Kramer, 1996). As a result, the literature on trust seems to have created the idea that building up trust again in relationships may prove too difficult and therefore "surprisingly few studies have directly examined how trust may be repaired" (Kim, Dirks, Cooper, & Ferrin, 2006, p. 50).

A self-interested perspective on restoring trust. As discussed earlier, impressive evidence exists that in interdependent settings in which valued resources are allocated, people's motives to protect and pursue their self-interest seems to loom larger than pursuing the interests of others and the community at large. In line with this assumption, trust has mainly been looked at from a rationalist perspective. This approach suggests that people's decisions to trust others is motivated by the self-interested motive to obtain material and financial resources when engaging in a trustworthy relationship with the other party (i.e., referred to as a *calculative perspective of trust*; see also Williamson, 1993, for the economist's view of trust as calculative). From a calculative perspective of trust, trust violation may lead to the perception of a loss of an economic relationship in which financial and tangible resources are exchanged. If this calculative motive is dominant, then satisfying economic needs may present a condition under which trust can be restored (e.g., returning money or giving a financial compensation or incentive may satisfy self-interest needs and thus promote the willingness to trust again).

Desmet, De Cremer, and van Dijk (2008) examined whether trust can indeed be bought back when dealing with other parties in mixed-motive settings. These authors made use of the dictator game (i.e., where the recipient cannot reject the offer) to examine whether the trust of recipients of unfair offers (which violate accepted moral standards such as the equal 50-50 split) can be promoted again by offering financial compensation. These authors examined the impact of partial compensation (i.e., giving something back but still leaving unequal final outcomes in favor of the transgressor), equal compensation (i.e., returning enough money so both parties receive equal final outcomes), or overcompensation (i.e., returning money to create unequal final outcomes in favor of the victim of the trust violation). The findings, across two experimental bargaining games, revealed that trust was promoted more by receiving overcompensation than exact compensation, but this effect only emerged when the intentions of the transgressor were unclear. That is, when it was uncertain whether the transgressor wanted to deceive and act unfairly, then overcompensations worked. In contrast, when it was clear that the transgressor had the intention to deceive, overcompensations were not more effective than equal compensations. It was as if in the case of clear deception, victims of the trust violation simply wanted their money back and did not wish to build a further relationship. In light of that idea, the overcompensation did not work as it would create a financial imbalance (even debt) with the violating party, which would mean that further interaction was needed.

The case of social and self-interested motives in restoring trust. However, concerns about tangible outcomes (as driven by a self-interest motive) are not the only concerns of human beings. Nontangible concerns (e.g., feeling respected and accepted) can also dictate people's behavior. For that reason, trust repair tactics are also needed that focus on the social motives of those whose trust is violated. Indeed, theoretical models and research on interpersonal phenomena, for example, social justice (Tyler & Lind, 1992), decision making within groups (e.g., De Cremer, 2002), and negotiations (Blount & Larrick, 2000) have shown that social motives go beyond the effect of economic concerns in explaining social preferences, behavior, and decisions. For example, in the context of negotiation situations, Lax and Sebenius (1986, p. 74) noted that "negotiator's interests can go beyond the obvious and tangible," noting, "take for example, the almost universal quest for social approval or the simple pleasure one derives from being treated with respect, even in a one-time encounter." Moreover, scholars have argued that trust violations do more than just inflict transaction losses on the victim (Tomlinson, Dineen, & Lewicki, 2004), so the question is whether these social motives should also be addressed.

One way these social motives can be addressed when trust is violated, is by offering an apology. Prior research in trust repair has already documented that apologies can indeed be an effective strategy for restoring trust (e.g., De Cremer & Schouten, 2008; Kim et al., 2004; Kim et al., 2006; Tomlinson et al., 2004; Schweitzer, Hershey, & Bradlow, 2006). In fact, when we look at the business world, the corporate apologies are piling up. For example, Apple CEO Steve Jobs apologized quickly for the discount action of Apple where an earlier priced iPhone of $599 was cut to $399 after their most dedicated customers waited in long lines to pay the higher price. Thus, violations of unfair allocations have to be accounted for by taking up responsibility and expressing remorse (Schweitzer & Gibson, 2008), as even done by Enron CEO Kenneth Lay, when he noted: "I take responsibility for what happened at Enron, both good and bad."

De Cremer (2009) attempted to examine when exactly apologies (operationalized by including the elements of taking up responsibility and expression of remorse; see Scher & Darley, 1997) and when financial compensations impact upon the trust perceptions of those whose trust was violated by receiving an inappropriate offer in a bargaining game. In his research, De Cremer manipulated whether the allocation of resources implied dividing losses or gains. He argued that the valence of resources (i.e., gains vs. losses) should influence whether people's self-interested motives (i.e., their tangible concerns) or their social motives (i.e., their nontangible concerns) would be activated and affect their willingness to trust others. This argument was based on a theory referred to as *prospect theory* (Kahneman & Tversky, 1979). This theory argues that losses loom larger than gains. In other words, people, in general, are more motivated to avoid losses than to pursue gains. Applying this idea to the allocation of resources suggests that when losses are allocated, people's behaviors should be driven more by self-interest. As a result, under these circumstances, financial compensations should be valued more by those whose trust was violated. Findings indeed revealed that in the case where losses were allocated, financial compensation (this time the financial compensation was aimed at giving money back to arrive at equal final outcomes) was more effective than the delivery of an apology. In the gain condition, however, both the equal financial compensation and the delivery of an apology were equally effective. The latter finding therefore suggests that when unfair allocations are made in the area of gains, then not only self-interested motives but also more social motives will influence the process of trust repair, whereas in the area of losses, primarily self-interested motives drive the trust repair process.

The power of a promise to avoid restoring trust. As the results of Desmet et al. (2008) and De Cremer (2009) show, in the context of allocating resources, the issue of trust repair can be an expensive one. To avoid making such large financial investments to build trust again it is therefore important to examine whether trust can be fostered before making (often tricky) allocation decisions. In other words, is it possible to convince others that one will be a trustworthy allocator? If one can succeed in establishing this perception beforehand, then bargaining may become more effective. In fact, this question is particularly relevant to managers and leaders as one of their important tasks is to create a trustworthy working climate in which decisions can be made in a legitimate manner (Tyler, 2006). To address this question, De Cremer, Reinders Folmer, Van Dijke, and Pillutla (2009) focused on the use of a social account (i.e., a repair tactic aimed at diminishing the fear of the other party) that could be used by those in charge to foster trust before making allocation decisions. Social accounts have been characterized as an important means to reduce fear of exploitation resulting from threatening interaction partners (Bies, 1987; Lewicki & Bunker, 1996). In organizations, often those in charge can be viewed as being interested in pursuing their own interests (which could potentially explain why they have ended up being in charge). As a result, subordinates often fear social conflicts in which they will end up being the "sucker." In order to deal with such potential future conflicts, it is advised that those in charge attempt to clarify, justify, or explain their intentions, a process that is referred to as a *social account* (De Cremer, van Dijke, & Pillutla, 2010). Thus, by giving an account, those in charge may seek to change how others perceive their motives (Sitkin & Bies, 1993). If the account is effective, it may change such perceptions, and thus may remove the risk of conflict.

The account that was used in the research of De Cremer, Reinders, van Dyke, and Pillutla (2009) concerns the use of a promise to assure the other party that fair and cooperative decisions will be made. A promise is a particularly useful social account to use when power or status differences exist between the allocator and the recipient. Indeed, making a promise to be fair and cooperative communicates information relevant to removing fear of being exploited and thus promoting the belief that the powerful allocator can be trusted. Even more so, making the explicit promise to be fair suggests that the allocating party is willing to take into account the interest of the other party as well, which is an important component of trustworthiness, referred to as *benevolence* (Mayer, Davis, & Schoorman, 1995). Thus, in the context of bargaining, the use of a promise can be seen as an important social account that can be used to *protect against* breaches of trust.

Employing the use of a promise in a dictator game, De Cremer, Reinders, van Dyke, and Pillutla (2009), first of all, found that those in charge (the powerful allocator in their studies) evaluated the use of a promise as an effective strategy to ensure that subordinates would trust them. However, their research also showed that when subordinates received a promise (relative to not receiving one) before the allocator made an offer, perceptions of suspicion and distrust were enhanced. In other words, although those in charge were of the opinion that a promise was the appropriate action, it turned out that the actual communication of a promise backfired in a way that, rather than fostering trust, enhanced perceptions of distrust.

Lessons to be Learned on Preventing and Dealing with Ethical Failures

If organizations pursue a strategy to prevent unethical behavior then some suggestions can be made in order to facilitate long-term success. First of all, managers and organizations often install means to prevent unethical behavior that signal that people cannot be trusted. In other words, sanctions and other regulation systems often communicate in an implicit way that they are installed because of the potential distrust and conflict that is present in the group, department, or organization. If this is the message that organizational members receive, chances are slight that unethical behavior is reduced, rather, it may even be increased. That is, if an (implicit) awareness is created that people cannot trust each other, then building up cooperative and trustworthy relationships over the long term may prove difficult. For that reason, the employment of sanctions to prevent unethical behavior needs to be accompanied by an explicit message that organizational members can comply with, consequently making the sanction legitimate in their eyes. One way to do this is to promote the procedural fairness of the sanction (De Cremer & Tyler, 2005). The benefits of this approach are that procedurally fair sanctions will increase commitment to the purpose of the sanction and at the same time also signals that the organization installing the sanction is a moral decision maker (Tyler & De Cremer, 2009). To put it briefly, preventing unethical behavior needs to be done in ways that motivate people intrinsically rather than extrinsically.

As pointed out earlier, it is not always possible to prevent the emergence of unethical decisions and behaviors. As a result, organizations and their leaders need to be capable of managing states of distrust. Our research shows that restoring trust involves a combination of tactics aimed at both self-interest and social motives, that is, satisfying the economic and the relational motives of the trust relationship that people have created with the organization. Under some circumstances, financial compensations work and under some they do not. Careful attention needs to be paid to determining an effective management style that adheres to situational cues when deciding whether financial compensations, apologies, or perhaps both are required. The above research suggests that when bad intentions are clear and unfair allocations are made in the area of gains, then apologies may significantly gain in value. Finally, managers and leaders should also realize that they should not quickly rush into the process of preventing distrust by making promises. As our research shows, promises may actually backfire if they raise suspicion. Being the one in charge may promote fear of exploitation, a state that may undermine the effectiveness of a promise (even if it is a sincere one). To avoid this, it is advised that the legitimacy of the power base of those in charge should be enhanced (French & Raven, 1959). If the power base is considered legitimate, then subordinates will frame promises more in terms of a cooperative intention rather than a competitive one.

In Conclusion

Taken together, the aim of the present chapter was threefold: (1) Highlight the importance of a descriptive approach, in addition to a prescriptive one, in developing the new area of behavioral business ethics (see De Cremer & Tenbrunsel, forthcoming). (2) Illustrate the importance of knowing more accurately the motives of people in modeling bad or good behavior to learn whether we should prevent negative behaviors or promote positive ones. (3) Highlight the lack of attention in the literature on how to remedy ethical failures. It is my hope that future researchers (a) adopt the new lenses provided by behavioral business ethics to pursue a synthesis between the descriptive and prescriptive approaches in order to arrive at a more complete understanding of (un)ethical behavior and (b) devote more attention to effective strategies that deal with ethical failures and restoring trust.

References

Baumeister, R. F., Bratlavsky, E., Finkenauer, C., & Vohs, K. (2001). Bad is stronger than good. *Review of General Psychology, 3*, 323–370.

Bazerman, M. H., & Banaji, M. R. (2004). The social psychology of ordinary ethical failures. *Social Justice Research, 17*, 111–115.

Bies, R. J. (1987). The predicament of injustice: The management of moral outrage. In L. L. Cummings & B. M. Staw (Eds.), *Research in organizational behavior* (Vol. 9, pp. 289–319). Greenwich, CT: JAI Press.

Blount, S., & Larrick, R. (2000) Framing the game: Examining frame choice in bargaining. *Organizational Behavior and Human Decision Processes, 81*, 43–71.

Carlsmith, K. M. (2006). The roles of retribution and utility in determining punishment. *Journal of Experimental Social Psychology, 42*, 437–451.

De Cremer, D. (2002) Respect and cooperation in social dilemmas: The importance of feeling included. *Personality and Social Psychology Bulletin, 28*, 1335–1341.

De Cremer, D. (2009). *Psychological perspectives on ethical behavior and decision making*. Greenwich: Information Age Publishing.

De Cremer, D., Mayer, D.M., & Schminke, M. (2010). On understanding ethical behavior and decision making: A behavioral ethics approach. *Business Ethics Quarterly, 20*, 1–6.

De Cremer, D., & Aquino, K. (2009). *Does one bad or good turn deserve another? Power and the application of the norm of negative and positive reciprocity.* Manuscript submitted for publication.

De Cremer, D., Reinders Folmer, C., van Dijke, M., & Pillutla, M. (2009). *On promises and power in bargaining: Do promises to make fair offers backfire or not?* Manuscript in preparation.

De Cremer, D., & Schouten, B. C. (2008). When apologies for injustice matter: The role of respect. *European Psychologist, 13*, 239–247.

De Cremer, D., Snyder, M., & Dewitte, S. (2001). The less I trust, the less I contribute (or not)? The effects of trust, accountability and self-monitoring in social dilemmas. *European Journal of Social Psychology, 31*, 93–107.

De Cremer, D., & Tenbrunsel, A. (forthcoming). *Behavioral business ethics: Ideas on an emerging field.* Taylor & Francis.

De Cremer, D., & Tyler, T. R. (2005). Managing group behavior: The interplay between procedural fairness, self, and cooperation. *Advances in Experimental Social Psychology, 37*, 151–218.

De Cremer, D., & van Dijk, E. (2005). When and why leaders put themselves first: Leader behavior in resource allocations as a function of feeling entitled. *European Journal of Social Psychology, 35*, 553–563.

De Cremer, D., & van Dijk, E. (2008). Leader-follower effects in resource dilemmas: The roles of selection procedure and social responsibility. *Group Processes and Intergroup Relations, 11*, 355–369.

De Cremer, D., & van Dijk, E. (2009). Paying for sanctions in social dilemmas: The effects of endowment asymmetry and accountability. *Organizational Behavior and Human Decision Processes, 109*, 45–55.

De Cremer, D., van Dijke., E., & Pillutla, M. (2010). Explaining unfair offers in ultimatum games and its effects on trust: An experimental approach. *Business Ethics Quarterly, 20*, 107–126.

De Cremer, D., van Dijk, E., & Reinders Folmer, C. P. (2009). Why leaders may feel entitled to take more: Feelings of entitlement as a moral rationalization strategy. In D. De Cremer (Ed.), *Psychological perspectives on ethical behavior and decision making.* Greenwich, CT: Information Age Publishing.

Desmet, P., De Cremer, D., & van Dijk, E. (2008). *In money we trust? When financial compensations matter in repairing trust perceptions.* Manuscript submitted for publication.

Ferrell, O.C., Fraedrich, J., & Ferrell, L. (2008). *Business ethics.* Boston: Houghton Mifflin Company.

Folger, R. (2001). Fairness as deonance. In S. W. Gilliland, D. D. Steiner & D. P. Skarlicki (Eds.), *Research in social issues in management* (Vol. 1, pp. 3–33). New York: Information Age Publishers.

Folger, R., & Salvador, R. (2008). Is management theory too "self-ish"? *Journal of Management, 34*, 1127–1151.

Forsyth, R., Horowitz, J. L., Savin, N. E., & Sefton, M. (1994). Fairness in simple bargaining experiments. *Games and Economic Behavior, 6*, 347–369.

French, J. R. P., & Raven, B. H. (1959). *The bases of social power*. In D. Cartwright (Ed.), Studies in social power (pp. 118–149). Ann Arbor, MI: Institute of social research.

Güth, W., Schmittberger, R., & Schwarze, B. (1982). An experimental analysis of ultimatum bargaining. *Journal of Economic Behavior and Organization, 3*, 367–388.

Hill, T. E. (2000). *Respect, pluralism, and justice*. Oxford: Oxford University Press.

Jones, E. E., & Davis, K. E. (1965). From acts to dispositions: The attribution process in person perception. In L. Berkowitz (Ed.), *Advances in experimental social psychology* (Vol. 2). Orlando, FL: Academic Press.

Kahneman, D., Knetsch, J. L., & Thaler, R. (1986). Fairness as a constraint on profit seeking: Entitlements in the market. *American Economic Review, 76*, 728–741.

Kahneman, D., & Tversky, A. (1979). Prospect theory: Analysis of decision under risk. *Econometrica, 47*, 263–291.

Kim, P., Dirks K., Cooper, C. & Ferrin D. (2006). When more blame is better than less: The implications of internal vs. external attributions for the repair of trust after a competence- vs. integrity-based trust violation. *Organizational Behavior and Human Decision Processes, 99*, 49–65.

Kim, P., Ferrin, D., Cooper, C., & Dirks, K. (2004). Removing the shadow of suspicion: The effects of apology versus denial for repairing competence- versus integrity-based trust violations. *Journal of Applied Psychology, 89*, 104–118.

Kramer, R. M. (1999) Trust and distrust in organizations: Emerging perspectives, enduring questions. *Annual Review of Psychology, 50*, 569–598.

Lax, D. A., & Sebenius, J. K. (1986). Interests: The measure of negotiation. *Negotiation Journal, 2*, 73–92.

Lerner, M. J. (2003). The justice motive: Where social psychologists found it, how they lost it, and why they may not find it again. *Personality and Social Psychology Review, 7*, 388–389.

Lewicki, R. J., & Bunker, B. B. (1996). Developing and maintaining trust in working relationships. In R. M. Kramer & T. R. Tyler (Eds.), *Trust in organizations: Frontiers of theory and research*. Thousand Oaks, CA: Sage.

Mayer, R. C., Davis, J. H., & Schoorman, F. D. (1995). An integrative model of organizational trust. *Academy of Management Review, 20*, 709–735.

Meyerson, D., Weick, K. L., & Kramer, R. M. (1996). Swift trust and temporary groups. In R. M. Kramer and T. R. Tyler (Eds.), *Trust in organizations* (pp. 166–195). Sage Publications: London.

Mulder, L., van Dijk, E., De Cremer, D., & Wilke, H. A. M. (2006). Undermining trust and cooperation: The paradox of sanctioning systems in social dilemmas. *Journal of Experimental Social Psychology, 42*, 147–162.

Mulder, L., Verboon, P., & De Cremer, D. (2009). Sanctions and moral judgments: The moderating effect of sanction severity and trust in authorities. *European Journal of Social Psychology, 39*, 255–269.

Pillutla, M. M., Murnighan, J. K., & De Cremer, D. (2009). *Transgressions as opportunities to build trust*. Unpublished manuscript, London Business School, U.K.

Rousseau, D. M., Sitkin, S.B., Burt, R. S., & Camerer, C. (1998). Not so different at all: A cross-discipline view of trust. *Academy of Management Review, 23*, 393–404.

Schweitzer, M. A., & Gibson, D. E. (2008). Fairness, feelings, and ethical decision-making: Consequences of violating community standards of fairness. *Journal of Business Ethics, 77,* 287–301.

Schweitzer, M. E., Hershey, J. C., & Bradlow, E. T. (2006). Promises and lies: Restoring violated trust. *Organizational Behavior and Human Decision Processes, 101,* 1–19.

Scher, S. J., & Darley, J. M. (1997). How effective are the things people say to apologize? Effects of the realization of the apology speech act. *Journal of Psycholinguistic Research, 26,* 127–140.

Sitkin, S. B., & Bies, R. J. (1993). Social accounts in conflict situations: Using explanations to manage conflict. *Human Relations, 46,* 349–370.

Skitka, L. J., Bauman, C. W., & Mullen, E. (in press). Morality and justice: An expanded theoretical perspective and empirical review. In K. A. Hedgvedt & J. Clay-Warner (Guest Editors). *Advances in group processes.* Greenwich, CT: JAI Press.

Tenbrunsel, A. E., & Smith-Crowe, K. (2008). Ethical decision-making: Where we've been and where we're going. *Academy of Management Annals, 2,* 545–607.

Tomlinson, E. C., Dineen, B. R., & Lewicki, R. J. (2004). The road to reconciliation: Antecedents of victim willingness to reconcile following a broken promise. *Journal of Management, 30,* 165–187.

Treviño, L. K. (2007). *Managing business ethics: Straight talk about how to do it right* (4ᵗʰ ed.). John Wiley & Sons, Inc.

Treviño, L. K., & Ball, G. A. (1992). The social implications of punishing unethical behavior: Observers' cognitive and affective reactions. *Journal of Management, 18,* 751–768.

Treviño, L. K. & Weaver, G. R. (1994). Business ETHICS/BUSINESS Ethics: One field or two? *Business Ethics Quarterly 4,* 113–128.

Treviño, L. T., Weaver, G., & Reynolds, S. J. (2006). Behavioral ethics in organizations: A review. *Journal of Management, 32,* 951–990.

Tyler, T. R. (2006). Legitimacy and legitimation. *Annual Review of Psychology, 57,* 375–400.

Tyler, T. R., & De Cremer, D. (2009). Ethics and rule adherence in groups. In D. De Cremer (Ed.). *Psychological perspectives on ethical behavior and decision making.* Greenwich, CT: Information Age Publishing.

Tyler, T. R., & Huo, Y. J. (2002). *Trust in the law.* New York: Russell-Sage Foundation.

Tyler, T. R., & Lind, E. A. (1992). A relational model of authority in groups. In M. Zanna (Ed.), *Advances in Experimental Social Psychology* (Vol. 25, pp. 115–191). New York: Academic Press.

Williamson, O. E. (1993). Calculativeness, trust and economic organization. *Journal of Law and Economics, 30,* 131–145.

7

Paved With Good Intentions: Unethical Behavior Conducted to Benefit the Organization, Coworkers, and Customers

Elizabeth E. Umphress
Texas A&M University
Joanna Tochman Campbell
Texas A&M University
John B. Bingham
Brigham Young University

News of unethical activity conducted within organizations seems to permeate the business landscape. Such reports of unethical acts create the loss of public trust and economic devastation. Because of the possible negative consequences of unethical acts, it is important to understand the potential types and causes of unethical behavior. Work on unethical behavior typically focuses on those unethical acts that have the potential to harm others (e.g., Folger & Baron, 1996; Neuman & Baron, 1997; O'Leary-Kelly, Griffin, & Glew, 1996) or to help the individual actor (e.g., Duffy, Ganster, & Pagon, 2002; Greenberg, 2002; O'Leary-Kelly & Bowes-Sperry, 2001) engaging in the unethical act. In contrast, in this chapter we focus on unethical conduct that is conducted to benefit others.

Umphress and Bingham (2009) described such unethical "actions that are intended to promote the effective functioning of the organization" (p. 6) as unethical prosocial behaviors (for related discussions, see also Brief, Buttram, & Dukerich, 2001; Vardi & Weitz, 2004). Umphress and Bingham (2009) argued that employees who conduct unethical prosocial behavior focus on the potential benefit, while ignoring or overlooking the ethicality associated with their actions. However, they did not consider specific targets of such behavior (i.e., coworkers, clients, etc.) nor the affective components that might foster unethical prosocial behavior. Drawing on and extending Umphress and Bingham (2009), we focus on unethical actions conducted by individual employees that are conducted to benefit three different groups: one's organization, coworkers, and customers/clients. In doing so, we highlight that behavior carried out to benefit others can also be unethical, which is a form of unethical behavior often neglected within the ethics literature.

Additionally, we illustrate potential motivators that may serve to encourage unethical acts intended to benefit others. In particular, we look to social exchange theory, social identification theory, and positive mood as influential antecedents to these types of unethical acts. The great majority of the work on social exchange theory, social identification theory, and positive mood tends to emphasize the positive consequences of these constructs. We do not dispute this previous evidence and we acknowledge that these constructs have positive consequences for individuals and organizations. Indeed, we concede that the positive effects of social exchange, social identification, and positive mood far outweigh any negative effects outlined in our current treatment of unethical employee behavior. Yet we believe it is important to highlight the possibility that these constructs may motivate unethical actions and we provide theoretical rationale for their potentially unintended negative consequences.

Our work contributes to the literatures in business ethics in two ways. First, we emphasize that employees conduct unethical acts to benefit their organization, coworkers, and customers/clients. In doing so, we extend beyond extant work that considers how employees attempt to harm their organizations and add to the growing literature on deviant, counterproductive, or unethical behaviors carried out with beneficial motives (Molinsky and Margolis 2005; Morrison, 2006; Vardi and Weitz, 2004; Warren 2003). Second, we highlight a potential "dark side" to constructs that are predominately considered beneficial for organizational functioning by proposing that these constructs could motivate unethical behavior to benefit others. Although typically thought to engender positive and ethical behavior for organizations (Ashforth & Mael, 1989; Cropanzano & Mitchell, 2005; Forgas & George, 2001), we argue that individuals with functional exchange relationships, strong identity attachments, and positive affect may also be the most likely to engage in unethical behavior with beneficial intentions.

This chapter will unfold as follows. First, we will discuss unethical behavior that is conducted to benefit the organization, coworkers, and customers/clients. Second, we will review work on social exchange theory, social identity theory, and positive mood, and discuss how these constructs might motivate these unethical acts. We will conclude with a discussion of the theoretical and practical implications of our work for organizations at multiple levels of analysis.

Unethical Behavior with the Intent to Benefit Others

Before addressing unethical acts intended to benefit others, it is important to define unethical behavior. We adopt Donaldson and Duffee's (1994) concept of hypernorms to aid in our definition. *Hypernorms* are globally held standards of ethical behavior judged in terms of justice, law, or widely held social norms that determine the morality of behavior, which include basic human rights and the obligation to treat others with respect and dignity (Donaldson & Dunfee, 1994). Using this frame of reference, we define unethical behaviors as those behaviors that violate hypernorms. Thus, unethical acts violate absolute societal standards (Donaldson & Dunfee, 1994) that govern whether a behavior is ethical or unethical, rather than merely violating a specific set of social benchmarks, such as organizational norms (Robinson & Bennett, 1995). Following from our preceding definition, we define unethical behavior to benefit others as behaviors that violate hypernorms with an intended positive or helpful consequence for others.

We provide four parameter conditions to our conceptualization of unethical behaviors that are conducted to help the organization, coworkers, or customers/clients. First, we recognize the possibility that employees may engage in unethical behavior without specific intentions to benefit or harm others (e.g., an employee failing to report a serious product defect to customers when that employee has no knowledge of the flaw). Also, we note that employees conduct work-related actions involving errors, mistakes, or unconscious negligence (e.g., Asare & Wright, 1995). Because these acts are not conducted to intentionally benefit others, they would not constitute the type of unethical behavior discussed in this chapter. Again, our focus here is on those behaviors that are purposely intended to benefit others.

Second, although employees may aim to help, the end result of their actions may be inconsistent with their intentions. For instance, an employee may choose to destroy potentially incriminating documents to protect the organization; however, the destruction of these documents may not result in any form of organizational benefit. Indeed, the unethical act may cause the organization to look more suspicious to external auditors, harming the organization in the long run. The end result of unethical actions is important and is the focus of other work (e.g., Treviño & Ball, 1992; Weaver, Treviño, & Cochran, 1999; Velasquez, 1996; Weaver, 2004). Our focus here is on the motivations behind unethical behavior that is conducted with the intention to benefit others.

Third, we acknowledge that employees may conduct unethical actions with the intent to benefit *only* themselves. Previous empirical and theoretical work has focused on the role of self-interested motives (e.g., Grover & Hui, 1994; Treviño & Youngblood, 1990). However, unethical behaviors conducted primarily with the intention of benefiting the self alone, and not others, would fall outside of our conceptualization. Our treatment of unethical behavior to benefit others assumes that employees' intentions are other-focused and any residual consequences that might benefit individuals personally would not be considered deliberate. Thus, self-interested motives fall outside the scope of our conceptual framework and will not be discussed in this chapter.

Finally, our notion of unethical behavior to benefit others may involve acts of commission—such as tampering with a manufacturer's expiration date to sell a perishable item—or omission—such as covering for coworkers by failing to fully inform organizational representatives about their unethical activities. Both unethical acts of commission and omission are included in our conceptualization of unethical behavior to benefit others.

Unethical Behaviors Directed Toward the Organization, Coworkers, and Clients/Customers

Anecdotal evidence, both prominent and subtle, exists for the notion that employees sometimes conduct unethical actions that have the potential to benefit the organization. We highlight several examples that illustrate our conceptualization. First, consider the Watergate scandal where former president Richard M. Nixon's closest advisors conducted burglary, campaign fraud, espionage, sabotage, illegal tax audits, and illegal wiretapping, all in the interests of advancing the interests of the Nixon administration (Rangell, 1980; Genovese, 1999). As Strother (1976) noted, "Watergate presents a similar paradox in the willingness of a number of the participants to jeopardize their careers through criminal acts which had no direct promise of personal gain" (p. 20).

More recently, New England Patriots video assistant Matt Walsh was charged for illegally filming coaching signals in walk-through practices in preparation for the Super Bowl. He apparently wore clandestine apparel (rather than his typical New England Patriots attire) to access information that could be used against the Patriots' competitor. Walsh said, "I had always been a big Patriots fan. I was very enthused, just to have the opportunity that I had and the job to work for them" (ESPN.com, 2008, p. 1). Walsh also told the *New York Times* that he was hired in 1999 and first filmed a game for New England in the 2000 preseason, against Tampa Bay. "Once I had done it for the first game, and I kind of understood a little bit of the process of how it was going, I actually asked one of our quarter-backs if the information that I provided was beneficial in any way," Walsh said. "He said, 'Actually, probably about 75 percent of the time, Tampa Bay ran the defense we thought they were going to run. If not more'" (ESPN. com, 2008, p. 1; Bishop, 2008). These examples illustrate that employees may conduct unethical behavior by focusing on the potential benefits of the behavior for the organization rather than the ethicality associated with the act.

Employees also may conduct unethical actions with the intention of benefiting coworkers such as covering for a coworker's unethical activity or making unethical decisions that might aid a coworker's career. Coworkers are a fundamental aspect of the working social environment because employees are not likely to function in isolation for most occupations. Coworkers likely become more important as organizations utilize team-based work and organizations employ flatter organizational structures. Due to the usual proximity of coworkers, employees are likely to witness or uncover the unethical behavior of their coworkers. For instance, employees may protect coworkers by failing to report when coworkers falsify the number of hours worked or embezzle money from the organization. Also, employees may actively engage in unethical activity for a coworker such as lying on behalf of coworkers, failing to inform supervisors or other organizational authorities of their coworkers' unethical activity, or exaggerating the contribution of the coworker to a team product. Although lying, exaggerating, or otherwise protecting coworkers might be considered "helping," (e.g., by limiting sanctions against them, etc.), such behaviors violate hypernorms of honesty, fairness, and accountability and would thus be considered unethical behavior on the part of the employee. Admittedly, employees might find it difficult to report the unethical activity of coworkers (Miceli & Near, 2005; Paul & Townsend, 1996), but by failing to do so, they could be considered complicit in the unethical act.

Finally, employees might conduct unethical behaviors with the intent to benefit customers and clients.[1] We focus particular attention on this type of unethical behavior because customers are a vital aspect of the organizational environment. In fact, as stated by one employee (Rafaeli, 1989, p. 259):

> Without the customers the store would never exist. Without the cashiers it might be hard. Without the manager—we get along, and you can always find a replacement for cashiers and managers. But not without the customers. They make the money.

Examples of unethical behaviors directed toward customers abound, from giving customers merchandise or offering services with an unreasonably high discount, to providing them free of charge. Also, employees may provide some customers with proprietary information, not available to other customers, such as alerting them of upcoming sales and advising to delay large purchases until then, or recommending that they purchase a given product or service elsewhere at a lower price. Some customers may also be given preferential treatment when they are late on their payments, or may be given more time to pay than other customers (for example, employees may be more likely to bend the rules for customers placing large orders). For instance, a number of studies investigate and document cases of employees unethically helping customers by passing cars in the vehicle inspection market (Gino & Pierce, 2009; Pierce & Snyder, 2008; Hubbard, 1998).

Jehn and Scott's (2008) research indicates that airline employees lie to protect passengers by reducing their anxiety and stress levels. For example, the authors report that in a particular case, damage to one engine was causing plane turbulence, but it was announced that it was due to weather problems. Moreover, the authors report that this type of lie—to benefit the passenger—is often appreciated by the airline's customers. This type of action saves the passengers from worry and increased anxiety, but violates the hypernorm of honesty.

Many potential situations for unethical prosocial behavior toward customers arise in the context of professional employees, such as accountants, lawyers, and medical professionals. As evidenced by the failure of Arthur Andersen to uncover major accounting irregularities at one of its largest clients, Enron, accountants may be willing to overlook earnings management on the part of the client, especially in the case of low-risk clients, where the auditor's acquiescence has a lower chance of being discovered (Brandon, Kerler III, Killough, & Mueller, 2007). Further, lawyers often find themselves at the crossroads of providing advice that is legal and leads to the optimal outcome for the client versus advice to undertake an action that is both legal and ethical. The context of commercial legal advice, where lawyers interact with firms and other professionals, may be particularly susceptible to professional advice that is within the realm of what is legal but falls outside the boundaries of what is ethical (Mescher, 2008). A number of lawyer–client ethical dilemmas strike at some of the most salient social hypernorms, such as the protection of human life, as in the case of death row volunteering, where the client wishes that his or her life be terminated (Harrington, 2000; Chandler, 1998). Moreover, the potential for unethical behaviors arises in the case of statisticians and other consultants who may break hypernorms of social justice by lying with the intent to benefit their clients while acting in the role of expert witness (Fisher, 1986; Meier, 1986). Finally, medical professionals may find themselves in situations where abiding by a patient's wishes, as in the case of euthanasia, may counter hypernorms of preserving human life (Asch & DeKay, 1997).

In summary, these numerous examples of unethical prosocial behavior conducted to benefit the organization, coworkers, and customers suggest that they are a not an uncommon part of daily events in organizational life. However, one might question the rationale for why employees might engage in these beneficial actions, even when the wrongful nature of such acts seems woefully apparent. In the following section, we turn to discussing potential motivators behind these types of behavior.

Potential Motivators of Unethical Acts Intended to Benefit Others

Social Exchange Theory

Social exchange theory focuses on the relationship cultivated by the exchange of resources between two parties (Blau, 1964; Emerson, 1976). According to this theory, individuals feel obliged to repay the benefits they receive from others (e.g., Blau, 1964; Emerson, 1976; Gouldner, 1960). Put succinctly, if one party provides a benefit, the other party is motivated to reciprocate by providing a benefit in return (Gouldner, 1960). Whereas parties can refuse to reciprocate benefits received from others (i.e., reciprocating benefits is voluntary), those who fail to reciprocate may incur penalties such as distrust, decreased reputation, denial of future benefits, as well as other sanctions (Gouldner, 1960). In contrast, those who choose to reciprocate can engage in a self-perpetuating system of exchange in which benefits, mutual trust, approval, and respect reside (Blau, 1964).

Social exchange relationships differ from purely economic exchange relationships in that social exchanges involve unspecified obligations in which the exact nature of exchange unfolds over time, whereas economic exchanges are short-term transactions in which both parties specify the exact nature of the exchange, such as payment or service, in advance (Blau, 1964). Further, social exchange relationships can involve the exchange of economically valued items and/or the exchange of less tangible resources such as esteem or recognition, whereas in economic exchange transactions involve merely the exchange of wealth or goods (Blau, 1964; see Cropanzano, Rupp, Mohler, & Schminke, 2001, for a review).

Social exchange relationships have particularly relevant implications within employment contexts. According to Gouldner (1960), individuals may comply with duties specified by their status (e.g., wife, father, employee) within society not only to fulfill their status duties, but also because others have fulfilled their duty to them. This reasoning implies that employees perform organizational duties not only to fulfill employment obligations, but also to repay considerate treatment from their supervisor, organization, or coworkers. Researchers in the organizational literature use social exchange theory to help explain the importance of beneficial treatment from others within organizations. These literatures include psychological contracts (e.g., Van Dyne & Ang, 1998), leadership (e.g., Pillai, Schriesheim, & Williams, 1999; Wayne, Shore, & Liden, 1997), perceived organizational support (e.g., Eisenberger, Huntington, Hutchison, & Sowa, 1986; Eisenberger, Armeli, Rexwinkel, Lynch, & Rhoades, 2001; Wayne et al., 1997), organizational justice (Organ, 1988; 1990), and trust (e.g., Whitener, Brodt, Korsgaard, & Werner, 1998).

Research on social exchange theory generally concludes that beneficial consequences accrue to both parties when positive social exchange relationships exist (see Cropanzano & Mitchell, 2005, for a review). For example, more favorable perceptions of leader–member exchange, fair treatment, and perceived organizational support create an open-ended and closer social exchange relationship between the employer and employee in which employees reciprocate favorable treatment by benefiting the organization or their manager (Cropanzano et al., 2001). Thus, social exchange researchers (e.g., Organ, 1988, 1990) predict, for example, that employees respond to favorable treatment with organizational citizenship behaviors (OCB) and increased performance (e.g., psychological contacts, Coyle-Shapiro, 2002; Turnley, Bolino, Lester, & Bloodgood, 2003; perceived organizational support, Eisenberger et al., 2001; Lynch, Eisenberger, & Armeli, 1999; Moorman, Blakely, & Niehoff, 1998; leader–member exchange, Masterson, Lewis, Goldman, & Taylor, 2000; Settoon, Bennett, & Liden, 1996; Wayne, Shore, & Liden, 1997; and organizational justice, Cohen-Charash & Spector, 2001; Kamdar, McAllister, & Turban, 2006; Tekleab, Takeuchi, & Taylor, 2005; Tepper & Taylor, 2003). Also, research suggests that employees with positive social exchange relationships are less likely to engage in unethical acts that may harm the organization, such as stealing, (e.g., Greenberg, 1993; Pearson, 1998; Townsend, Phillips, & Elkins, 2000), rule-breaking behavior directed toward production (e.g., substandard work, slowdowns, and insubordination), and damage to property (e.g., embezzlement, and vandalism; Hollinger, 1986). Additionally, work on social exchange has addressed employee–coworker relationships and employee–customer relationships. Perceived coworker support, or the extent to which coworkers provide emotional and work-related assistance, has been shown to influence employee role perceptions, work attitudes (Ng & Sorensen, 2008), withdrawal from work, and some types of job performance (Chiaburu & Harrison, 2008).

Employees have the time and opportunity to engage in positive social exchange relationships with the organization and coworkers, but not all employees may have the opportunity to form social exchange relationships with customers. As noted above, social exchange relationships form over time, and some employees do not have long-term relationships with customers. However, in instances in which employees interact repeatedly with the same customers, we believe it is likely that employees and customers will form positive social exchange relationships (see Morgan & Hunt, 1994).

Previous work in the marketing literature suggests that employees form relationships with customers via relationship marketing, or developing, retaining, and attracting customer relationships (e.g., Berry & Parasuraman, 1991). This literature acknowledges that social exchange constructs, such as trust and commitment between customers and the organization, enhance important outcomes such as productivity and cooperative behaviors (Morgan & Hunt, 1994; Sirdeshmukh, Singh, & Sabol, 2002). Specifically, researchers have investigated how an employee's tendency to aim to meet customer goals, or customer orientation, can influence employee behavior at work (Rafaeli, Ziklik, & Doucet, 2008). Rafaeli (1989), for example, in her analysis of the role of supermarket cashiers, finds that customers have immediate influence over cashier employees due to their physical proximity, amount of time cashiers spend interacting with customers, and exchanging information with and receiving immediate feedback from customers. Managerial influence, on the other hand, while legitimate, was found to be more remote. Those employees with high customer orientation or emphasis on customer value (Khalifa, 2004), especially if one adopts the "customer knows best" view, may be motivated to engage in unethical behavior aimed at helping customers.

In summary, employees might respond to social exchange relationships by engaging in unethical acts to benefit the organization, coworkers, and customers. After forming a positive social relationship, employees may choose to reciprocate those positive relationships by conducting unethical acts to help others. For instance, employees may choose to fail to issue refunds to customers as a way to reciprocate positive social exchange relationships with their employer. With regard to unethical acts to benefit coworkers, employees with strong positive relationships with a coworker might choose to help "cover" for their coworker by lying to supervisors concerning a coworker's performance. Finally, employees may step over ethical boundaries in order to "go the extra mile" for a frequent or long-time customer.

Social Identity Theory

According to social identity theory (Tajfel & Turner, 1986), part of an individual's self concept derives from membership with a social group or entity (Tajfel, 1981, p. 255). Individuals can perceive identification with different groups, such that a person has not one, "personal self," but rather several selves that correspond to identification with membership in different groups (Tajfel & Turner, 1986). People tend to favor ingroup members in terms of attributions, material resources, social support, and helping behavior (Tajfel & Turner, 1979; Brewer, 1979; Tajfel, Billig, Bundy, & Flament, 1971). This suggests that if an employee perceives high identification with their ingroup, then the employees will engage in helping behavior or other types of behavior to support members of that ingroup.

Organizational identification is one form of identification salient to our discussion, and it is defined as an employee's perception of belonging and membership to his or her employing organization (Ashforth & Mael, 1989; Dutton, Dukerich, & Harquail, 1994). Organizational identification enables individuals to both embody and support their organization (Ashforth & Mael, 1989; Turner, 1987). Employees who strongly identify with their organization internalize the organization's successes and failures as their own (Mael & Ashforth, 1992). Thus, they behave in ways that benefit the organization and that are consistent with organizational expectations, such as through higher loyalty, increased extra-role behaviors and job performance, and decreased turnover intentions (Mael & Ashforth, 1995; van Knippenberg & van Knippenberg, 2000; Wanhuggins, Riordan, & Griffeth, 1998). We also note, however, that one could identify with customers or coworkers if those individuals are members of a salient ingroup. For instance, customers and coworkers could share demographic characteristics such as gender, race, ethnicity, age, religion, or national origin. If the employee shares membership in a given ingroup with a customer or coworker, they might feel a sense of identification with the individual and behave in ways to benefit their ingroup.

Previous work has suggested that high levels of identification with an ingroup could encourage unethical behavior to enhance the status of the ingroup (e.g., Ashforth & Anand, 2003; Dukerich, Kramer, & Parks, 1998; den Nieuwenboer & Kaptein, 2008). Consistent with this logic, we consider how identification with organizations, coworkers, and customers may encourage unethical acts by employees in attempts to benefit these groups. Identification may compel employees to disregard ethical standards (e.g., personal values, norms, and cognitive processes) in favor of behaviors that help others. When one's social identity with a group is increasingly more important to the individual, employees may augment their own morality to coincide with the morality of their social ingroup (Banfield, 1958). Through a desire to protect the group's identity, individuals may place the interests of the group above those who could be harmed by the unethical act. Identification could allow employees to perceive unethical behaviors to help others as dutiful acts that serve their group (Ashforth & Anand, 2003). For instance, a highly identified employee may make false claims about the feature of a product to help make a sale to help their organization.

Given this potential, we propose that those who strongly identify with their organization, or an ingroup shared with fellow employees or customers, may disregard their own moral standards in favor of unethical acts that protect or help others. Consistent with our arguments, Dukerich et al. (1998, p. 253), suggest that overidentification, when the needs of the actor become secondary to the needs of the organization, may influence unethical acts performed on behalf of the organization (see also Elsbach, 1999). High levels of identification may cause employees to conduct unethical acts such as lying to protect or covering up evidence that might otherwise harm the organization, customers, or fellow employees. Therefore, we argue that identification could lead individuals to benefit their organization, customers, or fellow employees.

Positive Mood

Positive affect or mood is a mild affective state (i.e., feeling happy; Isen, 1999). Research demonstrates a number of beneficial consequences of being in a positive mood. For instance, positive mood enhances cognitive flexibility (Ashby, Isen, & Turken, 1999) and creative problem solving (Bass, De Dreu, & Nijstad, 2008). People in a positive mood tend to be judged as more interpersonally effective, more talkative, and disclose more information about themselves (Forgas, 2006). In a dispute resolution situation, those in a positive mood use more cooperative and less competitive problem-solving strategies (Forgas, 1998a). Further, positive mood influences evaluations of behavior, such that those in a positive mood rate themselves and others as more skilled and positive than those in a negative mood (Forgas, Bower, & Krantx, 1984). In an organizational context, positive affect is known to promote helpfulness in the form of organizational citizenship behavior and task performance at work (George, 1991; Tsai, Chen, & Liu, 2007). Due to its beneficial influence, it is generally perceived that employees in a positive mood are more productive employees, in that they demonstrate higher levels of performance and creativity, and have more positive experiences with customers (Forgas & George, 2001).

Some theoretical and empirical evidence suggests that positive mood may facilitate unethical behaviors (Treviño, Weaver, & Reynolds, 2006), and we argue that this possibility may be especially true for unethical behaviors that have the potential to benefit others. Positive mood is related to promotion focus in self-regulation, which is associated with accomplishments and aspirations, and is less associated with prevention focus, which is associated with safety and responsibility (Bass, et al., 2008). A prevention focus due to a positive mood may activate the idea that the situation is safe or satisfactory, which can trigger decision making based on heuristics or cognitive shortcuts (Fiedler, Asbeck, & Nickel, 1991; Fiedler, Pampe, & Scherf, 1986; Isen, 1984, 1987). Conversely, a negative mood indicates that something is problematic and promotes detailed assessment of information (Forgas, 1995; Forgas, 1992; Forgas & Bower, 1987; Ottaviani & Beck, 1988; Schwarz, 1990; Weary et al., 1991). That is, "the safety signal elicited by positive affective states should motivate those in such states to take advantage of the presumed safety by seeking stimulation and pursuing incentives, activities that would be ill advised under less benign circumstances" (Friedman, Förester, & Denzler, 2007, p. 143). Therefore, positive affect could influence unethical behavior because individuals may not recognize the potentially harmful or negative implications of their decisions and fail to recognize the ethical implications of their actions. This could be especially true for unethical behavior to benefit others because those in a positive mood may focus on the potential beneficial consequences of the unethical act, shielding the ethicality associated with their actions.

More direct evidence indicates that those in a positive mood may be receptive to unethical acts with the potential to benefit others. Research suggests that people in a positive mood are more likely to comply with an unconventional request from another person than those in a negative mood (Forgas, 1998b) and more likely to exhibit conformity to the group than those in a negative mood (Tong, Tan, Latheef, Slamat, & Tan, 2008). Recent research also suggests that those in a positive mood are less likely to detect the ethical behavior of others when compared to those in a negative mood. For instance, Forgas and East (2008) induced positive, neutral, and negative mood, and asked participants to watch video clips of individuals who were either deceptive or honest about denying a theft. Those in a positive mood were significantly less likely to detect deceptive communications than those in a negative mood. This work suggests that those in a positive mood are likely to trust others and be deceived by others when compared to those in a negative mood. With regard to unethical acts to benefit others, those in a positive mood may be more likely to conform to group norms to engage in unethical acts to benefit others and comply with unethical requests from others.

We have argued that positive mood may facilitate unethical behavior to benefit others. However, we acknowledge it is possible that the finding that positive affect increases creative problem solving also may allow employees to find a way to help others when asked to do something that does not include unethical behavior. Also, recent research suggests that mild positive affect leads individuals to be deliberative in their choices and enhances self-control (Isen, 2007); yet this work has not addressed helping behaviors toward others. Indeed, work on positive mood and unethical behavior is relatively scant. Therefore, we highlight the contribution of considering the role of positive affect on unethical behavior and we encourage future research to explore the conditions in which this type of unethical behavior could be enhanced or reduced by positive mood.

Theoretical Implications

Throughout history, individuals have found resourceful ways to commit unethical acts to help benefit others. Our focus in this chapter has been to extend how unethical behavior operates in organizations by describing how unethical behavior may be directed toward helping others. Drawing on and extending the work of Umphress and Bingham (2009), our treatment of unethical behavior directed toward the organization, other employees, and customers adds to both established (e.g., Finney & Lesieur, 1982) and recent (Pinto, Leana, & Pil, 2008) research addressing the motivations for unethical activity in organizations. Our conceptual arguments have the potential to add further insight about unethical behavior in varying levels of the organization. Specifically, we underscore several key theoretical implications for ethical behavior at the level of the individual and the organization.

Individual-Level Implications

At the individual level of analysis, research generally assumes that social exchange, organizational identification, and positive mood are related to constructive, ethical outcomes. For instance, research examining employee–organization and employee–supervisor relationships provides ample evidence that social exchange relationships generally lead to beneficial outcomes (see Cropanzano & Mitchell, 2005). Notwithstanding that, our theoretical logic suggests that employees may commit unethical behavior toward the organization, other employees, or customers and that both practitioners and researchers should consider this possibility in future treatments of unethical organizational behavior.

Whether directed at the organization or another organizationally relevant target, one might inquire about the mechanisms by which individuals choose to engage in unethical acts. Individuals are moral creatures and generally possess well-defined social controls (Sykes & Matza, 1957). Behaviors that counter hypernorms require justification so that individuals may shield themselves from self-blame (Bandura, 1999; Sykes & Matza, 1957) and dissonance (Festinger & Carlsmith, 1957). Individuals who choose to engage in unethical behaviors may continue to espouse strong personal values systems, even as they conduct unscrupulous deeds (Ashforth & Anand, 2003). Thus, our treatment of unethical behavior directed toward others has implications for individual-level values or cognitive processes that may influence whether and how employees decide to act.

Further, although not specifically discussed here, our arguments also have implications for the interactionist approach to morality (Bandura, 1999; Treviño, 1986), wherein moral decisions and behaviors emerge from the interplay of personal and contextual factors. Consistent with this view, we recognize that other factors such as organizational culture or climate may influence whether such relationships or affective states influence unethical behavior directed toward others. Indeed, we might gain a better understanding of unethical behavior directed toward others by considering influential contextual or situational factors. Future research might examine the conditions under and the processes through which employees carry out unethical behaviors with prosocial intentions.

Organizational-Level Implications

The literature on corporate social responsibility (CSR) started developing in the 1950s (Carroll, 1999). Despite this early scholarly attention, "CSR is still an embryonic concept in the academic literature" (McWilliams, Siegel, & Wright, 2006, p. 15), and the field is in its first stage of development, lacking a dominant paradigm (Lockett, Moon, & Visser, 2006). Whereas no universally accepted definition of corporate social responsibility exists (McWilliams, et al., 2006; Rodriguez, Siegel, Hillman, & Eden, 2006), one popular definition depicts CSR as firm "actions that appear to further some social good, beyond the interests of the firm and that which is required by law" (McWilliams & Siegel, 2001, p. 117).

Our examination of unethical prosocial behaviors toward customers and employees can add to the discourse on what precisely *is* a social good. Can unethical actions aimed at benefiting other employees or the firm's customers be socially responsible? In other words, does the end justify the means? Research evidence points to the existence of an *outcome bias* in individual decision making, whereby actions are more likely to be deemed ethical versus unethical if they result in a positive outcome, even if the outcome is largely based on chance (Gino, Moore, & Bazerman, 2008). This suggests that positive outcomes can impede ethical decision making, and a focus on the intended benefits of corporate social responsibility can hinder judgments as to the ethicality of the actions undertaken in order to help organizational stakeholders such as customers or groups of employees.

Potential research questions that arise include the following: What are the strategies firms use to engage in corporate social responsibility? Specifically, do some firms resort to unethical means in order to achieve ethical outcomes? For example, firms could use financial resources that were made available through potentially fraudulent accounting manipulation to fund their CSR programs. Also, how do shareholders and other stakeholders (e.g., regulators, suppliers, customers, and employees) react to firms' unethical practices with respect to corporate social responsibility initiatives? Does media portrayal play a role in how CSR practices are received and judged by a firm's various stakeholders by their framing of messages?

A greater awareness of unethical behaviors directed toward benefitting others can also extend our knowledge of the impact of agent-theoretic relationships on firm-level outcomes. Agency theory (Jensen & Meckling, 1976; Eisenhardt, 1989) deals with the problems created by the separation of ownership and control; it assumes that managers are boundedly rational, self-interested decision makers (Simon, 1957). Since its original conception, agency theory has also been applied at lower levels of the organization (e.g., Jones & Butler, 1992). Our examination of unethical prosocial behaviors points to the fact that costs to the firms can also accrue due to agent (employee) actions that are not motivated by self-interest, but rather by the desire to help others (through unethical means). If these unethical practices get exposed, they can deliver a significant blow to the focal organization's reputation, which is a unique and a relatively unexplored agency cost to the firm. Moreover, unethical helping behaviors can directly impact the organization's bottom line through heavily discounted merchandise and services, an overly generous return policy, or sales lost through employees' referrals to competitors due to their lower pricing.

There are a number of interesting research questions that arise in the context of agency theory and unethical prosocial behaviors. For example, how does leadership at the top of the organizational hierarchy impact employees' propensity to engage in these types of behaviors? Another potential line of inquiry would be to examine how monitoring and incentive alignment, central to agent-theoretic arguments, impact employees' engagement in unethical behaviors intended to benefit the organization, fellow employees, and customers. We encourage future research to consider these and related questions. In sum, we have offered a number of theoretical implications at the level of the individual and the organization. In the following section, we turn our attention to the practical implications of unethical prosocial behaviors.

Practical Implications

Major corporate scandals in recent years have brought public attention not only to the legality but also the ethicality of actions undertaken by firms' employees. Among the major contributors to the current worldwide financial crisis were legal but ethically questionable actions undertaken by multiple firms. Unethical behaviors with the intent to benefit others constitute a unique subset of unethical behaviors, which can nonetheless have significant impacts on individual- and firm-level outcomes. Our exposition of these types of unethical behaviors thus offers a number of implications for managerial practice.

We noted a potential "dark side" to social exchange, identification, and positive mood. We proposed the possibility that these constructs, generally considered beneficial, could influence unethical behavior to benefit others. To inhibit unethical behaviors to benefit others, we do not suggest that managers and organizations should attempt to experience negative relationships, promote low identification, and generate negative moods within the workplace. The benefits of positive social exchange relationships, identification, and positive mood in terms of increased job performance and ethical citizenship behaviors, will likely far outweigh any potentially negative consequence of unethical behaviors discussed here. Instead, we encourage managers and organizational leaders to consider that employees might conduct unethical actions to benefit others within situations that most managers would consider ideal, and to develop an organizational culture in which unethical acts (including those that benefit others) are not tolerated. Without an explicitly stated and carefully managed ethical culture, organizations may quickly join the corporate scandal headlines that have become so prevalent in recent years.

The number of service firms versus manufacturing firms has grown rapidly in the past several decades in most postindustrial economies, including the United States (Beckett-Camarata, Camarata, & Barker, 1998). Service encounters, such as customer interactions with clerks, bank tellers, cashiers, or other firm employees, are a ubiquitous part of a modern, service-oriented economy (Rafaeli, 1989; Czepiel, Solomon, & Surprenant, 1985). The strength and quality of a firm's relationship with customers is an important determinant of a firm's long-term survival (Conlon & Murray, 1996). Positive customer affect has been found to influence customer perceptions of service quality (Pugh, 2001). Further, research suggests that customer satisfaction leads to customer loyalty (Rust & Zahorik, 1993), and loyalty is in turn associated with revenue growth and firm profitability (Pugh, Dietz, Wiley, & Brooks, 2002). Finally, extant research suggests that customer orientation is related to customer commitment to the firm (Donavan & Hocutt, 2001). However, although customer orientation is related to many positive firm-level outcomes, it is important to draw the line between ethical and unethical behaviors intended to benefit customers in the pursuit of customer satisfaction. In this chapter, we identify one of the pitfalls of high customer orientation, whereby attempting to achieve customer satisfaction at all costs, employees may resort to unethical acts.

It is important to point out that unethical behaviors with the intent to benefit customers do not uniquely apply to service industries. Firms in manufacturing industries may be even more prone to these types of behaviors on the part of their employees, as many customer relationships in those settings are long term, with repeated interaction and an expectation of continuing the relationship in the future. Research on customer satisfaction indicates that customer expectations serve as standards against which experiences are judged, leading to satisfaction or dissatisfaction, and past experiences can contribute to expectations (Zeithaml, Berry, & Parasuraman, 1993). Therefore, previous unethical helping behavior could lead to customers' expectations of such behaviors in the future, which implies that each act of unethical prosocial behavior can set a dangerous precedent. This effect is likely to be further strengthened by word-of-mouth spillover effects, whereby one unethical act of helping raises multiple current and potential customers' expectations of receiving similar treatment.

Given the potential deleterious effects of unethical helping behaviors to firm reputation, we advance a number of suggestions for managerial consideration at the individual as well as organizational level. At the individual level, if organizational pressure is perceived to be high enough, the employee may in fact feel as if she/he has no choice but to satisfy the customer, even if it means breaking organizational and/or societal norms. Therefore, managers must "walk the line" when it comes to emphasizing the importance of customers and customer satisfaction, and motivating an appropriate level of compliance with customer's wishes. Further, organizations may take steps to reinforce frontline employees' organizational identity in an attempt to combat undue customer influence over employees. One potential way to achieve this would be to increase service employees' interaction with fellow employees as well as managers.

At the organizational level, top managers need to consider the ethicality of their actions separate from the intended outcomes. Adopting a holistic view of the impact of organizations on their stakeholders and the society, we posit that channeling good intentions into unethical means can deliver more harm than good. While short-term consequences of unethical prosocial behavior may appear beneficial, its long-run impact is uncertain and may prove disastrous to a firm's reputation and business-model sustainability. Again, we think that it is important for company leadership to emphasize ethical behavior, realizing that not all helpful behavior may be ethical.

Our work can also contribute to the discourse on the implications of corporate social responsibility. In addition to a host of individual empirical studies (e.g., Waddock & Graves, 1997; Russo & Fouts, 1997; Cochran & Wood, 1984), meta-analytic findings suggest that both corporate social performance, and to a lesser degree environmental performance, are likely to pay off in the form of corporate financial performance (Orlitzky, Schmidt, & Rynes, 2003). Due to the existence of an *outcome bias* in individual decision making, whereby actions are more likely to be deemed ethical if they result in a positive outcome (Gino, Moore, & Bazerman, 2008), managers should exercise added caution when it comes to corporate social responsibility initiatives, since their intended beneficial outcomes can cloud individual judgment concerning CSR-related actions.

In all, we wish to encourage organizational researchers and managers to consider that some unethical actions can be initiated with the intent to benefit the organization, coworkers, and customers. Employees with the best intentions might be engaging in unethical acts that threaten the reputation and productivity of the organization. We propose that these unethical acts could be motivated by social exchange relationships, identification, and positive mood. We see these as highly fruitful avenues of future research in organizational ethics and encourage researchers to investigate these and other possibilities.

Endnotes

1. Note that we will use the term "customers" to refer to customer and client relationships.

References

Asare, S. K., & Wright, A. (1995). Normative and substantive expertise in multiple hypotheses evaluation. *Organizational Behavior and Human Decision Processes, 64*, 171–184.

Asch, D. A., & DeKay, M. L. (1997). Euthanasia among US critical care nurses: Practices, attitudes, and social and professional correlates. *Medical Care, 35*(9), 890–900.

Ashby, F. G, Isen, A. M., & Turken, A. U. (1999). A neuropsychological theory of positive affect and its influence on cognition. *Psychological Review, 106*, 529–550.

Ashforth, B. E., & Anand, V. (2003). The normalization of corruption in organizations. In R. M. Kramer & B. M. Staw (Eds.), *Research in organizational behavior, Vol. 25* (pp. 1–52). Boston: Elsevier Science.

Ashforth, B. E., & Mael, F. (1989). Social identity theory and the organization. *Academy of Management Review, 14*, 20–39.

Bandura, A. (1999). Moral disengagement in the perpetration of inhumanities. *Personality and Social Psychology Review, 3*, 193–209.

Banfield, E. C. (1958). *The moral basis of backward society.* New York: Free Press.

Bass, M., De Dreu, C. K. W., & Nijstad, B. A. (2008). A meta-analysis of 25 years of mood-creativity research: Hedonic tone, activation, or regulatory focus. *Psychological Bulletin, 134*, 779–806.

Beckett-Camarata, E. J., Camarata, M. R., & Barker, R. T. (1998). Integrating internal and external customer relationships through relationship management: A strategic response to a changing global environment. *Journal of Business Research, 41*, 71–81.

Berry, L. L., & Parasuraman, A. (1991). *Marketing services*. New York: Free Press.

Bishop, G. (2008). Videotaper's inside view of the Patriot's spying. *New York Times*, May, 16. p. 1.

Blau, P. M. (1964). *Exchange and power in social life*. New York: John Wiley and Sons.

Brandon, D. M., Kerler III, W. A., Killough, L. N., & Mueller, J. M. (2007). The joint influence of client attributes and cognitive moral development on student's ethical judgments. *Journal of Accounting Education*, *25*, 59–73.

Brewer, M. B. (1979). In-group bias in the minimal intergroup situation: A cognitive-motivational analysis. *Psychological Bulletin*, *86*, 307–324.

Brief, A. P., Buttram, R. T., & Dukerich, J. M. (2001). Collective corruption in the corporate world: Toward a process model. In M. E. Turner (Ed.), *Groups at work: Theory and research. Applied social research*. (pp. 471–499). Mahwah, NJ: Lawrence Erlbaum Associates, Inc.

Carroll, A. B. (1999). Corporate social responsibility: Evolution of a definitional construct. *Business & Society*, *38*(3), 268–295.

Chandler, C. (1998). Voluntary executions. *Stanford Law Review*, *50*(6), 1897–1927.

Chiaburu, D. S., & Harrison, D. A. (2008). Do peers make the place? Conceptual synthesis and meta-analysis of coworker effects on perceptions, attitudes, ICBs, and performance. *Journal of Applied Psychology*, *93*, 1082–1103.

Cochran, P. L. & Wood, R. A. (1984). Corporate social responsibility and financial performance. *Academy of Management Journal*, *27*(1), 42–56.

Cohen-Charash, Y., & Spector, P. E. (2001). The role of justice in organizations: A meta-analysis. *Organizational Behavior and Human Decision Processes*, *86*, 278–321.

Conlon, D. E., & Murray, N. M. (1996). Customer perceptions of corporate responses to product complaints: The role of explanations. *Academy of Management Journal*, *39*(4), 1040–1056.

Coyle-Shapiro, J. A. M. (2002). A psychological contract perspective on organizational citizenship behavior. *Journal of Organizational Behavior*, *23*, 927–946.

Cropanzano, R., & Mitchell, M. S. (2005). Social exchange theory: An interdisciplinary review. *Journal of Management*, *31*, 874–900.

Cropanzano, R., Rupp, D. E., Mohler, C. J. , & Schminke, M. (2001). Three roads to justice. In G. Ferris (Ed.), *Research in personnel and human resources management* (pp. 101–113). Greenwich, CT: JAI Press.

Czepiel, J. A., Solomon, M. R., & Surprenant, C. F. (1985). *The service encounter*. Lexington, MA: Lexington Books.

Den Nieuwenboer, N. A., & Kaptein, M. (2008). Spiraling down into corruption: A dynamic analysis of the social identity processes that cause corruption in organizations to grow. *Journal of Business Ethics*, *83*, 133–146.

Donavan, D. T., & Hocutt, M. A. (2001). Customer evaluation of service employee's customer orientation: Extension and application. *Journal of Quality Management*, *6*, 293–306.

Donaldson, T., & Dunfee, T. W. (1994). Toward a unified conception of business ethics: Integrative social contracts theory. *Academy of Management Review*, *19*, 252–284.

Duffy, M. K., Ganster, D., & Pagon, M. (2002). Social undermining in the workplace. *Academy of Management Journal*, *45*, 331–351.

Dukerich, J., Kramer, R. M., & Parks, J. M. (1998). The dark side of organizational identification. In D. Whetten & R Godfrey (Eds.), *Identity in organizations: Developing theory through conversations* (pp. 245–256). Thousand Oaks, CA: Sage.

Dutton, J. E., Dukerich, J. M., & Harquail, C. V. (1994). Organizational images and member identification. *Administrative Science Quarterly, 39*, 239–263.

Eisenberger, R., Armeli, S., Rexwinkel, B. , Lynch, P. D., & Rhoades, L. (2001). Reciprocation of perceived organizational support. *Journal of Applied Psychology, 86*, 42–51.

Eisenberger, R., Huntington, R., Hutchison, S. , & Sowa, D. (1986). Perceived organizational support and employee diligence, commitment, and innovation. *Journal of Applied Psychology, 71*, 500–507.

Eisenhardt, K. M. (1989). Agency theory: An assessment and review. *Academy of Management Review, 14*(1), 57–74.

Elsbach, K. D. (1999). An expanded model of organizational identification. In R. I. Sutton & B. M. Staw (Eds.), *Research in organizational behavior, Vol. 21* (pp. 163–200). Stamford, CT: JAI Press.

Emerson, R. M. (1976). Social exchange theory. *Annual Review of Sociology, 2*, 335–362.

ESPN.com (2008). Walsh dismisses Pats' attempts to minimize illegal taping. May 15. http://sports.espn.go.com/nfl/news/story?id=3396731. Retrieved June 10, 2009.

Festinger, L., & Carlsmith, J. M. (1957). Cognitive consequences of forced compliance. *Journal of Abnormal and Social Psychology, 58*, 203–210.

Fiedler, K., Asbeck, J., & Nickel, S. (1991). Mood and constructive memory effects on social judgment. *Cognition and Emotion, 5*, 363–378.

Fiedler, K., Pampe, H., & Scherf, U. (1986). Mood and memory for tightly organized social information. *European Journal of Social Psychology, 16*, 149–164.

Finney, H. C., & Lesieur, H. R. (1982). A contingency theory of organizational crime. In S. B. Bacharach (Ed.), *Research in the sociology of organizations, Vol. 1* (pp. 255–299). Greenwich, CT: JAI Press.

Fisher, F. M. (1986). Statisticians, econometricians, and adversary proceedings. *Journal of the American Statistical Association, 81*(394), 277–286.

Folger, R., & Baron, R. A. (1996). Violence and hostility at work: A model of reactions to perceived injustice. In G. R. Van den Bos & E. Q. Bulatao (Eds.). *Violence on the job: Identifying risks and developing solutions* (pp. 51–85). Washington, DC: American Psychological Association.

Forgas, J. P. (1992). On bad mood and peculiar people: Affect and person typicality in impression formation. *Journal of Personality and Social Psychology, 662*, 863–875.

Forgas, J. P. (1995). Mood and judgment: The affect infusion model (AIM). *Psychological Bulletin, 117*, 39–66.

Forgas, J. P. (1998a). On feeling good and getting your way: Mood effects on negotiator cognition and bargaining strategies. *Journal of Personality and Social Psychology, 74*, 565–577.

Forgas, J. P. (1998b). Asking nicely? The effects of mood on responding to more or less polite requests. *Personality and Social Psychology Bulletin, 24*, 173–185.

Forgas, J. P. (2006) Affective influences on interpersonal behavior: Toward under-standing the role of affect in everyday interactions. In J. P. Forgas (Ed.), *Affect in social thinking and behavior* (pp. 269–289). New York: Psychology Press.

Forgas, J. P., & Bower, G. H. (1987). Mood effects on person perception judgments. *Journal of Personality and Social Psychology, 53*, 53–60.

Forgas, J. P., Bower, G. H., & Krantx, S. (1984). The influence of mood on perceptions of social interactions. *Journal of Experimental Social Psychology, 20*, 497–513.

Forgas, J. P, & East, R. (2008). On being happy and gullible: Mood effects on skepti-cism and the detection of deception. *Journal of Experimental Social Psychology, 44*, 1362–1367.

Forgas, J. P., & George, J. M. (2001). Affective influences on judgments and behav-ior in organizations. *Organizational Behavior and Human Decision Processes, 86*, 3–34.

Friedman, R. S., Förester, J., & Denzler, M. (2007). Interactive effects of mood and task framing on creative generation. *Creativity Research Journal, 19*, 141–162.

Genovese, M. A. (1999). *The Watergate crisis.* Westport, CT: Greenwood Press.

George, J. M. (1991). State or trait: Effects of positive mood on prosocial behaviors at work. *Journal of Applied Psychology, 76*, 299–307.

Gino, F., Moore, D. A., & Bazerman, M. H. (2008). *No harm, no foul: The outcome bias in ethical judgments.* Harvard Business School NOM Working Paper No. 08-080 (July 1, 2008). Available at SSRN: http://ssrn.com/abstract=1099464. Retrieved March 12, 2009.

Gino, F., & Pierce, L. (2009). *Robin Hood under the hood: Wealth-based discrimina-tion in illicit customer help.* Working paper. (January 6, 2009). Available at SSRN, http://ssrn.com/abstract=1157083. Retrieved March 12, 2009.

Gouldner, A. W. (1960). The norm of reciprocity: A preliminary statement. *American Sociology Review, 25*, 161–178.

Greenberg, J. (1993). Stealing in the name of justice: Informational and interper-sonal moderators of theft reactions to underpayment inequity. *Organizational Behavior and Human Decision Processes, 54*, 81–103.

Greenberg, J. (2002). Who stole the money, and when? Individual and situational determinants of employee theft. *Organizational Behavior and Human Decision Processes, 89*, 985–1003.

Grover, S. L., & Hui, C. (1994). The influence of role-conflict and self-interest on lying in organizations. *Journal of Business Ethics, 13*, 295–303.

Harrington, L. (2000). A community divided: Defense attorneys and the ethics of death row volunteering. *Law and Social Inquiry, 25*(3), 849–881.

Hollinger, R. C. (1986). Acts against the workplace: Social bonding and employee deviance. *Deviant Behav*ior, *7*, 53–75.

Hubbard, T. N. (1998). An empirical examination of moral hazard in the vehicle inspection market. *The RAND Journal of Economics, 29*(2), 406–426.

Isen, A. (1984). Towards understanding the role of affect in cognition. In R. S. Wyer & T. K. Srull (Eds.), *Handbook of social cognition, Vol. 3* (pp. 179–236). Hillsdale, NJ: Erlbaum.

Isen, A. (1987). Positive affect, cognitive processes and social behaviour. In L. Berkowitz (Ed.), *Advances in experimental social psychology, Vol. 20* (pp. 203–253). San Diego, CA: Academic Press.

Isen, A. M. (1999). Positive affect. In T. Dalgleish & M. Power (Eds.), *Handbook of cognition and emotion* (pp. 521–539). New York: Wiley.

Isen, A. M. (2007). Positive affect, cognitive flexibility, and self-control. In Y. Shoda, D. Cervone, & G. Downey (Eds.), *Persons in context: Building a science of the individual* (pp. 130–147). New York: Guilford Press.

Jehn, K. A., & Scott, E. D. (2008). Perceptions of deception: Making sense of responses to employee deceit. *Journal of Business Ethics, 80,* 327–347.

Jensen, M. C., & Meckling, W. H. (1976). Theory of the firm: Managerial behavior, agency costs and ownership structure. *Journal of Financial Economics, 3*(4), 305–360.

Jones, G. R., & Butler, J. E. (1992). Managing internal corporate entrepreneurship: An agency theory perspective. *Journal of Management, 18*(4), 733–749.

Kamdar, D., McAllister, D. J., & Turban, D. B. (2006). "All in a day's work": How follower individual differences and justice perceptions predict OCB role definitions and behavior. *Journal of Applied Psychology, 91,* 841–855.

Khalifa, A. S. (2004). Customer value: A review of recent literature and integrative configuration. *Management Decision, 42*(5), 645–666.

Lockett, A., Moon, J., & Visser, W. (2006). Corporate social responsibility in management research: Focus, nature, salience and sources of influence. *Journal of Management Studies, 43*(1), 115–136.

Lynch, P. D., Eisenberger, R., & Armeli, S. (1999). Perceived organizational support: Inferior versus superior performance by wary employees. *Journal of Applied Psychology, 84,* 467–483.

Mael, F. A., & Ashforth, B. E. (1992). Alumni and their alma-mater: A partial test of the reformulated model of organizational identification. *Journal of Organizational Behavior, 13,* 103–123.

Mael, F. A., & Ashforth, B. E. (1995). Loyal from day one: Biodata, organizational identification, and turnover among newcomers. *Personnel Psychology, 48,* 309–333.

Masterson, S. S., Lewis, K., Goldman, B. M., & Taylor, M. S. (2000). Integrating justice and social exchange: The differing effects of fair procedures and treatment on work relationships. *Academy of Management Journal, 43,* 738–748.

McWilliams, A., & Siegel, D. (2001). Corporate social responsibility: A theory of the firm perspective. *Academy of Management Review, 26*(1), 117–127.

McWilliams, A., Siegel, D. S., & Wright, P. M. (2006). Corporate social responsibility: Strategic implications. *Journal of Management Studies, 43*(1), 1–18.

Meier, P. (1986). Damned liars and expert witnesses. *Journal of the American Statistical Association, 81*(394), 269–276.

Mescher, B. R. (2008). The business of commercial legal advice and the ethical implications for lawyers and their clients. *Journal of Business Ethics, 81,* 913–926.

Miceli, M., & Near, J. P. (2005). Standing up or standing by: What predicts blowing the whistle on organizational wrongdoing? In J. J. Martocchio (Ed.), *Research in personnel and human resources management, Vol. 24* (pp. 95–136). Oxford: Elsevier.

Molinsky, A., & Margolis, J. (2005). Necessary evils and interpersonal sensitivity in organizations. *Academy of Management Review, 30,* 245–268.

Moorman, R. H., Blakely, G. L., & Niehoff, B. P. (1998). Does perceived organizational support mediate the relationship between procedural justice and organizational citizenship behavior. *Academy of Management Journal, 41,* 351–357.

Morgan, R. M., & Hunt, S. D. (1994). The commitment-trust theory of relationship marketing. *Journal of Marketing, 58*, 20–38.

Morrison, E. W. (2006). Doing the job well: An investigation of pro-social rule breaking. *Journal of Management, 32*, 5–28.

Neuman J. H., & Baron, R. A. (1997). Aggression in the workplace. In R. A. Giacalone & J. Greenberg (Eds.), *Antisocial behavior in organizations* (pp. 37–67). Thousand Oaks, CA: Sage Publications.

Ng, T. W. H., & Sorensen, K. L. (2008). Toward a further understanding of the relationships between perceptions of support and work attitudes. *Group & Organization Management, 33*, 243–268.

O'Leary-Kelly, A. M., & Bowes-Sperry, L. (2001). Sexual harassment as unethical behavior: The role of moral intensity. *Human Resource Management Review, 11*, 73–92.

O'Leary-Kelly, A. M., Griffin, R. W., & Glew, D. J. (1996). Organization-motivated aggression: A research framework. *Academy of Management Journal, 21*, 225–253.

Organ, D. W. (1988). *Organizational citizenship behavior: The good soldier syndrome.* Lexington, MA: Lexington Books.

Organ, D. W. (1990). The motivational basis of organizational citizenship behavior. In B. M. Staw & L. L. Cummings (Eds.), *Research in organizational behavior, Vol. 12* (pp. 43–72). Greenwich, CT: JAI Press.

Orlitzky, M., Schmidt, F. L., & Rynes, S. L. (2003). Corporate social and financial performance: A meta-analysis. *Organization Studies, 24*(3), 403–441.

Ottaviani, R., & Beck, A. T. (1988). Cognitive theory of depression. In K. Fiedler & J. Forgas (Eds.), *Affect, cognition and social behavior* (pp. 209–218). Göttingen, Germany: Hogrefe.

Paul, R. J., & Townsend, J. B. (1996). Don't kill the messenger? Whistle-blowing in America—A review and recommendations. *Employee Responsibilities and Rights Journal, 9*, 149–161.

Pearson, C. M. (1998). Organizations as targets and triggers of aggression and violence: Framing rational explanations for dramatic organizational deviance. In P. A. Bamberger & W. J. Sonnenstuhl (Eds.), *Research in the sociology of organizations: Deviance in and of organizations* (pp. 197–223). Greenwich, CT: JAI Press.

Pierce, L., & Snyder, J. (2008). Ethical spillovers in firms: Evidence from vehicle emissions testing. *Management Science, 54*(11), 1891–1903.

Pillai, R., Schriesheim, C. A., & Williams, E. S. (1999). Fairness perceptions and trust as mediators for transformational and transactional leadership: A two-sample study. *Journal of Management, 25*, 897–933.

Pinto, J., Leana, C. R. & Pil, F. K. (2008). Corrupt organizations or organizations of corrupt individuals? Two types of organization-level corruption. *Academy of Management Review, 33*, 685–709.

Pugh, S. D. (2001). Service with a smile: Emotional contagion in the service encounter. *Academy of Management Journal, 44*(5), 1018–1027.

Pugh, S. D., Dietz, J., Wiley, J. W., & Brooks, S. M. (2002). Driving service effectiveness through employee-customer linkages. *Academy of Management Executive, 16*, 73–84.

Rafaeli, A. (1989). When cashiers meet customers: An analysis of the role of supermarket cashiers. *Academy of Management Journal, 40*(3), 534–559.

Rafaeli, A., Ziklik, L., & Doucet, L. (2008). The impact of call center employees' customer orientation behaviors on service quality. *Journal of Service Research, 10*, 239–255.

Rangell, L. (1980). *The mind of Watergate: An exploration of the compromise of integrity.* New York: Norton.

Robinson, S. L., & Bennett, R. J. (1995). A typology of deviant workplace behaviors: A multidimensional scaling study. *Academy of Management Journal, 38*, 555–572.

Rodriguez, P., Siegel, D. S., Hillman, A., & Eden, L. (2006). Three lenses on the multinational enterprise: Politics, corruption, and corporate social responsibility. *Journal of International Business Studies, 37*(6), 733–746.

Russo, M. V. & Fouts, P. A. (1997). A resource-based perspective on corporate environmental performance and profitability. *Academy of Management Journal, 32*(2), 245–273.

Rust, R., & Zahorik, A. (1993). Customer satisfaction, customer retention, and market share. *Journal of Retailing, 69*(1), 193–215.

Schwarz, N. (1990). Feelings as information: Informational and motivational functions of affective states. In E. T. Higgins & R. Sorrentino (Eds.), *Handbook of motivation and cognition: Foundations of social behavior, Vol. 2* (pp. 527–562). New York: Guilford Press.

Settoon, R. P., Bennett, N., & Liden, R. C. (1996). Social exchange in organizations: Perceived organizational support, leader-member exchange, and employee reciprocity. *Journal of Applied Psychology, 81*, 219–227.

Simon, H. A. (1957). *Models of man.* New York: Wiley.

Sirdeshmukh, D., Singh, J., & Sabol, B. (2002). Consumer trust, value, and loyalty in relational exchanges. *Journal of Marketing, 66*, 15–37.

Strother, G. (1976). The moral codes of executives: A Watergate-inspired look at Barnard's theory of executive responsibility. *Academy of Management Review, 15*, 13–22.

Sykes, G., & Matza, D. (1957). Techniques of neutralization. *American Sociological Review, 22*, 664–670.

Tajfel, H. (1981). *Human groups and social categories: Studies in social psychology.* Cambridge, U.K.: Cambridge University Press.

Tajfel, H., Billig, M. G., Bundy, R. P., & Flament, C. (1971). Social categorization and intergroup behavior. *European Journal of Social Psychology, 1*, 149–178.

Tajfel, H., & Turner, J. C. (1986). The social identity theory of intergroup behavior. In S. Worchel & W. G. Austin (Eds.), *Psychology of intergroup relations* (2nd ed., pp. 7–24). Chicago: Nelson-Hall.

Tajfel, H., & Turner, J. C. (1979). An integrative theory of intergroup conflict. In W. G. Austin & S. Worchel (Eds.), *The social psychology of intergroup relations.* Monterey, CA: Brooks-Cole.

Tekleab, A. G., Takeuchi, R., & Taylor, M. S. (2005). Extending the chain of relationships among organizational justice, social exchange, and employee reactions: The role of contract violations. *Academy of Management Journal, 48*, 146–157.

Tepper, B. J., & Taylor, E. C. (2003). Relationships among supervisors' and subordinates' procedural justice perceptions and organizational citizenship behaviors. *Academy of Management Journal, 46*, 97–105.

Tong, E. M. W., Tan, C. R. M., Latheef, N. A., Selamat, M. F. B., & Tan, D. K. B. (2008). Conformity: Moods matter. *European Journal of Social Psychology, 38,* 601–611.

Townsend, J., Phillips, J. S., & Elkins, T. J. (2000). Employee retaliation: The neglected consequence of poor leader-member exchange relations. *Journal of Occupational Health and Psychology, 5,* 457–463.

Treviño, L. K. (1986). Ethical decision-making in organizations: A person-situation interactionist model. *Academy of Management Review, 11,* 601–617.

Treviño, L. K., & Ball, G. A. (1992). The social implications of punishing unethical behavior: Observers' cognitive and affective reactions. *Journal of Management, 18,* 751–769.

Treviño, L. K., Weaver, G. R., & Reynolds, S. J. (2006). Behavioral ethics in organizations: A review. *Journal of Management, 32*(6), 951–990.

Treviño, L. K., & Youngblood, S. (1990). Bad apples in bad barrels: A causal analysis of ethical decision-making behavior. *Journal of Applied Psychology, 75,* 378–385.

Tsai, W., Chen, C., & Liu, H. (2007). Test of a model linking employee positive moods and task performance. *Journal of Applied Psychology, 92,* 1570–1583.

Turner, J. C. (1987). *Rediscovering the social group: Self-categorization theory.* Oxford, U.K.; New York: Blackwell.

Turnley, W. H., Bolino, M. C., Lester, S. W., & Bloodgood, J. M. (2003). The impact of psychological contract fulfillment on the performance of in-role and organizational citizenship behaviors. *Journal of Management, 29,* 187–206.

Umphress, E. E., & Bingham, J. (2009). *When employees do bad things for good reasons: Examining unethical prosocial behaviors.* Unpublished manuscript.

Van Dyne, L., & Ang., S. (1998). Organizational citizenship behavior of contingent workers in Singapore. *Academy of Management Journal, 41,* 692–703.

Van Knippenberg, D., & van Knippenberg, B. (2000). Who takes the lead in risky decision making? Effects of group members' risk preferences and prototypicality. *Organizational Behavior and Human Decision Processes, 83,* 213–234.

Vardi, Y., & Weitz, Y. (2004). *Misbehavior in organizations: Theory, research, and management.* Mahwah, NJ: Lawrence Erlbaum Associates.

Velasquez, M. (1996). Why ethics matters: A defense of ethics in business organizations. *Business Ethics Quarterly, 6,* 201–223.

Waddock, S. A., & Graves, S. B. (1997). The corporate social performance–financial performance link. *Strategic Management Journal, 18*(4), 303–319.

Wanhuggins, V. N., Riordan, C. M., & Griffeth, R. W. (1998). The development and longitudinal test of a model of organizational identification. *Journal of Applied Social Psychology, 28,* 724–749.

Warren, D. E. (2003). Constructive and destructive deviance in organizations. *Academy of Management Review, 28,* 622–632.

Wayne, S. J., Shore, L. M., & Liden, R. C. (1997). Perceived organizational support and leader-member exchange: A social exchange perspective. *Academy of Management Journal, 40,* 82–111.

Weary, G., Marsh, K. L., Gleicher, F., & Edwards, J. A. (1991). Social cognitive consequences of depression. In G. Weary. F. Gleicher, & K. L. Marsh (Eds.), *Control motivation and social cognition* (pp. 121–142). New York: Springer.

Weaver, G. R. (2004). Ethics and employees: Making the connection. *Academy of Management Executive Journal, 18*, 121–126.

Weaver, G. R., Treviño, L. K., & Cochran, P. L. (1999). Corporate ethics programs as control systems: Influences of executive commitment and environmental factors. *Academy of Management Journal, 42*, 41–58.

Whitener, E. M., Brodt, S. E., Korsgaard, M. A., & Werner, J. M. (1998). Managers as initiators of trust: An exchange relationship framework for understanding managerial trustworthy behavior. *Academy of Management Review, 23*, 513–530.

Zeithaml, V. A., Berry, L. L., & Parasuraman, A. (1993). The nature and determinants of customer expectations of service. *Journal of the Academy of Marketing Science, 21*(1), 1–12.

8

Failures, Losses, and Fairness: The Customer's Perspective

Dr. Ronald L. Hess, Jr.
College of William & Mary

One of the most important events that can produce perceptions of inequity in a customer–organization exchange involves product and service failures. Failures are defined as any product or service performance that falls below the customers' expectations (Hoffman & Bateson, 1997). These events produce losses for customers that can result in negative outcomes for organizations if not properly addressed. Organizations attempt to restore customer losses with recovery strategies, which are the actions and efforts used to restore the losses produced by failures (Gronroos, 1988). Many types of recovery activities are available to organizations including free products, discounts, coupons, refunds, and apologies, among others.

Few organizations, however, have developed or implemented effective recovery strategies to handle failures. Evidence of poor recovery is pervasive across both the academic and popular presses. For example, Bitner, Booms, and Tetreault (1990) find that more than 50 percent of organizational recovery actually "escalates" the dissatisfaction produced by the initial failure. Furthermore, customer ratings of recovery collected by ACSI (American Customer Satisfaction Index) reveals that very few organizations score above 60 on the 100-point index (Fornell, 2007). Given these inadequate evaluations of organizational recovery and the negative impact that poor recovery has on many important organizational outcomes such as satisfaction, loyalty, and word-of-mouth recommendations (Fornell & Wernerfelt, 1987; Keaveney, 1995), a more thorough understanding of the failure–recovery process is essential.

A review of the present research on the failure–recovery process suggests that there are several important issues that require further attention. First, a more thorough understanding of the inequity caused by failures is necessary. One predominant view in marketing suggests that customers experience a "loss of resources" when failures occur that produces perceptions of inequity in the exchange (Smith, Bolton, & Wagner 1999;

Oliver 1997). Smith, Bolton, and Wagner (1999) contend that customers categorize these lost resources into two distinct accounts, economic (e.g., monetary, functional) and noneconomic (e.g., social, esteem, emotional). Unfortunately, these two categories do not adequately capture the multitude of losses that customers can experience during the failure–recovery process. Without a more comprehensive classification of customer losses, the development of a more effective recovery strategy is not possible.

The second issue requiring more attention by researchers involves developing and testing competing models of recovery. Presently, few theoretical models have been proposed or empirically tested in marketing to determine which most effectively restores the inequity caused by customer losses. One exception is a model offered by Smith, Bolton, and Wagner (1999) proposing that customer perceptions of fairness and satisfaction are enhanced whenever the recovery applied is "in kind" or matches with the type of loss (economic vs. noneconomic) experienced (p. 359). Thus, a poorly prepared meal, considered an economic loss, requires an economic recovery that may include a price discount, meal replacement, or complementary meal. Likewise, rude employee behavior, considered a noneconomic loss, requires a noneconomic recovery, such as an apology. Although this approach is well-accepted in the study of the failure–recovery process, the results of this study were mixed with most of the proposed relationships not supported in the restaurant context. Thus, the introduction of alternative models of recovery may be necessary if improvements to this process are to be achieved.

The purpose of this paper is to provide a more comprehensive examination of the various losses that can be experienced by customers during the failure–recovery process. Integrating existing consumer behavior research on prechoice perceived risk with anecdotal evidence of customer experiences of this process, a multidimensional conceptualization of customer losses will be introduced. In addition, a number of theoretically based models of recovery will be proposed that can be employed by organizations to more effectively restore customers' perceptions of equity, satisfaction, and loyalty. In the following section, a review of failure classifications and customer losses will be presented.

Categorization of Failure Types

Early research on the failure–recovery process attempted to categorize the types of failures that are experienced by customers (Bitner, Booms, & Tetreault, 1990; Kelley, Hoffman, & Davis, 1993; Keaveney, 1995). The predominant view of these researchers was that customers responded uniquely to different types of failures. Bitner, Booms, and Tetreault (1990) uncovered three general categories that caused customer dissatisfaction which include: (1) unacceptable responses to failures (i.e., recovery), (2) unresponsive to customer needs and requests, and (3) inappropriate employee treatment of customers. Their findings also revealed that unacceptable responses to failures (Category 1) occurred most frequently in the airline and hotel industries, while unresponsive responses to customer needs and requests (Category 2) occurred most often in the restaurant industry.

A similar study conducted within a retailing context showed that the unacceptable response to product defects (similar to Category 1 above but adapted for the retailing context) produced most (70.5%) of customers' dissatisfying incidents (Kelley, Hoffman, & Davis, 1993). These authors also collected and classified information regarding the recovery activities employed by retailers to respond to customers' failure experiences. The findings indicated that product replacement (26.2%), no recovery activity (17.2%), refund of purchase price (12.3%), and problem correction (12.3%) were the most frequently cited recovery activities provided by retailers. In addition, the authors paired specific failure types with the corresponding recoveries employed by retailers. The findings showed that a wide variety of recovery activities were applied to the same failure type suggesting that retailers generally disagreed about which recovery activities were most effective at restoring customer equity when failures occurred.

In a similar study of the behavioral consequences of failures, Keaveney (1995) revealed that core service failures (24.8%), unacceptable employee treatment of customers (19.1%), unfair pricing practices (16.7%), inconvenience (location, hours of operation, wait time) (11.6%), and unacceptable recovery (9.7%) were the most frequently cited incidents causing customers to switch to competitive firms. Most interesting, she also showed that most (55%) of the customers' switching behavior was produced by multiple failure types occurring during a single encounter with an organization. Thus, customers were much more likely to switch to the competition when, for example, they were charged an unfair price combined with unacceptable resolution of the price issue (i.e., recovery) during an encounter with the organization.

A second stream of research has more recently emerged in marketing that employs a more simplistic classification scheme to empirically examine whether customers respond differently to certain types of failures. Much of this research classifies failures based on the outcome (i.e., central benefits received or sought by customers) and process (i.e., how the service is delivered to customers) conceptualization of service delivery (Gronroos, 1988; Parasuraman, Zeithaml, & Berry 1985). For example, outcome failures are related to problems with the restaurant meal, hotel room, and haircut, while process failures involve problems with the way in which these services are delivered including the courtesy, responsiveness, and speed of delivery provided by the employee. Several different terms have been employed for outcome (e.g., core) and process (e.g., peripheral, service encounter), but the intended meanings are quite similar and often used interchangeably in the marketing literature.

Smith, Bolton, and Wagner (1999) use the outcome-process categorization of failures to examine which recovery activities are most effective in restoring customer perceptions of equity (i.e., distributive, procedural, and interactional fairness) and, in turn, satisfaction with the service encounter. Applying principals of resource exchange theory and mental accounting, these authors suggest that outcome failures will generate economic losses (e.g., monetary, functional), while process failures will produce noneconomic losses (e.g., social, esteem, emotional). They contend that recovery activities that are "in kind" or match the losses experienced by customers will lead to higher perceptions of fairness and postrecovery satisfaction. The findings of this study support this view within a hotel context but not within a restaurant context. The lack of support in the restaurant context will be explored in detail in a later section of this chapter.

In contrast to this outcome-process distinction, Hess, Ganesan, and Klein (2007) focus on a subset of process failures that they appropriately call *interactional failures*. Interactional failures are defined as the inappropriate or inadequate employee treatment of customers. They argue that a more precise classification of failures is needed because these types of failures *always* occur during "face-to-face" interactions between employees and customers. Thus, customers focus their responses on the focal employee by formulating causal attributions and evaluations about this individual. This response process differs significantly from other types of failures whereby customer attributions and evaluations focus on the organization and not the employee.

In this study, Hess, Ganesan, and Klein (2007) examined several factors that influence whether these employee-oriented attributions and evaluations would impact the organization. Their findings reveal that organizations are somewhat protected from the negative effects of interactional failures if customers have experienced excellent core and interactional service in the past from the organization. Although these authors did not focus on recovery activities in this study, their findings provide additional evidence that failure types play a significant role in the customer response process.

Limitations of the Loss of Resources View of Failures

As indicated in the previous section, the *loss of resources* view of failures has become well-accepted in the marketing literature and has guided much recent research on the failure–recovery process. This perspective is quite useful as the basis for how failures can produce perceptions of inequity within the customer–organization exchange. However, despite the importance of this perspective, several important limitations exist that must be addressed if the goal is to develop more effective organizational recovery strategies.

First, the contention that customer losses fit neatly into only two categories—economic and noneconomic—is unrealistic and incomplete. It is very common for customers to experience many different losses during the failure–recovery process. For example, valuable time and effort is required (and thus lost) when customers choose to complain about failures. These lost resources are often augmented with additional losses if an employee expresses reservations, verbally or nonverbally, about the validity of the customer's account of the failure event and treats the customer impolitely during the process.

Most important, customers' responses to feelings of self-doubt about the validity of their complaint will likely differ significantly from their responses to the poor treatment provided by the employee. The former may induce locus attributions concerning who is to blame for the failure event (i.e., consumer vs. organization), while the latter may prompt strong feelings of anger, betrayal, distrust, and dissatisfaction directed toward an employee or organization. Thus, given the distinct customer responses to these losses that have traditionally been classified broadly as *noneconomic* resources, a more thorough categorization of customer losses is necessary.

A second shortcoming to the economic–noneconomic distinction is that customers typically experience more than a single loss *simultaneously* during the failure–recovery process. Smith, Bolton, and Wagner (1999) suggest that each type of failure (outcome or process) can only generate a single economic or noneconomic loss. Thus, an outcome failure will only produce an economic loss and a process failure will only produce a noneconomic loss. This overly simplistic view of the failure–recovery process fails to consider that customers can experience a multitude of losses *simultaneously* for each failure event.

For example, it is not uncommon for customers to feel apprehension about expressing a complaint to a waiter as well as feel embarrassed about the possibility of generating unwanted attention from family, friends, and other restaurant patrons when their meal is improperly prepared. In this situation, the customer experiences *three* distinct losses (defined as performance, social, and psychological losses in Table 8.1), most of which are noneconomic, in response to a single outcome failure (i.e., considered an economic loss). As this example clearly demonstrates, customers can experience several losses simultaneously during a single failure–recovery event and, in many instances, these losses will not match the loss from the initial failure.

TABLE 8.1

Multidimensional Conceptualization of Customer Losses

Type of Loss	Definition	Postfailure	Prerecovery
Performance Loss	Functional losses incurred when product or service does not perform as expected or falls below expectations.	X	
Financial Loss	Economic losses incurred when the benefits desired from the product or service are not received or are viewed as inadequate or unacceptable. Includes the monetary expenses to secure replacement or return.	X	X
Experiential Loss	Loss of life experiences, enjoyment, and pleasure incurred from the failure of product/service.	X	
Physical Loss	Pain and suffering incurred from physical harm and/or injury to the customers' physical being, health, or safety.	X	
Social Loss	Loss of self-esteem and self-confidence based on the views of other customers, employees, friends, and family. Includes unwelcome attention from others during and after failure and suspicion from employees while voicing complaint.	X	X
Psychological Loss	Loss of self-esteem and self-confidence based on the harm incurred to the customer's ego.	X	X
Collateral Loss	Results from the indirect losses incurred from the failure of product/service.	X	
Convenience Loss[a]	Loss of personal time, effort exerted, and inconvenience incurred to file a complaint, secure a replacement, or return a product/service to the organization.		X

[a] Based on time loss (risk) identified by T. Roselius, "Consumer Rankings of Risk Reduction Methods," 1971, *Journal of Marketing, 35*, 56–61.

Given the limitations of the current classification of customer losses offered by Smith, Bolton, and Wagner (1999), a multidimensional categorization that captures a wide variety of losses that can be experienced simultaneously by customers will be introduced. A more specific classification of losses will greatly assist with the formulation of alternative recovery models that could more effectively restore customers' perceptions of equity and postrecovery satisfaction.

Multidimensional Categorization of Postfailure Customer Losses

For many years, marketing researchers have investigated the influence that customers' perceptions of risk have on their decision-making and pre-purchase behavior. *Perceived risk,* as employed in the context of consumer decision making, is defined as the probability of loss resulting from the purchase of a product or service (Jacoby and Kaplan, 1972; Roselius, 1971). Many researchers have identified a wide variety of risk types including financial, performance, social, psychological, physical, opportunity loss, and time (Jacoby and Kaplan, 1972; Roselius, 1971). Perceived risk has also been examined in terms of both the probability and importance of loss if an unfavorable purchase outcome occurs (Bettman, 1975; Peter & Tarpey, 1975). An investigation of customers' use of risk-reducing methods has also been conducted and finds that a familiar brand image, positive word-of-mouth recommendations, free samples, and premium priced brands are some of the most effective methods of relieving risk perceptions (Roselius, 1971). Given the obvious similarities between issues of perceived risk (i.e., the probability of losses involved with unfavorable purchase outcomes) and the actual losses incurred when unfavorable purchase outcomes occur (i.e., failures), the perceived risk framework will be employed as a foundation for a more comprehensive categorization of postfailure customer losses.

Table 8.1 presents the various losses that can be experienced by customers following failures. These include performance, financial, experiential, physical, social, psychological, convenience, and collateral losses. The table also specifies that some of these losses can result from the initial failure event (postfailure losses) and/or prior to recovery in the form of a supplementary loss (prerecovery losses). Prerecovery losses can only be incurred by customers if they take action or exert effort to resolve the initial failure event. Such losses often deter many customers from voicing a complaint when failures occur (Fornell, 2007). Indeed, evidence shows that less than 10% of customers complain about the failures they experience and only 35% complain about their *most* dissatisfying experiences (Richens, 1983). Addressing these types of losses may assist organizations in encouraging more customers to voice their complaints, giving them at least an opportunity to restore perceptions of inequity with effective recovery strategies.

The most obvious customer loss is *performance loss*, which is defined as the functional loss of resources incurred when a product or service either does not perform as expected or falls below expectations. Closely related to this loss is *financial loss*, which is the monetary loss experienced when the benefits received from the product or service are not received, are viewed as inadequate, or are unacceptable and requires additional funds for repurchase. Customers can also endure supplementary financial losses during the prerecovery stage of the process if additional economic resources are required (and thus lost) to complain to the organization about the failure. Such losses can entail the travel expenses required for a return trip to the place of business or lost wages incurred during this process. In some situations, these losses can become quite sizable for customers and can inhibit them from filing a complaint or attempting to acquire restitution following a failure event.

In addition, *experiential losses* can occur whenever customers are deprived of life experiences, enjoyment, and pleasure when a product or service failure occurs. For example, a nonfunctioning toy given as a gift to a child can spoil the valuable memories for the family during a holiday celebration. Losses such as these cannot be regained. The experiential benefits can often represent a significant share of the total benefits received from some products and services. For example, a fine dining experience involves a more complex set of benefits than simply the functional benefit of sustenance. A relaxing and/or romantic dining experience can be lost rather quickly when the waiter is not attentive or the meal is not properly prepared.

Another type of loss that can be experienced by customers is physical loss. These losses occur whenever failures cause physical harm to the customers' well-being, health, or safety, resulting in pain and suffering. *Physical losses* are often sustained when the nature of the service act involves the minds or bodies of customers. Customers are most susceptible to these losses in the health care, dental care, massage, beauty, and personal fitness service industries (Lovelock, 1983).

In addition to these losses, customers can also suffer *psychological losses* that involve harm to the customers' self-esteem and self-confidence. Psychological losses are particularly prevalent when customers interact with impolite or insulting employees (i.e., interactional failures). Customers often consider interactional failures as personal assaults and can be quite harmful to their sense of worth as individuals. Although no empirical verification has been conducted to my knowledge, researchers have suggested that customers may view psychological losses more nega-tively than other types of losses (Hess, Ganesan, & Klein 2007).

The type of losses that can be sustained from the disparaging or judg-mental views from employees, friends, family, and other customers are called social losses. *Social losses* can include the perceptions of suspicion from employees when customers voice complaints or the unwelcome atten-tion from other customers during and after a failure event. For example, a customer who receives a poor haircut must endure not only performance loss but also social losses from the unwanted observations and comments from friends and family. The resources lost from these experiences consist of affiliations and status as viewed by others.

Another important and frequently overlooked loss involves the collat-eral damage that can be incurred by some customers following failure events. *Collateral losses* are indirect losses resulting from the unforeseen consequences of failures and can become much more costly to customers than the direct losses associated with the initial failure event. For example, luggage that fails to arrive at baggage claim following a flight certainly produces several of the customer losses presented above. A passenger who inadvertently packs the car keys inside this lost luggage, however, will experience collateral losses if an automobile must be rented or a taxi must be contacted to return home from the airport. Such losses would not have been incurred by the customer if the luggage had arrived at baggage claim as promised.

The final type of loss is *convenience loss*, which is experienced whenever customers request redress from the organization about a failure event. These losses include the time, effort, and inconvenience incurred during the recovery process to file a complaint, secure replacement, or return products/services. Convenience is analogous to time loss introduced in the risk literature by Roselius (1971).

Organizations typically fail to consider or compensate customers for these types of losses. As a result, most recovery strategies, even when well-executed, fail to fully restore the inequity endured by customers fol-lowing failures. Research in marketing has predominantly employed a justice perspective to understand how customers evaluate organizational recovery activities following failures (Ambrose, Hess, & Ganesan, 2007; Homburg & Furst, 2005; Maxham & Netemeyer, 2002; Smith, Bolton, & Wagner, 1999; Tax, Brown, & Chandrashekaran, 1998; Blodgett, Hill, & Tax, 1997; Goodwin & Ross, 1992). Much of this research has focused on the three-factor model of justice which includes distributive, procedural, and interactional factors. However, many researchers agree that interactional justice has two distinct aspects: interpersonal sensitivity and explana-tions (Greenberg, 1993a). Recently, this four-factor model has empirically demonstrated a better fit to the data than the three-factor model of justice within a failure–recovery context (Ambrose, Hess, & Ganesan, 2007). Thus, the four-factor model of justice will be explored here to better understand how customers' perceptions of inequity can be restored given the broader categorization of losses discussed previously. In the following section, the four types of justice will be defined and the recovery activities most closely linked with each type of justice will be explored.

Service Recovery and Customer Perceptions of Fairness

Research in marketing demonstrates that customers' perceptions about the fairness of how their complaint is handled is an important determinant of several important outcomes such as customer satisfaction, loyalty, repurchase intentions, trust, and word-of-mouth recommendations (Ambrose, Hess, & Ganesan, 2007; Homburg & Furst, 2005; Maxham & Netemeyer, 2002; Smith, Bolton, & Wagner, 1999; Tax, Brown, & Chandrashekaran, 1998; Blodgett, Hill, & Tax, 1997; Goodwin & Ross, 1992). Four distinct types of perceived justice have been introduced to understand how customers respond to the recovery process. Table 8.2 provides a summary of the four types of fairness, conceptual definitions of each, and associated recovery activities that have been linked with each type of fairness.

Distributive justice is the perceived fairness of outcome allocations, and is typically evaluated with respect to the equity of those outcome distributions (Adams, 1965; Deutsch, 1985; Homans, 1961). Researchers in marketing have shown that recovery activities that involve tangible compensation in the form of reimbursement, product/service replacement, credit, repair, refund, correction, and additional tangible compensation positively impact customers' perceptions of distributive justice (Smith, Bolton, & Wagner, 1999; Tax, Brown, & Chandrashekaran, 1998; Goodwin & Ross, 1992). The second type is *procedural justice*, which refers to the perceived fairness of the processes by which allocation decisions are made (Lind & Tyler, 1988; Thibaut & Walker, 1975). Research demonstrates that when individuals believe that the procedures were fair, they were more satisfied with the outcome they received, even when the decision outcome was unfavorable (Lind & Tyler, 1988; Thibaut & Walker, 1975). Researchers in marketing have shown that customer perceptions of procedural justice are based on recovery activities such as convenience, flexibility, timeliness (of response), opportunity to voice, control over the process, process knowledge, helpfulness, efficiency, assumption of responsibility, and follow-up (Tax, Brown, & Chandrashekaran, 1998; Conlon & Murray, 1996; Clemmer, 1993; Goodwin & Ross, 1992).

In the traditional models of justice, individuals are also sensitive to *interactional justice*, which is the perceived fairness of the treatment that customers receive during the enactment of procedures (Smith, Bolton, &

TABLE 8.2

Relationship of Recovery Activities and Types of Justice

Types of Justice	Recovery Activities[a]
Distributive Justice[a]	
Perceived fairness of outcome allocations	• Tangible compensation in the form of reimbursement • Product/service replacement • Credit • Repair • Refund • Correction
Procedural Justice[a]	
Perceived fairness of the process(es) by which allocation decisions are made	• Convenience • Flexibility • Timeliness (of response) • Opportunity to voice • Process control • Process knowledge • Helpfulness • Efficiency • Assumption of responsibility • Follow-up
Interpersonal Justice[b]	
Perceived fairness of interpersonal treatment provided during the enactment of procedures and distributions of outcomes	• Empathy • Effort • Politeness • Friendliness • Sensitivity • Apology • Justification • Lack of bias • Honesty
Informational Justice[b]	
Perceived fairness of explanations and information	• Feedback • Postrecovery follow-up • Candid communication • Thorough explanation about procedures followed • Timely communication about procedures • Tailor communications to specific needs

[a] Based on taxonomy by S. Tax, S., Brown, W. W., & Chandrashekaran, M., "Customer Evaluations of Service Complaint Experiences: Implications for Relationship Marketing," 1998, *Journal of Marketing, 62*, 60–76; interactional justice is used in their study to represent a combination of interpersonal and informational justice.

[b] Allocation of recovery activities to interpersonal and informational justice was made by the author based on the conceptual definitions of each concept.

Wagner, 1999; Tax, Brown, & Chandrashekaran, 1998; Blodgett, Hill, & Tax, 1997; Bies & Moag, 1986). Most research on perceived justice in the management discipline treats interactional justice as the third type of justice while distinguishing between its two subdimensions: interpersonal sensitivity and explanations (Bies, 2001; Cropanzano, Byrne, Bobocel, & Rupp, 2001; Cohen-Charash & Spector, 2001; Greenberg, 1993a; Bies & Shapiro 1988). Research demonstrates that interpersonal sensitivity and explanations each affect perceptions of fairness (Greenberg, 1993b, 1994).

Greenberg (1993a) suggests that these two dimensions of interactional justice are better conceptualized as two distinct forms of justice: *interpersonal justice,* defined as the fairness of interpersonal treatment provided during the enactment of procedures and distributions of outcomes, and *informational justice,* defined as the fairness of explanations and information. Research linking the specific recovery activities with each type of justice (Tax, Brown, & Chandrashekaran, 1998) was performed before the distinction between interpersonal and informational justice was empirically demonstrated (Ambrose, Hess, & Ganesan, 2007; Colquitt, 2001).

Using the conceptual definitions of each concept as a guide, recovery activities such as employee empathy, effort, politeness, friendliness, sensitivity, apology, lack of bias, and honesty should be linked with customers' perceptions of interpersonal justice. In contrast, timely feedback, postrecovery follow-up, a thorough explanation of the process followed, justification for the decision that was made, candid communication, timely communication about procedures, and tailored communications about the customers' circumstances should be related to informational justice (Clemmer, 1993; Conlon & Murray, 1996; Goodwin & Ross, 1992; Smith, Bolton, & Wagner, 1999; Tax, Brown, & Chandrashekaran, 1998).

Using the four types of justice defined above and summarized in Table 8.2, several theoretically based models of recovery will be presented in the next section. Each model offers a different viewpoint about how recovery activities should best be applied to restore customers' perceptions of these four types of justice, satisfaction, and loyalty. As discussed previously, very few theoretical models of recovery have been proposed in previous research. The model introduced earlier by Smith, Bolton, and Wagner (1999), referred to here as the matching model of recovery will begin this discussion.

The Matching Model of Recovery

As discussed previously, the matching model proposed by Smith, Bolton, and Wagner (1999) suggests that customer fairness is maximized when the recovery activity offered matches the type of loss experienced from the failure. The authors contend that outcome failures will result in economic losses and recovery activities in the form of compensation or economic resources should be used by organizations to restore these lost resources. In contrast, process failures will create noneconomic losses, which are best restored with recovery activities involving noneconomic resources.

To validate this model of recovery, Smith, Bolton, and Wagner (1999) examined the moderating effects of type of failure (outcome vs. process) on the relationships among four recovery activities (compensation, response speed, apology, and recovery initiation) and three types of justice (distributive, procedural, and interactional). Compensation represented an economic resource while the three other recovery activities, response speed, apology, and recovery initiation, represented noneconomic resources.

Specifically, these authors hypothesized that recovery compensation would have a greater positive effect on distributive justice for an outcome (versus process) failure. In contrast, a recovery initiated by the organization and including an apology would have a greater positive effect on interactional fairness for a process (versus outcome) failure. A similar relationship between speed of recovery and procedural justice was also expected for process (versus outcome) failures. Although the results of this study support these relationships within the hotel context, only a single interaction (compensation × outcome failure interaction → distributive justice) was supported in the restaurant context.

Earlier in this paper, several important limitations were presented about this matching of losses with recovery resources. These limitations may offer some explanation about why many of these proposed relationships did not hold in the restaurant context. Recall that one of the primary limitations is that the matching model, as tested by Smith, Bolton, and Wagner (1999), fails to consider the multitude of losses that are possible during the failure–recovery process. The second limitation is that the matching model fails to consider that customers can experience several losses simultaneously during any given failure episode. Most important, the direct resources lost from the failure may not "match" the resources of these simultaneous losses.

It is this limitation that may offer the most plausible explanation for why these results were not supported in the restaurant context. The consumption of certain services, such as restaurants, entails an *experiential exchange* that can be considered by many customers as more valuable than the fundamental benefit sought from the purchase (Nelson, 1974; Darby & Karni, 1973). For example, the benefit gained from a dining experience can transcend what is gained from the consumption of the food. The social interaction with friends or family and the serenity of a romantic night out to reconnect with a spouse is often the actual benefit being sought by customers during this service experience. Thus, the losses experienced from a poorly prepared meal can be viewed in economic terms, but the noneconomic losses can possibly be considered more valuable to customers in certain situations.

A revised matching model that differentiates products and services along experience properties (Nelson, 1974; Darby & Karni, 1973) and also recognizes the additional losses presented in Table 8.1 may improve the validity of the matching model for developing effective recovery strategies. Recovery activities must be identified that "match" the complex set of resources lost when failures occur. In addition, a determination of the specific set of losses that apply to certain types of failures will help significantly in the further development of this model. For example, if findings show that the primary customer loss suffered during a failure involving a fine restaurant meal is an experiential loss, a special invitation for a unique dining experience on a different night may more effectively restore this loss and also provide the restaurant another opportunity to restore customer trust and confidence in the abilities of the restaurant. A recovery that simply employs compensating the customer with free meals or discounted items may not be appropriate or may be ineffective when the primary customer losses are experiential. Providing the customer another opportunity for an enjoyable experience may be more effective in this situation.

Also important however, is the possibility that additional simultaneous losses occurred during the failed dining experience. For example, social losses may have been incurred during the dining experience if the customer was embarrassed by the attention from family and friends when complaining to the waiter about the meal. Diverting attention from the incident by apologizing and offering the table complementary drinks may be quite effective at restoring the social losses incurred by the failure. Overall, this revised matching model, which considers a wider variety of losses that are possible during a failure event, may offer some promise for developing an effective recovery strategy for organizations. A variation on this perspective is the general-specific purpose model of recovery, which will be explored next.

The General-Specific Purpose Model of Recovery

The general-specific purpose model of recovery suggests that certain recovery activities represent *general purpose* resources that should be applied by organizations to address *any* type of customer loss, while others are *special purpose* resources that should only be offered to customers for specific types of losses. The general-specific model was originally introduced by Roselius (1971) in a study testing the effects of risk-reducing methods on customers' perceptions of predecision risk. In this study, the author included four types of risk (e.g., time, hazard, ego, and money risk) and eleven risk-relieving methods (e.g., endorsements, brand loyalty, major brand image, private testing, store image, free samples, money-back guarantee, government testing, comparison shopping, highest priced, word-of-mouth recommendations) to determine which methods were the most useful at reducing customers' prepurchase risk.

The findings of this study reveal that brand loyalty (i.e., past purchase experience with brand) and major brand image (i.e., major, well-known brand name) are effective risk relievers for all four types of risk. Roselius (1971) refers to these as general purpose methods of risk relief. However, he also demonstrates that for certain types of prepurchase risk, special purpose risk-relieving methods become highly effective. Specifically, he shows that in the case of hazard risk (i.e., risk of harm to health or safety), customer loyalty to a previously purchased brand and well-known brand remain effective, but government testing (i.e., tested and approved by government agency) emerges as a very powerful risk-relieving method for this type of loss. Roselius (1971) appropriately call these special purpose methods because they become important under special circumstances.

This general-specific purpose concept may also be especially appropriate in a failure–recovery context. There are many recovery activities that researchers have suggested should be considered as general purpose and thus should be applied for every failure event. It is likely that customers will expect organizations to provide a recovery that is convenient, timely in response, and provides an opportunity to express their views about the failure. Customers may also expect employees to be empathetic and offer an apology for the inconvenience caused by the unfortunate event. A small form of tangible compensation may also be quite effective and highly advisable for all failures. In addition, postrecovery follow-up in the form of an e-mail, telephone call, or note to ensure that the customers complaints were handled to their satisfaction may also be a necessary component of every recovery regardless of failure type or loss endured. Other recovery activities may be special purpose resources and only applied under certain circumstances. Central to the general-specific purpose model of recovery is the verification of general purpose and special purpose recovery activities.

A review of previous research on the failure–recovery process suggests that there could be some merit to the general-specific model of recovery. Blodgett, Hill, and Tax (1997) examined the effects of distributive, procedural, and interactional justice on repurchase and negative word-of-mouth intentions. The context of the study involved the customers' dissatisfaction with a poorly produced pair of athletic shoes. The authors experimentally manipulated each type of justice by providing different levels of recovery activities that most closely apply to each type of justice. For distributive justice, customers were offered: full refund of the purchase price, 50% discount, or 15% discount on their next purchase. A sincere apology or rude employee behavior was used for interactional justice. Finally, for procedural justice, the store manager was physically present in the store and available to help the customer or was not present and the customer was required to return to the store the next day to resolve the issue.

The results showed that distributive and interactional justice were both significantly related to repurchase and negative word-of-mouth intentions; however, procedural justice was not significantly related to these outcomes. The interactional effects of distributive and interactional effects were also examined showing that higher perceptions of interactional justice enhanced the impact of distributive justice on repurchase and negative word-of-mouth intentions. Although the manipulation for procedural justice is obviously problematic because one of the treatments entail the customer to accrue additional losses to resolve the problem (i.e., required to return to the store the next day), the recovery activities used for distributive (i.e., full refund, 50% discount, or 15% discount) and interactional justice (i.e., apology or rude employee behavior) may represent specific purpose resources and those used for procedural justice (i.e., store manager available or not present) may represent general purpose resources in this situation.

Other research demonstrates a similar pattern of results with regard to distributive, interactional, and procedural justice. For example, Smith, Bolton, and Wagner (1999) and Smith and Bolton (2002) both found that interactional and distributive were more strongly related to satisfaction with recovery than procedural justice within a restaurant and hotel context. Furthermore, within a new home construction context, Maxham and Netemeyer (2002) showed that only distributive justice was significantly related to satisfaction with recovery, repurchase intentions, and word-of-mouth recommendations. Taken together, these divergent results could provide some evidence that some recovery activities, through their effects on distributive, procedural, and interactional justice, could be considered as general purpose resources while others should be considered special purpose resources.

The final model that will be explored in this paper focuses on the order in which the recovery activities are offered to customers following failures.

The Sequential Model of Recovery

The sequential model of recovery suggests that the ordering of recovery activities is important for restoring the inequity experienced by customers following failures. This perspective is founded on the research of van den Bos, Vermunt, and Wilke (1997) who examined the effects of outcome favorability (favorable versus unfavorable outcome), and procedural accuracy (accurate versus inaccurate) and the procedure–outcome sequence (outcome before procedure versus procedure before outcome) on perceptions of procedural justice and distributive justice. The context used for this study involved a job interview.

The findings of this study revealed several important issues that are quite applicable to the examination of the failure–recovery process. First, the results showed that a favorable outcome has a greater impact on procedural and distributive justice if an outcome–procedure sequence rather than a procedure–outcome sequence is followed. The sequence was not relevant for unfavorable outcomes. Next, the accuracy of the procedures had a significant impact on perceptions of justice. Specifically, an unfavorable outcome had a more strongly negative effect on procedural and distributive justice when inaccurate procedures were followed as to accurate procedures. Furthermore, these results were more pronounced when the procedure was followed by the outcome. Finally, procedures in general (regardless of accuracy) had a greater impact on both distributive and procedural justice when the procedure was presented prior to the outcome.

The findings of this study are quite important for a better understanding of the failure–recovery process. The order in which recovery activities are offered to customers may be quite important for restoring perceptions of equity, satisfaction, and loyalty. Recovery may be perceived more effective if a favorable outcome decision is offered before the procedure is explained. In addition, given the influence that the accuracy of procedures has on perceptions of justice, the procedures followed by employees to make such outcome decisions must be carefully constructed, extremely precise, and clearly reflect the customers' account of the failure.

Little or no evidence exists for the potential validity of the sequential model of recovery. In fact, few authors have even proposed these types of effects. Yet this model offers some significant insights about how customers may respond to the sequencing of different recovery activities offered by organizations following failures. The model may be especially helpful to organizations when unfavorable outcomes must be conveyed to customers. Accurate procedures actually may protect organizations from negative responses from customers when unfavorable decision outcomes must be made to address customers' complaints.

However, the influence of procedures in the recovery process may be especially noteworthy given the poor quality of recovery procedures used at most organizations currently. The simple act of voicing a complaint is often a significant obstacle for many customers and many choose instead to allow failure issues to remain unresolved. It is quite unfortunate that customers must experience these unacceptable procedures prior to outcome decisions during the failure–recovery process. As shown by van den Bos, Vermunt, and Wilke (1997) the procedure–outcome sequence consistently leads to significantly *lower* perceptions of distributive and procedural justice regardless of the outcome decision. Thus, organizations could gain significant positive benefits simply through improvements in any aspect of the recovery process that enhances customer convenience and ease of communicating failures—those aspects of the recovery that precede any decisions that must be made about the failure event.

Managerial Implications and Conclusions

Despite the well-documented negative consequences of poorly addressing customer complaints, very few organizations have implemented an effective recovery strategy to handle such events. As indicated previously, evidence of customers' dissatisfaction with organizational recovery efforts is well-documented in both the academic and popular presses. Fornell (2007), for example, reports that organizations in industries such as life insurance, e-commerce auctions, airlines, hospitals, and health care insurance consistently score under 50 on a 100-point index on complaint handling satisfaction. The purpose of this paper, therefore, is to provide managers with a better understanding of the failure–recovery process and to assist them with the development of recovery strategies that more effectively address the failures (and losses) that customers experience.

The overall objective for organizations should be to fully restore the losses and resulting inequities that customers perceive when failures occur. Yet most recovery activities only restore a fraction of the losses experienced and thus most customers remain dissatisfied. Without a clear understanding of the full array of losses that are possible, an effective recovery strategy is not possible. Adapting previous research on perceived risk as well as using anecdotal observations of customer experiences with failures, a multidimensional conceptualization of customer losses was introduced. As Table 8.1 presents, customers can experience many different types of losses including performance, financial, experiential, physical, social, psychological, collateral, and convenience.

Managers must also be mindful of the fact that customers often endure more than one of these losses simultaneously during a failure event. Thus, a poorly prepared meal (performance loss) can produce several additional losses such as experiential (loss of life experiences, enjoyment, and pleasure), social (loss of self-esteem and self-confidence based on the views of others), psychological (loss of self-esteem and self-confidence based on the harm to one's ego), and convenience (loss of personal time and effort to file complaint) losses. Many of these losses are less tangible and may appear less important to customers; however, such losses can be extremely damaging to the customer–organization relationship if not fully restored through organizational recovery activities. Organizational sensitivity to the breadth of losses that are possible and the administration of recovery activities to fully remunerate customers for all of these losses will likely result in considerable benefits for organizations.

Using this conceptualization of customer losses as a foundation, several theoretical models of recovery were proposed that included the revised matching model, general-specific model, and sequential model (see Table 8.3 for summary). The revised matching model is an adaptation of previous research by Smith, Bolton, and Wagner (1999). These authors claimed that customers expected recovery activities that were "in kind" with the type of loss experienced by the customer. The revised matching model introduced in this paper suggested that recovery activities must match a wider variety of customer losses (see Table 8.1) in order to be effective. Thus, organizations that only offer customers a complementary meal when the initial order is improperly prepared fail to restore the social and experiential benefits that are often lost during a couple's romantic dining experience. Instead, organizations should provide a more complete

TABLE 8.3

Summary of Three Theoretical Models of Recovery

Matching Model of Recovery

- *Customer Loses*—Many types of resources are lost by customers when failures occur, causing perceptions of inequity in the customer–organization exchange. The revised matching model presented here recognizes the multitude of losses that can occur simultaneously during a single failure event (see Table 8.1).
- *Loss-Matching Recovery Resources*—Apply recovery activities that "match" the customer losses experienced by the customer.

General-Specific Purpose Model of Recovery

- *General Purpose Recovery Activities*—Certain recovery activities may be equally effective across all types of losses.
- *Specific Purpose Recovery Activities*—Certain recovery activities will differ in terms of relevance/effectiveness depending upon types of loss/failure that is experienced by customers.

The Sequential Model of Recovery

- *Outcome-Process Sequence*—Fairness is maximized if favorable decision outcomes are presented before the process is described.
- *Accuracy of Procedures*—Offering accurate (versus inaccurate) procedures about how an outcome decision is made minimizes the negative effect of unfavorable decision outcomes on perceptions of fairness.
- *Process-Outcome Sequence*—Procedures have a significant impact on perceptions of fairness when process is presented before the outcome is described.

---

recovery by offering the couple an exclusive dinner invitation with a special menu and seating location, at no charge. These efforts will likely be much more effective at restoring the social and experiential experiences lost during the failure.

The second theoretical model of recovery explored in this paper was the general-specific model. This model, based on the work on perceived risk by Roselius (1971), suggests that certain recovery activities can be effective across all types of losses, while others should be applied for specific types of losses. This model suggests that customers may expect certain types of recovery activities (i.e., general recovery activities) by organizations regardless of the types of losses that they experience, while others (specific recovery activities) are contingent upon the situation or some other criteria. For example, customers may expect an opportunity to express their views about the failure situation, timely resolution, and a sincere apology for the trouble caused by the failure. Thus, organizations should be prepared to provide these activities for every situation. In contrast, specific types of recovery activities may depend upon the type of failure experienced, type of product or service, or tangibility of the product or service.

It is possible that the general-specific and matching models advocate similar recovery activity recommendations. However, these models could also provide very different recovery recommendations as well. For example, customers may expect some form of compensation (e.g., percentage discount, free items, coupon, etc.) regardless of the type of losses experienced. The application of compensation to address all failure situations is inconsistent with the principals of the matching model because this advocates offering compensation to restore losses that are at times non-economic (e.g., impolite or unhelpful employee behaviors).

The final model introduced was the sequential model of recovery based on the research of van den Bos, Vermunt, and Wilke (1997). The basic principle of this model is that the sequence with which the recovery is presented to customers may influence their perceptions of fairness. These authors found that perceptions of fairness may be maximized if the outcome is presented prior to the description of the procedures. They also revealed, however, that a description of procedures prior to providing an unfavorable decision outcome may have a positive influence on fairness perceptions. Within a failure–recovery context, it is possible that the sequence of recovery activities may influence customers' perceptions of fairness. Thus, the presentation of a free meal followed by a sincere apology from the employee may lead to greater fairness perceptions than the opposite sequence. The sequential model of recovery may be best subsumed within either the general-specific or revised matching models, as the order of presentation may influence the effectiveness of both of these recovery models.

References

Adams, J. S. (1965). Inequity in social exchange. In L. Berkowitz (Ed.), *Advances in experimental social psychology* (Vol. 2, pp. 267–299). New York: Academic Press.

Ambrose, M., Hess, R. L., & Ganesan, S. (2007). The relationship between justice and attitudes: An examination of justice effects on event and system-related attitudes. *Organizational Behavior and Human Decision Processes, 103*, 21–36.

Bettman, J. R. (1975). Information integration in consumer risk perception: A comparison of two models of component conceptualization. *Journal of Applied Psychology, 60*, 3, 381–385.

Bies, R. J. (2001). Interactional (in)justice: The sacred and the profane. In J. Greenberg and J. Colquitt (Eds.) *The handbook of organizational justice: Fundamental questions about fairness in the workplace* (pp. 89–118). Lawrence Erlbaum Associates, Mawheh: New Jersey.

Bies, R. J., & Moag, J. S. (1986). Interactional justice: Communication criteria for fairness. In B. Sheppard (Ed.), *Research on negotiation in organizations* (Vol. 1, pp. 43–55). Greenwich, CT: JAI Press.

Bies, R. J., & Shapiro, D. L. (1988). Voice and justification: Their influence on procedural fairness judgments. *Academy of Management Journal, 31*, 676–685.

Bitner, M., Booms, B. M., & Tetreault, M. S. (1990). The service encounter: Diagnosing favorable and unfavorable incidents. *Journal of Marketing, 54*, 71–85.

Blodgett, J. G., Hill, D. J., & Tax, S. S. (1997). The effects of distributive, procedural and interactional justice on post-complaint behavior. *Journal of Retailing, 73*, 2, 185–210.

Clemmer, E. C. (1993). An investigation into the relationships of justice and customer satisfaction with services. In R. Cropanzano (Ed.), *Justice in the workplace: Approaching fairness in human resource management* (Vol. 5, pp. 197–207). Hillsdale, NJ: Erlbaum.

Cohen-Charash, Y., & Spector, P. E. (2001). The role of justice in organizations: A meta-analysis. *Organizational Behavior and Human Decision Processes, 86*, 278–321.

Colquitt, J. A. (2001). On the dimensionality of organizational justice: A construct validation of a measure. *Journal of Applied Psychology, 86*, 386–400.

Conlon, D. E., & Murray, N. M. (1996). Customer perceptions of corporate responses to product complaints: The role of explanations. *Academy of Management Journal, 39*, 1040–1056.

Cropanzano, R., Byrne, Z. S., Bobocel, D. R., & Rupp, D. R. (2001). Moral virtues, fairness heuristics, social entities, and other denizens of organizational justice. *Journal of Vocational Behavior, 58*, 164–209.

Darby, M. R., & Karni, E. (1973). Free competition and the optimal amount of fraud. *Journal of Law and Economics, 16*, 67–86.

Deutsch, M. (1985). *Distributive justice*. New Haven, CT: Yale University Press.

Fornell, C. (2007). *The satisfied customer: Winners and losers in the battle for buyer preference*. New York: Palgrave MacMillan.

Fornell, C., & Wernerfelt, B. (1987). Defensive marketing strategy by customer complaint management: A theoretical analysis. *Journal of Marketing Research, 24*, November, 337–346.

Goodwin, C., & Ross, I. (1992). Consumer responses to service failures: Influence of procedural and interactional fairness perceptions. *Journal of Business Research, 25*, 149–163.

Greenberg, J. (1993a). The social side of fairness: Interpersonal and informational classes of organizational justice. In R. Cropanzano (Ed.), *Justice in the workplace: Approaching fairness in human resource management* (pp. 79–103). Hillsdale, NJ: Lawrence Erlbaum Associates.

Greenberg, J. (1993b). Stealing in the name of justice: Informational and interpersonal moderators of theft reaction to underpayment inequity. *Organizational Behavior and Human Decision Processes, 54*, 81–103.

Greenberg, J. (1994). Using socially fair treatment to promote acceptance of a work site smoking ban. *Journal of Applied Psychology, 79*, 288–297.

Gronroos, C. (winter, 1988). Service quality: The six criteria of good perceived service quality. *Review of Business, 9*, 10–13.

Hess, R. L., Ganesan, S., & Klein, N. M. (2007). Interactional service failures in a pseudo-relationship: The role of organizational attributions. *Journal of Retailing, 83*, 1, 79–95.

Hoffman, K. D., & Bateson, J. E. J. (1997). *Essentials of services marketing*. Fort Worth, TX: Dryden Press.

Homans, G. C. (1961). *Social behavior: Its elementary forms*. New York: Harcourt, Brace & World.

Homburg, C., & Furst, A. (2005). How organizational complaint handling drives customer loyalty: An analysis of the mechanistic and organic approach. *Journal of Marketing, 69*, 3, July, 95–114.

Jacoby, J., & Kaplan, L. (1972). The components of perceived risk. In M. Venkatesan (Ed.), *Proceedings, third annual conference, association for consumer research* (pp. 382–393). Chicago: University of Chicago Press.

Keaveney, S. M. (1995). Customer switching behavior in service industries: An exploratory study. *Journal of Marketing, 59*, April, 71–82.

Kelley, S. W., Hoffman, K. D., & Davis, M. A. (1993). A typology of retail failures and recoveries. *Journal of Retailing, 69*, 429–452.

Lind, E. A., & Tyler, T. R. (1988). *The social psychology of procedural justice*. New York: Plenum.

Lovelock, C. H. (summer, 1983). Classifying services to gain strategic marketing insights. *Journal of Marketing, 47*, 9–20.

Maxham, J. G., & Netemeyer, R. G. (2002). Modeling customer perceptions of complaint handling over time: The effects of perceived justice on satisfaction and intent. *Journal of Retailing, 78*, 239–252.

Nelson, P. (1974). Advertising as information. *Journal of Political Economy, 81*, 729–754.

Oliver, R. (1997). *Satisfaction: A behavioral perspective on the consumer*. New York: McGraw-Hill Companies, Inc.

Parasuraman, A., Zeithaml, V. A., & Berry, L. L. (fall, 1985). A conceptual model of service quality and its implications for future research. *Journal of Marketing, 49*, 41–50.

Peter, J. P., & Tarpey, L. X. (1975). A comparative analysis of three consumer decision strategies. *Journal of Consumer Research, 2*, 1, 29–37.

Richens, M. (winter, 1983). Negative word-of-mouth by dissatisfied customers: A pilot study. *Journal of Marketing, 47,* 68–78.

Roselius, T. (January 1971). Consumer rankings of risk reduction methods. *Journal of Marketing, 35,* 56–61.

Smith, A. K., Bolton, R. N., & Wagner, J. (1999). A model of customer satisfaction with service encounters involving failure and recovery. *Journal of Marketing Research, 36,* 356–372.

Tax, S. S., Brown, W. W., & Chandrashekaran, M. (1998). Customer evaluations of service complaint experiences: Implications for relationship marketing. *Journal of Marketing, 62,* 60–76.

Thibaut, J. & Walker, L. (1975). *Procedural justice: A psychological analysis.* Hillsdale, NJ: Lawrence Erlbaum Associates.

van den Bos, K., Vermunt, R. & Wilke, H. A. M. (1997). Procedural and distributive justice: What is fair depends more on what comes first than what comes next. *Journal of Personality and Social Psychology, 72,* 1, 95–104.

9

Advances in Research on Punishment in Organizations: Descriptive and Normative Perspectives

Linda Klebe Treviño
The Pennsylvania State University
Gary R. Weaver
University of Delaware

Introduction

Punishment is an often-used management tool that has been the subject of increasing research attention. We define punishment as "the manager's application of a negative consequence or withdrawal of a positive consequence from someone under his or her supervision" (Treviño, 1992, p. 649). Given this definition, punishment may include relatively mild actions such as verbal reprimands as well as more serious actions such as withholding a pay raise or bonus, or suspending or even terminating an employee. Our discussion begins with a brief review of the once-conventional behaviorist view of punishment in organizations. We then contrast this to current empirical research and theory, which has placed greater emphasis on the context surrounding punishment events, and on participants' and observers' cognitive and affective states. Finally, we introduce normative views of punishment adapted from philosophical and criminological writings about punishment in society. These views suggest new ways of thinking about punishment in organizations and new venues for future empirical research.

Descriptive/Empirical Perspectives

Behaviorism and Organizational Behavior

For many years the organizational behavior literature represented punishment in organizations from a behaviorist learning theory perspective (Skinner, 1953). Behaviorist-based punishment studies focused on the punishing stimulus and the behavioral response of the punishment target. Behaviorism treated cognitions as scientifically unknowable and therefore unworthy of study. Basic principles derived from behaviorist research provided the conventional wisdom about how managers should (but mostly should not) use punishment (e.g., Luthans & Kreitner, 1985). The focus was on the supervisor/subordinate dyad and, in particular, on the subordinate's negative behavioral and emotional reactions to punishment. Managers were advised to refrain from punishing subordinates unless absolutely necessary because punishment would necessarily produce unwanted negative side effects (e.g., anger, sabotage). Instead of punishment, managers were strongly encouraged to use positive reinforcement. Where punishment was unavoidable, managers were to follow a series of principles based upon operant conditioning research, principles that would increase the likelihood of behavior change without producing negative side effects. For example, managers were told to be sure that the punishment was timely so that the punished employee would connect the punishment with the undesirable behavior. Some of these traditional punishment recommendations (e.g., timeliness) have been supported in recent research on effective discipline methods (e.g., Brett, Atwater, & Waldman, 2005).

Beyond Behaviorist Approaches

Questioning of the behaviorist conventional wisdom began with a celebrated paper by Solomon (1964) in which he reviewed the research on punishment and proposed that Skinner had created a "legend" that punishment didn't work. Skinner (1953, pp. 182–183) had written: "In the long run punishment, unlike reinforcement, works to the disadvantage of both the punished organism and the punishing agency." Solomon argued that Skinner's conclusions were not based upon the research evidence and had failed to take into account a number of complexities, including the kind and intensity of punishment used, the kinds of subjects, and a number of other factors (cf. Newman, 1985), and he called for additional research.

Nearly two decades later, in the management literature, Arvey and Ivancevich (1980, p. 123) observed that "the topic of punishment has received essentially no attention from organizational researchers." They also highlighted the lack of empirical evidence to support the conventional wisdom. Based upon key insights learned in various areas of organizational research, they outlined a number of research propositions that pointed toward research efforts to come. For example, they explored the importance of the quality of the relationship between the punisher and the punished person, as well as the importance of offering a rationale or explanation for the punishment. In recent years, theorizing and empirical research on punishment in organizations have advanced considerably, generally supporting the notion that punishment need not have negative effects. Researchers have begun to look more broadly at the social setting surrounding punishment, more deeply at the characteristics of the disciplinary approach used, and at the role of cognitions (i.e., justice evaluations) and affect in explaining reactions to punishment (Arvey & Ivancevich, 1985; Ball & Sims, 1991). This is consistent with the general trend toward a more cognitive/affective approach to the study of organizational behavior, and toward more complex understandings of the interaction between individual behavior and social context.

Justice Perspectives

The social and organizational justice literatures suggest that subordinates' reactions to punishment are likely based on justice evaluations that consider the perceived fairness of the outcomes (distributive justice) of punishment, the processes by which outcome decisions are made (procedural justice), and the interpersonal treatment received (interactional justice). The underlying thesis argues that employees assess the *justice* of punishment along numerous justice dimensions, and persons' reactions to punishment need not be negative if the punishment is perceived to be fair. For example, verbal expressions such as, "I had it coming," "I asked for it," or "I deserved it" suggest that individuals sometimes take responsibility for misconduct and conclude that their punishment is justified. Accordingly, Cole (2008) found that when individuals accept personal responsibility for their misbehavior, they perceive punishment for misconduct to be more just. And, Atwater and colleagues (Atwater, Camobreco, Dionne, Avolio, & Lau, 1997) found that punished military cadets actually sympathized with their leader and rated the leader more highly in reaction to punishment that was clearly contingent on misconduct (compared to noncontingent punishment).

Ball, Treviño, and Sims (1992, 1993, 1994) proposed and found that punished subordinates' affective and behavioral reactions to punishment are based upon evaluations of the distributive and procedural justice characteristics of disciplinary events. In their work, punished subordinates and their supervisors completed surveys about the same punishment incident. Supervisors were asked to report on the subordinate's postpunishment work performance and organizational citizenship behaviors. Punished subordinates reported on their perceptions of the incident and their subsequent attitudinal reactions. The studies (Ball et al., 1993, 1994) found that a distributive characteristic of the punishment, harshness, negatively influenced subsequent performance, perceptions of both distributive and procedural justice, trust in the supervisor, and organizational commitment. Harshness was defined as the subordinate's perception that the punishment was too severe given what others had received and too severe given the misconduct.

Subordinates' perceptions of the procedural aspects of the punishment were also important. Subordinates' perceptions of control (that they had input and that their input was considered) positively influenced their citizenship and satisfaction with the supervisor. Perceptions of arbitrariness (lack of adherence to organizational rules) negatively influenced perceptions of procedural and distributive justice. Perceptions that the punishment was adequately explained also positively influenced perceptions of procedural justice. Finally, perceptions that the supervisor used a constructive, counseling approach with the subordinate positively influenced trust in and satisfaction with the supervisor, and negatively influenced subordinate intentions to leave. In several studies by Baron (1988), destructive approaches to criticism resulted in anger, as well as lower goals and self-efficacy. In the research by Ball and colleagues, the subordinate's perception that the supervisor's demeanor was negative was inversely associated with trust in and satisfaction with the supervisor (Ball et al., 1994). Subsequent research has extended these findings. For example, Bennett (1998) found that consistently allocated punishment produced more positive effects. Cole (2008) found that fairness perceptions were lower when punishment was perceived to be severe, but they were enhanced when employees were given explanations for their discipline and when a constructive counseling orientation was used. Brett and colleagues (Brett et al., 2005) found that postdiscipline behavior improved when supervisors engaged in two-way discussions with disciplined employees. A recent meta-analysis (Podsakoff, Bommer, Podsakoff, & MacKenzie, 2006) also found that punishment that is clearly contingent on poor performance produces more favorable outcomes, and that fairness perceptions are a key mediating cognition of the contingent punishment–outcome relationship. Finally, Atwater and colleagues (Atwater, Waldman, Carey, & Cartier, 2001) concluded that, although punishment can produce negative recipient reactions, when employees perceive punishment to be fair, fewer negative outcomes result. These findings suggest that how punishment is administered matters greatly if punishment is to be effective, and that justice evaluations are extremely important to subordinates' reactions. Based upon the combination of research evidence, we now know that supervisors can avoid potential negative side effects of punishment by:

- making punishment clearly contingent on poor performance or rule violation
- matching the severity of the punishment to the severity of the misconduct
- making punishment consistent with what others have received
- providing the subordinate with input into the punishment decision-making process
- using a constructive counseling orientation and avoiding negative emotional displays in interactions with the subordinate around the disciplinary event
- adequately explaining the punishment in a way that clearly ties it to the misconduct
- punishing in private

Cole and Latham (1997) followed this advice in designing training in procedurally just disciplinary techniques for supervisors in a union setting. Compared to untrained supervisors, when these trained supervisors conducted employee discipline, employees perceived it to be fairer.

Clearly, taking justice concerns into account has contributed to our understanding of subordinates' reactions to punishment and has provided support for a justice perspective on punishment in organizations. Understanding reactions to punishment requires an examination of how punished employees make sense of what has happened to them and points to an emphasis on cognition in punishment research.

Recently, researchers have begun to ask whether demographic differences such as race and gender influence disciplinary practices and employee reactions to punishment. For example, considering gender effects, Cole (2004) found that female supervisors in a union environment were more likely (than men) to use disciplinary behaviors that employees perceived to be fair. By contrast, Brett and colleagues (2005) found that males and females did not discipline differently. But, when female managers were rated lower on the extent to which they used two-way discussion (an interactional justice characteristic), punishment was more likely to have negative outcomes. Further, Atwater and colleagues (Atwater, Waldman, Carey, & Waldman, 2001) found that disciplined employees were less likely to perceive their punishment to be fair when the supervisor was female, and female recipients of punishment were more likely to perceive their punishment to be unfair, resulting in negative feelings toward the supervisor and organization. Punishment research is also beginning to consider race effects. For example, Thau, Aquino, and Bonner (2008) found that noncontingent punishment decreased citizenship behaviors only among whites. They argued that blacks may have adapted to being mistreated because of past experiences and, as a result, noncontingency has less of an impact on their behavior. These findings suggest that sense-making around punishment may depend upon social identity. Thus, future research should continue to consider the potential effects of demographic differences on punishment practices and employee reactions.

In a broader application of the justice perspective on punishment, Treviño (1992) proposed that punishment in organizations should be conceptualized as a social phenomenon rather than merely a dyadic incident involving a supervisor and a subordinate. When punishment is conceptualized in these broader social terms, observers' evaluations of punishment and their learning from others' punishment become important. Based upon theorizing and research from the social, organizational, and criminal justice literatures, Treviño (1992) proposed that retributive justice (discussed in more detail below) is as important in organizations as it is in society. Organizational observers expect serious wrongdoers to be punished, a proposition supported by Niehoff and colleagues (Niehoff, Paul, & Bunch, 1998). Organization members are disappointed or even outraged when wrongdoers are not disciplined, feeling as if they, rather than the wrongdoers, have been punished. Observers' cognitive, affective, and behavioral reactions are more positive when they perceive that misconduct in the organization is punished fairly and, interestingly, this often means severely (Treviño & Ball, 1992; Niehoff et al., 1998). Treviño and Ball (1992) found that observers responded most positively when punishment of ethical rule violators was severe and they considered the severest punishment (dismissal with legal action) to be the most fair. Similarly, Niehoff and colleagues (1998) found that observer perceptions of fairness were stronger with increased punishment severity and severity was associated with more positive attitudes toward the supervisor and lower intent to leave the organization. A number of other studies have supported the idea that if observers perceive punishment and other negative outcomes to be fair, they are more likely to express satisfaction, trust, commitment, and lower turnover intention, and their motivation and work performance are higher (Alexander & Ruderman, 1987; Brockner et al., 1987, 1990; O'Reilly & Puffer, 1989; O'Reilly & Weitz, 1980; Schnake, 1986). One important question for future research involves balancing this concern with punishment's potentially positive impact on observers with the common recommendation, noted above, that punishment should be conducted in private.

Recent research has taken this social perspective even further, noting that teams have been given more responsibility for performance management, including punishment. But group disciplinary decisions do not differ significantly from those made by managers. Both rely on attributions of performance seriousness to make their punishment decisions (Liden et al., 1999).

These findings support the notion that punishment can usefully be thought of as a social phenomenon that provides important learning for coworkers and the entire social group. Moreover, unpunished wrongdoing can be a source of moral outrage and perceptions of injustice in the social group. This concern with the broader implications of punishment for larger organization units, and for people's sense of justice and injustice, further distinguishes recent work in organizational punishment from earlier accounts. Recognition of this broader range of issues also contributes to our ability to provide managers with realistic and useful advice.

Punishment research has also taken the manager's perspective. A qualitative study of managers' reactions to their own experiences with punishment (Butterfield, Treviño, & Ball, 1996) found that managers are also quite aware of justice concerns. Seventy-six managers were interviewed and asked to discuss an "effective" and "ineffective" punishment incident. The results suggested that a number of justice-related concerns differentiated the two types of incidents. First, managers took subordinates' justice reactions into account when deciding whether and how much to punish the subordinate. Also, in support of a more cognitive approach, managers noted that employees sometimes accepted responsibility for their misconduct and expected to be disciplined for what they did. Further, managers recognized the social implications of punishment. They were aware that their other subordinates expected them to punish misconduct and that doing so was perceived to be fair. Managers also expressed their own justice concerns when making decisions about whether and how to punish. They discussed issues of equity and severity, as well as constructiveness, privacy, and timing. Interestingly, they talked most about the importance of following prescribed punishment procedures. Managers seemed to be more concerned about procedural justice than they were about the distributive issues that appear to be most important for punished subordinates' attitudes and behaviors (Ball et al., 1993, 1994).

Expansion of punishment research to include the broader social environment, justice concerns, and the manager has contributed significantly to our understanding of punishment from a descriptive/empirical perspective. Yet many questions remain about how managers can balance individual learning, satisfaction, and justice evaluations with work group learning and justice evaluations, and also with managers' own needs and concerns. Additional research will be needed to address these complex issues. For example, the punished employee, the leader, and the work group may react differently to specific punishments. Are there circumstances under which the manager should be more concerned with the particular employee or with the group? Or, is there some ideal level of punishment or approach to punishment that produces the best combination of reactions from punished subordinates, managers, and observers?

Given the increasing importance of affect in organizational behavior research (e.g., see Barsade & Gibson, 2007), future investigations should also take affect more into account in understanding reactions to punishment. Individual differences, such as negative affectivity, have been shown to influence reactions to punishment (Ball et al., 1994). And, in their qualitative study, Atwater and colleagues (Atwater et al., 2001) found a variety of emotional responses to punishment on the part of both managers and punished employees.

Social Context Issues

Future research on punishment should consider broadening the focus even more. For example, most of the research has focused on formal punishment by authority figures within established hierarchical structures. However, much punishment actually occurs more informally as when free riders in groups are punished by peers (Fehr, 2004), whistleblowers are ostracized by work group members (Warren & Smith-Crowe, 2008), or supervisors use informal means to bring deviant subordinates into line (Fortado, 1994). In such instances, contextual factors such as organizational culture, informal norms, and peer-based modes of punishment may be more important than formal punishment procedures. Further, various forms of self-discipline on the part of employees may make extensive punishment regimes unnecessary in an organization. Grey (1994), for example, argued that the well-defined career tracks in professional accounting firms constitute an internalized system of organizational discipline. Again, more research is needed to understand these alternative approaches to punishment and reactions to them from subordinates, observers, and managers themselves.

With few exceptions (e.g., Klaas & Dell'Omo, 1997), research has seldom considered why particular punishment practices are adopted in organizations. Research might, for example, consider how organizational technologies affect systems of punishment. Do certain systems of production make certain modes of punishment necessary, possible, or impossible? Do organizational technologies influence the impact that different modes of punishment have within organizations?

Similar questions may be raised about the impact of extraorganizational context on punishment practice. For example, how do punishment practices diffuse across organizational fields? Consider how the U.S. government has played an active role in influencing organizations to adopt specific disciplinary practices. Under advisory guidelines developed in 1991 by the congressionally chartered United States Sentencing Commission, organizations have financial incentives for efforts taken to ensure compliance with the law by the organization and its members. Courts are allowed to adjust fines levied for organizational violations of federal law, with the extent of adjustment dependent on the kinds of actions a firm has taken in order to ensure legal compliance. A firm's adoption and application of well-defined penalties for employees who contribute to illegal organizational behavior serves to mitigate the fines to which the offending organization is subject. This requirement of discipline is coupled with other organizational structures and policies (e.g., investigatory offices and procedures), which together constitute the outlines of a disciplinary system.

Finally, cross-cultural differences in individual behavior and societal culture also suggest important new questions about punishment, especially in light of increasing globalization of business. Cultures differ in their standards of justice, members' attachment to organizations, attributions of responsibility, and beliefs about status, authority, and power. For example, national cultures vary in the degree to which they emphasize individualism or collectivism. Individualism subordinates collective purposes to personal goals (Triandis, 1984, 1989; Triandis, Brislin, & Hui, 1988), while collectivism does the opposite. In terms of the implications for punishment in organizations, individualism, with its emphasis on autonomy and competitiveness, encourages an adversarial approach to conflict, while collectivism, with its emphasis on collective purposes and group harmony, encourages a conciliatory approach to conflict within the group (Trubinsky, Ting-Toomey, & Lin, 1991).

These differences have several implications for the practice of punishment in organizations. First, persons from individualistic cultures may respond more positively to punishment that addresses personal interests, whereas collectivists may respond more positively to punishment that appeals to group norms and interests (Bontempo, Lobel, & Triandis, 1990). Further, where punishment occurs within collectivist societies, it may be more likely aimed at reaffirming or reestablishing group harmony, than is characteristic in individualistic cultures. Also, collectivist organizations may more commonly direct punishment toward groups (e.g., work groups, departments) rather than individuals. Research has begun to investigate a phenomenon known as *co-punishment*. With co-punishment, coworkers of a perpetrator who are themselves not guilty of any violation or offense are held accountable and disciplined for the peer's misconduct. This practice is likely more common in some collectivist culture settings (e.g., the Taiwanese military) than in individualistic cultures. In a study conducted in the Taiwanese military, justice perceptions depended upon collective responsibility norms. Perceived collective responsibility had a stronger impact on procedural justice perceptions where collective responsibility norms were strong (Chi, Lo, Tsai, & Niehoff, 2008).

Cultures also differ in what is referred to as *power distance*. A culture's power distance "indicates the extent to which a society accepts the fact that power in institutions and organizations is distributed unequally" (Hofstede, 1980b, p. 45). High power distance reveals a culture's acceptance of inequality and respect for the bounds of social status or class. High power distance is reflected in hierarchical organizational relationships, such that organizational superiors are treated as irreproachable and entitled to their organizational power. By contrast, low power distance cultures minimize inequalities and deemphasize status and class roles (Hofstede, 1980a, 1980b). These differences in attitudes toward authority, power, and status can affect the degree to which an organization member is seen as entitled to levy punishment or liable to receive punishment. They also indicate potential variation in the degree to which punishment decisions may be challenged by organization members. Future research on how punishment in organizations relates to national culture could be extremely helpful to global businesses that are attempting to create human resource practices that can cross national borders or that are at least sensitive to cultural differences.

In summary, empirical research on punishment in organizations has followed the more general transition of social science research away from early-twentieth-century behaviorist models, and toward increasing emphases on cognition, affect, and the complex interactions of individuals with their social context. Although this broader perspective has received empirical attention (e.g., justice-based reactions to punishment) over the past decade, many opportunities remain to expand our understanding.

Bridging Descriptive/Empirical and Normative Perspectives

The recent focus on justice in understanding reactions to punishment offers a bridge between descriptive/empirical approaches and normative/ prescriptive perspectives because a justice approach to punishment indicates that many parties are concerned about the ethics of punishment (what is right), as well as its instrumental outcomes (what works). Ideas about actual and idealized punishment practices have long occupied social theorists and philosophers. We next turn to some of these as a means of further developing theoretical insights, which may inform future research. Attending more consciously to normative issues can bring to light previously ignored assumptions and can open the door to important venues for further research and greater understanding (Weaver & Treviño, 1994). Indeed, recently Cropanzano and Stein (2009) have argued that the primary moral assumption undergirding much organizational justice research is essentially a narrowly focused, self-interested one, reflecting organizational justice research's origins in the self-interested concerns of equity theory. If so, attention to normative theory can help to broaden our perspective of issues relevant to future empirical punishment research. Because our primary interest here is in informing future empirical research, we will not consider how empirical research might inform normative thinking about punishment in organizations. Nevertheless, we acknowledge that empirical and normative theories may mutually inform each other. This clearly has occurred in regard to societal-level questions of punishment (cf., Duff & Garland, 1994; Garland, 1990; Braithwaite & Pettit, 1990).

Management researchers have not explicitly discussed the normative question of what constitutes just punishment in organizations, perhaps assuming that such concerns were more properly the domain of philosophers and social theorists. For example, empirical researchers often seek to evaluate the effectiveness of various modes of punishment in organizations. But against what criteria is effectiveness to be judged? What is the point of punishment in organizations—to achieve managerial goals? What about the goals of labor or of society in general? Although these kinds of questions have been debated often in the context of societal crime and punishment, they are rarely explicitly considered in reference to punishment in organizations.

But normative claims are not entirely alien to descriptive/empirical theories of punishment in organizations, although they are generally assumed rather than openly stated. Consider how the conventional wisdom about punishment in organizations admonished managers not to punish because it wouldn't produce the outcomes they desired—a strictly instrumental rather than justice-oriented rationale. Management researchers were quick to accept this conventional wisdom despite its lack of empirical support in work organizations. This acceptance may have occurred because the prescriptions generated by the conventional wisdom were consistent with the underlying assumptions and accepted management values of the Human Relations movement and its characteristic concern for good relationships between managers and subordinates (see Lawrence, 1987). Prescriptions to avoid punishment and to focus on positive reinforcement were acceptable to management scholars who believed that managers should be engaged in developing their subordinates toward self-actualization. On the other hand, these underlying assumptions and values were not voiced or consciously addressed. In fact, the prescriptions were presented in instrumental terms consistent with a managerial ideology; "avoid punishment because it won't achieve the outcome you desire" not "avoid punishment because it has problematic ethical status" or because it is inconsistent with the normative principles of the human relations movement. If pressed to express their beliefs, researchers in the human relations school may have viewed punishment as highly manipulative and thus unethical, but they did not need to reject punishment as a form of control on ethical grounds. Rather, they could argue against punishment on grounds of "ineffectiveness" without having to face the conflict between their supposed scientific objectivity and their normative beliefs.

Normative/Prescriptive Perspectives on Punishment

Even if the existence of punishment, as a social practice, might be explainable in natural or social scientific terms (e.g., as an evolutionary response to the failure of simple one-on-one reciprocity game strategies when applied to large numbers of actors [Sripada, 2005]), punishment nevertheless raises moral questions. Analyses of the ethics of punishment typically are informed by a number of commonly held moral intuitions: that punishment involves suffering; that punishment is an inappropriate response to involuntary actions for which a person is not responsible; that only offenders should be punished; that punishment should be, in some sense, proportional to the offense; that punishment should occur after an offense (rather than being anticipatory); that successful offenses require more punishment than failed attempts; that the punisher must have appropriate moral standing to apply punishment in the situation at hand (Matravers, 2006); and so on (see, e.g., Rogers, 2007, pp. 85–86). The difficulty in analyzing the ethics of punishment lies in the fact that it is difficult to articulate a single, top-down (Tasioulas, 2006) framework or principle that adequately accounts for all of these common moral intuitions. Yet, at the same time, it is not tenable to simply create a superficial hybrid of different ethical theories and positions without regard for the internal coherence of the hybrid and of the distinct theories we might attempt to force into it (even though textbook treatments of ethics in business, and some efforts to empirically measure ethical behavior (e.g., Reidenbach & Robin, 1990), sometimes appear to suggest that one create just this sort of theoretical mix. Tasioulas (2006, p. 281), following Hampshire (1983, p. 148), refers to this as the "no-shopping" principle with regard to normative theories of punishment.

In what follows we review both historically prominent and more recent moral theories of punishment. We have grouped the normative/prescriptive perspectives on punishment into four general categories—consequentialist, retributive, expressive, and reintegrative/restorative. Although most normative scholarship on punishment has addressed it in the context of societal-level institutions (e.g., punishment for legal crimes), these different stances each suggest important issues and venues for theory and research on punishment in organizations.

Consequentialist Theories of Punishment

Consequentialist theories judge the propriety of punishment in terms of its consequences. Some consequentialist theories focus on particular acts of punishment and their consequences. Others focus on the consequences of a system of, or set of rules for, punishment. In either variant a punishment act or punishment rule is justified if it generates a better set of consequences than any feasible alternative. Consequentialist theories differ in terms of what they judge to be the relevant good consequences. For classical utilitarians (e.g., Bentham, 1789; Mill, 1863), the good consequences to be achieved are defined in terms of societal happiness or welfare (though this idea should *not* be uncritically understood in terms of the popular but imprecise notion of the "greatest good for the greatest number," as utilitarianism confronts a variety of important questions about just how to tally societal welfare). Other consequentialist standards are possible, at least in theory (e.g., acting [or punishing] so as to maximize the number of peanuts in the world *is* a consequentialist standard, although no theorist has been known to hold to that position). In general, consequentialist views are considered forward looking; that is, punishment is justified by its instrumental contribution to some future state of affairs. For example, in popular discussions of punishment, the presumed effectiveness of punishment in incapacitating and/or reforming offenders and deterring others constitutes the consequentialist justification for criminal punishment. But other outcomes could include effects on a larger social entity (e.g., increases in social solidarity) or effects on other individuals (such as emotional satisfaction experienced by a punisher (cf. Cottingham, 1979; Walker, 1999).

As noted previously, early management literature adopted the behaviorist understanding of punishment in organizations. With its emphasis on questions of effective punishment and counterproductive side effects, this approach at least implicitly embodies a consequentialist view of punishment. Punishment is justified, in this view, if it achieves a manager's or an organization's desired outcomes. If the normative rationale for punishment is, as management writings generally assume, to control, change, or deter actions for organizational ends, it is appropriate then for empirical inquiry to focus on the effectiveness of punishment as a means or mechanism of behavioral control, change, or deterrence. But this is a particularly narrow consequentialist view because organizational ends may conflict with the needs of individuals or society (the latter being the focus of utilitarian ethical theory). After all, what is a positive outcome for a particular manager or organization may represent a negative outcome for society as a whole. Therefore, consequentialist theories arguably require a broader perspective on the consequences that matter. A particular manager's need to control a particular subordinate's conduct may pale in comparison with the potential consequences for the work group, the organization, and society. Research that broadens the study of punishment beyond the superior/subordinate dyad, then, is on the right track—although from the standpoint of moral theory, it needs to look beyond other intraorganizational impacts to consider extraorganizational impacts as well. For example, research could consider the consequential role of intraorganizational punishments on the process by which entire organizations restore their legitimacy, in the eyes of outsiders, and reintegrate themselves into the larger organizational environment following some breach of moral or legal standards (Pfarrer et al., 2008).

Criticism of any particular consequentialist view of punishment often focuses on whether or not it in fact is effective in achieving its intended aim. Social science research on the outcomes of punishment in organizations, of the sort discussed earlier in this chapter, is relevant in addressing this question. But consequentialist views of punishment—including, by extension, typical managerial justifications of punishment in terms of its outcomes—face a more significant set of problems that arise regardless of whether particular outcomes are achieved. Critics of consequentialist positions often argue that they take an unjustifiably manipulative approach to people, treating the offender as an object of others' wishes rather than as a subject worthy of respect. In the extreme, critics claim that consequentialism justifies the punishment of innocents for the sake of some good consequence—as in a case wherein one could achieve a desired outcome more efficiently by framing an innocent person than by discovering and punishing the true offender. Not surprisingly, some consequentialist views of punishment therefore limit what may be done for the sake of beneficial consequences (e.g., invoking rules such as that there be no punishment of innocents; Hart, 1968). Such limits sometimes are accused of amounting to arbitrary and ultimately untenable hybrids (Bennett, 2004). Others propose that there is nothing too unusual about innocent suffering as a (regrettable) human condition, and that many nonpunishment decisions we make involve such suffering (Bagaric, 2001). But such defenses of consequentialism are debatable, because normally these other situations of harm to innocents do not involve the direct, intentional harming of innocents (though harm to innocents might be an unintended side effect) (Duff, 1990; Moore, 1997). But even apart from the harm-to-innocents issue, consequentialism is criticized on grounds that the offender is not treated with respect as an agent capable of making moral choices, but rather as an object whose moral choices can be ignored for the sake of producing some consequence judged beneficial by others. In short, a consequentialist view of punishment is not "consistent with respecting each other as moral agents" (Bennett, 2004, p. 325).

In organizational contexts, one might reject these criticisms on the grounds that on joining a work organization, people to some degree surrender claims to be treated as moral subjects rather than as means to organizational ends. However, empirical research discussed earlier suggests that organization members expect fair treatment—importantly including respect as persons rather than as objects—for themselves and others. So, regardless of the outcome of philosophical debates about the propriety of consequentialist punishment, organizations still need to consider their members' nonconsequentialist justice expectations. Although some kinds of justice expectations may be held in abeyance (e.g., it may be fair to distribute some resources within organizations in ways that are unfair outside organizations; it may be fair procedurally for the military to use different means of discipline than are used in civilian life), not all such concerns are left at the door upon entering an organization. Insofar as the "respecting each other as moral agents" criticism of consequentialist views of punishment holds, organizational researchers need to consider carefully the tension between respecting an employee as a moral agent and viewing discipline of that (or any) employee in the consequentialist fashion that undergirds common organizational outlooks. But if we raise questions of nonconsequentialist moral limits on punishment, we open the door to considering other moral justifications for punishment that are independent of concerns for or reactions to consequences. We turn to those views now.

Retributive Theories of Punishment

Historically, the most prominent nonconsequentialist views of punishment are retributive theories. Whereas consequentialist views are essentially forward looking—justifying punishment by future consequences, conventional retributive views typically are backward looking—justifying punishment on the grounds that an offender's past actions warrant a particular punishment regardless of the outcome of that punishment, as when someone argues that convicted murderers simply deserve to die. But what is the basis of this reasoning? There are multiple varieties of retributivism, varying according to how this question is answered (Cottingham, 1979; Walker, 1999). In some varieties, the justification for punishment resides in some ideal of balance or payback in response to a wrong, such that the punishment provides a kind of moral compensation to immoral actions—for example, "when you do undeserved harm to someone you deserve to have harm … inflicted upon you in return" (Rogers, 2007, p. 81; see also Ellis, 1995, Moore, 1997, and Walker, 1999 for descriptions of other versions of this general outlook). In other varieties, the fundamental retributive idea involves compensating for the unfair advantage the wrongdoer appropriates to him- or herself by virtue of the wrongdoing; punishment, in this view, restores a degree of "fair play" (Cottingham, 1979; Murphy, 1973). Intuitive as these positions are in some respects, they leave questions unanswered. Why, for example, is a past event "sufficient justification for the present infliction of suffering?" (Rogers, 2007, p. 81). And the "fair play" argument that punishment reestablishes a level playing field between the offender, who has unilaterally taken on a personal advantage through improper behavior, and other, nonoffending persons presumes that those other persons and the offender in fact all aim at the same goal, or are all engaged in the same activity (with the only difference being that the offender does not "follow the rules"). This is doubtful; at least sometimes offenders clearly have goals radically different from those sought by other persons; they are not all engaged in the same basic activity (Duff, 1986).

Other retributive theorists (e.g., Moore, 1997) address the question of justifying punishment in terms of core ideas of what offenders deserve, where claims that an offender deserves punishment are viewed (for example) as founded in basic moral intuitions, or as arising naturally from a sense of self-blame or guilt. In the latter case, if guilt is understood as an affective state indicating that the guilt holder deserves to be punished, and if we assume an egalitarian stance, then—it is argued—anyone must make a similar judgment about other similarly situated people (Moore, 1997). Alternative emotion-oriented accounts focus on more emotions such as revenge, resentment, or vindictiveness, and treat them as legitimate bases for punishment because these emotions undergird important values such as self-respect and moral order. That is, these punishment-driving emotions reflect an emotional allegiance to what is right (i.e., the emotions embody a moral position; see, e.g., Murphy, 2003). Appeals to basic intuitions and moral emotions as foundations for moral judgment meet with much criticism, however, on grounds that the mere fact that an outlook or attitude is deeply held or emotionally embedded does not make it right. Thus as much as consequentialist views face a serious problem insofar as consequentialist punishment violates moral agency or dignity, retributive views face ongoing difficulty in providing justification for the common intuitions about desert that undergird retribution (see Bennett, 2004, p. 326).

Some social science research seems to parallel the kinds of concerns animating retributive theories of punishment. But appearances can be somewhat deceiving. For example, social justice theorists (Hogan & Emler, 1981) have acknowledged the importance of retributive justice concerns, and their work informed Treviño's (1992) arguments about the importance of observers' justice evaluations of organizational punishment. People in groups are motivated to maintain social cohesion and rule violations threaten that cohesion. Group members desire punishment and believe it is just because, when rules have been violated, punishment serves to reinforce the standards and symbolizes the value of conformity to the rules (Blau, 1964). Punishment also makes an example of the rule violator and contributes to the perception of the organization as a place where people get their just desserts (Lerner, 1977). Failure to punish rule violators leaves the behavioral standards open to question and the social order unbalanced. And so it appears that this social justice/group cohesion approach is about retribution. In a limited sense, this is true, as these theories focus on situations in which people look backward to assign blame, and consider how people think about the relationships among wrongdoing, responsibility, and punishment. But according to these theories, looking backward to assign blame (and punish) serves a forward-looking function—reinforcement of group norms, maintenance of social order and cohesion, and so on. Thus, their concern ultimately is with consequences, even if the consequences are not typically managerial ones.

More in parallel with fundamentally retributive moral theory is recent social science work on moral intuition, moral emotion, and moral identity (e.g., Aquino & Reed, 2002; Blasi, 1984; Haidt, 2001). This research treats moral behavior (such as retributive behavior) as arising in often automatic fashion, and as reflecting deeply ingrained tendencies toward thought and action. It is possible that these kinds of approaches to moral action might put social scientific "flesh" on the conceptual "skeleton" of some retributive theories, which appear, in the end, to appeal to some set of deeply entrenched moral intuitions and emotional stances toward responsibility and punishment. And so there is ample opportunity for a merging of retributive theory's various articulations of moral intuitions and emotions with social scientific accounts of the factors influencing the formation of those intuitions, and their influence on behavior (including individual and organization-level punishment practices).

Mixed Consequentialist/Retributive Theories

It is difficult to defend hybrids of what normally are seen as fundamentally different types of moral theories. But this does not prevent the effort with regard to punishment, especially given that both consequentialist and retributivist views both can point to some fundamentally plausible foundations (respectively, that consequences matter, and that punishment should only be applied to persons who deserve punishment), and to some fundamental problems in the opposing view (i.e., that moral agency and dignity matter, and that judgments of desert need some justification). Often these attempted hybrids involve the imposition of consequentialist constraints on retribution, or vice versa. Thus, that a person deserves punishment might be viewed as a necessary but not sufficient condition for punishment, with consequences being viewed as the basis for determining what kind of punishment to apply in a given situation given that the person deserves some kind of punishment or other. Some of these hybrids are not necessarily as ad hoc as they might appear. For example, Rogers' "mixed" position holds that punishment must be deserved (in keeping with retributivism, although Rogers focuses on bad character in the present rather than specific wrongful actions in the past), but also holds that it is a contingent, consequentially guided judgment as to whether any particular institution (the state, in her case, or an organization, for our purposes) should have standing to impose that punishment. In short, there really are two different decisions, and two different moral judgments, in play in any given punishment situation, and each raises concerns unique to itself. This kind of complexity in turn opens interesting venues of organizational research. Researchers can consider not only retributive questions of which kinds of events are viewed by organization members as warranting punishment, but can also address questions as to which forms and methods of punishment (or nonpunishment) are appropriate from a consequentialist standpoint (e.g., whether frontline managers have standing to punish particular types of offenses).

Another example of a hybrid approach generally is referred to as the *communicative theory of punishment*. In what is probably the most familiar of these, von Hirsch's account (e.g., 1993; summarized succinctly in Bennett, 2004), the view of punishment is developed on the foundation of a particular view of human nature—that people are neither angels nor beasts. Punishment, in this view, provides moral censure, "addresses the understanding of the offender as a moral agent," and "aims to gain her acceptance of her need for punishment, thus treating her as a moral agent who can see the justice of what is done to her" (Bennett, 2004, p. 328). In short, punishment appeals to the "angelic" side of people, and in doing so it is solely communicative in intent, incapable of justifying hard treatment. But we are also beasts whose understanding does not fully control behavior. And thus punishment needs to appeal to that side of humanity by providing prudential reasons for doing what one should. Put differently: "[W]ere we angels—perfect moral agents—the threat element would be unnecessary; were we brutes—entirely lacking in moral agency—the censure would be unnecessary" (Bennett, 2004, p. 329). Thus, the censure and hard treatment aspects of punishment are conceptually distinct, with unique foundations, even though in actual human conditions they are unavoidably concurrent. From the standpoint of empirical research in organizations, this particular approach suggests considerations of the complexities of identity dimensions and their connection to motivation (or lack thereof) as relevant to thinking about punishment. For example, perhaps in dealing with offenders who have an otherwise strong moral identity, censure alone is appropriate and justified, whereas in other cases more onerous forms of punishment are in order. Moreover, it is likely that particular forms of hard treatment might enhance or undermine the goal of communicating censure and appealing to understanding, even if they adequately guide the "beast" in an offender. Thus, it appears that this particular approach to punishment could be well served by attention to how organizational punishments not only influence behavior but also influence cognition.

Expressive Theories of Punishment

The communicative theory mentioned above is related to a larger perspective on punishment often referred to as *expressive theories*. This alternative to the conventional consequentialist/retributivist divide centers on the expressive role of punishment (e.g., Feinberg, 1970). At the individual level, punishment may be seen as an expression of outrage and blame (Tunick, 1992), or an expression of the sense that something wrong has been done (von Hirsch, 1985) and should be denounced (Primoratz, 1989). The general idea is that "punishment is a particularly emphatic way of expressing criticism and some wrongs call for a degree of criticism that can only be expressed by punishment" (Hanna, 2008, p. 128). At the collective level, expressive theories have represented punishment as an expression of a community's solidarity in the face of challenge or threat. This stance is neither traditionally consequentialist nor conventionally retributive; it departs from conventional retributivism because it is concerned with an outcome (e.g., expression of outrage), and because it requires a public response to wrongdoing (whereas pure retribution could be carried out in secret [see Walker, 1999, pp. 602–603]). But it is not typically consequentialist, because it is the punishment act itself that fulfills the cognitive or affective purpose of punishment, rather than some subsequent consequence of punishment distinct from the act itself (Duff & Garland, 1994, p. 8). Expressive theories typically are challenged with regard to their claim that certain types of wrongdoing require criticism by means of punishment rather than criticism by other means; for example, why not just rely on symbolic censure (Hanna, 2008; Tasioulas 2006)? Expressive theorists typically argue that punishment is uniquely capable of expressing certain forms of serious censure or outrage.

For punishment in organizations, expressive theories suggest attention be given to punishment's effects on the affective and cognitive status of persons other than an offender, and also suggest a research agenda focused not on the performance-oriented outcomes of punishment, but on how punishers and observers make sense of a particular incident (Weick, 1979) and their emotional reactions to it. This is similar to the approach taken by Treviño in her emphasis on observers' reactions to punishment and the approach taken by Butterfield and colleagues (Butterfield et al., 1996) in their study of managers' reactions to effective and ineffective punishment incidents. Importantly for organizational settings, however, is the fact that this justification of punishment might have implications for the way punishment is conducted—for example, that punishment involve public forms of censure.

Reintegrative and Restorative Theories of Punishment

Retributive theories often have difficulty handling cases of repentant and reformed wrongdoers who have not been punished for a long-ago misdeed. Once detected, should such persons now be punished, despite their present good character and social contributions? Put differently, standard retributive views seem to be relatively uninterested in the present condition of a past wrongdoer (Rogers, 2007). One response to this is to argue that it is bad character in the present, rather than bad acts at some past time, which deserves punishment (Rogers, 2007). But the problem of reformed but unpunished offenders also points to a very different view of punishment, one that sees social reintegration or restoration as its goal. Thus, some theorists frame their justification of punishment in terms of its penitential and educative role, which in turn reintegrates offenders into a social group (Duff, 1986; Hampton, 1984; Reitan, 1996). If we assume a group of individuals united by some set of values, offenses against those values either create a gulf between the offender and that group, or reflect a preexisting gulf. Punishment can bridge that gulf, restoring individuals to the group by removing the stigma attached to offenders (Reitan, 1995) or by awakening a sense of morality within the offender (Hampton, 1984). When punishment viewed this way is successful, the offender will come to see the punishment as a form of penance (Duff, 1986). Although in a broad sense such views are consequentialist, it is cognitive and affective, rather than behavioral consequences, which are the primary focus of attention. Because reintegrative views often incorporate ideas such as guilt and stigma (i.e., conditions that a person might *deserve* to suffer), they can be viewed as more similar to retributive theories than to consequentialist approaches.

Restorative theories go beyond the question of reintegrating offenders and focus on the general restoration of relationships that were affected by an episode of wrongdoing (e.g., Braithwaite, 1999). Not only are offenders reintegrated into the social group (by acceptance of responsibility, remorse, and penance), but both victims and the larger social unit involved receive some kind of restoration or reestablishment (such as by tangible or intangible restitution, and the restoration of trust within the group). Walker (2006) refers to the entire process as one of "moral repair," which she summarizes as "restoring or creating trust and hope in a shared sense of value and responsibility" (p. 28), such that stable moral relations can again hold.

Reintegrative and restorative theorists acknowledge that conventional punishments in society typically do not achieve penitential, restorative, and reintegrative results, but use this as a basis for proposing reforms (Duff, 1986). They ask whether these results can be achieved by means other than actual punishment (e.g., victim–offender reconciliation programs, or victim support programs). The same issue arises in organizations; reintegration might be more achievable by forgiveness rituals, for example, than by punishment (although forgiveness of an offender might risk violating the justice expectations of other organization members, unless forgiveness norms are embedded in the organizational culture). A modest amount of empirical research has begun to address such alternative perspectives in organizational contexts, primarily with regard to the occurrence of forgiveness in workplace settings (Aquino, Grover, Goldman, & Folger, 2003; Aquino, Tripp, & Bies, 2001, 2006; Bradfield & Aquino, 1999; Tripp, Bies, & Aquino, 2007). Needed, however, is research that examines not just extant situational influences on forgiving and reconciling behavior in organizations, but research that attends to a wide range of organizational, and specifically managerial, processes that might have such restorative outcomes. Goodstein and Butterfield (2009), reviewing the concept of restorative justice, suggest multiple respects in which this idea is relevant to, and can redirect, organizational research: (a) multilevel research on the "aftermath of unethical behavior" rather than simply the causes of unethical behavior, (b) research on "righting wrongs" and moral repair processes, (c) reconceptualizing incidents of unethical behavior as restorative failures, (d) attention to processes of redemption and reintegration, and (e) the role of entire social units in the process of restoration. This last concern, in turn, has the potential to spread the initial research question of within-organization restoration processes beyond organizational boundaries, because the behavior and attitudes of external actors can be crucial, in some cases, for the legitimacy and effectiveness of practices adopted within organizations.

Alternatives to Punishment, and Alternative Roles of Punishment

Restorative justice theory and this general review of normative theories of punishment, point toward a larger range of questions concerning punishment in organizations: can morally proper practices and outcomes be achieved by means other than conventional punishments? What alternative practices might exist for expressing societal or within-organization disapproval of certain actions? Is punishment even appropriate in organizations, or should consideration be given to an abolitionist position (as sometimes is argued with regard to societal-level punishment)? After all, existing punishment practices might embody latent organizational roles removed from their manifest "official" rationale. Rusche and Kirchheimer (1939), for example, argue that criminal punishment practices reflect labor market conditions; regimes of punishment constitute means for economic systems to adjust to changing economic conditions as they affect the relative supply of labor and employment. Punishment might also function to divert attention from issues over which key actors in a society or organization are powerless (Matheisen, 1974). We might think similarly about organizational punishment practices. In the manner of *scapegoating*, punishment could constitute a kind of symbolic management, which might reassure organizational members and constituents that something is being done about an organizational problem regardless of whether it is effectively being resolved (Pfeffer, 1981). Punishment also might serve to reinforce existing distinctions of power and status within organizations, given that even less overtly punitive organizational practices (e.g., "soft bureaucracy") can represent various forms of political interest and power centers in organizations (Robertson & Swan, 2004). Along these lines, future research should consider the more latent roles potentially played by punishment in organizations.

Conclusion

Research on punishment in organizations has advanced significantly in recent years through attention to justice cognitions and the broader social context within which punishment occurs. Our analysis of the descriptive/empirical research suggests that this work needs to expand even more to include more affective considerations, macro-organizational issues (e.g., organizational culture, technology), and even extraorganizational issues (e.g., national culture, interorganizational fields).

In addition, we took the opportunity to consider a number of normative perspectives on punishment and to consider how they might inform descriptive/empirical work. A number of ideas emerged. A focus on consequentialist theories suggested the need to consider a broader set of consequences than has been considered in the past and the need to understand more deeply the kinds of justice expectations organization members hold. Retributive theories led to a whole set of research questions about observers' reactions to punishment, responsibility attributions, and how observers think about the appropriate match between offenses and punishments (Treviño, 1992). Expressive theories focused attention on affect, in particular the affect of the punisher, which has only begun to be studied empirically (Butterfield, Treviño, & Ball, 1996). Reintegrative reform theories pointed to concerns that have not been addressed in organizational research as far as we know. They suggested particularly interesting research questions about what punishment practices might work best if reintegration were the goal. Finally, the normative literature suggests that we should also consider alternatives to punishment and the latent roles punishment may play in organizations.

Taken together, all of these theories and perspectives on punishment indicate that punishment in organizations remains an active and important area of study, with much remaining in the way of interesting questions, potential synergies, and new perspectives arising from the juxtaposition of different perspectives. At the same time, the most interesting, valuable, and productive new directions for the future might prove the most difficult to follow, insofar as they would require scholars to step out of the conventional boundaries of particular (and comfortable) theories or disciplines, so that they conduct their research in ways informed by both descriptive and normative insights.

References

Alexander, S., & Ruderman, M. (1987). The role of procedural and distributive justice in organizational behavior. *Social justice research, 1*, 177–198.

Aquino, K., & Reed, A., II. (2002). The self-importance of moral identity. *Journal of Personality and Social Psychology, 83*, 1423–1440.

Aquino, K., Grover, S. L., Goldman, B., & Folger, R. (2003). When push doesn't come to shove: Interpersonal forgiveness in workplace relationships. *Journal of Management Inquiry, 12*, 209–216.

Aquino, K., Tripp, T. M., & Bies, R. J. (2001). How employees respond to personal offense: The effects of victim and offender status on revenge and reconciliation in the workplace. *Journal of Applied Psychology, 86*, 52–59.

Aquino, K., Tripp, T. M., & Bies, R. J. (2006). Getting even or moving on: Power, procedural justice, and types of offense as predictors of revenge, forgiveness, reconciliation, and avoidance in organizations. *Journal of Applied Psychology, 91*, 653–668.

Arvey, R. D., & Ivancevich, J. M. (1980). Punishment in organizations: A review, propositions, and research suggestions. *Academy of Management Review, 5*, 123–132.

Arvey, R. D. & Jones, A. P. (1985). The use of discipline in organizational settings: A framework for future research. In B. Staw & L.L. Cummings (Eds.), *Research in organizational behavior* (volume 7, pp. 367–408). Greenwich, CT: JAI Press.

Atwater, L. E., Camobreco, J. F., Dionne, S. D., Avolio, B. J., & Lau, A. N. (1997). Effects of rewards and punishments on leader charisma, leader effectiveness and follower reactions. *Leadership Quarterly, 8*, 133–152.

Atwater, L. E., Waldman, D. A., Carey, J. A., & Cartier, P. (2001). Recipient and observer reactions to discipline: Are managers experiencing wishful thinking? *Journal of Organizational Behavior, 22*, 249–270.

Atwater, L. E.., Waldman, Carey, J. A., & Waldman, D. A. (2001). Gender and discipline in the workplace: Wait until your father gets home. *Journal of Management, 27*, 537–561.

Bagaric, M. (2001). *Punishment and sentencing: A rational approach.* London: Cavendish Publishing.

Ball, G. A., & Sims, H. P., Jr. (1991). A conceptual analysis of cognition and affect in organizational punishment. *Human Resource Management Review, 1*, 227–243.

Ball, G. A., Treviño, L. K., & Sims, H. P., Jr. (1992). Understanding subordinate reactions to punishment incidents: Perspectives from justice and social affect. *Leadership Quarterly, 3*(4), 307–333.

Ball, G. A., Treviño, L. K., & Sims, H. P., Jr. (1993). Justice and organizational punishment: Attitudinal outcomes of disciplinary events. *Social Justice Research*, 6(1), 39–67.

Ball, G. A., Treviño, L. K., & Sims, H. P., Jr. (1994). Just and unjust punishment: Influences on subordinate performance and citizenship. *Academy of Management Journal*, 37(2), 299–322.

Baron, R. A. (1988). Negative effects of destructive criticism: Impact on conflict, self-efficacy, and task performance. *Journal of Applied Psychology*, 73, 199–207.

Barsade, S. G., & Gibson, D. E. (2007). Why does affect matter in organizations? *Academy of Management Perspectives*, 21, 36–59.

Bennett, C. (2004). Punishment. *Philosophical Books*, 45, 324–334.

Bennett, R. J. (1998). Taking the sting out of the whip: Reactions to consistent punishment for unethical behavior. *Journal of Experimental Psychology: Applied*, 4, 248–262.

Bentham, J. (1789/1970). *An introduction to the principles of morals and legislation*, J. H. Burns & H. L. A. Hart, (Eds.). London: Methuen.

Bies, R. J. (1986). The predicament of injustice. In B.M. Staw & L.L. Cummings (Eds.), *Research in organizational behavior* (volume 9, pp. 290–318). Greenwich, CT: JAB Press.

Bies, R. J., & Moag, J. S. (1986). Interactional justice: Communications criteria of fairness. In R. J. Lewicki, B. H. Sheppard, and M. H. Bazerman (Eds.), *Research on negotiations in organizations* (volume 1, pp. 43–55). Greenwich, CT: JAI Press.

Blasi, A. (1984). Moral identity: Its role in moral functioning. In W. Kurtines & J. Gewirtz (Eds.), *Morality, moral behavior and moral development* (pp. 128–139). New York: Wiley.

Blau, P. M. (1964). *Exchange and power in social life*. New York: Wiley.

Bontempo, R., Lobel, S., and Triandis, H. (1990). Compliance and value internalization in Brazil and the U.S. *Journal of Cross-Cultural Psychology*, 21, 200–213.

Bradfield, M., & Aquino, K. (1999). The effects of blame attributions and offender likableness on revenge and forgiveness in the workplace. *Journal of Management*, 25, 607–631.

Braithwaite, J. (1999). Restorative justice: Assessing optimistic and pessimistic accounts. *Crime and Justice*, 25, 1–127.

Braithwaite, J., & Pettit, P. (1990). *Not just desserts: A republican theory of criminal justice*. Oxford: Oxford University Press.

Brett, J. F., Atwater, L. E., & Waldman, D. A. (2005). Effective delivery of workplace discipline. *Group and Organization Management*, 30, 487–511.

Brockner, J., Grover, S., Reed, R., DeWitt, R. L., & O'Malley, M. (1987). Survivors' reactions to layoffs: We get by with a little help for our friends. *Administrative Science Quarterly*, 32, 526–541.

Brockner, J., DeWitt, R. L., Grover, S., & Reed, T. (1990). When it is especially important to explain why: Factors affecting the relationship between managers' explanations of a layoff and survivors' reactions to the layoff. *Journal of Experimental Social Psychology*, 26, 389–407.

Butterfield, K. D., Treviño, L. K., & Ball, G. A. (1996). Punishment from the manager's perspective: A grounded investigation and inductive model. *Academy of Management Journal*, 39,1479–1512.

Chi, S. S., & Lo, H. (2003). Taiwanese employees' justice perceptions of co-workers' punitive events. *Journal of Social Psychology, 143,* 27–42.

Chi, S. S., Lo, H., Tsai, M., & Niehoff, B. P. (2008). Bystanders' reactions towards co-punishment events in the Taiwanese military: Examining the moderating effects of organizational norms. *Asian Journal of Social Psychology, 11,* 274–278.

Cole, N. D. (2004). Gender differences in perceived disciplinary fairness. *Gender, Work, and Organization, 11,* 254–279.

Cole, N. D. (2008) Consistency in employee discipline: An empirical exploration. *Personnel Review, 37,* 109–117.

Cole, N. D., & Latham, G. P. (1997). Effects of training in procedural justice on perceptions of disciplinary fairness by unionized employees and disciplinary subject matter experts. *Journal of Applied Psychology, 82,* 699–705.

Cottingham, J. (1979). Varieties of retribution. *Philosophical Quarterly, 29,* 238–246.

Cropanzano, R., & Stein, J. H. (2009). Organizational justice and behavioral ethics: Promises and prospects. *Business Ethics Quarterly, 19,* 193–234.

Duff, R. A. (1986). *Trials and punishments.* Cambridge: Cambridge University Press.

Duff, R. A. (1990). *Intention, agency, and criminal liability: Philosophy of action and the criminal law.* London: Blackwell.

Duff, R. A., & Garland, D. (1994). Introduction: Thinking about punishment. In R. A. Duff & D. Garland, (Eds.), *A reader on punishment* (pp. 1–143). Oxford: Oxford University Press.

Ellis, A. (1995). Recent work on punishment. *Philosophical Quarterly, 45,* 225–233.

Fehr, E. (2004). Don't lose your reputation. *Nature, 25,* 449–450.

Feinberg, J. (1970). The expressive function of punishment. In J. Feinberg, *Doing and deserving: Essays in the theory of responsibility* (pp. 95–118). Princeton, NJ: Princeton University Press.

Fortado. B. (1994). Informal supervisory social control strategies. *Journal of Management Studies, 31*(2), 251–274.

Garland, D. (1990). *Punishment and modern society.* Chicago, IL: University of Chicago Press.

Goodstein, J., & Butterfield, K. (2009). *Extending the horizon of business ethics: Restorative justice and the aftermath of unethical behavior.* Working paper.

Grey, C. (1994). Careeer as a project of the self and labor process discipline. *Sociology, 28,* 479–498.

Haidt, J. (2001). The emotional dog and its rational tail: A social intuitionist approach to moral judgment. *Psychological Review, 108,* 814–834.

Hampshire, S. (1983). *Morality and conflict.* London: Blackwell.

Hampton, J. (1984). The moral education theory of punishment. *Philosophy and Public Affairs, 13,* 208–238.

Hanna, N. (2008). Say what? A critique of expressive retributivism. *Law and Philosophy, 27,* 123–150.

Hart, H. L. A. (1968). Prolegomenon to the principles of punishment. In H. L. A. Hart, *Punishment and responsibility,* (pp. 1–27). Oxford: Oxford University Press.

Hofstede, G. (1980a). *Culture's consequences: International differences in work-related values.* Beverly Hills, CA: Sage.

Hofstede, G. (summer 1980b). Motivation, leadership and organization: Do American theories apply abroad? *Organizational Dynamics, 9,* 42–63.

Hogan, R., & Emler, N. P. (1981). Retributive justice. In M. J. Lerner and S. C. Lerner (Eds.), *The justice motive in social behavior: Adapting to times of scarcity and change* (pp. 125–143). New York: Plenum Press.

Klaas, B. S., & Dell'omo, G. G. (1997). Managerial use of dismissal: Organizational-level determinants. *Personnel Psychology, 50,* 927–954.

Lawrence, P. (1987). Historical development of organizational behavior. In J. Lorsch (Ed.) *Handbook of organizational behavior* (pp. 1–9). Englewood Cliffs, NJ: Prentice-Hall.

Lerner, M. J. (1977). The justice motive: Some hypotheses as to its origins and forms. *Journal of Personality, 45,* 1–52.

Liden, R. C., Wayne, S. J., Judge, T. A., Sparrowe, R. T., Kraimer, M. L., & Feranz, T. M. (1999). Management of poor performance: A comparison of manager, group member, and group disciplinary decisions. *Journal of Applied Psychology, 84,* 835–850.

Luthans, F., & Kreitner, R. (1985). *Organizational behavior modification and beyond.* Glenview, IL: Scott, Foresman.

Mathiesen, T. (1974). *The politics of abolition.* New York: Wiley.

Matravers, M. (2006). "Who's still standing?" A comment on Antony Duff's preconditions of criminal liability. *Journal of Moral Philosophy, 3,* 320–330.

Mill, J. S. (1863/2002). *Utilitarianism.* Indianapolis, IN: Hackett.

Moore, M. S. (1997). *Placing blame: A theory of criminal law.* Oxford: Oxford University Press.

Murphy, J. G. (1973). Marxism and retribution. *Philosophy and Public Affairs, 2,* 217–243.

Murphy, J. G. (2003). *Getting even: Forgiveness and its limits.* Oxford: Oxford University Press.

Newman, G. (1985). *The punishment response.* New York: Harrow & Heston.

Niehoff, B. P., Paul, R. J., & Bunch, J. F. S. (1998). The social effects of punishment events: The influence of violator past performance record and severity of the punishment on observers' justice perceptions and attitudes. *Journal of Organizational Behavior, 19,* 589–602.

O'Reilly, C. A., III, & Puffer, S. M. (1989). The impact of rewards and punishments in a social context: A laboratory and field experiment. *Journal of Occupational Psychology, 62,* 41–53.

O'Reilly, C. A., III, & Weitz, B. A. (1980). Managing marginal employees: The use of warnings and dismissals. *Administrative Science Quarterly, 25,* 467–483.

Ouchi, W. G. (1980). Markets, bureaucracies and clans. *Administrative Science Quarterly, 25,* 129–141.

Pfeffer, J. (1981). Management as symbolic action. *Research in Organizational Behavior, 3,* 1–52.

Pfarrer, M. D., DeCelles, K. A., Smith, K. G., & Taylor, M. S. (2008). After the fall: Reintegrating the corrupt organization. *Academy of Management Review, 33,* 730–749.

Podsakoff, P. M., Bommer, W. H., Posdakoff, N. P., & MacKenzie, S. B. (2006). Relationships between leader reward and punishment behavior and subordinate attitudes, perceptions, and behaviors: A meta-analytic review of existing and new research. *Organizational Behavior and Human Decision Processes, 99,* 113–142.

Primoratz, I. (1989). *Justifying legal punishment*. Atlantic Highlands, NJ: Humanities Press.

Reidenbach, R. P., & Robin, D. E. (1990). Toward the development of a multidimensional scale for improving evaluations of business ethics. *Journal of Business Ethics, 9*, 639–653.

Reitan, E. (1996). Punishment and community: The reintegrative theory of punishment. *Canadian Journal of Philosophy, 26*, 57–82.

Robertson, M., & Swan, J. (2004). Going public: The emergence and effects of soft bureaucracy within a knowledge-intensive firm. *Organization, 11*, 123–148.

Rogers, K. A. (2007). Retribution, forgiveness, and the character creation theory of punishment. *Social Theory and Practice, 33*, 75–103.

Rusche, G., & Kirchheimer, O. (1939). *Punishment and social structure*. New York: Columbia University Press.

Schnake, M. E. (1986). Vicarious punishment in a work setting. *Journal of Applied Psychology, 71*, 343–345.

Skinner, B. F. (1953). *Science and human behavior*. New York: Macmillan.

Solomon, R. L. (1964). Punishment. *American Psychologist, 19*(4), 239–252.

Sripada, C. S. (2005). Punishment and the strategic structure of moral systems. *Biology and Philosophy, 20*, 767–789.

Tasioulas, J. (2006). Punishment and repentance. *Philosophy, 81*, 279–322.

Thau, S., Aquino, K., & Bommer, W. H. (2008). How employee race moderates the relationship between non-contingent punishment and organizational citizenship behaviors: A test of the negative adaptation hypothesis. *Social Justice Research, 21*, 297–312.

Treviño, L. K. (1992). The social effects of punishment in organizations: A justice perspective. *Academy of Management Review, 17*(4), 647–676.

Treviño, L. K., & Ball, G. A. (1992). The social implications of punishing unethical behavior: Observers' cognitive and affective reactions. *Journal of Management, 18*(4), 751–768.

Triandis, H. C. (1984). A theoretical framework for the more efficient construction of culture assimilators. *International Journal of Intercultural Relations, 8*, 301–330.

Triandis, H. C. (1989). The self and social behavior in differing cultural contexts. *Psychological Review, 96*, 506–520.

Triandis, H. C., Brislin, R., & Hui, C. H. (1988). Cross-cultural training across the individualism-collectivism divide. *International Journal of Intercultural Relations, 12*, 269–289.

Tripp, T. M., Bies, R. J., & Aquino, K. (2007). A vigilante model of justice: Revenge, reconciliation, forgiveness, and avoidance. *Social Justice Research, 20*, 10–34.

Trubinsky, P., Ting-Toomey, S., and Lin, S. (1991). The influence of individualism-collectivism and self-monitoring on conflict styles. *International Journal of Intercultural Relations, 15*, 65–84.

Tunick, M. (1992). *Punishment: Theory and practice*. Berkeley: University of California Press.

von Hirsch, A. (1985). *Past or future crimes: Deservedness and dangerousness in the sentencing of criminals*. New Brunswick, NJ: Rutgers University Press.

von Hirsch, A. (1993). *Censure and sanctions*. Cambridge: Cambridge University Press.

Weaver, G. R., & Treviño, L. K. (1994). Normative and empirical business ethics: Separation, marriage of convenience, or marriage of necessity? *Business Ethics Quarterly, 4*, 129–143.

Walker, M. U. (2006). *Moral repair: Reconstructing moral relations after wrongdoing.* Cambridge: Cambridge University Press.

Walker, N. (1999). Even more varieties of retribution. *Philosophy, 74*, 595–605.

Warren, D. E., & Smith-Crowe, K. (2008). Deciding what's right: The role of external sanctions and embarrassment in shaping moral judgments in the workplace. In A. P. Brief & B. M. Staw (Eds.), *Research in organizational behavior* (volume 28, pp. 81–105). Amsterdam: Elsevier.

Weick, K. (1979). *The social psychology of organizing.* New York: Random House.

Section III

New Theoretical Perspectives

10

Social Hierarchies and the Evolution of Moral Emotions

Robert Folger
University of Central Florida
Russell Cropanzano
University of Arizona

The condition of man ... is a condition of war of everyone against everyone.

—**Thomas Hobbes,** *Leviathan* **(1651, Part I, Chapter 4)**

The strongest is never strong enough to be always the master, unless he transforms his strength into right, and obedience into duty.

—**Jean-Jacques Rousseau,** *Du Contrat Social* **(1762, Part I, Chapter 1)**

This chapter analyzes how the sentiments known as moral emotions relate to a sense of ethical obligation. In recent years scholars have begun to place great emphasis on the role of emotion in behavioral ethics. This research has taken two broad perspectives, analyzing both the impact of emotion on individual moral judgments (e.g., Connolly & Hardman, 2009; Haidt, 2006; Shweder & Haidt, 1993), and the enforcement of moral norms (e.g., Ketelaar, 2006; Pillutla & Murnighan, 1996). Historically, these kinds of questions have tended to be posed at the level of individual psychology (cf., see Cropanzano, Stein, & Goldman, 2007; Folger & Salvador, 2008; Skitka, 2003). There is also, however, a long philosophical tradition of asking about the social group. In his *Politics,* Aristotle (350 b.c.e.) famously asserted that "man is by nature a political animal." Most researchers agree with Aristotle's view, in the sense of accepting that human beings are biologically and emotionally built for social living (e.g., Cacioppo & Patrick, 2008; Goleman, 2006) and that this influences our sense of what of is moral (Gazzaniga, 2008). Our analysis of this issue is organized around a question asked by Boehm (1999, p. 1): "Are we by nature hierarchical or egalitarian?" These group-level questions have sparked answers ranging between the polar extremes indicated by our opening quotes from Thomas Hobbes (1651) and Jean-Jacques Rousseau (1762).

As is true for questions of individual moral motivation, it is a mistake to treat this as dichotomous either/or options (cf. Skitka, 2003, 2009). Rather, there seems to be a continuum that at one end pushes us to dominate others, whereas at the opposite end we are encouraged to acquiesce to others' desires. Life is a mixed-motive game, and both situational and dispositional factors can push us one way or the other (Hamburger, 1979). For example, depending upon the particular facets of an interactive decision, people might be prone to compete or cooperate (Miller, 2003). Likewise, there seem to be variations in personality that predict how individuals treat others (e.g., social value orientations; cf. Van Lange & Kuhlman, 1994). Hence, there seems to be some variation within particular individuals and also across situations. Even a cursory look at human social life indicates that we are both hierarchical and egalitarian animals. A comprehensive understanding requires that we take these often competing, but sometimes complementary, orientations into account (Fiske, 1991).

Addressing moral emotions in the context of social hierarchies will be the topic of this chapter. We address such questions from the perspective of Boehm's (1989, 1999, 2000) *ambivalence-compromise* model ("Potentially we are all both doves and hawks," says Boehm, 1999, p. 227). That model emphasizes certain human predilections constituted by our evolutionary history—the poles of the kinds of continua we mentioned above. But the model goes beyond this, also paying special attention to the human capacity for behavioral liability that allows for variations along those continua individually and as a function of the circumstances.

We can begin with the observation that human social groups contain both "haves" and "have-nots." Power, prestige, and status can be rank-ordered along a dimension of better-off to worse-off. Some people will always be bigger and stronger than others. Some will be smarter, more creative, and so on. Moreover, a human capacity to perceive hierarchical differentiation is probably universal (Fiske, 1991), even though responses to such differentiation may vary. We follow Boehm's lead by focusing on variations in the ways that social hierarchies can function.

As noted above, the emphasis we place on hierarchy, however, stems from our interest in addressing another set of questions as well. In fact, these questions will constitute the focal point of our analysis. Why are moral norms associated with some emotions (e.g., varieties of outrage) and not others? What functional role has moral sentiment played in evolutionary survival that can be differentiated from the functional role played by other emotions? In this chapter we address such questions in the context of a theory of deonance (Folger, 1994, 1998, 2001; Folger & Salvador, 2008), which takes its name from the Greek word for duty (*deon*) and emphasizes the role of moral obligations in social life. We integrate Boehm's (1989, 1999, 2000) model of hierarchy with Folger's concept of deonance by analyzing how certain categories of emotions relate to the perceived moral dictates of social life in its various hierarchical forms.

Social Hierarchy and Human Dispositions

The *ambivalence-compromise* model of hierarchy (Boehm, 1999) portrays the social life of humans as reflecting a dynamic tension between a tendency to dominate and a tendency to submit. As a consequence, we reach semistable social equilibrium through ambivalent-compromises. A *compromise*, of course, refers to a sort of satisfying settlement that is acceptable but not necessarily fully optimal to all parties involved (Friedman, Tidd, Currall, & Tsai, 2000; Pruitt, 1983; Pruitt & Carnevale, 1993). It is likely to be *ambivalent*, in the sense that the parties to the settlement will have some reservations and concerns about the agreement. They will likely show at least some caution. As Boehm (1999, p. 149) summarizes the matter:

> I suggest that the views of Rousseau and Hobbes may reflect human nature quite accurately—but only if we combine their contradictory viewpoints, rather than allowing them to compete. Humans do seem to enjoy autonomy and serenity. At the same time, they seem to have a competitive penchant for domination that leads to conflict and creates a need for governance. Natural selection is the agency responsible for both facets, so we must look to the evolutionary basis of our political nature if we are to understand these opposing tendencies.

We shall develop these ideas in the two sections that follow. First, we shall take a historical perspective, analyzing how the dynamics of this ambivalence have manifested themselves in the social structure of human groups. Next, we shall provide a more focused analysis, describing the evolution of these opposing tendencies.

Orthodox and Reverse-Dominance Hierarchies

In developing his analysis, Boehm (1999, 2000) distinguished between two types of hierarchies—*orthodox* and *reverse-dominance*. An *orthodox* hierarchy is an extreme hierarchical form known as a strict "pecking order," which is common in a variety of species. A somewhat less extreme version exists in the chain-of-command structure of the military or in highly centralized, mechanistic organizations. Orthodox hierarchies thus display fairly clear differentiations of rank and the type of social order in which those at lower ranks tend to defer to those at the higher ranks. A *reverse-dominance* hierarchy, on the other hand, exists when a cabal of "weaker" members organizes itself so as to upset the rule of the alpha animal. In a reverse-dominance hierarchy the weaker, acting as a team, have more power than the stronger. Hence, "all human societies involve some kind of political hierarchy, whether reversed or orthodox … with either the rank and file or the despot in question winning out" (Boehm, 1999, p. 237). The same human attributes can produce quite distinct social arrangements. This historical appearance of each hierarchy can be diagramed as a sort of "U" (Knauft, 1991), with the orthodox hierarchy emerging at each end and the reverse-dominance hierarchy manifesting itself in the trough.

At the earliest times in our prehistory, our primate progenitors and postneolithic humans in chiefdoms lived under the conditions of a rather orthodox hierarchy. Although orthodox hierarchies were common in such circumstances, our ancestors would have had the latent ability to transcend them. For example, our close cousins, the modern chimpanzees, show that coalitions of the weak can form alliances that displace the strong (Van Lawick-Goodall, 1971). In other words, our progenitors began as social groups with high power distance but with the cognitive architecture to at least partially blunt the abuse of power by dominant animals (de Waal, 1996).

As our progenitors became hunter gatherers, the hierarchy began to change. Conventions among hunter gatherers tended to blunt the expression of this autocratic tendency, producing highly egalitarian (for *Homo sapiens)* collectives (e.g., Berry, 1967, 1979). These successful coalitions-of-the-weak created *reverse-dominance* hierarchies. Boehm (1999, 2000) argued that when nomadic hunter-gatherers coped with the living conditions prevalent during Paleolithic times they found it adaptive to operate as relatively egalitarian, cohesive bands (Berry, 1967, 1979; Thomas, 2006). This in turn required the group as a whole to be "dominant" over any given individual, especially those who might otherwise seek to impose their will on the majority. Notice that there is still a sort of hierarchy, but one in which the majority rules over the autocrat.

Later, when agricultural settlements were established, hierarchy began to reassert itself. Boehm also noted how this description constituted an interesting puzzle: What could account for the shift from autocracy toward egalitarianism and back to autocracy again? Boehm's approach to the enigma involved acknowledging that "We always live with *some* type of hierarchy" (1999, p. 237), but that any given social structure represents a compromise between polar opposites on a hierarchical continuum. Boehm (1999, p. 65) summarized the matter as follows:

> The curve began with strong degrees of despotism [such as seen in the African great apes and the common ancestor they shared with

humans] ... then dipped to represent a protracted period of hunter-
gatherer egalitarianism [which Boehm identifies chiefly with the
Paleolithic era]. Not too long after the domestication of plants and
animals [begun during the Neolithic], the curve climbed steeply to
encompass not only hierarchical chiefdoms, but eventually civiliza-
tions and nations.

Human social life is hierarchical and has always been hierarchical.
However, this simple statement misses an important point—there are at
least two different types of hierarchies—orthodox and reverse-dominance.
These produce very different living arrangements, although people seem
to have managed comfortably and for a long time with each. We shall now
consider how these seemingly conflicting tendencies have come about.

Evolutionary Reasons for Our Social Hierarchies

Boehm (1989, 2000) argued that variations in the nature of social hierarchies are best understood by taking into account some fundamental predispositions laid down as part of the evolutionary history of a species.
Contributions to the gene pool obviously come only from organisms that
survive and reproduce (Wood, 2005; Wade, 2006). Selective pressures in
the environment dictate at least some degree of competition over scarce
resources (for survival) and mating opportunities (for reproductive success) (Miller & Kanazawa, 2007). It seems reasonable, therefore, to assume
the existence of a major human tendency as involving *dispositions to dominance* as one component of our nature (Boehm, 1999, p. 234).

Consider the consequences that would accrue if status rivalries were to
escalate to the point of a Hobbesian war of all against all. As Hobbes (1651)
noted, the result would be "continual fear, and danger of violent death: and
the life of man, solitary, poor, nasty, brutish and short" (Hobbes, Ch. 12).
Homo sapiens need to blunt a predilection for runaway competition (Wade,
2006) and build cooperation (Shermer, 2008; Wright, 1994); otherwise our
species could not survive. One solution to this problem can be seen in
the ways that conflicts are sometimes resolved when animals compete for
dominance: Once defeat seems likely, the weaker displays signs of submissiveness to the stronger, and the fight ceases. This has a major adaptive
advantage because even the victor in such a contest might sustain lethal
injuries if it were to continue to the bitter end. It seems likely, therefore,
that the pressures of natural selection would also have provided humans
with *submissive dispositions* (Boehm, 1999, p. 235).

Carried to the extreme, such submissiveness might create risks for
both the group and the individual. For those individuals who are overly
compliant, there is a risk that none of their needs will ever be met, and
that they will find themselves subject to the most severe of reproductive

disadvantages. Human beings have a submissive tendency to defer to authority, but if this predilection were unchecked, our species would not have long endured. Indeed, postulating the existence of dispositions to be dominant over others implies its complement, namely a *disposition to dislike domination* (Boehm 1999, p. 234). The overall result among human beings, therefore, is a "triadic pull between dominance, resentment of domination [i.e., a desire for autonomy], and submission" (Boehm, p. 242). In the case of the reverse-dominance hierarchies of hunter-gatherers, the resentment of domination simply resulted in a kind of "majority rule" that kept would-be dominants in line (Thomas, 2006).

Order Despite Tension: The Role of Moral Obligation

We argue that moral norms play a key role in allowing coordinated activities within human groups despite the tensions of a triadic pull regarding dominance, dislike of dominance, and submission (Wilson, 1993). In essence we argue that norms of moral obligation occupy a symbolically dominant position in a psychic hierarchy that operates in conjunction with the status differentiations of a social group. Moral rules, metaphorically speaking, function in much the same way as leaders or rulers. In an orthodox hierarchy they act to support the ruler's (or ruling class's) dominance by legitimizing authority and submission to it. In the egalitarian social order of a reverse-dominance hierarchy, would-be rulers—or even those who happen to be more advantaged relative to others—become subject to the demands of moral obligation. An example of the latter situation is the moral obligation known as *noblesse oblige*, or the norm of sharing generously and caring for the needy by virtue of one's own more abundant resources (a norm that tends to encourage a more egalitarian distribution of goods).

To illustrate how moral norms can be fitted into a human hierarchy, it is worthwhile to consider Heider's (1958) chapter on "Ought and Value," originally appearing in *The Psychology of Interpersonal Relations*. Heider (p. 219) wrote that "In the case of ought ... it is not a particular somebody that is felt to want or command people to do *x*, but some suprapersonal objective order." Note in that passage the idea of an "order" characterized as having a *supra*personal quality, such that its status is "above" that of the status possessed by any given person. We suggest, therefore, that a moral obligation in effect occupies a position of high status or dominance, and that people who internalize its value will subordinate themselves to it.

We thus see a connection between Boehm's (1999) ideas about social hierarchies and Folger's theory of deonance (1994, 1998, 2001; Folger & Salvador, 2008), which is about the psychology of moral obligation. To examine this connection, we propose a conceptual alignment between the orthodox/reversed distinction and a distinction about moral obligations made by Immanuel Kant (1797/1991), namely between what he called *perfect* duties and those he called *imperfect*. As we see it, the former align with the kinds of norms that would help hold together the social order of an orthodox hierarchy, whereas the latter align with norms more characteristic of reverse-dominance hierarchies. Given the "triadic pull," both types of duties should be commonly observed.

To make our case, we proceed in the following fashion. First, we say a bit more about the role of morality as a means of striking a balance among the competing tendencies of dominance assertion, subordination acceptance, and autonomy maintenance (resistance to domination). In that vein we elaborate on what it means for cultures to be characterized by various moral norms. Next, we provide some exegesis on Kant's perfect/imperfect distinction. Finally, we devote separate sections to addressing how perfect duties act in a fashion analogous to the role of traditional rulers in orthodox hierarchies, whereas imperfect duties function in ways consistent with the egalitarian tendencies seen in reverse-dominance hierarchies.

Moral Norms

Reproductive fitness can be maximized when the three opposing forces are in dynamic equilibrium. The problem, of course, is that a dynamic equilibrium is inherently unstable. Keeping it relatively stable, therefore, requires a certain amount of effort and skill. Maintaining a stable hierarchy is more than an interpsychic problem. In fact, it invariably leads to actual conflicts, as one person or coalition tries to assert itself at the expense of others. How did our ancestors, and how do we ourselves, manage this terrain?

Different societies establish moral rules that balance the expression of the three aforementioned predispositions. The cultural standards themselves are not identical, of course, and a good deal of variation exists (cf. Moghaddam, Taylor, & Wright, 1993; Smith & Bond, 1994). *Homo sapiens* do not have rigid genetic programming. Rather, we are predisposed to learn moral rules from others in our societies (e.g., Wilson, 1993; Wright, 1994). This influence is especially strong when we are growing up (Pinker, 2002). There is good evidence for this. Acceptance of moral sentiments is a cultural universal, found throughout the world (Brown, 1991; Shermer, 2008). These tend to emerge early in childhood (Skitka, Bauman, & Mullen, 2008), and even our close primate relatives have a rudimentary sense of justice (Brosnan, 2006). Learning morality, in other words, is akin to learning language (Mikhail, 2009). We are predisposed to learn language but are flexible as to the specific content. Many different languages exist, but all human cultures have at least one. This is not to say that our morality is infinitely pliable. There seem to be some norms that are more easily internalized than others. For example, *Homo sapiens* appear to have an inborn taboo against incest (Haidt, 2006). In any case, all cultures will need some sort of moral norms that balance the influence of these three tendencies (cf. Fiske, 1991).

These norms serve as (hopefully) flexible guidelines for resolving the tensions that necessarily arise as communities attempt to balance the three propensities described above. Such rules tend to be highly abstract, symbolic, and/or ideological. Interestingly, the rule exists apart from a particular person or setting. Thus, a moral norm can define what constitutes a legitimate leader. This can strengthen the hand of dominant individuals. This could be a good thing for the collective, if strong leadership is needed. On the other hand, this also provides those at the lower levels a "legitimate" and "justifiable" basis for challenging, and collectively exerting negative social sanctions against, those at the higher levels who violate moral norms (Boehm, 1999). As such, moral norms can also strengthen the cause of individual autonomy. In this way, an ethical proscription can push on any of these inclinations—submissiveness (you have an obligation to obey), power seeking (you have a legitimate right to lead), or autonomy (you have the right to disobey). If the rules are properly calibrated, they provide an ethical "language" or framework, which members of a given community can use to navigate conflicts that arise in regard to the social hierarchy.

Perfect and Imperfect Duties

The key, as we have just stated, is to have the moral rules properly calibrated. Those norms most critical to submission tend to err on the rigid side, but other norms seem more akin to advisory guidelines. This possibility maps nicely onto the dichotomy between *perfect* and *imperfect* duties, a distinction originally made by Kant (1797/1991); for an analysis relevant to this point, see Trafimow & Trafimow, 1999. A *perfect duty* has an absolutist quality about it. Perfect duties are often stated as proscriptions, as in "thou shalt not" murder, steal, commit adultery, and so on. The moral obligation not to impose negative harms on others clearly has a perfect-duty quality to it. If everyone had an emotional urge to harm others, social life would be impossible, so it must have experienced strong selection pressure. An *imperfect duty* allows relatively more discretion and personal autonomy about ways of properly exhibiting respect for the given obligation in question. Imperfect norms are often stated as positive affirmations. For example, "one should help those who are less fortunate," but need not give all that one has or more than one can afford. Imperfect norms allow for different types of resolutions of ambivalences about the degree of stringency required.

The flexibility of imperfect moral obligations makes them interesting and, to be sure, evolutionarily adaptive. To continue the example above, the obligation to do positive things for those in need would be consistent with the band's looking out for its young. Sharing child-rearing duties is a major advantage of group living, unless it goes too far. Some degree of discretion seems necessary, lest so much of one's own inclusive fitness be exhausted as to preclude passing on one's genes to the next generation in the gene pool (i.e., you can't be so unselfish as to die, and not reproduce, while trying to benefit others). Interestingly, our inclinations toward autonomy comprise a sort of imperfect duty to ourselves, at least in some respects. True, one cannot be so self-aggrandizing as to be shunned or exiled. This would constitute a loss of the necessary benefits and protections that come from living in a social band. On the other hand, one's personal genetic fitness matters as well, and it is likely that many a biological saint failed to pass on his or her genes. (This may explain why there are so few saints among us.)

Next, we turn to some conjectures about relations between orthodox hierarchies and perfect duties, followed by a discussion about possible relations between reverse-dominance hierarchies and imperfect duties. We suggest that orthodox hierarchies make severe demands upon subordinates for obedience to authority. Those at the top of the hierarchy will enforce strict obedience, which is best achieved if those beneath tend to internalize their submissiveness. In reverse-dominance hierarchies, the pressure to conform acts on those who would otherwise be dominant, but the nature of this pressure is not as strong as in the case of orthodox hierarchies. We pursue this line of argument in an attempt to indicate why evolutionary pressures might have led to proscriptions against vice (perfect duties) and prescriptions for virtue (imperfect duties) as ways of achieving social order.

Orthodox Hierarchies and Perfect Duties

To the extent that the weaker are content to be submissive to the stronger, strict, or "orthodox" hierarchies will tend to be relatively stable. An extreme resentment of domination, however, could continually threaten to undermine any social order that was dependent entirely on physical force. Nonetheless, the existence of orthodox hierarchies in the "U" of evolutionary history suggests that this type of semistable equilibrium is possible despite dispositional tendencies otherwise capable of tearing the social fabric apart. Indeed, in many social settings it might even be preferred (Udy, 1959).

Because an orthodox (top–down) hierarchy is undoubtedly subject to dynamic tensions, and thus represents only a semistable equilibrium, we suggest that more than one mechanism of social order needs to be at work. First of all, the strong can gain submission from the weak by the use of physical force and other means of coercion. An armed police officer, for example, has the physical means by which to subdue an unarmed suspect. Indeed, French and Raven (1959) described coercive power as a way that a leader can gain conformity and obedience from followers.

The construct of conformity, however, can also be dissected into varieties that Kelman (1974) identified as ranging from mere compliance to internalized influence: There can be extrinsically motivated reasons to follow a leader (as one who provides rewards or threatens punishment), but these can also be supplemented by intrinsic motivations such as admiration for the leader or allegiance to the ideals that he or she exemplifies. We say colloquially that you can lead a horse to water but can't make it drink. Put another way, physically forcing a horse toward a stream will not accomplish the desired result without the horse's desire to comply. When a horse is thirsty enough, however, it is not even necessary to use force. Similarly, dominance becomes easier when others are inclined to be submissive.

We suggest that Rousseau (1762) expressed a similar idea as seen in our opening quote from his writings. In his words, obedience can be obtained by creating a sense of duty, making it less necessary to rely on brute strength. Norms of moral obligation provide a powerful source for social order, and they can thereby serve to bolster acceptance of the stratifications inherent in orthodox hierarchy. Indeed, the feudal order is a classic example of a castelike society in which serfs seem to have internalized their low status as simply the way things were meant to be—or in other words, the way things *ought* to operate (Bernstein, 2004).

Note also that Rousseau (1762) referred to transforming strength into right. We might restate this by saying that obedience can be turned into duty only if a firm sense of right and wrong is in play. This seems to be consistent with what Kant (1797/1991) had in mind when he described some duties as having an absolute or "perfect" quality to them. Similarly, a ruler in an orthodox hierarchy must command absolute allegiance. Disobedience can be punishable by death. The upshot is that subordinates cannot be too tempted to disobey the ruler or disregard the requisite call for deference. To restate the idea of both extrinsic and intrinsic controls we might say that extrinsic norm enforcement (e.g., a ruler's power) works best when complemented by norm acceptance, and that the greater the degree to which internalized acceptance is "perfect" (obeyed without question), the easier it is for the powerful to stay in power.

Reverse-Dominance Hierarchies and Imperfect Duties

The classic example of an imperfect duty is the norm of generosity. Interestingly enough, precisely that kind of obligation looms large within the egalitarian groups that Boehm (1999) characterized as reverse-dominance hierarchies. A degree of leadership is tolerated, but only if those who would lead a group show some willingness to share with others in need. Note that we say *some* willingness, which coincides with the idea that imperfect duties do not make demands in nearly as absolute a fashion as perfect duties.

Boehm's (1999, 2000) analysis of hierarchy was based on the assumption that present-day nomadic foragers would give us an idea of what it must have been like for the hunter-gatherers of Paleolithic times. From data collected widely on the basis of numerous anthropological studies, Boehm (2000) concluded that virtually all such groups shared a very similar view about the qualities someone should have in order to be considered influential in the group. As imperfect duties, the norms for leader conduct in reverse-dominance hierarchies are "moral codes [that] regularly work to suppress hedonistic [e.g., self-aggrandizing, anti-egalitarian] or aggressive behavior tendencies that generate social problems" (Boehm, 1999, p. 229). Norms of obligation (as perfect duties) apply mainly to those at the bottom when the hierarchy is orthodox, but they apply mainly to those at the top (as imperfect duties) when a reverse-dominance hierarchy is in place.

What are the kinds of norms among hunter-gatherers that might qualify as imperfect duties? Among others, these include ideals "convincing people that generosity toward other group members is desirable" (Boehm, 1999, p. 245). In a more extended passage of his 1999 book, Boehm summarized his earlier commentary as follows (p. 246):

> That the positive side of moral manipulation is substantial [cf. imperfect duty] is borne out by the patterns that appeared when I surveyed desired and undesired leadership qualities in the chapters on hunter-gatherers and tribesmen. We saw that these egalitarians heavily emphasized positive role features [norms of moral conduct], notably generosity and even temper, and appeared to think of them at least as frequently as negative features such as stinginess or overbearingness. It was clear that, in a typical ethos, altruistic generosity oriented to the entire group was an extremely important attribute.

Indeed, those allowed informal roles of leadership might achieve that status partly based on skills such as hunting, but it was also important for them to display "generosity, kindness, and freedom from bad temper" and to be "self-effacing" (Boehm, 1999, p. 33, quoting Service, 1975).

Again we think that there are two ways in which such attributes might be instilled—via extrinsic and intrinsic routes. On the one hand, rank-and-file members of the group might try to coerce the more advantaged members, or those with higher status, to share and be generous. On the other hand, such efforts would have a greater chance of being effective if evolution had provided a mechanism whereby those at the top internalized feelings consistent with sharing and generosity.

Self-Regulation and Regulation by Others

Up to this point we have referred to the concept of internalization in two ways. First, we suggested that the internalization of submissiveness makes evolutionary sense when, as with orthodox hierarchies, subordinates might need to fear the wrath of the bigger, stronger, and more powerful. Similarly, the absolute authority of perfect duties requires an internalized mechanism of self-regulation to avoid the wrath of those outraged by the violation of such duties. Second, we argued that it is the relatively advantaged in a group who would need to internalize norms of sharing, generosity, and concern for the unfortunate—norms that correspond to imperfect duties. Although the stringency of those kinds of social obligations is not so absolute as in the case of perfect duties, it is clear that the less advantaged might experience at least some degree of resentment when those obligations are not met.

Notice, however, that we have actually smuggled into our arguments *two* sets of internalizations: one on the part of those who are held accountable for conforming to moral norms (meeting obligations), and one on the part of those who hold others accountable. To put it another way, the enforcement of moral norms requires an internalized sense that those kinds of norms *should* be enforced (i.e., feeling that something needs to be done about violations). The capacity to feel certain kinds of emotions plays a key role in both kinds of internalizations, and that is the topic to which we turn next.

Moral Emotions: Some General Thoughts

The philosophers David Hume (1740, 1777) and Adam Smith (1759) had specific candidates for the job of internalization. They referred to them as "moral sentiments," though in modern terminology there are more likely to be thought of as "moral emotions" (Tangney, Stuewig, & Mashek, 2007). In an interesting paper, Ketelaar (2006) asserts that moral sentiments exert their constraining effect in two ways. The self-conscious emotions tend to provide an internal regulator of one's own conduct (Tracy, Robins, & Tangney, 2007). These include such things as guilt, shame, and embarrassment (Gilbert, 2003; Tangney, Miller, Flicker, & Barlow, 1996). Ketelaar (2006, p. 102) refers to the self-conscious emotions as "self-focused" and "norm-obeying." He argues that these are only one element in maintaining social norms. Ketelaar (p. 105) observes that some other emotions are best described as "other-focused" and "norm-enforcing." These include indignation, contempt (Ekman & Heider, 1988), and disgust (Chapman, Kim, Susskind, & Anderson, 2009).

By means of this twin set of emotions, nature has given us a hammer and an anvil to maintain dynamic equilibrium in our social hierarchies. The experience of self-focused emotions, such as shame and guilt, helps motivate us in ways that guide our behavior and that provide occasions for self-restraint. Similarly, when other people experience other-focused emotions such as resentment or indignation in response to our moral transgressions, they are apt to give us social-conduct feedback in an attempt to impose constraints on our behavior. To be sure, the particulars of these feelings are culturally socialized, but they are made possible by adaptive features of our neural architecture (Wilson, 1993; Wright, 1994).

Perfect Duties, Imperfect Duties, and Moral Emotions

Thus far we have seen that there are two types of emotions—the set of norm-obeying or self-conscious emotions that regulate the self, and norm-enforcing or other-focused emotions that regulate the behavior of other people. We argue that these two types of emotional experience can be linked conceptually to the constructs of perfect and imperfect duties. As shown in Table 10.1, some emotions are associated with perfect duties, whereas others are associated with imperfect duties. This depends further on whether one is focusing on the self or on another person. (The table also has arrows that go with S for Self and O for Other, but we postpone our discussion of that feature momentarily.)

We must also emphasize that these guilt, shame, resentment, and indignation labels are conceptually driven and the respective emotions conceptually defined. That is, those terms need not coincide with the looser connotations of ordinary language. Guilt and shame are words that are often used interchangeably in everyday discourse, for example, whereas here they represent separate constructs. What we mean by guilt is, as noted earlier, analogous to what "transgressors" at the *top* of a reverse-dominance hierarchy might feel.

TABLE 10.1

Moral Emotions and Moral Duties

Moral Impetus	Type of Duty	
	Imperfect Duty	**Perfect Duty**
Self-restraint	Guilt (S↑)	Shame (S↓)
Other-constraint	Resentment (O↓)	Indignation (O↑)

Note: "S" refers to Self and "O" refers to Other. The arrows designate the "position" of Self and Other relative to one another (see accompanying text).

The quality of emotion that we call shame, on the other hand, is analogous to what those at the *bottom* of an orthodox hierarchy might feel if they transgressed.[1] In addition, the 2 × 2 classification system should not be taken to imply that these emotional categories represent wholly distinct emotional experiences. Even as conceptualized according to the present framework, for example, feelings of "guilt" can co-occur with feelings of "shame."

Suppose that a transgression has occurred. The wrongdoer will likely feel an emotion—guilt if she violated an imperfect duty, but shame if she violated a perfect one (see Table 10.1). An observer will also feel an emotion—resentment if the violation was against an imperfect duty but indignation if it was against a perfect one. To the extent that both individuals, the actor and the observer, have internalized the norm, they are apt to feel their respective emotions such that the feelings of the actor are reinforced by the feelings of the observer.

Consistent with the perspective we have drawn from Boehm's (1999, 2000) analysis as applied to moral norms, we think the connections to perfect and imperfect duties are aligned as indicated in Table 10.1. The former constitutes a much stronger type of obligation, with not much discretion involved. To be sure, there are some exceptions to this rigidity, but these are rare and can call for excuses or justifications that seem valid. We suggest that a sense of shame is aligned more readily with those obligations that fall into the category of perfect duties, whereas guilt is felt more readily in conjunction with imperfect duties.

Self-Focused and Other-Focused Emotions Work in Tandem

Another part of Table 10.1 introduces a schematic in which S (Self as Actor) and O (Other as Observer) are represented in hierarchical relation to one another. We propose that this schematic is useful for understanding the moral emotions of guilt, shame, resentment, and indignation as we conceptualize them. Conceptualizing moral emotions as a function of the relative "positions" of Self and Other (the respective "status" of each) is also consistent with recognizing hierarchy as a central feature of sociality in group-living species.

The schematic works this way. If you feel ashamed ($\downarrow S$), it is because you have *done* something "disreputable" or otherwise fallen "below" some standard regarding what people can and should do. You also cause others to infer that you might *be* a certain kind of disreputable or inadequate person as result. You do not "measure up." The greater the extent to which your conduct is shameful in a moral sense (as the violation of a perfect duty), the more likely it is that you will elicit indignation from others. That is, they will feel morally superior ($\uparrow O$) or at least in some sense have a "stature" from which they might "look down upon" you.

If you feel guilty (↑S), you are in some sense better off—in a better position than—someone else, especially as regards the resources you *have*. It should not be surprising, therefore, that disadvantaged others (↓O) might resent your advantaged position; they do not have as many resources and are relatively worse off than you. This pair of emotions is "moralized" in the sense that something akin to an imperfect duty is at stake. We examine the Shame/Indignation and then the Guilt/Resentment pair (Allred, 1999) in the following sections.

Shame

Our analysis has emphasized hierarchical relations. We think these help contribute to the biological preparedness for shame. Fessler (2004) has argued that ordinary (nonmoralized) shame is likely to have evolved prior to guilt. In part, we think that's true because shame (especially as Fessler conceptualizes it) grows almost directly out of the deference that animals show to those of higher rank. If you're around the alpha male or the tribe's elders, you'd better be careful how you behave! The right to criticize under such circumstances flows in only one direction. As members of traditional cultures, we would "bow down" to those "above" us in class or caste. Such behavioral tendencies are not unlike the kinds ascribed to shame proneness (e.g., withdrawal and avoidance; cf. Tangney et al., 2007).

Shame, whether moralized or not, reflects position, status, stature, standing, and the like. This vertical dimension is not unlike that associated with the up–down nature of power, and hence the relationship to honoring and being respectful. In addition to other people, we can also be respectful of ideas and ideologies. The duty/obligation to honor a matter of principle is an example, as is allegiance to a cause. Not to display those kinds of allegiance to certain *protected* or *sacred values* is to be regarded as "less" of a person. What we *do* on such occasions reflects on who we are considered to *be*. In fact, we might generally honor a principle (or "protect" a value, Skitka, 2002; Skitka & Mullen, 2008) and yet have a deficient character attributed to us for even a single lapse (Riskey & Birnbaum, 1974). Research by Trafimow and Trafimow (1999) in fact shows that perfect duties are those for which a single negative behavior can create the inference of a negative trait. For that reason we associate shame with the failure to observe a perfect duty, as distinguished from guilt as a shortcoming with regard to an imperfect duty.

Indignation

Indignation as moral sentiment ("righteous indignation," "moral outrage," or perhaps mere contempt) is thus the other side of the coin, so to speak, vis-à-vis shame. The indignant feel they have a right to "put down" those who act shamefully, and displaying indignation can do just that. Note that the indignant person does not have to be someone in any way harmed by the shameful act (cf. Ellard & Skarlicki, 2002; Folger, 2001; Skarlicki & Kulik, 2005; Turillo et al., 2002). We can be indignant or morally outraged about something that happens on the other side of the planet, as with acts by people who "should be ashamed of themselves"—what they have done seems outrageous, at least by our lights (the moral high ground on which we stand). In traditional cultures of many varieties, of course, a higher class or caste will indeed feel entitled to be righteously indignant at those who do not honor and respect them to the degree deemed appropriate. Moral standards are not unlike that: The relevant moral sentiment is that they deserve our honor and respect, so others have a right to castigate us for being the kinds of people who do not live up to such standards.

Moralized shame may have grown out of deference-based shame, just as Rozin (1999) attributes moralized disgust to the kind that relates only to bodily protection (for empirical evidence supporting this point, see Chapman et al., 2009). A fully moralized shame experience, therefore, represents perhaps an extreme variety on some continuum—or perhaps it is a variation and represents a slight qualitative variation.

Guilt

The experience of guilt as we conceptualize it is rather unusual, and that is part of the reason why we tend to agree with Fessler's (2004) thoughts about it. Fessler has several reasons for arguing why guilt should be differentiated from shame. For one thing, guilt probably represents a more recent evolutionary development, perhaps even having not as much to do with the ordinary selective pressures of evolution as with some sort of gene-culture co-evolution process. Tangney's work (e.g., Tangney et al., 2007), and the work of others whom she credits, is also persuasive to a degree, at least as far as the sense in which she has pointed to different categories of behavioral tendencies. We have been influenced by what we consider to be other pieces of the puzzle as well.

One is the so-called "guilt-compliance" literature in social psychology, ably reviewed by Baumeister, Stillwell, and Heatherton (1994). The social psychological studies show that when people are made to feel guilty (via experimental manipulations in the laboratory), they become especially responsive to a variety of needful requests. There are a couple of things noted by Baumeister et al. that relate to this perspective. First, the feeling of guilt extends beyond simply making up for any problems caused to a given person as a result. People made guilty are more responsive to almost any kind of request from anyone! Second, the effect is not 100% consistent in the literature. It seems as if *accidentally* caused harm tends to produce the compliance effect with a greater degree of regularity than does harm for which the research participants are made to feel more directly responsible in some sense. This is an odd finding. Intuitively, it would seem that one would bear more guilt, and hence a greater obligation for restitution, when the harm was deliberate.

It seems that when a person causes accidental harm, he or she may experience guilt as a result. This has also been found in research on *survivor guilt*. The term survivor guilt was "first used to describe the guilt that people may feel when literally surviving the death of another ... [and currently] expanded to include guilt about any advantage a person believes they have when compared with others, such as success, superior abilities, or a greater degree of health and well-being" (O'Conner, Berry, & Weiss, 2000, p. 519). As one can see, survivor guilt and guilt compliance share an element of chance. Once more we see this counterintuitive finding; this is quite the opposite of analyses that link guilt to personal causation. It is possible, of course, that there are different varieties of guilt; scholars (and laypeople) could be using the same word to mean somewhat different things. Even were this to be the case, it would not change our present analyses. At least two powerful phenomena—guilt compliance and survivor guilt—seem to result when an individual gains an *accidental* advantage over another person.

A related insight regarding guilt can be found in Adams's (1963, 1965) early work on equity theory. When a person was inequitably well-off (*overreward*), Adams proposed that he or she would experience guilt. Consistent with compliance guilt research, this guilt could be alleviated by working harder in trying to make up for the undeserved outcomes received. Consistent with our analysis here, Adams's view of guilt was implicitly hierarchical. To illustrate, we use the ↑S (relative to ↓O) notation for guilt: You are better-off than you deserve (just your dumb luck, and other people's bad luck); you feel bad about it; you wish you could do something about it, even if you can't (e.g., your friend is dead); when presented with an opportunity to do something that helps "pay back" the world for what you've been handed, you jump at the opportunity.

Resentment

As with its partner, guilt, the term *resentment* is a moral emotion in our analysis. That is, resentment is the righteous anger that results when someone achieves an outcome that is more favorable than deserved. Related emotions, such as jealousy and envy, are similar but less moralized. To understand how resentment complements guilt, recall from the preceding text that the guilt-compliance effect is stronger when the original harm was accidental. Likewise, people may feel survivor guilt when they have been fortunate but done nothing wrong. Resentment is the flip side of this. The *disadvantaged* party may feel resentment at another individual's success, even though that success was purely fortuitous. Put differently, the outcome is unfair because the beneficiary did nothing special to deserve it. The less-fortunate person feels resentment because he or she was not the lucky one.

Adams's (1963, 1965) analysis of inequity applies here. Experimental manipulations of disadvantageous inequity in the laboratory are just that—states brought about by the design of the investigator, rather than being based on anything the participants have done (which is also the case for manipulations of overpayment guilt). Note that resentment is not a purely individual-level phenomenon. Entire groups of people can feel resentment simply by becoming aware of others who are well-off all of a sudden, as when the most salient comparison referent changes abruptly and a sense of relative deprivation ensues (cf. James & Cropanzano, 1990).

Of course, shame and guilt can also be mixed together as emotions. After all, both are confronting essentially the same functional issue—how to get along in a group, in the sense of those emotions' ancestral origins. Transgressions against other people, which some take as the principle defining features of moral norms,[2] will often arouse guilt as well as shame, and for good reason. On the one hand, there is one type of danger: We may become victims of someone's wrath. In our model, this can be understood as righteous indignation—moral outrage aimed at one who has violated a perfect-duty norm and thereby engaged in shameful conduct. On the other hand, there is another type of danger: We may become the target of resentment, with the implication that we should be generous and self-sacrificing. Caught between a rock and a hard place, we may vacillate, throw the dice, and pick one response type rather than the other, try to do some of both, and so on. In other words, we may feel both types of emotions in the same circumstances and may have some impulses that point in both directions.

Shame, Guilt, and Management
Responses to Ethical Challenges

Homo sapiens are unique animals (Gazzaniga, 2008) who use their minds and bodies to actively create their environment (Blakeslee & Blakeslee, 2007; Johnson, 2004). For that reason, people do not (only) passively respond to one another, they also mount active challenges (Allred, 1999). Such challenges can create conflicts and bring about change (Bies & Tripp, 2002; Tripp & Bies, 1997), though how this plays out will depend on the responses chosen by each party. As we shall see, the evolutionary history of our species sometimes leads us astray.

To illustrate this point, let us consider the situation where leaders in government or in business have done something that is ethically dubious. Sad to say, any number of examples present themselves (Ermann & Lundman, 1987), such as fraudulent accounting (Eichenwald, 2005), wasteful spending (Stossel, 2004), self-serving actions by regulatory agencies (McWilliams, 1996), and deceitful political ads (Westin, 2007). In situations such as these, the organization is likely to face challenges from the public. These challenges will involve explicit or implicit accusations and can run the gambit from the minor (e.g., responding to a complaint letter) to some that are quite major (e.g., responding to a scandal). Here the analysis of shame and guilt seems especially apropos because the organization does indeed find itself in a situation that involves potential loss of "face" (reputation), the possibility of financial loss, or even jail sentences. Organizational leaders are put into positions that might make them feel ashamed, but how will they respond?

In these situations, the most effective strategy for lessening negative consequences could well be a display of remorse, such as a request for forgiveness (Tripp & Bies, 2008; Tripp, Bies, & Aquino, 2007). These displays of genuine penitence are effective in lessening the negative consequences that might otherwise ensue (e.g., McCullough, Rachal, Sandage, Worthington, Brown, & Hight, 1998; McCullough & Worthington, 1995; McCullough, Worthington, & Rachal, 1997). But this is not the way things often work out. Despite this, power holders often neglect to apologize; the very kinds of responses most likely to ameliorate resentment are often the ones that leaders are least likely to provide. For example, when conducting layoffs, managers often display uncivil treatment toward workers (e.g., see Folger & Pugh, 2002; Folger & Skarlicki, 1998). Our model sheds light on this gap between the *typical* behavior and the *optimal* behavior.

Guilt, Shame, and Humiliation

At first glance the discrepancy between what works and what is often done may seem surprising (Folger & Skarlicki, 2001). However, it is important to recognize the hierarchical aspects of guilt and shame. According to the framework presented here, a guiltlike response is needed in these kinds of situations. One feels guilty when he or she has an illegitimate advantage. As we have seen, the behavioral response is to comply with requests (Baumeister et al., 1994; Tangney & Dearing, 2002). In other words, a guiltlike response would, in a gracious manner, show a willingness to give up something—to swallow one's pride, as we say colloquially (cf. Tangney et al., 1996). The rank of the guilty person is acknowledged, and all parties can go forward (cf. Tripp et al., 2007).

While a guiltlike response is called for, situations involving public accusations often elicit shamelike responses instead. When an individual is made to feel ashamed, this experience is one of *humiliation*. This is very aversive, to say the least. It is hard, therefore, to exhibit the sense of *humility* that is actually called for in the situation. The resulting behavioral tendencies can be less than helpful. When we are ashamed, our tendency is not to welcome others with open arms. Rather, shameful situations involve a sense of threat. When we are ashamed, we want to avoid, hide, flee, and so forth (Tangney & Dearing, 2002; Tangney et al., 2007).

These shame-related behaviors seem sadly characteristic of the times when leaders must face charges of misconduct. They do not prompt open communication, and this may cause the conflict to escalate (Allred, 1999). The party making the accusation, in turn, is likely to respond with additional charges of "stonewalling" and cover-up, as officials seek to deny or obfuscate. The public-relations literature is also replete with instances in which what leaders say publicly only enflames the outrage that already exists (e.g., Boyd, 2001; Kauffman, 1999; Wise, 2004). For example, during the height of the California energy crisis, for which Enron energy traders were partially responsible (McLean & Elkind, 2003), CEO Jeff Skilling was asked to provide his views. He retorted with an insensitive joke that blamed the victim: "You know what the difference is between the state of California and the *Titanic*? ... At least when the *Titanic* went down, the lights were on" (reported by Eichenwald, 2005, p. 464). On other occasions, officials try to get off the hook by means of proffered justifications that in fact seem either unjustifiable or even illegitimate.

Situations That Provoke Shame and Guilt

As observed by others (e.g., Tangney et al., 2007), guilt seems to be the more promising emotion when it comes to promoting constructive responses to wrongdoing. It is noteworthy that many leaders manage to respond in a guilt-oriented, not shame-oriented, fashion. The response of Johnson and Johnson to the Tylenol crisis is instructive in this regard. Rather than focus blame somewhere else (which would have been perfectly legitimate), the company made a dramatic, costly sacrifice. Such a response is a classic example of the guilt mode of freely giving up something in a generous, gracious manner (Baumeister et al., 1994). For that reason, it is worthwhile to identify situations that provoke shame, distinguishing them for those that provoke guilt.

Shame situations. In accordance with our model, shamelike responses occur in situations experienced subjectively as if they involved competition to be on top, to win, to come out ahead, and so on. These feelings that can be engendered in situations associated with the experience of losing a competition. Because economic exchange can be seen as a zero-sum game, a shame-based orientation might be the default when leaders perceive that their organization is under attack by virtue of accusations brought against it. When relations with the public are viewed in purely economic (i.e., competitive) terms, therefore, a defensive posture may be a quite natural response. Add to that the competition with other firms in the same business or between politicians aspiring to the same office, and orienting in a manner consistent with shame-based defensiveness may seem not only natural but also very reasonable. That might help to explain why such behavior is so surprisingly common, even when it turns out to be dysfunctional.

Guilt situations. What would turn the situation into one where a guilt-like orientation is more likely? If the evolutionary and social-functional basis for the experience of guilt is a situation in which people have more than their share and feel some need to make sacrifices graciously for the sake of relationships, then this suggests that something similar might be aroused when an organization is more relationship oriented vis-à-vis essential stakeholders, such as customers and workers. These would be institutions whose business is such that loyalty and long-term relationships are paramount.

Perhaps there is another aspect of the origins of guilt that is relevant as well. As Boehm (2000) has noted, hunter-gatherers would need a "social insurance policy" because resources such as large game could be obtained only on an uncertain, irregular basis by even the best of hunters. Long-term relationships are important. Rather than risk being resented, the most successful hunters on a given occasion would display modesty and would share willingly the food they had been fortunate enough to obtain. This could have a payoff in future times that were less fortunate for the hunter. Similar cultural practices have been documented in modern-day groups of hunter-gatherers (Thomas, 2006). This suggests that guilt-oriented responses are especially important when (a) a long-term trusting relationship is of practical value and (b) the economic position of the organization is strong so that it is a less critical concern. Let us take these features one at a time.

First, a long-term trusting relationship can be an economic asset (Morris, 1997). The way that Johnson and Johnson handled the Tylenol scare illustrates the point. That firm's advertising refers to it as "a family company," and the nature of its business relates to meeting the health-care needs of its customers. Building up and sustaining a reputation for trustworthiness is required by that type of relationship with the public (e.g., Tomlinson & Mayer, 2009; Bryce, 2007). Trust grows as a relationship grows but can be shattered if betrayed, whereupon it becomes hard to restore. For that reason, it could be more important to make sure that the relationship is sustained, even if it requires acting in a self-sacrificial way. Under these conditions, the guilt-based motive of wanting to ensure reconciliation becomes especially relevant.

Second, and conversely, some organizations may be under more economic pressure than others. When an organization is in lean times, leaders are apt to feel vulnerable and under attack. When times are better, the organization may be more willing to accept responsibility, admit wrongdoing, make concessions, apologize, and the like. These organizations can afford to be "vulnerable." They willingly allow themselves to have some of their advantages be temporarily reduced if that is what it takes to restore the public's trust. This suggests that companies in financial difficulty, in highly competitive industries, and so on, may not feel sufficiently advantaged to allow for the spirit of guilt and its self-sacrificial concomitants.

Conclusion

In this chapter we explored how the sentiments known as moral emotions pertain to perceived norms of moral obligation. We first considered the evolutionary basis for such obligations as they might relate to issues of hierarchy in social life. Following Boehm (1999), we noted how tensions involving three underlying human dispositions (the desire to dominate, a willingness to be dominated, and an aversion to being dominated) might have given rise to two major forms of hierarchy, namely orthodox and reverse-dominance variations. That distinction in turn led us to consider how each form of hierarchy might call for its own set of normative obligations—in particular, moral norms that apply to different positions in a status hierarchy.

We went on to speculate that moral norms have their influence by virtue of intrinsic/extrinsic emotional pairings. Ketelaar (2006) has called these *norm-obeying* moral emotions (self-focused, such as guilt) and *norm-enforcing* moral emotions (other-focused, such as indignation). We linked them to positions in social hierarchies. Finally, we addressed how the functioning of moral emotions might influence the reactions of executives to challenges from the public.

Human beings have evolved a set of complementary emotional tools that can help to resolve moral dilemmas and maintain ethical workgroups. When properly harnessed, these predispositions can build more ethical work organizations. We have sought to place such emotional tendencies in evolutionary perspective and to analyze their relation to the ever-present context of social hierarchy.

Endnotes

1. Of course, not all uses of the word *shame* in everyday conversation are tied to moral transgressions. Asked to recall shame incidents in studies by de Hooge, Zeelenberg, and Breugelmans (2007), for example, the respondents often wrote about academic or athletic failures. These probably represent a case in which people might expect something more like (nonmoral) contempt than (moral) indignation. There is also a moralized version of contempt, however, and we think moralized shame fits into a hierarchical schema.

2. We do not share this view because moral norms typically involve some adherence to a rule of conduct. This is an old idea in social psychology. Fritz Heider (1958) devoted an entire chapter of *The Psychology of Interpersonal Relations* to "Ought and Value." This chapter dealt extensively with the role of moral norms in human society. Although he distinguished between the moral sense of *ought* and its broader possible applications (e.g., "I ought to carry an umbrella because it might rain"), the passages we quote are especially apropos to the former. Furthermore, "In the case of [a moral] ought, … it is not a particular somebody that is felt to want or command people to do *x*, but some suprapersonal objective order" (Heider, 1958, p. 219). Note that the idea of an "order" is characterized as having a *supra*personal quality, such that its status is "above" that of the status possessed by any given person.

   Another important feature of Heider's analysis relates to the notion of the *objective* quality of moral norms (oughts). "Oughts are impersonal," he wrote, and have "the validity of objective existence"—that is, moral principles "refer to standards … independent of the individual's wishes" (1958, p. 219). He noted that what a person ought to do "has a significance beyond personal concerns" (p. 220), which means that moral norms seem objective in the sense that they exhibit an intersubjectively validated reality. Put another way, this "requirement of a suprapersonal objective order" is one "whose validity therefore transcends the point of view of any one person" (p. 222). Thus moral norms are consensually shared values because "ought has interpersonal validity. … it is … universal and should look alike to everybody," and "attributing ought to an objective order requires that people in general should concur in its directives" (p. 222).

References

Adams, J. S. (1963). Toward an understanding of inequity. *Journal of Abnormal and Social Psychology, 47*, 422–436.

Adams, J. S. (1965). Inequity in social exchange. In L. Berkowitz (Ed.), *Advances in experimental social psychology* (pp. 267–299). New York: Academic Press.

Allred, K. G. (1999). Anger and retaliation: Toward an understanding of impassioned conflict in organizations. In R. J. Bies, R. J. Lewicke, & B. H. Sheppard (Eds.), *Research on negotiation in organizations* (pp. 27–58). Stamford, CT: JAI Press.

Aristotle. (350 b.c.e/1943). *Politics.* (Benjamin Jowett, Trans.). New York: Modern Library.

Baumeister, R. F., Stillwell, A. M., & Heatherton, T. F. (1994). Guilt: An interpersonal approach. *Psychological Bulletin, 115,* 243–267.

Berry, J. W. (1967). Independence and conformity in subsistence level societies. *Journal of Personality and Social Psychology, 7,* 415–418.

Berry, J. W. (1979). A cultural ecology of social behavior. In L. Berkowitz (Ed.), *Advances in experimental social psychology* (Vol. 12, pp. 177–207). New York: Academic Press.

Bernstein, W. J. (2004). *The birth of plenty: How the prosperity of the modern world was created.* New York: McGraw-Hill.

Bies, R. J., & Tripp, T. M. (2002). "Hot flashes and open wounds": Injustice and the tyranny of its emotions. In S. W. Gilliland, D. D. Steiner, & D. P. Skarlicki (Eds.), *Emerging perspectives on managing organizational justice* (pp. 203–221). Greenwich, CT: Information Age Publishing.

Blakeslee, S., & Blakeslee, M. (2007). *The body has a mind of its own: How body maps in your brain help you do (almost) everything better.* New York: Random House.

Boehm, C. (1989). Ambivalence and compromise in human nature. *American Anthropologist, 91,* 921–939.

Boehm, C. (1999). *Hierarchy in the forest.* Cambridge, MA: Harvard University Press.

Boehm, C. (2000). Conflict and the evolution of social control. In L. D. Katz (Ed.), *Evolutionary origins of morality: Cross-disciplinary perspectives* (pp. 79–101). Bowling Green, OH: Imprint Academic.

Boyd, J. (2001). The rhetoric of arrogance: The public relations of the Standard Oil Trust. *Public Relations Review, 27,* 163–178.

Brosnan, S. F. (2006). Nonhuman species' reactions to inequity and their implications for fairness. *Social Justice Research, 19,* 153–185.

Brown, D. E. (1991). *Human universals.* New York: McGraw-Hill.

Bryce, H. J. (2007). The public's trust in nonprofit organizations: The role of relationship marketing and management. *California Management Review, 49,* 112–125.

Cacioppo, J. T., & Patrick, W. (2008). *Loneliness: Human nature and the need for social approval.* New York: W. W. Norton & Company.

Chapman, H. A., Kim, D. A., Susskind, J. M., & Anderson, A. K. (2009). In bad taste: Evidence for the oral origin of moral disgust. *Science, 323,* 1222–1226.

Connolly, T., & Hardman, D. (2009). "Fools rush in": A JDM perspective on the role of emotions in decisions, moral and otherwise. In D. M. Bartels, C. W. Bauman, L. J. Skitka, & D. L. Medin (Eds.), *The psychology of learning and motivation* (Vol. 50, pp. 25–306). Burlington, VT: Academic Press.

Cropanzano, R., Stein, J., & Goldman, B. M. (2007). Individual aesthetics: Self-interest. In E. H. Kessler & J. R. Bailey (Eds.), *Handbook of organizational and managerial wisdom* (pp. 181–221). Los Angeles, CA: Sage Publications.

De Hooge, I. E., Zeelenberg, M., & Breugelmans, S. M. (2007). Moral sentiments and cooperation: Differential influences of shame and guilt. *Cognition and Emotion, 21,* 1025–1042.

De Waal, F. (1996). *Good natured: The origins of right and wrong in humans and other animals.* Cambridge, MA: Harvard University Press.

Eichenwald, K. (2005). *Conspiracy of fools: A true story.* New York: Broadway Books.

Ekman, P., & Heider, K. G. (1988). The universality of a contempt expression: A replication. *Motivation and Emotion, 12,* 303–308.

Ellard, J. H., & Skarlicki, D. P. (2002). A third-party observers' reactions to employee mistreatment: Motivational and cognitive processes in deservingness assessments. In S.W. Gilliland, D. D. Steiner, & D. P. Skarlicki (Eds.), *Research in social issues in management* (pp. 133–158). Greenwich, CT: Information Age Publishing.

Ermann, M. D., & Lundman, R. J. (Eds.). (1987). *Corporate and governmental deviance: Problems of organizational behavior in contemporary society* (3rd ed). Oxford, UK: Oxford University Press.

Fessler, D. M. T. (2004). Shame in two cultures: Implications for evolutionary approaches. *Journal of Cognition and Culture, 4,* 207–262.

Fiske, A. P. (1991). *Structures of social life: The four elementary forms of human relations.* New York: The Free Press.

Folger, R. (1994). Workplace justice and employee worth. *Social Justice Research, 7,* 225–241.

Folger, R. (1998). Fairness as a moral virtue. In M. Schminke (Ed.), *Managerial ethics: Moral management of people and processes* (pp. 13–34). Mahwah, NJ: Erlbaum.

Folger, R. (2001). Fairness as deonance. In S. W. Gilliland, D. D. Steiner & D. P. Skarlicki (Eds.), *Research in social issues in management* (Vol. 1, pp. 3–33). New York: Information Age Publishers.

Folger, R., & Pugh, S. D. (2002). The just world and Winston Churchill: An approach/avoidance conflict about psychological distance when harming victims. In M. Ross & D. T. Miller (Eds.), *The justice motive in social life: Essays in honor of Melvin Lerner* (pp. 168–186). Cambridge: Cambridge University Press.

Folger, R., & Salvador, R. (2008). Is management theory too "self-ish"? *Journal of Management, 34,* 1127–1151.

Folger, R., & Skarlicki, D. P. (1998). When tough times make tough bosses: Managerial distancing as a function of layoff blame. *Academy of Management Journal, 41,* 79–87.

Folger, R., & Skarlicki, D. P. (2001). Fairness as a dependent variable: Why tough times can lead to bad management. In R. Cropanzano (Ed.), *Justice in the workplace (Volume 2): From theory to practice* (pp. 97–118). Mahwah, NJ: Erlbaum.

French, J. R. P., Jr., & Raven, B. (1959). The basis of social power. In D. Cartwright (Ed.), *Studies in social power* (pp. 150–167). Ann Arbor, MI: Institute for Social Research.

Friedman, R. A., Tidd, S. T., Currall, S. C., & Tsai, J. C. (2000). What goes around comes around: The impact of personal conflict style on work conflict and stress. *The International Journal of Conflict Management, 11,* 32–55.

Gazzaniga, M. S. (2008). *Human: The science behind what makes us unique.* New York: HarperCollins.

Gilbert, P. (2003). Evolution, social roles, and the differences in shame and guilt. *Social Research, 70,* 1205–1230.

Goleman, D. (2006). *Social intelligence: The new science of human relationships.* New York: Bantam Books.

Haidt, J. (2006). *The happiness hypothesis: Finding modern truth in ancient wisdom.* New York: Basic Books.

Hamburger, H. (1979). *Games as models of social phenomena.* New York: W. H. Freeman & Company.

Heider, F. (1958). *The psychology of interpersonal relations.* Hillside, NJ: Erlbaum.

Hobbes, T. (1651/2009). *Leviathan, the matter, forme and power of a common wealth ecclesiasticall and civil.* [Edited by J. C. A. Gaskin.] Oxford, U.K.: Oxford University Press.

Hume, D. (1740/1978). *A treatise on human nature.* Oxford, U.K.: Clarendon Press.

Hume, D. (1777/1996). *Enquiries concerning human understanding and concerning the principles of morals.* Oxford, U.K.: Oxford University Press.

James, K., & Cropanzano, R. (1990). Focus of attention and locus of control as moderators of fraternal justice effects. *Social Justice Research, 4,* 69–185.

Johnson, S. (2004). *Mind wide open: Your brain and the neuroscience of everyday life.* New York: Scribner.

Kant (1797/1991). *The metaphysics of morals.* (M. Gregor, Trans.). Cambridge, U.K.: Cambridge University Press.

Kauffman, J. (1999). Adding fuel to the fire: NASA's crisis communications regarding Apollo 1. *Public Relations Review, 25,* 421–432.

Kelman, H. G. (1974). Further thoughts on the process of compliance, identification, and internalization. In J. T. Tedeschi (Ed.), *Perspectives on social power* (pp. 125–171). Chicago, IL: Aldine.

Ketelaar, T. (2006). The role of moral sentiments in economic decision making. In D. De Cremer, M. Zeelenberg, & J. K. Murnighan (Eds.), *Social psychology and economics* (pp. 97–116). Mahwah, NJ: Erlbaum.

Knauft, B. M. (1991). Violence and sociality in human evolution. *Current Anthropology, 32,* 391–428.

McClean, B., & Elkind, P. (2003). *The smartest guys in the room: The amazing rise and scandalous fall of Enron.* New York: Portfolio Books.

McCullough, M. E., Rachal, K. C., Sandage, S. J., Worthington, E. L., Jr., Brown, S.W., & Hight, T. L. (1998). Interpersonal forgiving in close relationships II: Theoretical elaboration and measurement. *Journal of Personality and Social Psychology, 75,* 1586–1603.

McCullough, M. E., & Worthington, E. L., Jr. (1995). Promoting forgiveness: A comparison of two brief psychoeducational interventions with a waiting-list control. *Counseling and Values, 40,* 55–68.

McCullough, M. E., Worthington, E. L., & Rachal, K. C. (1997). Interpersonal forgiving in close relationships. *Journal of Personality and Social Psychology, 73,* 321–336.

McWilliams, P. (1996). *Ain't nobody's business if you do: The absurdity of consensual crimes in our free country.* Los Angeles, CA: Prelude Press.

Mikhail, J. (2009). Moral grammar and intuitive jurisprudence: A formal model of unconscious moral and legal knowledge. In D. Bartels, C. W. Bauman, L. J. Skitka, & D. Medin (Eds.), *Moral judgment and decision making: Psychology of learning and motivation.* San Diego, CA: Psychology Press.

Milgram, S. (1974). *Obedience to authority.* New York: Harper & Row.

Miller, A. S., & Kanazawa, S. (2007). *Why beautiful people have more children: From dating, shopping, and praying to going to war and becoming a billionaire. Two evolutionary psychologists explain why we do what we do.* New York: Perigee Books.

Miller, J. 2003. *Game theory at work: How to use game theory to outthink and outmaneuver your competition.* New York: McGraw-Hill.

Moghaddam, F. M., Taylor, D. M., & Wright, S. C. (1993). *Social psychology in cross-cultural perspective.* New York: W. H. Freeman.

Morris, T. (1997). *If Aristotle ran General Motors: The new soul of business.* New York: Heny Holt & Company.

O'Conner, L. E., Berry, J. W., & Weiss, J. (2000). Survivor guilt, submissive behavior and evolutionary theory: The down-side of winning in social comparison. *British Journal of Medical Psychology, 73,* 519–530.

Pillutla, M. M., & Murnighan, J. K. (1996). Unfairness, anger, and spite: Emotional rejections of ultimatum offers. *Organizational Behavior and Human Decision Processes, 68,* 208–224.

Pinker, S. (2002). *Blank slate: The modern denial of human nature.* New York: Viking Press.

Pruitt, D. G. (1983). Strategic choice in negotiation. *American Behavioral Scientist, 27,* 167–194.

Pruitt, D. G., & Carnevale, P. J. (1993). *Negotiation in social conflict.* Pacific Grove, CA: Brooks/Cole.

Riskey, D. R., & Birnbaum, M. H. (1974). Compensatory effects in moral judgment: Two rights don't make up for a wrong. *Journal of Experimental Psychology, 103,* 171–173.

Rousseau, J.-J. (1762/1968). *The social contract, or principles of political right.* (Maureen Cranston, Trans.). New York: Penguin Classics.

Rozin, P. (1999). The process of moralization. *Psychological Science, 10,* 218–221.

Shermer, M. (2008). *The mind of the market: Compassionate apes, competitive humans, and other tales from evolutionary economics.* New York: Times Books.

Shweder, R. A., & Haidt, J. (1993). The future of moral psychology: Truth, intuition, and the pluralist way. *Psychological Science, 4,* 360–365.

Skarlicki, D. P., & Kulik, C. (2005). Third party reactions to employee mistreatment: A justice perspective. In B. Staw & R. Kramer (Eds.), *Research in organizational behavior* (Vol. 26, pp. 183–230). Greenwich, CT: JAI Press.

Skitka, L. J. (2002). Do the means always justify the ends, or do the ends sometimes justify the means? A value protective model of moral reasoning. *Personality and Social Psychology Bulletin, 28,* 588–597.

Skitka, L. J. (2003). Of different minds: An accessible identity model of moral reasoning. *Personality and Social Psychology Review, 7,* 286–297.

Skitka, L. J. (2009). Exploring "lost and found" of justice theory and research. *Social Justice Research, 22,* 98–116.

Skitka, L. J., Bauman, C. W., & Mullen, E. (2008). Morality and justice: An expanded theoretical perspective and empirical review. In K. A. Hedgvedt & J. Clay-Warner (Guest Editors). *Advances in group processes,* Vol. 25 (pp. 1–27).

Skitka, L. J., & Mullen, E. (2008). Understanding judgments of fairness in a real-world political context: A test of the value protective model of justice reasoning. *Personality and Social Psychology Bulletin, 28,* 1419–1429.

Smith, A. (1759/2000). *The theory of moral sentiments*. New York: Prometheus.

Smith, P. B., & Bond, M. H. (1994). *Social psychology across cultures: Analysis and perspectives*. Boston, MA: Allyn & Bacon.

Stossel, J. (2004). *Give me a break*. New York: HarperCollins.

Tangney, J. P., & Dearing, R. L. (2002). *Shame and guilt*. New York: The Guilford Press.

Tangney, J. P., Miller, R. S., Flicker, L., & Barlow, D. H. (1996). Are shame, guilt, and embarrassment distinct emotions? *Journal of Personality and Social Psychology, 70,* 1256–1269.

Tangney, J. P., Stuewig, J., & Mashek, D. J. (2007). Moral emotions and moral behavior. In S. T Fiske, A. E. Kazdin, & D. L. Schacter (Eds.), *Annual review of psychology* (Vol. 58, pp. 345–372). Palo Alto, CA: Annual Reviews, Inc.

Thomas, E. M. (2006). *The old way: A story of the first people*. New York: Picador.

Tomlinson, E. C., & Mayer, R. C. (2009). The role of causal attribution dimensions in trust repair. *Academy of Management Review, 34,* 85–104.

Tracy, J. L., Robins, R. W., & Tangney, J. P. (2007). (Eds.) *The self-conscious emotions: Theory and research*. New York: Guilford Press.

Trafimow, D., & Trafimow, S. (1999). Mapping perfect and imperfect duties onto hierarchically and partially restrictive trait dimensions. *Personality and Social Psychology Bulletin, 25,* 686–695.

Tripp, T. M., & Bies, R. J. (1997). What's good about revenge? The avenger's perspective. In R. J. Lewicki, R. J. Bies, & B. H. Sheppard (Eds.), *Research on negotiation in organizations* (Vol. 6, pp. 145–160). Greenwich, CT: JAI Press.

Tripp, T. M., & Bies, R. J. (2008). *Getting even: The truth about workplace revenge—and how to stop it*. New York: John Wiley & Sons.

Tripp, T. M., Bies, R. J., & Aquino, K. (2007). A vigilante model of justice: Revenge, reconciliation, forgiveness, and avoidance. *Social Justice Research, 20,* 10–34.

Turillo, C. J., Folger, R., Lavelle, J., Umphress, E., & Gee, J. (2002). Is virtue its own reward? Self-sacrificial decisions for the sake of fairness. *Organizational Behavior and Human Decision Processes, 89,* 839–865.

Udy, S. W., Jr. (1959). *Organization of work: A comparative analysis of productive among nonindustrial peoples*. New Haven, CT: Hraf.

Van Lange, P. M. F., & Kuhlman, D. M. (1994). Social value orientations and impressions of partner honesty and intelligence: A test of the might versus morality effect. *Journal of Personality and Social Psychology, 67,* 126–141.

Van Lawick-Goodall, J. (1971). *In the shadow of man*. Boston, MA: Houghton Mifflin.

Wade, N. 2006. *Before the dawn: Recovering the lost history of our ancestors*. New York: The Penguin Press.

Westin, D. (2007). *The political brain: The role of emotions in deciding the fate of the nation*. New York: PublicAffairs.

Wilson, J. Q. (1993). *The moral sense*. New York: The Free Press.

Wise, K. (2004). Attribution versus compassion: The City of Chicago's response to the E2 crisis. *Public Relations Review, 30,* 347–356.

Wood, B. (2005). *Human evolution: A very short introduction*. Oxford, U.K.: Oxford University Press.

Wright, R. (1994). *The moral animal: The new science of evolutionary psychology*. New York: Pantheon Books.

11

Free Riders as a Blind Spot of Equity Theory: An Evolutionary Correction

Michael E. Price
Brunel University

Over the past several decades, equity theory (Adams, 1963, 1965)—which predicts that members of organizations will strive to be rewarded equitably, rather than under- or overrewarded—has established itself as a foundational theory in organizational behavior and management. While equity theory has been highly successful in many respects, it has also been criticized for various reasons. The purpose of this chapter is to suggest that one of these criticisms—equity theory's unreliability in situations of overreward—could be met more effectively if organizational scholars reformulated equity theory from an evolutionary psychological perspective. Equity theory would gain increased predictive power from this reformulation, because it would become better able to address the tendency of members to seek overreward—a tendency that has been recognized for decades in the social sciences as the "free rider problem" (Olson, 1965). An improvement in equity theory's ability to address the free rider problem would significantly enhance the theory's usefulness because the free rider problem is not just a trivial detail that equity theory overlooks. On the contrary, overcoming this problem is central to the health and success of any organization (Olson, 1965; Albanese & Van Fleet, 1985; Ostrom, Walker, & Gardner, 1992), and the reasons for this problem's centrality are thrown into relief by the evolutionary psychological perspective (Price, Cosmides, & Tooby, 2002; Tooby, Cosmides, & Price, 2006). An evolutionarily updated equity theory would help to explain both why free rider problems commonly occur at all organizational levels (including managerial levels, as will be emphasized at the conclusion of this chapter), and also how solving these problems can be a key to improving organizational productivity.

Equity Theory: Summary and Predictions

The core elements of classic equity theory (Adams, 1963, 1965), hereafter CET, are as follows. Members engage in a process of social exchange with their organization in which they offer *inputs* for *outcomes*. Inputs are defined as the member's perceived contributions to the organization (e.g., work effort, skills), and outputs are things that the member receives from the organization (e.g., salary, social status). A member (referred to by Adams as "Person") compares his or her own outcome-to-input ratio with those of a referent individual or group (called "Other"). Other is usually another individual; for example, a coworker who performs a similar role as Person, but Other may also be Person in another context such as a previous job. Consistent with the theory of cognitive dissonance (Festinger, 1957), members should become distressed when their outcome-to-input ratio is unequal to those of others, and should attempt to rectify this inequity. For example, imagine that Person perceives himself to have an outcome-to-input ratio of 1:1; for purposes of illustration, let's say that he receives one unit of payment in exchange for one full day's work. If Person perceives that Other's ratio is 2:1—that is, that Other receives two units of payment in exchange for one full day's work—then Person will perceive himself to be relatively underrewarded, and will attempt to reduce this discrepancy. One way he could accomplish this would be by acting to alter the values of his own inputs and outcomes and those of Other. That is, he could strive to increase his own outcome, decrease his own input, increase Other's input, or decrease Other's outcome. Other options would be to distort cognitively the values of any of these inputs or outcomes (for example, he could perceive his own inputs to be lower), change to a different referent Other whose outcome-to-input ratio was closer to his own, or leave the field entirely (for example, by quitting his job).

In situations in which Person perceives himself to be overrewarded rather than underrewarded compared to Other, CET's predictions remain fundamentally the same. If Person again perceives his own outcome-to-input ratio to be 1:1, but now perceives Other's ratio to be 1:2, then he will perceive himself to be relatively overrewarded. He should again feel distress, and be motivated to relieve it by promoting equity via the same methods he would use in the case of underreward. One feature that Adams does suggest should differ between situations of underreward and overreward is the negative emotion that causes distress in Person and thus motivates him to promote equity: Person should experience anger when underrewarded and guilt when overrewarded.

Assessing the Predictiveness of Equity Theory

In evoking the concept of the relative outcome-to-input ratio, CET sketches the psychological computational processes that members must experience in order to judge the fairness of their exchange relationship with their organization. CET is remarkably parsimonious for a social science theory, and it has generally proved useful for predicting behavior. A relatively objective assessment of CET's value is provided by Miner (2003), who had 71 organizational behavior scholars rate the importance of 73 organizational behavior theories on a 7-point scale. Ratings ranged from 2.71 to 5.97, and CET scored a 5.93, for third place overall. Miner also included CET in his list of the 25 organizational behavior theories with the highest scientific validity. The numerous research reviews that have been published on CET (e.g., Greenberg, 1990; Ambrose & Kulick, 1999; Colquitt, Conlon, Wesson, Porter, & Ng, 2001; Mowday & Colwell, 2003; Colquitt, Greenberg, & Zapata-Phelan, 2005; Bolino & Turnley, 2008) generally echo the sentiment that CET has been one of the more important and successful theories in organizational behavior. However, these reviews also acknowledge that CET has attracted a number of consistent criticisms. Bolino & Turley (2008) summarize these reviews in their list of the four most common criticisms of CET: First, CET is underspecified, particularly in terms of predicting reactions to inequity; second, it only considers equity rules, as opposed to other kinds of distribution rules (e.g., equality, need); third, it considers only distributive justice, to the exclusion of procedural and interactional justice; and fourth, it is significantly more accurate in predicting behavior in cases of underreward than in cases of overreward. While all of these criticisms are important, they each target a distinct problem that can be addressed individually, and the remainder of this chapter will focus on addressing the last one on this list.

CET's reduced predictiveness in situations of overreward has always been a bit awkward for the theory. As noted above, CET is rooted in cognitive dissonance theory, and since situations of underreward are just as dissonant as those of overreward, there is no principled reason from this perspective why the former should be more objectionable than the latter. Nevertheless, Adams did state that situations of underreward should be less tolerable than those of overreward. This prediction "is derived from two assumptions: first ... that the threshold for the perception of inequity is higher when Person is overrewarded than when he is underrewarded; secondly ... that Person is motivated to minimize his costs and to maximize his gains" (Adams, 1965, p. 284). In these sentences, Adams establishes what Lakatos (1978) would consider to be an auxiliary or ad hoc hypothesis, as opposed to a core hypothesis, of CET. This auxiliary hypothesis helps CET accommodate the relative tolerability of overreward, but it is by definition difficult to integrate an auxiliary hypothesis into a central theory, and so some unresolved questions remain. For example, is there any principled rationale behind the first assumption above, that "the threshold for the perception of inequity is higher when Person is overrewarded"? Perhaps it could be explained in terms of the second assumption ("Person is motivated to minimize his costs and to maximize his gains"); however, if members are motivated to minimize costs and maximize gains, why does CET theory predict in the first place that they should be motivated to *avoid* (rather than seek) overreward situations?

In practice, when tests of CET have shown members to be more tolerant of overreward than underreward, Adams's auxiliary hypothesis has been implicitly or explicitly invoked, often expressed in terms of egocentric bias (e.g., Greenberg, 1981, 1983; Loewenstein, Thompson, & Bazerman, 1989; Lerner, Somers, Reid, Chiriboga, & Tierney, 1991; Thompson & Loewenstein, 1992; Diekmann, Samuels, Ross, & Bazerman, 1997; Leung, Tong, & Ho, 2004). As a result, CET plus egocentric bias (in cases of overreward) has been established as a useful theory of how members perceive their exchange relationships with organizations. While CET loses some symmetry and simplicity from this bolting-on of egocentric bias, it gains a significant amount of predictive power. This seems like a reasonable trade-off, because prediction is, after all, the scientific bottom line. To paraphrase Einstein (1934), a theory should be as simple as it can be, without sacrificing any predictive power.

However, although the egocentric bias auxiliary hypothesis does help CET navigate through situations of overreward, it may not go far enough. CET may have an underlying flaw in its foundation, of which its struggles with overreward are merely symptomatic. Despite CET being supplemented with egocentric bias, one of its fundamental assumptions remains intact: *members prefer equity and are averse to inequity.* They may be *more* averse to underreward than to overreward, but nevertheless, they prefer equity over both. Although this core hypothesis does contain some important elements of truth about human behavior in organizations, it also contains a serious error (Olson, 1965; Ostrom et al., 1992), an error that is avoided by taking an evolutionary psychological perspective on cooperation in groups (Price et al., 2002; Tooby et al., 2006).

Evolutionary Equity Theory (EET)

Organizations are cooperative groups, often large and complex enough to contain many smaller nested cooperative groups (departments, teams, committees, etc.). Evolutionary psychology makes a set of general predictions about behavior in cooperative groups that are in some ways consistent with the predictions of CET, and in other ways quite different. These differences may help resolve some of the issues that have challenged CET. Because the simple theory that will be sketched here has some fundamental aspects in common with CET, it is perhaps best regarded as an evolutionarily informed update of CET, as opposed to a radical new theory. For that reason, the updated theory will be referred to as *evolutionary equity theory* (hereafter EET). Before presenting EET, it would help to review briefly some of the basic assumptions of evolutionary psychology.

From an evolutionary psychological perspective (Tooby & Cosmides, 1992, 2005), human minds are composed of information-processing mechanisms (adaptations) that were designed by natural selection primarily to promote the survival and reproduction of the individual in ancestral environments. Psychological adaptations can be thought of as "if, then" devices, which process informational inputs from the environment and respond by producing the psychological and behavioral outputs that would have been, on average, the adaptive response to such information in the ancestral past (e.g., IF you see a snake, THEN experience fear and back off). Because behavior is governed by these psychological adaptations, people behave in ways that, in ancestral environments, allowed them to acquire personal adaptive advantages and overcome personal adaptive problems. Contributing to a group cooperative effort would have provided ancestral humans with valuable opportunities to engage in contribution-for-benefit exchange (analogous to CET's input-for-outcome exchange). However, it would also have presented them with a unique set of risky adaptive problems and tempting opportunities for adaptive advantage.

The Free Rider Advantage, the Exploitation Problem, and the Consequences Problem

Ethnographic and archaeological evidence suggests that in ancestral environments, humans formed cooperative groups for the purpose of, for example, foraging for food, waging war, building structures, defending against predators, and developing political alliances (Lee & DeVore, 1968; Kelly, 1995). EET is based on consideration of the kinds of adaptive advantages and problems that would have been encountered by individual members of these cooperative groups.

In typical group cooperative interactions, members who reap the highest personal advantages, at least in the short term, are those whose benefit-to-contribution ratios are the highest. This principle has been studied for decades in social science, usually in the context of collective actions for the production of public goods (Olson, 1965; Hardin 1968). When the benefit produced is a public good (i.e., a resource to which all members have equal access), all members benefit equally, so those who contribute the least to production (free riders) have the highest benefit-to-contribution ratios. CET is usually applied to situations involving private goods (e.g., salaries, which can differ across individuals), but private goods situations can involve free rider problems as well, because benefit-to-contribution ratios can vary in private goods situations just as they can in public goods situations (an assumption on which CET is, of course, founded). Because natural selection is influenced primarily by the survival and reproduction of individuals as opposed to groups (Darwin, 1859; Williams, 1966; Tooby & Cosmides, 1992), it would have initially rewarded group members who preferred to have relatively high benefit-to-contribution ratios (Price, 2006a; Tooby et al., 2006), an opportunity which can be referred to as the *free rider advantage*.

In pursuing their advantage, free riders would have presented an immediate adaptive problem for more cooperative co-members (i.e., members with lower benefit-to-contribution ratios): in order to contribute adaptively, members would have had to ensure that their own benefit-to-contribution ratios did not disadvantage them relative to free riders. A standard finding of formal models of the evolution of cooperation is that free riders, if unchecked, will eventually exploit cooperators to extinction (e.g., Boyd & Richerson, 1988; Henrich, 2004). Therefore, selection would have disfavored members who were apathetic about being exploited by free riders, and would have favored those who were motivated to avoid such exploitation (Price, 2006b; Price et al., 2002). The danger that free riders pose to cooperators can be labeled the *exploitation problem*.

In order to solve the exploitation problem, evolution designed people to be averse to having benefit-to-contribution ratios that are lower than those of co-members. When members perceived that they were being exploited, the anger they experienced would have motivated them to try and reduce their disadvantages relative to free riders. They could have done so by striving to increase their own benefits and/or decrease their own contributions. However, they could also have directed this anger toward the free riders themselves, and tried to lower free riders' benefits and/or increase free riders' contributions. For example, by directing punishment strategically at free riders, they might have been able to lower free riders' net benefits while at the same time inducing them to contribute more (Price et al., 2002; Tooby et al., 2006). The anger of exploited members would also have led them to ostracize free riders from future cooperative interactions; the more a member acquired a reputation for free riding, the fewer exchange opportunities he would have had. In summary, because free riders presented an adaptive problem for co-members, they risked punishment and ostracism; and the more they acquired a reputation for free riding, the greater these costs would have been. Free riders thus faced a potential *consequences problem*.

According to EET, the evolutionary cat-and-mouse dynamic between cooperators and free riders would have designed the set of psychological mechanisms that governs the behavior of the average member of a modern human group. Because of the exploitation problem, members object when they perceive co-members' benefit-to-contribution ratios to be higher than their own. At the same time, because of the free rider advantage, members are more likely to seek relatively high benefit-to-contribution ratios when they perceive the social risks of free riding to be lower. Finally, when these social risks are perceived to be higher, members are more averse to having relatively high benefit-to-contribution ratios, because they strive to avoid the consequences problem.

Comparing the Predictions of CET and EET

CET and EET agree that in order for a member to assess the extent of his advantage or disadvantage relative to others, he needs to compare his own benefit-to-contribution ratio to those of others. Further, the two theories overlap to a large extent in their predictions about how that member should react if he perceives himself to be relatively underrewarded. If Member A perceives his own benefit-to-contribution ratio to be 1:1, and Member B's to be 2:1, then both theories predict that A will experience anger and be motivated to equalize the ratios. The main difference in the theories is that A's motivation to achieve equity is explained by CET in terms of aversion to cognitive dissonance and by EET in terms of aversion to the exploitation problem.

Diverging Predictions in the Case of Overreward (Free Riding)

In the case of overreward, the predictions of CET and EET begin to diverge. If Member A perceives that his own benefit-to-contribution ratio is 1:1, and that B's ratio is 1:2, then CET predicts that A should be motivated by guilt to equalize the ratios; however, A's motivation threshold for seeking equity in this situation will be higher than it is in the case of underreward. CET explains A's motivation to achieve equity again in terms of A's desire to avoid cognitive dissonance, and explains A's higher threshold for pursuing equity in terms of egocentric bias. CET does not predict that A will be motivated to pursue or maintain situations of overreward for himself, or that A's appetite for overreward will be influenced by his perception of the extent to which free riding entails social risks. EET, in contrast, makes both of these predictions.

According to EET, the free rider advantage will make being overrewarded seem appealing to some extent, but this extent will be limited by the degree to which free riding makes one vulnerable to the consequences problem. Thus, in order for Member A to decide how to react to being overrewarded, he will need to assess the likelihood that his free riding will be monitored and discovered by others, and evaluate others' willingness and ability to ostracize or punish him in retaliation for free riding. For example, others' willingness to punish may depend on their anger levels, and others' ability to punish may depend on the probability that they will interact in the future with A, or on their formidability relative to A. When detection and punishment are more likely, the consequences problem will be more salient, and A's preference for equity over overreward will increase. When the consequences problem is less relevant, A will more likely strive to maintain or even increase the extent of his free riding.

The Collapse of Cooperation When Free Riding Goes Unpunished

Because CET and EET make different predictions about how members react to situations of overreward, they also make different assessments about the extent to which free riding threatens the health of organizations. To a greater extent than EET, CET predicts that inequity in organizations is an automatically, efficiently self-correcting phenomenon. For example, imagine an organization in which unfairness is rampant: half the members perceive themselves to be underrewarded, and half perceive themselves to be overrewarded. Both halves should be motivated to seek equity: anger should motivate the underrewarded half to (e.g.,) work less hard, and guilt should motivate the overrewarded half to (e.g.,) work harder, until equity emerges as if from organic self-organization. With CET's egocentric bias auxiliary hypothesis, the picture loses some of its idealized symmetry, because the overrewarded half will need to perceive a relatively high level of overreward before they are motivated to strive for equity. Nevertheless, CET assumes a relatively high level of equitable self-correction in organizations, because it proposes that equity-oriented influences (the emotions of anger and guilt) are located entirely within the psychologies of members themselves, and are experienced automatically upon the perception of inequity.

EET, on the other hand, emphasizes that organizations will often not spontaneously and efficiently self-correct towards greater equity. In the half-underrewarded, half-overrewarded organization, EET predicts that the underrewarded half will indeed be motivated to increase equity; they will respond to the exploitation problem by (e.g.,) working less hard. However, the motivation of the overrewarded to increase equity will depend on how they answer questions related to the consequences problem: Has anyone noticed my free riding and will they notice it in the future? If so, will they have any desire or power to punish or ostracize me? Do I perceive these potential costs to be lower than the advantage of free riding? When the answers to such questions are more likely to be "no," free riding is more likely to persist or increase, and the motivation of the underrewarded will therefore continue to decay.

Unchecked free riding may ultimately cause cooperation in the organization to unravel completely, as members compete with one another in pursuit of the free rider advantage. The worse free riding gets, the more one has to free ride in order to maintain a free rider advantage (i.e., in order to be advantaged over someone with a very high benefit-to-contribution ratio, your ratio must be higher still). The result can be a negative feedback loop that is disastrous for the organization as a whole: as free riders become increasingly exploitative, their co-members increasingly lose motivation, and overall productivity continuously declines. EET suggests that the way to avoid this collapse is to increase the salience of the consequences problem for would-be free riders. Unless free riding is perceived as being sufficiently socially risky, a significant fraction of members will seek overreward. Their sense of guilt will often not in itself be sufficient to eliminate this temptation, contrary to the implications of CET.

Existing Evidence for Testing EET Against CET

As noted above, the predictions of CET and EET tend to converge in situations of underreward, and to diverge in situations of overreward. The emphasis here will be on evidence pertaining to the latter type of situation, because this kind of evidence permits an assessment of which theory is more predictive. In general, this evidence suggests that in many different types of groups and in many different cultures, members are often motivated to seek benefit-to-contribution ratios that endow them with a free rider advantage, unless their pursuit of this advantage is thwarted by the consequences problem.

The threat posed by the free rider problem to organizations has been recognized in the management literature for years, particularly in prominent reviews by Albanese & Van Fleet (1985) and Kidwell & Bennett (1993). Outside of the field of management, there is a huge literature on the free rider problem, going back at least as far as the classic works by Olson (1965) and Hardin (1968). Some more recent documenters of free riding's negative relationship with organizational productivity have been the political scientist Elinor Ostrom (e.g., Ostrom, 1990, 2000, 2009; Ostrom et al., 1992) and the numerous experimental economists who are cited below. Much of this research on the free rider problem has focused on public goods situations, in which a group cooperative effort produces a resource that is equally shared by each group member. As noted above, because public goods are distributed equally among members regardless of contribution, all members end up with equal outcomes. Public goods distribution systems are thus, in an important sense, different from the private goods systems envisioned by CET. Nevertheless, CET should be as capable of making predictions in public goods systems as is it in equity-based systems; it simply has to consider that in public goods systems, all group members have equal outcomes. In public goods situations, then, CET predicts that members will strive to equalize their inputs with those of co-members, in order to match their equal outcomes. In contrast, EET predicts that in public goods situations, the less members perceive that their free riding will entail negative social consequences, the more they will strive for inputs that are lower than those of co-members.

Free Riders in Public Goods Games

The public goods game, a standard paradigm from experimental economics, has produced evidence that is especially illuminating and relevant for testing CET versus EET. A public goods game is essentially an experimental collective action, in which members of small (usually four-person) groups are given an endowment of real money and have the opportunity to contribute toward the production of a public good. At the end of the game, whatever public good has been produced by the group is redistributed equally among all members, regardless of the extent to which a member contributed toward its production.[1] Thus, members who contribute the least reap the highest net benefits. The game is designed to create a free rider advantage, and so it presents an ideal context for testing the CET prediction that people will shun rewards that are proportionally greater than those received by others: if players are in fact often motivated to *seek* relative overreward, this game gives them the opportunity to do so.

Results from public goods games consistently show that many players are indeed motivated to seek overreward, and that this free riding is a chronic problem in the maintenance of group productivity. The standard pattern of contributing is as follows. Contributing is highest at the outset of the game; players apparently realize that cooperation is potentially productive, and begin by contributing on average about 40 to 60% of their endowment. However, some players contribute less than others, and continue to undercontribute as the game progresses, even after they have received feedback about the relative meagerness of their contributions. In response to this free riding, the higher contributors lower their own contributions, in order to mitigate their own exploitation. Thus, as the result of persistent free riding, average contributions dwindle as the game progresses, and group productivity decays gradually over time (e.g., Andreoni, 1988;

Croson, 2007; Croson, Fatas, & Neugebauer, 2005; Fehr & Gächter, 2000; Fischbacher, Gächter, & Fehr, 2001; Isaac & Walker, 1988; Masclet, Noussair, Tucker, & Villeval, 2003; Page, Putterman, & Unel, 2005).

However, even if free riding is a persistent problem in these games, that pattern does not mean that the majority of players are motivated to free ride. It could just be a few bad apples who ruin the production effort for everyone else, by behaving exploitatively and thus provoking lowered contributions from annoyed co-players. What do the data suggest about the percentage of players who free ride? The answer to this question is actually a bit more complicated than it may first appear. Researchers usually define a free rider as a player who consistently contributes below the mean co-player contribution, while those who contribute at or above this mean are considered cooperators. Studies that have attempted to classify players into different categories have sometimes concluded that free riders are in the minority (e.g., Fischbacher et al., 2001; Kurzban & Houser, 2005; Gunnthorsdottir, Houser, & McCabe, 2007). However, how far below the mean co-player contribution a player can go before he or she is considered a free rider rather than a cooperator, is necessarily arbitrary to some degree (Gunnthorsdottir et al., 2007). Further, the percentage of players who free ride does not remain constant across all public goods game conditions. Indeed, a major goal of public goods game research is to discover the conditions that influence the extent of free riding. So in addressing the issue of the prevalence of free riding, for now we will just note that it is common enough to damage group productivity significantly, and that its prevalence depends in large part on the conditions under which the game is played. The most important of these conditions is reviewed below.

Punishment as a Deterrent to Free Riding

Punishment of free riders is the most basic and effective solution to the free rider problem that experimental economists have investigated. That is not to say that punishment is the only possible solution; other solutions that have been proposed and explored include, for example, allowing greater verbal communication among players (e.g., Ostrom et al., 1992; Bochet, Page, & Putterman, 2006), manipulating the extent to which players can develop stable reputations (e.g., Andreoni, 1988; Croson, 1996), and presenting players with cues suggesting that they are being monitored (Haley & Fessler, 2005; Burnham & Hare, 2007). Punishment is not even the only kind of social sanction that may help prevent free riding; positive sanctions (rewards) may be effective as well, although studies of this effectiveness have produced mixed conclusions (Andreoni, Harbaugh, & Vesterlund, 2003; Sefton, Shupp, & Walker, 2007). However, punishment's power to deter free riding has been studied relatively extensively and documented relatively convincingly, so in consideration of space constraints, it will be the focus here. It should be noted that much of this research on punishment has been motivated explicitly by evolutionary considerations (e.g., Barclay, 2006; Boyd, Gintis, Bowles, & Richerson, 2003; Price et al., 2002; Price, 2005). This is true because an evolutionary approach, with its emphasis on the free rider problem and the consequences problem, suggests that a consequence like punishment, when severe enough to negate the advantage of free riding, will be an effective solution to the free rider problem. The idea of punishment as a solution to the free rider problem is thus highly compatible with EET.

Through punishment, public goods game players are given the opportunity to retaliate against undercontributing co-players by imposing some sort of cost on them, often in the form of a monetary fine. Fining interactions typically involve above-mean contributors imposing endowment-reducing fines on below-mean contributors, so these fines can appropriately be considered punishment of free riders (Ostrom et al., 1992; Fehr & Gächter, 2000, 2002; Nikiforakis, 2008; however, fining of above-mean contributors also occurs, often by individuals who have themselves been fined previously, and who presumably want revenge on their perceived punishers). The imposition of these fines is usually made to be costly, and players who choose to punish other players must use their own funds to pay for it. Despite this costliness, many players willingly pay to punish free riders, and punishment of free riders generally turns out to be a highly effective way of keeping contributions high, and so of staving off the decay of cooperation that usually characterizes public good games (e.g., Fehr & Gächter, 2000, 2002; Masclet, Noussair, Tucker, & Villeval, 2003; Sefton et al., 2007; Yamagishi, 1986; Ostrom et al., 1992; Nikiforakis, 2008). Because punishment prevents the cooperative interaction from unraveling due to free riding, the threat of being punished seems to motivate higher contributions from players who would otherwise free ride. Punishment is thus group-beneficial: contributions are higher when punishment is possible, so each group member's share is larger. Because punishment is group-beneficial and costly to impose, it is sometimes referred to as *altruistic punishment* (e.g., Fehr & Gächter, 2002; Boyd et al., 2003; Barclay, 2006), and seen as a kind of second-order contribution to the public good (Yamagishi, 1986).

Besides monetary sanctions, nonmonetary social sanctions also seem to be fairly effective ways of eliciting higher contributions from would-be free riders in public goods games. For example, Masclet et al. (2003) allowed standard monetary sanctions in some rounds and nonmonetary sanctions in others. In the nonmonetary rounds, players could sanction free riders by assigning points, which indicated "disapproval" of the free riding but had no monetary consequences. These nonmonetary sanctions affected contributions positively, although less positively than did the monetary sanctions. Ostracism is another kind of social sanction that can help prevent free riding. A public goods game study by Cinyabuguma,

Page, & Putterman (2005), which included a baseline treatment with no sanctioning and an expulsion treatment in which players could vote to expel free riders from their group, found that contributions were significantly higher in the expulsion treatment. Further, in public goods games where players are given access to information about the past behavior of their potential co-players, and then allowed to choose their co-players, free riders tend to be left out in the cold. Higher contributors tend to choose one another and end up forming the most cooperative and productive groups, while free riders are left behind to form less-productive groups (Ehrhart & Keser, 1999; Sheldon, Sheldon, & Osbaldiston, 2000; Page et al., 2005; Barclay & Willer, 2007). Thus, partner choice helps solve the free rider problem because it allows cooperators to ostracize free riders, and to thus put themselves in situations where they can contribute without fear of exploitation.

The evidence suggests that the free rider problem, as well as punishment's effectiveness as a solution to this problem, are both cross-culturally universal. This universality has been demonstrated not only in the above-cited public goods games with punishment played throughout North America, Europe, and Japan, but also via methods besides those of experimental economics. For example, comparative studies conducted among Californians and indigenous Shuar in the Ecuadorian Amazon suggest that in both cultures, punitive sentiment toward free riders is highest among those who are themselves the most willing to contribute to collective actions (Price et al., 2002; Price, 2005). And Ostrom, who has probably conducted more cross-cultural research on collective action than anyone else, notes that "in all known self-organized resource governance regimes that have survived for multiple generations, participants invest resources in monitoring and sanctioning the actions of each other so as to reduce the probability of free riding" (Ostrom, 2000, p. 138). The universality of free riding, and of free rider punishment, is consistent with the idea that these behaviors are the products of species-typical psychological mechanisms, and thus consistent with EET.

Finally, a crucial caveat about punishment must be stated: if administered unnecessarily or for the wrong reasons, punishment can backfire and actually have a negative effect on productivity in collective actions. There is a risk that external incentives like punishments will crowd out voluntary cooperativeness among participants (Titmuss, 1970; Vollan, 2008). Those who are already disposed toward contributing, and who do not need an external incentive to induce them to do so, may regard punishment as unwarranted coercion and contribute less under the threat of punishment than they would have in the absence of this threat. Punishment can also be detrimental if it is administered in a way that seems unfair or illegitimate; for example, in a way that suggests overly selfish motives on the part of the punisher (Fehr & Rockenbach, 2002).

Is the Above Evidence More Consistent with CET or EET?

One general behavior pattern, present in the cross-cultural evidence from the public goods game and other studies, is consistent with both CET and EET: group members are averse to being underrewarded. Relatively high contributors to public goods games, for example, will voluntarily act to punish and avoid co-players who have higher benefit-to-contribution ratios (free riders), and will reduce their own contributions if they become trapped in a group with such co-players. However, another major behavior pattern observed in the above studies seems compatible with EET but not with CET: the less of a risk there is that free riding will be punished in some way, the more likely group members will be to actively seek relative over-reward. This pattern is consistent with EET, which sees pursuit of the free rider advantage as a predictable outcome in the absence of the consequences problem. However, active free riding seems to undermine CET since CET predicts aversion to overreward, even if this aversion should be reduced relative to the extent to which it occurs in underreward situations.

As noted above, social scientists have long been aware of the theory that free riding poses a problem for group cooperative interactions. Indeed, the pioneering theoretical statements about this problem (Olson, 1965; Hardin, 1968) are only slightly younger than CET itself. Literature on the free riding problem has also been reviewed and discussed in mainstream management publications for years (e.g., Albanese & Van Fleet, 1985; Kidwell & Bennett, 1993). However despite the visibility of the free rider problem to management and organizational behavior audiences, little effort has been made to address the incompatibility of the free rider problem with CET. This oversight could be corrected fairly easily, by replacing CET's traditional foundation, rooted in cognitive dissonance theory, with a foundation that is based in evolutionary theory and that identifies the adaptive advantages and problems that members of cooperative groups would have faced in ancestral environments.

Applying EET in Organizations

As mentioned above, there have been notable efforts to raise the awareness of management scholars about the relevance of the free riding problem to organizational productivity (Albanese & Van Fleet, 1985; Kidwell & Bennett, 1993). Nevertheless, this problem has received relatively little attention compared to the large amount of research that has been inspired by, and has often been interpreted as being largely supportive of, CET.

Consequently, many researchers may be biased in favor of CET's view that inequity in organizations is to a large extent self-correcting. However, if EET is correct, then this CET perspective overestimates the extent to which overreward situations will self-correct, and underestimates the potential of the free riding tendency to infect an organization. Consequently, advice to managers that is rooted in CET, without due regard for the kinds of corrections offered by EET, could fail to diagnose one of the most significant threats to sustained productivity in cooperative groups.

Managers should be made aware of the universal pervasiveness of the free riding problem and of the corrosive effects it can potentially have at all organizational levels. But if free riding is not a problem that will just solve itself, then what can managers do to solve it? As noted above, various solutions to the problem have been proposed and explored, but the effectiveness of punishment has been especially well studied and well documented, so it will be the focus here. More specifically, the focus will be on what punishments for free riding should be explicitly designed to accomplish, and what they should be designed to avoid.

The ultimate goal of free rider punishment should be not to harm the guilty, but rather to maintain the health of the organization as a whole, by creating an environment in which people can contribute without fear of exploitation. If some members of an organization perceive that they are being exploited by others, it may be necessary for management to step in and demonstrate that taking advantage of contributors will not be tolerated. This approach to solving the exploitation problem for high-contributing workers does not mean that managers must adopt an overly cynical philosophy of human nature. It would be inaccurate, for example, for managers to assume that all of their employees are striving to exploit one another; research suggests that there is considerable variation in the extent to which individuals are motivated to free ride, and that substantial numbers of people may lack this motivation (Fischbacher et al., 2001; Kurzban & Houser, 2005; Gunnthorsdottir et al., 2007). Nevertheless, managers must expect that free riding strategies may well be pursued commonly and vigorously in organizations in which they are permitted to flourish. To expect otherwise could lead to results that are demoralizing for high-contributing employees and thus dangerous for the organization.

However, although managers should not underestimate the potential of free riding to become a problem, it is equally important that they avoid overestimating this potential, and that they strive to ensure that punishments for free riding are necessary and fair. Free riding may sometimes be perceived to be a larger problem than it actually is, and as noted above, punishments that are perceived as unnecessary or as overkill can crowd out genuine desires to contribute voluntarily. For example, for noncontribution to be true free riding, it must be intentional, and not be due to (e.g.,) illness or injury (Price, 2006a). Punishments directed at unintentional noncontribution will generally be perceived as unfair and demoralizing. It should be clear to everyone in the organization that punishments are directed only toward individuals who have intentionally pursued above-mean benefit-for-contribution ratios, and that the purpose of the punishment is to solve the exploitation problem for higher contributors and to thus promote the health of the organization as a whole. Punishments will be more likely to backfire if they are perceived as having additional, more selfish motives (e.g., if they are seen as a way for management to extract an amount of effort out of workers that is disproportionately large, given the extent of the workers' free riding).

What About When the Worst Free Riders Are the Managers Themselves?

The fact that free riding is a very real problem in organizations (Albanese & Van Fleet, 1985; Kidwell & Bennett, 1993; Ostrom, 2009), even at the very highest levels of organizational structure, has been illustrated repeatedly and vividly over the past several months of the global financial crisis, as leaders of various failed institutions have been accused of happily accepting "reward for failure." A dramatic recent example is Sir Fred Goodwin, who led the Royal Bank of Scotland to the largest annual corporate loss in U.K. history (£24.1 billion), before stepping down to receive an annual pension of about £700,000 (Treanor, 2009). From the perspective of the typical observer, it seems as though Sir Fred received a very large benefit in exchange for a massively negative contribution. This situation has inspired outrage among most British citizens, who regard Sir Fred as a kind of ultimate free rider, and has also prompted a desperate search by Gordon Brown's government to find some way of legitimately punishing Sir Fred, who apparently did not break any laws. In the absence of any legitimate threat of punishment, Sir Fred has appeared quite willing to seek and accept what most regard as a perversely unfair benefit-to-contribution ratio. While his is an extreme case, his behavior nevertheless seems to contradict CET and be consistent with EET. (The fact that EET sees this free riding as "natural" does not excuse it, of course; after all, it is just as "natural" to want to punish Sir Fred as it is for him to want to free ride.)

The phenomenon of top-level free riding underlines the fact that managers who are interested in punishing free riding fairly will often find themselves in the position of having to go after those at the very highest levels of an organization. It is important to emphasize this fact because it is often underappreciated. In the management literature, reviews of the free rider problem (e.g., Albanese & Van Fleet, 1985; Kidwell & Bennett, 1993) have tended to focus on what managers can do to prevent free riding by employees. But although the term free rider may conjure up an image in the minds of some of shirking workers at lower organizational levels, this assumption is likely false. Indeed, in a culture such as the United States in the early twenty-first century, when it is not unusual for the salaries of top management to be hundreds of times higher than those of the average worker, managers would seem to be in a relatively good position to acquire disproportionately high benefit-to-contribution ratios, if their contributions are not actually hundreds of times higher than those of the workers. It should be noted that that is a big "if." As Novak (1991) points out, the decisions of a talented manager can enrich a company to an extent that easily justifies, at least in financial terms, a salary that seems astronomical when compared to the average worker. Therefore, because the talent of managers is often an extremely valuable input, their extremely high salaries should not necessarily seem objectionable from the perspective of classic or evolutionary equity theory. On the other hand, higher salaries put management under greater pressure to perform well, because there is more opportunity for their inputs to fall short of their outcomes. The perception that this shortfall is occurring should become more likely when general economic conditions are bad, because in these times it becomes harder for management to make company-enriching decisions. That is probably why anger about high executive pay has become more common during the financial crisis of recent months. This idea—that managers are more likely to be perceived as free riders when times are bad—is quite interesting and probably underresearched ("What's Behind the Rise in CEO Pay?," 2005).

Sir Fred Goodwin was mentioned above primarily because his case provides a colorful and timely illustration of top-level free riding. One could question the appropriateness of using his case as an example, however, because much of the most visible outrage he has inspired (for example, from the British public) has been extraorganizational. Perhaps it would be more appropriate to regard the "organization" in this illustration not as RBS but as the larger British society, with Sir Fred being seen by many British citizens as having been lavishly rewarded for damaging British society (that is not to suggest, of course, that Sir Fred's behavior could not also have inspired anger within RBS). Regardless, evidence does suggest that the perception of managerial free riding probably is a common and potentially damaging within-organization phenomenon. When top management salaries are perceived to exceed their inputs, it can create distributive justice concerns among middle managers and lower-level workers (Cowherd & Levine, 1992; Wilhelm, 1993), which may produce cynicism (Andersson & Bateman, 1997), lack of commitment, and lower product quality (Cowherd & Levine, 1992). Although management researchers do not usually use the term *free riders* to describe managers in this context, the term is probably apt as a generic descriptor of members whose benefit-to-contribution ratios are perceived to be inequitably high.

As noted above, while free riding can occur at any organizational level, the management literature has tended to focus on lower-level rather than top-level free riding. The focus here on top-level free riding has been an effort to correct that, and there is also one further reason why the problem of top-level free riding merits special attention: top-level free riding will usually be more difficult to police and control than lower-level free riding. With lower-level free riding, management can be expected to step in and solve the problem because they have incentives to do so: by ending free riding they can benefit themselves as well as their whole organization. However, when it is the managers themselves who have been seduced by the free rider advantage, their interests (at least in the short term) will lie in allowing their own free riding to persist. Because free riders cannot be relied upon to police and punish themselves, the problem of top-level free riding is better solved by shareholders whose interests lie in promoting success for the whole organization (and not just for a particular individual or group within the organization), and who understand that free rider problems at any level will likely impede this success.

Endnote

1. A more detailed description of the public goods game follows. The game typically involves a group of participants in a lab who are subdivided into several game-playing groups; for example, 16 participants may compose 4 separate 4-player public goods games. Games are played via the lab's computer network for at least 10 rounds, under essentially anonymous conditions; players are known to co-players only by handles such as Player One, Player Two, etc. Each round, players are granted an endowment of tokens that are exchanged for real cash at the end of the game. Each player can choose whether to contribute none, some, or all of his tokens toward the production of a public good. The game's parameters are set to create a situation in which individuals gain an advantage from free riding. More formally, the rules of this game are as follows: in a game involving a group of n members, a player's individual contribution c is multiplied by m to create a public good mc, which is shared equally by all players. The value of m is always greater than 1.0, so that contributions actually do produce resources for the group. However, m is also always less than n, which means that one can profit more individually if one fails to contribute, and instead free rides on the contribution efforts of co-members. (If $m > n$, in contrast—i.e., if contributions are multiplied in an extremely productive way—then individuals gain more from contributing than from free riding). At the end of each round, whatever public good has been produced by all players' contributions is redistributed equally among all group members regardless of whether they contributed or

not. Following this redistribution, players are informed of the contribution and share sizes of co-players, and so are able to adjust their behavior based on the behavior of others.

References

Adams, J. S. (1963). Toward an understanding of inequity. *Journal of Abnormal and Social Inequity, 67*, 422–436.

Adams, J. S. (1965). Inequity in social exchange. In L. Berkowitz (Ed.), *Advances in experimental social psychology* (Vol. 2, pp. 267–299). New York: Academic Press.

Albanese, R., & Van Fleet, D. D. (1985). Rational behavior in groups: The free-riding tendency. *Academy of Management Review, 10*, 244–255.

Ambrose, M. L., & Kulick, C. T. (1999). Old friends, new face: Motivation research in the 1990s. *Journal of Management, 25*, 231–292.

Andersson, L. M., & Bateman, T. S. (1997). Cynicism in the workplace: Some causes and effects. *Journal of Organizational Behavior, 18*, 449–469.

Andreoni, J., (1988). Why free ride? *Journal of Public Economics 37*, 291–304.

Andreoni, J., Harbaugh, W., & Vesterlund, L. (2003). The carrot or the stick: Rewards, punishments, and cooperation. *The American Economic Review 93*, 893–902.

Barclay, P. (2006). Reputational benefits for altruistic punishment. *Evolution and Human Behavior, 27*, 325–344.

Barclay, P., & Willer, R. (2007). Partner choice creates competitive altruism in humans. *Proceedings of the Royal Society of London Series B, 274*, 749–753.

Bochet, O., Page, T., & Putterman, L. (2006). Communication and punishment in voluntary contribution experiments. *Journal of Economic Behavior & Organization, 60*, 11–26.

Bolino, M. C., & Turnley, W. H. (2008). Old faces, new places: Equity theory in cross-cultural contexts. *Journal of Organizational Behavior, 29*, 29–50.

Boyd, R., Gintis, H., Bowles, S., & Richerson, P. J. (2003). The evolution of altruistic punishment. *Proceedings of the National Academy of Sciences USA, 100*, 3531–3535.

Boyd, R., & Richerson, P. J. (1988). The evolution of reciprocity in sizable groups. *Journal of Theoretical Biology, 132*, 337–356.

Burnham, T., & Hare, B. (2007). Does involuntary neural activation increase public goods contributions in human adults? *Human Nature, 18*, 88–108.

Cinyabuguma, M., Page, T., & Putterman, L. (2005). Cooperation under the threat of expulsion in a public goods experiment. *Journal of Public Economics, 89*, 1421–1435.

Colquitt, J. A., Conlon, D. E., Wesson, M. J., Porter, O. L. H., & Ng, K. Y. (2001). Justice at the millennium: A meta-analytic review of 25 years of organizational research. *Journal of Applied Psychology, 86*, 425–445.

Colquitt, J. A., Greenberg, J., & Zapata-Phelan, C. P. (2005). What is organizational justice? A historical overview. In J. Greenberg & J. A. Colquitt (Eds.), *Handbook of organizational justice* (pp. 3–56). Mahwah, NJ: Lawrence Erlbaum Associates.

Cowherd, D. M., & Levine, D. I. (1992). Product quality and pay equity between lower-level employees and top management: An investigation of distributive justice theory. *Administrative Science Quarterly, 37*, 302–320.

Croson, R. T. A. (1996). Partners and strangers revisited. *Economics Letters, 53*, 25–32.

Croson, R. T. A. (2007). Theories of commitment, altruism and reciprocity: Evidence from linear public goods games. *Economic Inquiry, 45*, 199–216.

Croson, R. T. A., Fatas, E., & Neugebauer, T. (2005). Reciprocity, matching and conditional cooperation in two public goods games. *Economics Letters, 87*, 95–101.

Darwin, C. (1859). *On the origin of species*. London: Murray.

Diekmann, K. A., Samuels, S. M., Ross, L., & Bazerman, M. H. (1997). Self-interest and fairness in problems of resource allocation: Allocators versus recipients. *Journal of Personality and Social Psychology, 72*, 1061–1074.

Ehrhart, K., & Keser, C. (1999). *Mobility and cooperation: On the run*. Working Paper 99s-24, CIRANO, Montreal.

Einstein, A. (1934). On the method of theoretical physics. *Philosophy of Science, 1*, 163–169.

Fehr, E., & Gächter, S. (2000). Cooperation and punishment in public goods experiments. *American Economic Review, 90*, 980–994.

Fehr, E., & Gächter, S. (2002). Altruistic punishment in humans. *Nature, 415*, 137–140.

Fehr, E., & Rockenbach, B. (2002). Detrimental effects of sanctions on human altruism. *Nature, 422*, 137–140.

Festinger, L. (1957). *A theory of cognitive dissonance*. Evanston, IL: Row, Peterson.

Fischbacher, U., Gächter, S., & Fehr, E. (2001). Are people conditionally cooperative? Evidence from a public goods experiment. *Economics Letters, 71*, 397–404.

Greenberg, J. (1981). The justice of distributing scarce and abundant resources. In M. J. Lerner & S. C. Lerner (Eds.), *The justice motive in social behavior* (pp. 289–316). New York: Plenum.

Greenberg, J. (1983). Overcoming egocentric bias in perceived fairness through self-awareness. *Social Psychology Quarterly, 46*, 152–156.

Greenberg, J. (1990). Organizational justice: Yesterday, today and tomorrow. *Journal of Management, 16*, 399–432.

Gunnthorsdottir, A., Houser, D., & McCabe, K. (2007). Disposition, history and contributions in public goods experiments. *Journal of Economic Behavior & Organization, 62*, 304–315.

Haley, K. J., & Fessler, D. M. T. (2005). Nobody's watching? Subtle cues affect generosity in an anonymous economic game. *Evolution and Human Behavior, 26*, 245–256.

Hardin, G. (1968). The tragedy of the commons. *Science, 162*, 1243–1248.

Henrich, J. (2004). Cultural group selection, coevolutionary processes and large-scale cooperation. *Journal of Economic Behavior & Organization, 53*, 3–35.

Isaac, R. M., & Walker, J. M. (1988). Group size effects in public goods provision: The voluntary contributions mechanism. *The Quarterly Journal of Economics, 103*, 179–199.

Kelly, R. L. (1995). *The foraging spectrum: Diversity in hunter-gatherer lifeways.* Washington, DC: Smithsonian.

Kidwell, R. E., & Bennett, N. 1993. Employee propensity to withhold effort: A conceptual model to intersect three avenues of research. *Academy of Management Review, 18*, 429–456.

Kurzban, R., & Houser, D. (2005). Experiments investigating cooperative types in humans: A complement to evolutionary theory and simulations. *Proceedings of the National Academy of Science, 102*, 1802–1807.

Lakatos, I. (1978). *The methodology of scientific research programmes, Volume 1.* Cambridge, U.K.: Cambridge University Press.

Lee, R. B., & DeVore, I. (1968). *Man the hunter.* New York: Aldine de Gruyter.

Lerner, M., Somers, D. G., Reid, D., Chiriboga, D., & Tierney, M. (1991). Adult children as caregivers: Egocentric biases in judgments of sibling contributions. *The Gerontologist, 31*, 746–755.

Leung, K., Tong, K., & Ho, S. S. (2004). Effects of interactional justice on egocentric bias in resource allocation decisions. *Journal of Applied Psychology, 89*, 405–415.

Loewenstein, G., Thompson, L., & Bazerman, M. (1989). Social utility and decision making in interpersonal contexts. *Journal of Personality and Social Psychology, 57*, 426–441.

Masclet, D., Noussair, C., Tucker, S., & Villeval, M. (2003). Monetary and nonmonetary punishment in the voluntary contributions mechanism. *The American Economic Review, 93*, 366–380.

Miner, J. B. (2003). The rated importance, scientific validity, and practical usefulness of organizational behavior theories: A quantitative review. *Academy of Management Learning and Education, 2*, 250–268.

Mowday, R. T., & Colwell K. A. (2003). Employee reactions to unfair outcomes in the workplace: The contributions of Adams's equity theory to understanding work motivation. In L. W. Porter, G. A. Bigley, & R. M. Steer (Eds.), *Motivation and work behavior* (7th ed., pp. 65–82). Boston: McGraw-Hill.

Nikiforakis, N. (2008). Punishment and counter-punishment in public good games: Can we really govern ourselves? *Journal of Public Economics, 92*, 91–112.

Novak, M. (1991). *The spirit of democratic capitalism.* London: The IEA Health and Welfare Unit.

Olson, M. (1965). *The logic of collective action: Public goods and the theory of groups.* Cambridge, MA: Harvard University Press.

Ostrom, E. (1990). *Governing the commons: The evolution of institutions for collective action.* New York: Cambridge University Press.

Ostrom, E. (2000). Collective action and the evolution of social norms. *Journal of Economic Perspectives, 14*, 137–158.

Ostrom, E. (2009). Building trust to solve commons dilemmas: Taking small steps to test an evolving theory of collective action. In Simon Levin, (Ed.), *Games, groups, and the global good* (pp. 207–228). New York: Springer.

Ostrom, E., Walker, J., & Gardner, R. (1992). Covenants with and without a sword—self governance is possible. *American Political Science Review, 86*, 404–417.

Page, T., Putterman, L., & Unel, B. (2005). Voluntary association in public goods experiments: Reciprocity, mimicry and efficiency. *The Economic Journal, 115*, 1032–1053.

Price, M. E. (2005). Punitive sentiment among the Shuar and in industrialized societies: Cross-cultural similarities. *Evolution and Human Behavior, 26*, 279–287.

Price M. E. (2006a). Judgments about cooperators and free riders on a Shuar work team: An evolutionary psychological perspective. *Organizational Behavior and Human Decision Processes, 101*, 20–35.

Price M. E. (2006b). Monitoring, reputation and "greenbeard" reciprocity in a Shuar work team. *Journal of Organizational Behavior, 27*, 201–219.

Price M. E., Cosmides L., & Tooby J. (2002). Punitive sentiment as an anti-free rider psychological device. *Evolution and Human Behavior, 23*, 203–231.

Sefton, M., Shupp, R., & Walker, J. M. (2007). The effect of rewards and sanctions in provision of public goods. *Economic Inquiry, 45*, 671–690.

Sheldon, K. M., Sheldon, M. S., & Osbaldiston, R. (2000). Prosocial values and group-assortation within an N-person prisoner's dilemma. *Human Nature, 11*, 387–404.

Thompson, L. L., & Loewenstein, G. (1992). Egocentric interpretations of fairness and interpersonal conflict. *Organizational Behavior and Human Decision Processes, 51*, 176–197.

Titmuss, R. M. (1970). *The gift relationship: From human blood to social policy*. London: George Allen and Unwin.

Tooby, J., & Cosmides, L. (1992). The psychological foundations of culture. In J. H. Barkow, L. Cosmides, & J. Tooby (Eds.), *The adapted mind: Evolutionary psychology and the generation of culture* (pp. 19–136). New York: Oxford University Press.

Tooby, J., & Cosmides, L. (2005). Conceptual foundations of evolutionary psychology. In D. M. Buss (Ed.), *The handbook of evolutionary psychology*, (pp. 5–67). Hoboken, NJ: Wiley.

Tooby J., Cosmides L., & Price M. E. (2006). Cognitive adaptations for *n*-person exchange: The evolutionary roots of organizational behavior. *Managerial and Decision Economics, 27*, 103–129.

Treanor, J. (2009). RBS record losses raise prospect of 95% state ownership. *The Guardian*, February 26, 2009.

Vollan, B. (2008). Socio-ecological explanations for crowding-out effects from economic field experiments in southern Africa. *Ecological Economics, 67*, 560–573.

What's behind the rise in CEO pay? (2005). Retrieved July 01, 2009 from http:// knowledge.emory.edu/article.cfm?articleid=861.

Wilhelm, P. G. (1993). Application of distributive justice theory to the CEO pay problem: Recommendations for reform. *Journal of Business Ethics, 12*, 469–482.

Williams, G. C. (1966). *Adaptation and natural selection*. Princeton, NJ: Princeton University Press.

Yamagishi, T. (1986). The provision of a sanctioning system as a public good. *Journal of Personality and Social Psychology, 51*, 110–116.

12

From Proscriptions to Prescriptions: A Call for Including Prosocial Behavior in Behavioral Ethics

David M. Mayer
University of Michigan

How do most behavioral ethics articles begin? They generally note the growing interest in ethics in organizations due to the number of corporate indiscretions and scandals discussed in the media in recent years. Indeed, in a review of the field of behavioral ethics, Treviño, Weaver, and Reynolds (2006, p. 951) commence in the following way: "High impact scandals in organizations from businesses to athletic teams and religious organizations have generated widespread interest in ethical and unethical behavior in organizations." Although few would doubt that such scandals have promoted interest in behavioral ethics, I argue that by focusing almost exclusively on unethical behaviors, the field has inadvertently become narrower than perhaps it ought to be.

Indeed, the majority of work in the field of behavioral ethics has focused on *proscriptions*, defined as behaviors one *should not* engage in. For example, proscriptions involve lying, stealing, cheating, and harming someone else. Kant (1797/1991) refers to such behaviors as "perfect duties" (Trafimow, Bromgard, Finlay, & Ketelaar, 2005; Trafimow & Trafimow, 1999) because they are behaviors that should never be demonstrated. In contrast, there is considerably less research on *prescriptions*, defined as behaviors one *should* engage in. Examples of prescriptions include donating money to charity, helping someone in need, and whistle-blowing. Kant describes such behaviors as "imperfect duties" because although most would view it as desirable that people engage in these behaviors, they are not necessarily required all of the time.

As the field of behavioral ethics takes shape, it is important to consider ways for the domain to continue to grow and flourish. In this chapter I make the case that one way to help the field to continue to blossom is to add to our focus on proscriptions (i.e., unethical behavior) by also delving into the world of prescriptions (i.e., prosocial behavior). This idea has been expressed by other behavioral ethics scholars who encouraged future research to focus on "positive behaviors" as well (Treviño et al., 2006, p. 974). The purpose of this chapter is to provide a number of suggestions for how behavioral ethics research can be integrated with the literature on prosocial behavior. The hope is that these ideas will stimulate research that will help the field of behavioral ethics to expand. In addition, I highlight some practical managerial implications of this integration.

Integrating Prosocial Behavior into Behavioral Ethics

In what follows, I briefly describe a number of possible directions for integrating prosocial behavior into the behavioral ethics literature. The suggestions I provide do not represent a comprehensive list of topics, but rather a brief taste that I hope will whet the appetite of scholars interested in taking a prosocial approach to the study of behavioral ethics.

How Can the Whistle-Blowing Domain be Expanded?

A discussion of the integration of behavioral ethics and prosocial behavior should begin with perhaps the only topic that has already begun to do this—whistle-blowing (Gundlach, Douglas, & Martinko, 2003; Mesmer-Magnus & Viswesvaran, 2005; Near & Miceli, 1985). Whistle-blowing is defined as, "the disclosure by organization members (former or current) of illegal, immoral, or illegitimate practices under the control of their employers to persons or organizations that may be able to effect action" (Near & Miceli, 1985, p. 4). Whistle-blowing represents the quintessential example of how behavioral ethics and prosocial behavior can be integrated. Although we have learned a lot about the antecedents and consequences of whistle-blowing over the past couple of decades (see Mesmer-Magnus & Viswesvaran, 2005 for a meta-analytic review), many questions still remain unanswered.

Whistle-blowing is typically described in terms of reporting an unethical act to someone outside the organization, such as the media. Some research examines internal reporting, which involves reporting unethical behavior to organizational authorities (Treviño & Victor, 1992). However, in addition to whistle-blowing, research has traditionally failed to consider other prosocial or constructive responses to unethical behavior in organizations. Examples could include a direct conversation with the wrongdoer, standing up for someone else in a polite way, or providing emotional support to someone in need. Interestingly, these types of constructive responses to others' unethical behavior are simply not examined in our literature. It is easy to find a measure of deviance or more destructive responses to unethical behavior. However, there is a dearth of measures aimed at examining constructive responses to others' unethical behavior. It is important to understand such constructive responses because they likely lead to the best outcome for the whistle-blower, victim, and the organization.

Another relevant issue with respect to whistle-blowing is whether the harm is done to oneself or to a third party. A growing body of work in the organizational justice literature on the deontic model of justice (Folger, 1994, 1998, 2001) highlights that people often respond to others' unjust treatment. It would be interesting to see if there are different antecedents of whistle-blowing reactions to one's own mistreatment as compared to witnessing another being treated unethically. What drives a person to blow the whistle or to have a constructive response to someone else being treated in an unethical manner? This is an important avenue for future research on whistle-blowing.

Finally, organizational structures such as ethics hotlines provide an opportunity for individuals who have witnessed unethical behavior to "safely" report the behavior. It would be interesting if organizations had a hotline that encouraged stories of heroism and courage. Perhaps providing an outlet to discuss prosocial behaviors could encourage future prosocial acts as well as promote pride and a sense of identification with the company.

In general, the whistle-blowing literature sits nicely at the crossroads of ethics and prosocial behavior. However, I argue that much more can be done to further wed these areas. Such advances could involve expanding the domain to additional prosocial or constructive responses to unethical behavior, examining how reactions may differ to one's own vs. someone else's unethical treatment, and celebrating prosocial acts that take place in the organization. By taking a prosocial lens, a host of new questions related to whistle-blowing emerge.

Are There Distinct Moral Disengagement Mechanisms for Why People Fail to Engage in Prosocial Behaviors?

One of the most important and influential behavioral ethics theories is *moral disengagement* (Bandura, 1986, 1990a, 1990b, 1999, 2002). Moral disengagement presumes that individuals are normally able to self-regulate their moral behavior. Because humans seek to behave in ways that are consistent with internalized moral standards, individuals administer self-sanctions for engaging in unethical acts. For example, we may feel guilty if we deceive someone else. However, sometimes our moral functioning is set askew, and we are unable to regulate our moral behavior. Bandura refers to this as moral disengagement and describes a number of mechanisms that lead to failure in ethical self-regulation.

These mechanisms fall into three broad categories. The first category refers to cognitively restructuring the unethical behavior to seem less harmful. Mechanisms in this category include *moral justification* (i.e., framing unethical behavior as serving a greater good), *euphemistic labeling* (i.e., using language to make harmful acts appear more benign), and *advantageous comparison* (i.e., comparing one's act to a more egregious act). The second category involves obscuring the moral agency of the transgressor. A *displacement of responsibility* (i.e., blaming authority figures for one's own behavior) and *diffusion of responsibility* (i.e., spreading responsibility for one's own unethical behavior across a number of individuals) are the two main mechanisms in this category. The third category involves minimizing the distress caused to the victim. These mechanisms include *distortion of consequences* (i.e., reducing the seriousness of the offense), *dehumanization* (i.e., considering the victim undeserving of appropriate treatment), and *attribution of blame* (i.e., blaming the victim as deserving of the inhumane treatment). These eight mechanisms help explain how moral functioning may fail and unethical behavior may occur (Moore, Detert, Treviño, & Sweitzer, 2009).

Although research on moral disengagement has gained much traction in recent years (Aquino, Reed, Thau, & Freeman, 2007; Detert, Treviño, & Sweitzer, 2008), the research has typically been used to explain unethical behavior and has failed to consider a lack of prosocial behavior as an outcome. Interestingly, Bandura notes that moral agency can take two forms: (1) *inhibitive* (i.e., power to refrain from inhumane behavior) and (2) *proactive* (i.e., power to be humane). Curiously, research on moral disengagement, and the mechanisms themselves, tends to focus more on why someone engages in unethical behavior, as opposed to understanding why someone does not "do good" (i.e., engage in prosocial behavior). Although this distinction may be subtle, it is an important one. It begs the question: What would the moral disengagement mechanisms look like if they focused on why people sometimes fail to act in a prosocial manner? It is possible that a host of additional moral disengagement mechanisms exist to help explain why individuals fail to "do good" as opposed to doing unethical things.

One possible mechanism could include doubt that one's prosocial act will do any good. For example, if I give money to a homeless person I could assume that s/he will just use the money to buy alcohol. Or if I donate money to a charity, perhaps I believe only a small percentage of my money goes to help the people in need. In some cases, these may be accurate statements, but they are also useful justifications for not engaging in prosocial behavior.

A second mechanism is that another individual does not actually want your assistance. As an example, maybe you think your prosocial efforts would be viewed as pity and you personally would never like to be pitied.

Or you feel that helping would be viewed as paternalistic by the person in need and thus you believe the person would not want help. Thus, one reason people may not be prosocial is because of a belief that the other individual does not want your help.

A third mechanism is that we are helpful in one domain so that we are not responsible for helping in another domain. For example, if we are prosocial in terms of helping a spouse, child, or close friend, this may release the burden of being prosocial to other people or entities. If individuals have a prosocial identity because of their treatment of one set of individuals, they may feel less of an obligation to be of aid to others in need. This mechanism is consistent with theory and research on *moral credentialing*, a phenomenon whereby people are more likely to behave unethically (i.e., in a prejudiced manner) if their prior behavior establishes that they are in fact ethical (Monin & Miller, 2001). For example, in a series of three experiments, individuals who voted for Barack Obama were more likely to believe a job description better suited white applicants than black applicants and were more likely to give money to an organization that serves whites at the expense of an organization that serves blacks (Effron, Cameron, & Monin, 2009). Thus, believing one is ethical by behaving in a moral way in one domain can have the counterintuitive effect of making an individual less likely to behave in an unethical manner subsequently.

A fourth mechanism may involve questioning whether one is certain that unethical behavior took place. As an example, an employee in an organization may overhear what appears to be sexual harassment, but may question whether that is indeed what is going on. Alternatively, an employee may hear from another employee that the harassment took place, but because s/he is not certain, s/he decides not to report the behavior to organizational authorities. Thus, this mechanism concerns discounting knowledge about the veracity of unethical behavior.

A fifth mechanism is convincing oneself that reporting unethical behavior will be futile, could lead to some negative repercussions, and thus it is not worth speaking up about wrongdoing. Indeed, the whistle-blowing literature highlights that a belief that reporting will be futile (i.e., nothing will be done about it) and a fear of retaliation are the strongest predictors of failing to blow the whistle (Mesmer-Magnus & Viswesvaran, 2005; Near & Miceli, 1985; Treviño et al., 2006). Further, employees may rationalize not reporting unethical behavior by embracing a belief that their reporting will not be kept confidential. Although these concerns may be realistic and legitimate, they are also useful tools for deciding not to speak up in defense of a mistreated colleague and/or an unethical policy or procedure enacted by management.

These five proposed moral disengagement mechanisms focusing on why people fail to act in a prosocial manner are not meant to be an exhaustive list. Rather, they are presented here to illustrate some examples of how the mechanisms of moral disengagement may look different (or perhaps be expanded) if the goal is to understand why people fail to do good, as opposed to act in an unethical manner. Highlighting a comprehensive set of prosocial-related moral disengagement mechanisms is a promising area for future theory and research as it helps build on Bandura's desire to develop a theory not only about why people do bad things, but also why they fail to do good at times.

Are Unethical and Prosocial Behavior Separate Ends of the Same Continuum or Are They Distinct Constructs?

Another interesting conceptual (and empirical) issue relates to the relationship between unethical and prosocial behavior. Scholars have yet to clearly articulate whether unethical and prosocial behavior are separate ends of the same continuum or whether both unethical and prosocial behavior should be thought of as being on their own continua. Some scholars have broached this topic, although a definitive conclusion has yet to be reached. For example, Warren (2003) highlights a distinction between constructive and destructive deviance suggesting that acting outside norms can be either prosocial or unethical. Similarly, Umphress and Bingham (2009) introduce the concept of *prosocial unethical behavior,* again suggesting that unethical behavior can occur with a prosocial motivation in mind. In addition, Greenbaum and Folger (2009) make the case that unethical leader behavior is qualitatively different from ethical leader behavior, implying that unethical and ethical behavior should be considered as separate continua.

It would be beneficial to develop a detailed framework for how unethical and prosocial behavior fit together. A number of questions still need to be addressed. Should unethical and ethical behavior be thought of as two distinct constructs? Are ethical behavior and prosocial behavior one in the same? Can behaviors be prosocial and unethical at the same time? These are questions that would be useful to address conceptually as well as empirically.

Are the Typical Antecedents (e.g., Personal, Organizational) of Unethical Behavior the Same for Prosocial Behavior or Are They Different?

Typically, behavioral ethics research does not examine both unethical and prosocial behavior in the same study (Treviño et al., 2005). The research that examines both generally does not differentiate between the antecedents (Mayer, Kuenzi, Greenbaum, Bardes, & Salvador, 2009). The antecedents of unethical and prosocial behavior typically include personal characteristics (e.g., personality, values, moral development, identity) and organizational characteristics (e.g., leadership, climate, culture, norms, peers). It would be interesting to examine whether there are different antecedents of unethical and prosocial behavior. For example, is unethical leadership more predictive of unethical follower behavior, whereas ethical leadership is more strongly related to prosocial behavior? Is ethical climate more strongly associated with unethical behavior, and norms for citizenship more strongly related to prosocial behavior? It is important for both conceptual and practical reasons to tease apart whether these two types of behaviors have different precipitating variables.

Are the Processes Linking Personal and Organizational Variables to Unethical Behavior the Same for Prosocial Behavior or Are They Different?

A related idea involves the mechanisms that link personal and organizational variables to unethical and prosocial behavior. It is commonplace to use a number of theories interchangeably to explain the effects of personal and organizational characteristics on unethical and prosocial behavior. These theories include social exchange (Blau, 1964), social identity (Tajfel, 1978), and social information processing (Salancik & Pfeffer, 1978), among others. However, scholars generally do not delineate whether the mechanisms differ when unethical or prosocial behavior are the outcomes of interest. In an effort to explore how unethical and prosocial behaviors are similar and distinct, it is important to examine whether the mechanisms that link antecedents to such behaviors are driven by different mechanisms.

Are Automatic, Affective Reactions or Deep-Level Processing More Likely to Influence Unethical and Prosocial Behavior?

Traditionally, models of ethical decision making have focused on rational effortful processing. For example, Rest's (1986) four steps of ethical decision making include moral awareness, judgment, motivation, and ultimately behavior. However, recent theorizing in the behavioral ethics domain suggests that many reactions are automatic and affective in nature (Haidt, 2001; Sonenshein, 2007). This new perspective integrating affect into behavioral ethics is interesting and provides a nice contrast to more rational models of ethical decision making. However, the vast majority of theory and empirical research has focused on reactions to unethical behavior, as opposed to reactions to prosocial behavior. Further, most affective reactions such as guilt, shame, or disgust tend to be reactions to one's own or others' unethical behavior.

One important question is whether prosocial behaviors tend to be motivated by deep processing whereas unethical behavior is motivated by more immediate affective reactions. For example, the decision regarding whether to blow the whistle or not usually involves serious consideration. Given the risks associated with whistle-blowing it is perhaps not surprising that people have tended to provide a detailed rationale for not blowing the whistle (Mesmer-Magnus & Viswesvaran, 2005). In contrast, seeing a commercial of someone in need may evoke a reaction of compassion and may stimulate prosocial behavior. So, the question remains: Is unethical behavior more likely driven by automatic affective reactions and prosocial behavior driven by deeper-level processing?

Another potentially interesting way to integrate emotions into behavioral ethics is to examine affective reactions to prosocial behavior. Whereas unethical behaviors may promote feelings of disgust, contempt, or shame, it is possible that prosocial behavior could promote more positive moral emotions (Tangney, Stuewig, & Mashek, 2006). Examples of positive energizing moral emotions believed to stem from prosocial acts include awe, elevation, and admiration (Keltner & Haidt, 2003). Research on these positive moral emotions could be a fruitful area of future work.

Are Perceptions of an Organization's Ethicality Driven More by Prosocial or Unethical Behavior?

When key stakeholders (e.g., employees, customers, shareholders, etc.) evaluate an organization in terms of ethics, is the focus more on not engaging in unethical behavior or actually engaging in prosocial behavior? This is an important question that has yet to be examined in the behavioral ethics literature. Is it enough for an organization to do no wrong or must it also do some good? For example, if an applicant is interested in a company because he views the organization as ethical, is that perception influenced more by an absence of any ethical and legal violations or because the company is socially responsible and donates money to important causes? Is it necessary for an organization to both not do anything unethical and also engage in prosocial behavior to be viewed as ethical? Understanding how unethical and prosocial behaviors jointly influence perceptions of an organization's ethicality is a potentially interesting area of future inquiry.

How Can Virtues be Further Integrated into the Behavioral Ethics Literature?

One domain of ethics that is related to prescriptions involves organizational virtues. For example, Solomon (1992, 1999, 2000, 2004) developed a virtue-based theory of business ethics. The crux of this theory is that in order to excel in terms of moral behavior, organizations must have certain virtues. Recently, some behavioral ethics scholars have sought to integrate the literature on organizational virtues. Kaptein (2008) recently developed a measure of ethical culture based on Solomon's virtue-based theory. This measure assesses a number of different virtues, such as clarity, congruency, feasibility, supportability, transparency, discussability, and sanctionability. The virtues highlight prosocial ways the organization should behave (as opposed to unethical behaviors they should not engage in). Similarly, Cameron, Bright, and Caza (2004) introduced the concept of *organizational virtuousness* highlighting ways organizations can do good.

These examples help illustrate how the integration of virtues and behavioral ethics is possible and fruitful. Future research should empirically examine which of these virtues are most strongly related to positive perceptions of organizations. In addition, future work can examine how virtues influence prosocial behaviors in organizations and specify which virtues matter most.

Practical Managerial Implications

The ideas expressed in this chapter have a number of practical implications for organizations to not only reduce the level of unethical behavior but to increase the amount of prosocial behavior. Given that prosocial behavior has been linked to many valuable outcomes at the individual and organizational level, it is critical to understand how to promote prosocial behavior in organizations (Podsakoff, Blume, Whiting, & Podsakoff, 2009).

One important tactic for increasing prosocial acts is to develop an organizational ethical environment that encourages doing good. For example, consistent with prescriptions from Treviño and Nelson (1999), organizations can create an ethical climate by considering prosocial personality at the recruitment and selection phase, and to reinforce the importance of being prosocial through orientation and training programs and through reward and punishment systems. Further, structures should be in place to ensure that employees are held accountable and responsible for being prosocial. Finally, the importance of doing good—whether it be helping a coworker or serving a customer—can be emphasized when making decisions. Thus, the ethical climate of an organization plays a large role in encouraging prosocial behavior.

In addition to the ethical climate, ethical leaders are also critical in encouraging prosocial behavior (Brown, Treviño, & Harrison, 2005). Ethical leaders serve as role models for employees in terms of appropriate ways to behave. Ethical leaders who emphasize the importance of doing good, of being a helpful colleague, and of considering the effects of one's actions on key stakeholders, can encourage prosocial behavior in organizations.

The ethical climate and ethical leadership can help promote positive or constructive responses to unethical behavior. For example, when an organization has an ethical climate and leadership that supports doing the right thing, it will be easier for employees to speak up (i.e., whistle-blow) and report such misconduct to the proper organizational authorities. In addition, employees may feel comfortable having direct conversations with their coworkers or supervisors to address the inappropriate conduct in a constructive manner before it becomes a bigger problem.

If an organization wants to promote the value of doing good or acting in a heroic or courageous manner, structures can be put into place to help achieve this objective. For example, instead of an ethics hotline to report wrongdoing, a hotline could be established to report prosocial behavior as well. This information could then be relayed back to organizational members. This process helps management communicate to employees that the organization values virtuous behavior.

Another implication for management that can be taken from this chapter is that mission statements and organizational policies for proper conduct should focus not only on not doing bad things but also promoting prosocial behavior. For example, a mission statement can emphasize prosocial characteristics it values from employees. It should be noted that a mission statement alone is unlikely to have a strong influence on behavior, but shaping a climate around a mission statement by reinforcing it can be beneficial. Further, codes of conduct can emphasize not only what behaviors employees should not engage in, but can also detail the types of prosocial behaviors that are encouraged and valued.

In addition to the implications for developing an ethical organizational environment, this chapter has implications for how an organization is seen by various stakeholders. For example, in order to recruit the most talented applicants, organizations may need to be seen as not only failing to do unethical behavior but also as socially responsible—doing good for the local community, for example. Individuals like to be associated with organizations that instill pride and for many people a company that has a positive impact on society is important. Also, other stakeholders such as customers and shareholders are increasingly interested in the effect organizations have on a larger society. Thus, in an effort to be thought of as an ethical company that stakeholders are attracted to, oftentimes it is important to engage in prosocial behavior that promotes the greater good as opposed to only failing to be caught up in a scandal.

Conclusions

The field of behavioral ethics is in the relatively early stages of development and has clearly attracted considerable interest from scholars for both theoretical and practical reasons. Although the field of behavioral ethics has traditionally been a study of *proscriptions*, examining unethical behavior that occurs in organizations, in this chapter I argue that including *prescriptions*, a focus on prosocial behavior, should help broaden this domain.

Acknowledgments

I would like to thank Rob Folger who greatly influenced my thinking in this area. I also appreciate Marshall Schminke's constructive feedback on a prior version of this chapter.

References

Aquino, K., Reed, A., Thau, S., & Freeman, D. (2007). A grotesque and dark beauty: How moral identity and mechanisms of moral disengagement influence cognitive and emotional reactions to war. *Journal of Experimental Social Psychology, 43*, 385–392.

Bandura, A. (1986). *Social foundations of thought and action: A social cognitive theory.* Englewood Cliffs, NJ: Prentice-Hall.

Bandura, A. (1990a). Mechanisms of moral disengagement. In W. Reich (Ed.), *Origins of terrorism: Psychologies, ideologies, states of mind* (pp. 161–191). New York: Cambridge University Press.

Bandura, A. (1990b). Selective activation and disengagement of moral control. *Journal of Social Issues, 46*, 27–46.

Bandura, A. (1999). Moral disengagement in the perpetuation of inhumanities. *Personality and Social Psychology Review, 3*, 193–209.

Bandura, A. (2002). Selective moral disengagement in the exercise of moral agency. *Journal of Moral Education, 31*, 101–119.

Blau, P. (1964). *Exchange and power in social life.* New York: John Wiley.

Brown, M. E., Treviño, L. K., & Harrison, D. A. (2005). Ethical leadership: A social learning perspective for construct development and testing. *Organizational Behavior and Human Decision Processes, 97*, 117–134.

Cameron, K. S., Bright, D., & Caza, A. (2004). Exploring the relationship between organizational virtuousness and performance. *American Behavioral Scientist, 47*, 766–790.

Detert, J. R., Treviño, L. K., & Sweitzer, V. L. (2008). Moral disengagement in ethical decision making. *Journal of Applied Psychology, 94*, 374–391.

Effron, D. A., Cameron, J. S., & Monin, B. (2009). Endorsing Obama licenses favoring Whites. *Journal of Experimental Social Psychology, 45*, 590–593.

Folger, R. (1994). Workplace justice and employee worth. *Social Justice Research, 7*, 225–241.

Folger, R. (1998). Fairness as a moral virtue. In M. Schminke (Ed.), *Managerial ethics: Moral management of people and processes* (pp. 13–34). Mahwah, NJ: Erlbaum.

Folger, R. (2001). Fairness as deonance. In S.W. Gilliland, D. D. Steiner, & D. P. Skarlicki (Eds.), *Research in social issues in management* (pp. 3–33). New York: Information Age Publishers.

Greenbaum, R. L., & Folger, R. (2009). *Perceptions of supervisors' morally questionable expediency: A review of an antecedent and some consequences.* Unpublished manuscript.

Gundlach, M. J., Douglas, S., & Martinko, M. J. (2003). The decision to blow the whistle: A social information processing framework. *Academy of Management Review, 28,* 107–123.

Haidt, J. (2001). The emotional dog and its rational tail: A social intuitionist approach to moral judgment. *Psychological Review, 108,* 814–834.

Kant, I. (1797/1991). The metaphysics of morals. In H. Reiss (Ed.), *Kant's political writings.* Cambridge: Cambridge University Press.

Kaptein, S. P. (2008). Developing and testing a measure for the ethical culture of organizations: The corporate ethical virtues model. *Journal of Organizational Behavior, 29*(7), 923–947.

Keltner, D., & Haidt, J. (2003). Approaching awe, a moral, spiritual, and aesthetic emotion. *Cognition and Emotion, 17,* 297–314.

Mayer, D. M., Kuenzi, M., Greenbaum, R. L., Bardes, M., & Salvador, R. (2009). How low does leadership flow? Test of a trickle-down model. *Organizational Behavior and Human Decision Processes, 108,* 1–13.

Mesmer-Magnus, J. R., & Viswesvaran, C. (2005). Whistleblowing in organizations: An examination of correlates of whistleblowing intentions, actions, and retaliation. *Journal of Business Ethics, 62,* 277–297.

Monin, B., & Miller, D. T. (2001). Moral credentials and the expression of prejudice. *Journal of Personality and Social Psychology, 81,* 33–43.

Moore, C., Detert, J. R., Treviño, L. K., & Sweitzer, V. L. (2009). *Correlates and consequences of the propensity to morally disengage.* Unpublished manuscript.

Near, J. P., & Miceli, M. P. (1985). Organizational dissidence: The case of whistleblowing. *Journal of Business Ethics, 4,* 1–16.

Podsakoff, N. P., Blume, B. D., Whiting, S. W., & Podsakoff, P. M. (2009). Individual- and organizational-level consequences of organizational citizenship behaviors: A meta-analysis. *Journal of Applied Psychology, 94,* 122–141.

Rest, J. R. (1986). *Moral development: Advances in research and theory.* New York: Praeger.

Salancik, G. R., & Pfeffer, J. (1978). A social information processing approach to job attitudes and task design. *Administrative Science Quarterly, 23,* 224–253.

Solomon, R. C. (1992). Ethics and excellence. New York: Oxford University Press.

Solomon, R. C. (1999). *A better way to think about business: How personal integrity leads to corporate success.* New York: Oxford University Press.

Solomon, R. C. (2000). Business with virtue: Maybe next year. *Business Ethics Quarterly, 10,* 319–331.

Solomon, R. C. (2004). Aristotle, ethics and business organizations. *Organization Studies, 25,* 1021–1043.

Sonenshein, S. (2007). The role of construction, intuition, and justification in responding to ethical issues at work: The sensemaking-intuition model. *Academy of Management Review, 32,* 1022–1040.

Tajfel, H. (1978). *Differentiation between social groups: Studies in the social psychology of intergroup relations*. London: Academic Press.

Tangney, J. P., Stuewig, J., & Mashek, D. J. (2006). Moral emotions and moral behavior. *Annual Review of Psychology, 58*, 345–372.

Trafimow, D., Bromgard, I. K., Finlay, K. A., & Ketelaar, T. (2005). The role of affect in determining the attributional weight of immoral behaviors. *Personality and Social Psychology Bulletin, 31*, 935–948.

Trafimow, D., & Trafimow, S. (1999). Mapping perfect duties onto hierarchically and partially restrictive trait dimensions. *Personality and Social Psychology Bulletin, 25*, 686–695.

Trevino, L. K., & Nelson, K. A. (1999). *Managing business ethics: Straight talk about how to do it right*. New York: Wiley, John & Sons, Inc.

Treviño, L. K., & Victor, B. 1992. Peer reporting of unethical behavior: A social context perspective. *Academy of Management Journal, 35*, 38–64.

Treviño, L. K., Weaver, G. R., & Reynolds, S. J. (2006). Behavioral ethics in organizations: A review. *Journal of Management, 6*, 951–990.

Umphress, E., and Bingham, J. (2009). When organizational citizens do bad things for good reasons: Examining unethical prosocial behaviors. In M. Schminke (Ed.), *Managerial ethics: Moral management of people and processes* (2nd ed.). Hillsdale, NJ: Erlbaum.

Warren, D. E. 2003. Constructive and destructive deviance in organizations. *Academy of Management Review, 28*, 622–632.

13

A Review and Assessment of Ethical Decision Making Models: Is a Garbage Can Approach the Answer?

Marshall Schminke
University of Central Florida

Alex Vestal
University of Central Florida

James Caldwell
Southeast Missouri State University

Organizations are not rational places. They teem with egos, deadlines, politics, errors, uncertainty, and hidden agendas. It is therefore unreasonable to expect that managers should always behave like rational decision makers, impartially identifying problems, gathering full information, and making optimal decisions. In fact, often they do not.

However, many traditional approaches to ethical decision making assume managers engage in a rational, linear decision process when addressing ethical dilemmas. That is, managers first correctly identify ethical dilemmas, then evaluate alternative solutions to them, and finally, choose the best alternative. But if that process does not reflect how managers actually make other decisions, it probably does not accurately describe how they make ethical decisions either.

In the closing chapter of the first edition of *Managerial Ethics*, Schminke (1998) addressed this issue by proposing an alternative "nonrational" approach to ethical decision making. This model, based on Cohen, March, and Olsen's (1972) garbage can model of decision making, addressed a series of concerns about the process by which real managers confront ethical problems in real-world settings.

In this chapter, we revisit, revise, and extend Schminke's (1998) work. We do so by providing an updated review of traditional rational models of ethical decision making. We add to this a brief review of more contemporary models that begin to call into question the traditional rational approach. These provide the backdrop against which we consider nonrational approaches to decision making, and how nonrational approaches might inform our thinking about how ethical decision making actually occurs. We provide a description of Cohen et al.'s (1972) garbage can model of decision making and a review of its broad application to a variety of organizational issues and problems. Finally, we integrate the issues of ethical decision making and nonrationality, resulting in a garbage can model of ethical decision making.

"Rational" Models of Ethical Decision Making

Traditionally, scholars interested in understanding ethical decision making have embraced a rational perspective. Rational models are those that reflect—either explicitly or implicitly—the orderly, reasoned, linear decision processes that underlie most traditional economic decision models: correctly identifying the problem, knowing all relevant alternatives, identifying all relevant criteria, accurately weighting the importance of the criteria, accurately assessing each criteria vis-à-vis relevant goals, and accurately calculating and choosing the optimal alternative (Friedman, 1957).

Four approaches to modeling ethical decision making from a rational perspective have emerged in the literature. The first focuses on the characteristics of the individual making the decision. The second includes the setting or context in which the decision is made. The third goes beyond the individual and the context, focusing on the characteristics of the ethical issue or event itself. The fourth integrates both content concerns (What factors influence ethical decision making?) and process concerns (How are ethical decisions made?) in an attempt to understand how conflicts within the ethical decision process are resolved. In the following sections we briefly summarize some of the major models represented by each approach.

Models That Focus on Individuals

Scholars interested in understanding ethical decision making first focused on understanding the impact of individual attributes. Four of these have received particularly strong attention in the literature: Hogan's (1973) dialectical approach, Forsyth's (1980) moral judgment model, Kohlberg's (1981) cognitive moral development approach, and Rest's (1986) "four component" model.

Hogan (1973) presented the strongest view of the potency of individual traits on moral behavior. He focused on individuals' moral maturity, and in defining its parameters, he began with an image of humans as rule-formulating and rule-following animals. He then characterized how individuals differ across five dimensions, which capture their reactions to rule-governed behavior: moral knowledge, socialization, empathy, autonomy, and moral judgment.

Moral knowledge is the extent to which one understands the "rules" of moral behavior. Socialization describes the extent to which one believes these rules apply to him or her. Empathy reflects an individual's capacity to perceive situations from others' perspectives. Autonomy reflects the degree to which one's moral decisions are driven by a personal sense of duty, rather than peer or societal pressures. Finally, moral judgment addresses whether one considers human-generated laws (an ethic of responsibility) or higher-order "natural" law (an ethic of personal conscience) as providing the more appropriate guide for behavior. Hogan presented specific assessment devices for each dimension, and was clear that these individual-level characteristics dictate moral behavior regardless of setting. He suggested this model "should help to explain moral conduct in *any* socio-cultural context" (1973, p. 220, emphasis added).

Forsyth (1980) explored a different set of individual-level dimensions of ethical ideologies. His Ethics Position Questionnaire (EPQ) reflected a belief that variations in individuals' moral judgment may be described by two dimensions: relativism and idealism. Relativism reflects the extent to which one rejects the premise that universal rules or principles of ethical behavior exist. Idealism reflects the extent to which one believes that doing the right thing will always lead to desirable consequences. The resulting two-by-two matrix (high or low on each of the two dimensions) created a taxonomy of four ethical ideologies: situationists (high relativism and idealism), subjectivists (high relativism, low idealism), absolutists (low relativism, high idealism), and exceptionists (low relativism and idealism).

Forsyth (1980) tied each of these ideologies to existing ethical perspectives. For example, he related both the situationist and subjectivist perspectives (the high relativist ideologies) to ethical skepticism. He identified subjectivists as pragmatic ethical egoists, whose moral standards are relevant only with respect to one's own behavior. He linked situationist thinking with Fletcher's (1966) situation ethics, that morality is not so much a question of right and wrong as it is of a "fit" between one's actions and the context in which they occur. He likened absolutists to deontological thinking, in which one rejects considering the consequences of actions in determining the morality of actions. Finally, he suggested that exceptionists endorse teleological beliefs, in which the consequences of actions determine the morality of actions.

Probably the best-known individual-level approach to ethical decision making is Kohlberg's (1981) cognitive moral development (CMD) framework. Based on Piaget's (1932/1948) early work on moral development, Kohlberg suggested that CMD, or moral maturity, is reflected in six stages, across three levels of moral reasoning. The preconventional level contains

Stage 1 (punishment and obedience orientation) and Stage 2 (instrumental relativist orientation). At this level, individuals define morality in terms of the consequences of actions (e.g., reward and punishment) or the moral positions of authority figures. The conventional level includes Stage 3 ("good boy–nice girl" orientation) and Stage 4 (law and order orientation). Here, peer influences as well as family and societal norms become more instrumental in determining what constitutes moral behavior. This conventional reasoning defines morality in terms of maintaining family or social structures. Finally, the postconventional level includes Stage 5 (social contracts, legalistic orientation) and Stage 6 (universal ethical principles orientation). At this level, individuals define moral principles independently from self-interest, authority figures, and societal pressures. The postconventional individual defines morality in terms of personal conscience and universal principles.

Rest (1986) presented a similar framework of CMD. His description mirrored Kohlberg's (1981) in its emphasis on justice as the central criteria of morality and in its six-stage structure. However, Rest's approach differed from Kohlberg's in two important ways. First, although Rest's approach is a justice-based one, it reflected individuals' increasingly sophisticated thinking about how social cooperation can be organized. By contrast, Kohlberg's stages reflected a sense of justice in formalist terms (reversibility, universality, and prescriptivity). Therefore, Rest's conceptualization emphasized justice as social cooperation, whereas Kohlberg's conceptualization reflected justice in more individual terms, including individual rights and responsibilities, both societally and self-imposed. Second, Kohlberg's approach emphasized a more rigid (hard-and-fast) stage structure. That is, individuals are either in or out of a particular stage and do not float between multiple stages. Rest's model embraced a softer stage structure reflecting ranges of responses to ethical dilemmas. Individuals' ethical reasoning may be affected by more than one stage influence at a time.

Rest (1986, 1994) took the CMD approach a step further in creating what he called a four-component model. He suggested that moral development (i.e., moral judgment) is not enough to ensure moral behavior. Rather, moral judgment is only one of four individual-level psychological factors that contribute to moral behavior. The others include moral sensitivity, moral motivation, and moral character. Moral sensitivity addresses the extent to which an individual is aware that his or her actions might impact others. In other words, are moral issues even on the individual's "ethical radar screen"? Moral motivation reflects the extent to which moral values are accorded greater or lesser importance than one's other values (e.g., self-actualization, wealth, power, or self-preservation). Finally, moral character captures the extent to which an individual shows the fortitude or courage to carry out the actions he or she has defined as moral. In all, Rest's model significantly expanded our thinking about individual characteristics that may affect moral behavior. However, like the others, it is limited to individual-level characteristics. The next section briefly reviews models that also consider the role of situational context.

Models That Include Situational Effects

Treviño's (1986) "person-situation interactionist" model was among the first to consider not only the person facing the ethical dilemma, but also the setting in which that dilemma occurs (cf. Treviño & Youngblood, 1990; Treviño & Victor, 1992). Treviño suggested that moral cognitions (like those proposed by Kohlberg) drive ethical behavior, but this relationship is moderated by two factors. The first set of moderators includes other individual characteristics like ego strength, field dependence, and locus of control. The second set of moderators includes situational factors like job context (reinforcement contingencies and other pressures), organizational culture (including norms, values, obedience), and work characteristics (role taking and moral conflict resolution). Most adults operate from Kohlberg's conventional level of moral development, in which peer and social influences play a large role in determining what constitutes moral behavior (Treviño, 1986; Weber, 1990). Therefore, these situational influences should be especially salient in work settings, and thus impact the relationship between CMD and ethical behavior.

Others have considered both individual and organizational factors in models of ethical decision making. For example, Ferrell and Gresham's (1985) framework included individual factors such as the teleological (outcome-based) and deontological (rules-based) assumptions individuals use for making ethical decisions, as well as individual knowledge, values, and attitudes. Situational factors include the ethical beliefs and actions of significant others as well as the opportunity for action.

Building on earlier work, Bommer, Gratto, Gravander, and Tuttle (1987) proposed an even broader model of situational and individual influences on ethical decision making. The individual attributes in this model include level of moral development, personality traits (like locus of control), demographics (age, sex, education), motivational orientation (safety versus esteem), personal goals and values, and other factors like life experiences and intelligence. Situational factors cut across five different contextual environments. An individual's personal environment includes family and peer influences on the ethical decision process. The professional environment reflects codes of conduct, licensing requirements, and the influence of professional meetings. The work environment may influence ethical decision making though stated policies, corporate culture, and pressures of corporate goals. The governmental and legal environment includes laws and regulations resulting from legislation, administrative agencies, and the judicial system. Finally, the social environment addresses the influence resulting from religious, humanistic, cultural, and societal values.

Several recent attempts to model ethical decision making have centered on the theory of reasoned action (TRA) (Ajzen & Fishbein, 1980; Fishbein & Ajzen, 1975). The goal of TRA is to predict and understand a person's behavior, focusing on behavioral intent as the best predictor of that behavior. Intent, in turn, is influenced by both individual and situational factors. Individual factors include behavioral beliefs (Will the action lead to certain outcomes?), outcome evaluations (Are those outcomes positive or negative?), and attitudes toward the behavior itself. Situational factors include subjective norms like whether significant others think the behavior should or should not be performed.

Some TRA-based models of ethical behavior have held closely to the Fishbein and Ajzen framework (e.g., Dubinsky and Loken, 1989). Others have included a number of additional individual and situational factors. For example, Kurland (1995) proposed a model based on both TRA and the theory of planned behavior (Ajzen, 1991), which added perceived behavioral control to the situational constraints on behavior. Similarly, Hunt and Vitell (1986) proposed a general theory of marketing ethics based on TRA that included sociocultural, industry and organizational norms, and individual factors like deontological and teleological reasoning. Jones's (1991) model (which we revisit below) fits this categorization as well, in that it resulted from a synthesis of several models (Dubinsky & Loken, 1989; Ferrell & Gresham, 1985; Hunt & Vitell, 1986; Rest, 1986; Treviño, 1986), embedding Rest's four components and TRA-based approaches in a broader situational context. Finally, Ferrell, Gresham, and Fraedrich (1989) integrated three approaches into a single model of ethical decision making. Specifically, they combined Hunt and Vitell's TRA-based model with Ferrell and Gresham's (1985) model, and added Kohlberg's CMD framework to create what they termed a synthesis of ethical decision models.

Models That Focus on the Ethical Issue

Subsequently, authors began to expand their view of potential influences on ethical behavior. These works go beyond the influence of individual differences and the setting or situation in which the event occurs, to consider the nature of the ethical event itself. One example of this movement is Brady's (1990) "Janus-headed" view of ethical decision making. Although Brady's approach focused on individuals and their underlying ethical predispositions, its application required consideration of the particular ethical event.

Brady contended that individuals have two ethical "faces," one formalist and the other utilitarian (which he views as roughly synonymous with deontological and teleological approaches, respectively). Formalist reasoning reflects an inclination to follow rules or principles in determining what constitutes ethical behavior. Utilitarian reasoning evaluates the results of actions as ethical or not, rather than the actions themselves. Critical to Brady's approach is that formalism and utilitarianism do not represent opposite ends of a single continuum. Rather, individuals possess both formalist and utilitarian tendencies, and each has the capacity to play a greater role, depending on whether the issue at hand involves primarily formalist or utilitarian concerns.

In fact, many issues contain both formalist and utilitarian concerns. Brady (1990) illustrated this point in areas like whistleblowing, overseas corporate bribery, pollution, corporate trade secrets, and software piracy. In each of these issues, formalists might seek a set of rules to help best balance the rights of various stakeholders whose interests are mutually incompatible. On the other hand, utilitarians might seek to maximize the net social good (or minimize the net social harm) arising from such conflicts of interest.

Brady (1990) noted that not all issues reflect formalist and utilitarian concerns equally. For example, most of the ethical discussion surrounding new genetic engineering technologies has tended to focus on utilitarian concerns: Do the potential benefits of manipulating genetic structures in laboratory settings outweigh the potential harm (known and unknown) that might result from such tinkering? Likewise, nuclear power and nuclear weapons also seem to generate largely utilitarian discussions, while debate on employment discrimination seems to center around formalist issues: Should an employer have the right to hire anyone she pleases? Must employment selection be job-task related? In all, Brady's Janus-headed model suggested that individuals have the capacity to deal with both formalist and utilitarian concerns. However, it is the nature of the issue itself that determines the decision-making perspective from which an individual will address the dilemma.

Jones (1991) also looked beyond the individual and the setting in modeling how ethical decisions are made, proposing an issue-contingent model of ethical decision making. In it, he suggested that the moral intensity of a situation—the extent to which an issue-related moral imperative exists—is a multidimensional construct that "focuses on the moral issue, not on the moral agent or the organizational context" (Jones, 1991, p. 373). He argued that six dimensions characterize the moral intensity of an event. First, the *magnitude of the consequences* of an event are the sum of the harms (benefits) done to its victims (beneficiaries). Greater harms or benefits translate to greater moral intensity. Second, *social consensus* reflects the degree of social agreement that an act is good or bad. Greater consensus results in greater moral intensity. Third, *probability of effect* includes both the uncertainty of whether the event will take place and the likelihood that the predicted harm or benefits will occur if it does take place. Greater probability of effect will result in greater moral intensity. Fourth, *temporal immediacy* indicates the length of time between the act and the onset of its expected outcomes. Increased immediacy yields greater moral intensity. Fifth, *proximity* reflects the feeling of closeness (social, cultural, psychological, or physical) the decision maker has for the beneficiaries or victims of the act. Increased closeness results in greater moral intensity. Finally, *concentration of effect* reflects the degree to which a small or large number of individuals will be affected by an act of a given magnitude. Greater concentration results in greater moral intensity. Building on Rest's (1986) four-component model, Jones (1991) suggested that moral intensity may affect ethical decision making at any stage of the decision-making process—recognizing that a moral issue exists, making moral judgments, establishing moral intent, or actually engaging in moral behavior.

Models That Focus on Resolving Conflict

The models reviewed thus far have focused on either content factors (those that describe what kinds of things influence ethical decision making), process factors (those that discuss how decisions are made), or both. However, none of these models explicitly considers the role of conflict in the ethical decision-making process.

McDevitt, Giapponi, and Tromley (2007) developed a model of ethical decision making that addresses this issue. The McDevitt et al. (2007) approach recognizes that managers do not always face clear-cut choices when making ethical (and other) decisions. Risks associated with a particular decision may be uncertain, as may be its costs, not just financial, but emotional and reputational as well. Further, even in settings in which ethical values dominate those for power or achievement, the question of which ethical values should be adhered to often remains. Additionally, managers may be uncertain about their own or their employees' efficacy in bringing about desired outcomes.

In all, managers facing conditions like these may feel a great deal of anxiety or concern about whether the outcomes they seek are those that will actually emerge. Thus, McDevitt et al. (2007) argue that an effective model of ethical decision making must be capable of addressing the process by which individuals actually work out solutions to such ethical conflicts. They offer such a model based on Janis and Mann's (1977) model of decision making in the context of conflict, choice, and commitment. By integrating content variables with process variables involved in the decision-making process, this model is capable of addressing how inherent conflicts arise at various points along the decision cycle.

Models of Ethical Decision Making: An Evolution

In all, most models of ethical decision making have until recently been guided by traditional, linear, rational approaches to decision making. Each of the approaches outlined above operates under an assumption of systematic, rational decision making on the part of the individual facing the ethical dilemma. At times that assumption is implicit, but other times it is quite explicit. For example, in describing the theory of reasoned action, Ajzen and Fishbein (1980, p. 5) state:

> [T]he theory is based on the assumption that human beings are usually quite rational and make systematic use of information available to them. We do not subscribe to the view that human social behavior is controlled by unconscious motives or overpowering desires, nor do we believe that it can be characterized as capricious or thoughtless. Rather, we argue that people consider the implications of their actions before they decide to engage or not engage in a given behavior.

Even McDevitt et al.'s (2007) model, which allows for considerable uncertainty and conflict in the ethical decision-making process, embraces a linear, rational, process, as illustrated in their work by a flow chart that guides the decision maker through the multiple conflict points of the ethical decision process. However, these rational models have done little to explain why it is that when explaining their decisions, managers often find themselves using phrases such as "I had a gut feeling" or "I can't really explain why, but it just seemed like the right thing to do."

Recently, scholars have begun to embrace models of ethical decision that are capable of speaking to issues like these. They have done so by exploring alternatives to the linear, rational decision processes presented in previous work. These include models that address the role of emotion in the ethical decision process, as well as those that embrace nonlinear decision systems, such as retrospective sense-making.

Emotion in Ethical Decision Making

In recent years, scholars have pointed to the dual roles played by reason and emotion in decision making (Damasio, 1994), thereby challenging the traditional view of ethical decision making solely as a reasoned, deliberative process. Some scholars have even argued that emotional factors play a positive role in making better ethical decisions. For example, Etzioni (1988) noted that emotion "provides a constructive basis for behavior and decision making" (p. 138).

The dual roles played by reason and emotion have been embraced in the ethical decision-making literature as well. Scholars observe that simultaneous concerns about reason and emotion reflect a long-standing philosophical debate about the foundations of morality. For example, Rozin, Lowery, Imada, and Haidt (1999) point to historical tensions about the foundations of morality reflected in rational (e.g., Kant, 1789/1959) versus emotional (e.g., Hume, 1740/1969) perspectives on ethics. As a result, many ethics scholars have embraced emotion as a critical component of the process of making better moral judgments and decisions (Eisenberg, 2000; Pizarro, 2000).

Although formal models of ethical decision making that explicitly consider the role of emotion are still rare (see Gaudine and Thorne [2001] for an exception), considerable empirical evidence speaks to its importance. Studies spanning a variety of literatures including psychology (Moore, Clark, & Kane, 2008), organizational studies (Sekerka & Bagozzi, 2007), business (Connelly, Helton-Fauth, & Mumford, 2004), education (Morton, Worthley, Testerman, & Mahoney, 2006), and neuroscience (Greene, Sommerville, Nystrom, Darley, & Cohen, 2001) have supported the idea that reason and emotion represent simultaneously important components of the moral judgment process.

Retrospection in Ethical Decision Making

Scholars have also begun to reconsider the traditional belief that ethical decision making reflects a linear reasoning process, considering instead the possibility that retrospective processes might also play a role in ethical decision making. For example, Tenbrunsel (1998) found support for the idea that a decision to behave unethically led to a justification for the behavior rather than the justification for the behavior leading to a decision to behave unethically.

Other scholars have also questioned the assumption that ethical decision making is a deliberate and ordered process. Reynolds (2006), for example, presented a neurocognitive model of ethical decision making that embraced such retrospective processes explicitly. His model suggests that ethical decision making involves reasoned analysis as well as intuitive and retrospective components. Each operates through distinct but related decision-making cycles, one a higher-order conscious cycle involving reasoned analysis (the C-system) and the other a reflexive pattern-matching cycle involving intuition and retrospection (the X-system). This neurocognitive model contributes to our understanding of ethical decision making in at least two important ways. First, it accounts for searching, information structuring, and prototype matching that occurs before an active moral judgment even begins. Such processes are absent from traditional models like Rest's (1986) four-component model. Second, it makes explicit the reflexive or retrospective processes by which actors rationalize ethical decisions, rather than making deliberate, active moral judgments.

Another recent model that focuses on post hoc explanation and justification of ethical decisions was proposed by Sonenshein (2007). This sense-making-intuition model (SIM) not only proposes a final retrospective sense-making activity in the decision-making process, but also suggests that the process relies heavily on the decision maker's intuition. The SIM model outlines a three-stage process involving issue construction, intuitive judgment, and finally, explanation and justification.

During the first stage, social stimuli help individuals construct issues in environments that Sonenshein (2007) characterizes as equivocal and uncertain. The second stage involves intuitive judgment, which he describes as an automated, affect-based judgment. The mechanisms by which this judgment is made involve approach and avoidance behaviors as reactions to valences. Negative valances are associated with an "ethically questionable" judgment and positive valences are associated with an "ethically acceptable" judgment. In the third stage, individuals explain and justify the intuitive judgments they have made about the ethical issues they have constructed.

Integrative Models of Ethical Decision Making

At least one scholar has integrated both emotion and nonlinear, retrospective decision processes into a single framework. Haidt (2001) provided a social intuitionist model in which he proposed that moral judgments are directly caused by moral intuition (an emotion-based process) and that moral reasoning takes place in an *ex post facto* process when justification, explanations, or rationalizations are required by the social context. Haidt noted that in a sense, "one becomes a lawyer trying to build a case rather than a judge searching for the truth" (Haidt, 2001. p. 814).

Finally, Tenbrunsel and Smith-Crowe (2008) attempted to bridge some of the intricate differences among the traditional and emerging models of ethical decision making. In particular, their work seeks to integrate descriptive and normative approaches. Their inductively generated framework identifies three key components of the ethical decision-making process: moral awareness, moral decision making, and amoral decision making. In doing so, it distinguishes between the process that produces the decision (moral or amoral) and the resulting decision itself (ethical or unethical).

The Tenbrunsel and Smith-Crowe (2008) model also considers the decision frames of the decision maker; that is, the nature of the situation in which decision makers have been placed. Decision makers can be affected by a variety of frames (e.g., business, legal, and moral), and to the extent that the moral frame has influence, the decision maker will perceive the decision to be a moral decision. If, however, a frame other than a moral one exerts influence on the decision maker, then decision makers will not be morally aware. This theme of considering amoral decision making in tandem with moral decision making may be the most important contribution made by the Tenbrunsel and Smith-Crowe model. Notably, the authors argue that although moral awareness is important, it is not a prerequisite to an ethical outcome. A decision that begins with an amoral frame (e.g., business), in which there is thus no moral awareness, may still have moral implications and may still lead to an ethical (or unethical) decision. In other words, whether a decision has ethical ramifications is something of which decision makers may or may not be aware.

Nonrational Managerial Decision Making

Models like these provide breaches in the literature through which scholars may begin to consider models of ethical decision making that do not conform to the traditional, linear, rational perspective. Scholars involved in understanding managerial decision processes in general have long held that many decision processes operate outside of what is considered "rational" decision making, and that strict rationality does not describe many decision processes in real organizational settings (March & Simon, 1958). The next section summarizes several "nonrational" approaches to managerial decision making, which we explore with the hope of expanding our view of the processes that underlie them.

Before examining models of nonrational managerial decision making, an important point needs to be made. *Nonrational* decision making is not synonymous with *irrational* decision making. That is, nonrational models do not imply any sort of mental ineptitude, instability, incompetence, or lunacy on the part of decision makers. Rather, nonrational models recognize that in real organizational settings, real managers with limited cognitive resources seldom engage in the step-by-step, linear decision processes that underlie most traditional economic decision models. Four approaches to describing nonrational decision making have emerged in the literature: bounded rationality, incrementalism, biases and heuristics, and escalation. We explore each briefly.

The earliest models of nonrational decision making operate from a premise of "bounded rationality" (Simon, 1957; March & Simon, 1958), that decision makers lack information concerning the problem, alternative solutions, and relevant criteria. Further, time and cost constraints may limit their search process. Finally, limited perceptual and cognitive abilities constrain decision makers' abilities to calculate optimal solutions (Bazerman, 1986). Thus, managers may employ less than optimal or less than fully "rational" decision models. Rather, they tend to "satisfice" (selecting the first acceptable solution to a decision that comes along) rather than optimize (which requires exploring and evaluating all possible alternatives fully before selecting the best one) when facing many decisions.

In another view of nonrational decision making, Mintzberg and his colleagues described incremental decision approaches (e.g., Mintzberg, Raisinghani, & Theoret, 1976). An incremental approach recognizes that managers are often incapable of addressing large-scale, complicated issues in a single decision cycle. Alternatively, they may muddle through a series of subissues, with no clear endgame in mind. As outside observers, we may monitor an organization's actions as it moves from position A to, say, position E. It may appear to us that a well-reasoned decision-making process allowed the organization to take the large step from A to E. However, it is more likely that the company moved incrementally, from A to B, then from B to C, then from C to D, and finally, from D to E. What to an outsider may have appeared to be a revolutionary leap (from A to E) was in reality a series of smaller evolutionary steps, as managers sought to reduce major decisions to smaller, more manageable portions.

A third view of nonrational decision making considers the shortcuts—and possible resulting decision errors—inherent in many decision processes. Tversky and Kahneman (1974) outlined several biases and heuristics in decision making that include representativeness, availability, and anchoring and adjustment. *Representativeness* reflects managers' tendencies to be swayed by stereotypes. *Availability* denotes managers' inclination to give greater weight to more recent or easily recalled events. Finally, *anchoring and adjustment* reflects an individual's tendency to be influenced by initial figures in, say, negotiation settings, even when those figures are "objectively" irrelevant. Each of these denotes strategies that individuals use to simplify the decision process. However, each may also lead to biased decisions or even serious, systematic errors (Bazerman, 1986).

In a fourth example of nonrational decision making, Staw and others have described the escalation phenomenon in decision making (e.g., Staw, 1981). Research shows that managers often display escalating commitment even to a failing course of action. Ignoring the financial adage that "sunk costs are irrelevant," managers often throw good money after bad, and this commitment to the failed action may increase as the sunk costs increase.

Of course, all of these issues—bounded rationality, incrementalism, biases and heuristics, and escalation—are present in the sticky world of ethical decision making. We believe ethical decision making is no more or less rational than any other type of managerial decision making, and is thus guided by similar nonrational processes. Making matters even more complicated, managers facing ethical dilemmas often confront ambiguity not only about what constitutes a correct or moral course of action, but even about how to decide what constitutes moral behavior. One non-rational decision model in particular—the garbage can model (Cohen, March, & Olsen, 1972)—has contributed substantially to addressing the practical problems faced by managers trying to make quality decisions while operating in turbulent and uncertain environments. We believe the garbage can model may help organize our thinking about ethical decision making as well.

A Garbage Can Model of Decision Making

The garbage can model of decision making examines how managers make decisions under conditions of high uncertainty. In developing the model, Cohen et al. (1972) described a type of high uncertainty setting they call *organized anarchies*. Organized anarchies reflect three traits: problematic preferences, unclear technologies, and fluid participation. *Problematic preferences* imply that individuals' preference sets are unclear; the organization operates under a set of inconsistent and ill-defined goals and desires on the part of its members or coalitions of members. The organization or decision situation reflects a loose collection of ideas rather than a single, coherent structure. *Unclear technologies* indicate that even organization members find the decision processes to be ambiguous. Decisions are made but the process by which that occurs is not well understood. *Fluid participation* suggests that participants vary in the amount of time and effort they devote to various issues. This variation may also extend to the makeup of the decision team itself.

The garbage can approach notes four forces flowing through these organized anarchies: problems, solutions, participants, and choice opportunities. *Problems* represent the concerns for organization members—issues that require attention. *Solutions* are answers. However, these answers are not static, nor are they necessarily linked to the specific questions that generated them. *Participants* enter and exit the mix. A variety of demands on members' time and resources requires that they constantly reevaluate their involvement with different projects or issues. Finally, *choice opportunities* present themselves on occasion when a decision or action is called for.

Cohen et al. (1972) view organizations as large garbage cans, into which streams of these four elements flow. The four ingredients mix and swirl over time, but this churning process does not follow a linear, "rational" pattern in which participants with choice opportunities discover decision alternatives, anticipate the likely outcomes of those alternatives, evaluate those outcomes relative to set goals, and finally reach a decision. Rather, the model views the process as much more random; organizations become "collections of choices looking for problems, issues and feelings looking for decision situations in which they might be aired, solutions looking for issues to which they might be the answer, and decision makers looking for work" (p. 2).

Garbage can decision processes have described some famous outcomes. For example, 3M's ubiquitous Post-it sticky notes grew from a new adhesive polymer developed by chemist Spencer Silver in 1964. However, it sat as a solution without a problem until ten years later, when another chemist, Arthur Fry, came up with a problem for Spencer's solution: bookmarks that kept falling out of his Sunday hymnal. After six more years of testing and marketing, Post-its finally saw national distribution (Mingo, 1994).

Similarly, Kimberly-Clark, a paper manufacturer in Wisconsin since 1872, began developing paper-based substitutes for cotton absorbing materials in 1914. As World War I escalated, cotton shortages led Kimberly-Clark to develop a variety of uses for the new product (Cellucotton) including bandages and gas mask filters. After the war ended, they owned a solution for which few problems remained. In response, they produced Cellucotton in thin sheets, which became known as Kleenex tissues. Kimberly-Clark marketed the new product narrowly as a way to remove cold cream. Later, marketing research revealed that two thirds of their customers did not use the product to remove cold cream at all, but rather as disposable handkerchiefs. After developing a new marketing campaign (that also encouraged using Kleenex as coffee filters!), sales soared (Mingo, 1994).

Applications of the Garbage Can Model

Individual level. Shortly after its inception, the garbage can model began to contribute to scholars' thinking on a variety of questions involving decision making under uncertainty at a variety of levels. Some of these applications involved individual-level decision making. For example, Decrop and Snelders (2005) crafted a typology of decision making in the tourism industry. They applied the garbage can approach to describe an "opportunistic" type of vacationer who responds to the co-occurrence of vacation needs and vacation choice solutions. Similarly, Bitektine (2009) applied the garbage can model to understand how researchers in the social sciences make decisions about specific research topics. This model suggests that the faddishness sometimes apparent in social science research may be the result of researchers responding to the confluence of three domain-specific factors (relevant research questions, legitimate research methodologies, and available research data) rather than a reasoned assessment of which projects hold the greatest potential for making real long-term contributions. In the education literature, Bartunek and Keys (1979) drew upon the model to explain individuals' decisions to participate in decision-making processes in schools.

Organization level. Scholars have applied the garbage can approach to understanding decisions made at the organizational level as well. For example, scholars have explored strategic decision making from the garbage can perspective (Eisenhardt & Zbaracki, 1992; Hickson, 1987), as well as entrepreneurial strategies like entry into new markets (Backer & Clark, 2008) and creating ventures where markets do not yet exist (Sarasvathy, 2001). It has also been applied successfully to technology application issues, including Masuch and LaPotin's (1989) application in exploring artificial intelligence choice systems for organizations, Davern and Kauffman's (2000) work on understanding investments in information technology, and Chenhall's (2003) research on understanding managerial decisions when implementing management control systems. (In an interesting reversal, Browning, Soernes, Stephens, and Saetre [2006] explored the impact of technology choice on the dynamics of garbage can decision making.) Education scholars have modeled the diversity of programs and courses offered in U.S. colleges and universities with a garbage can approach. Waguespack (2006) found that a garbage can process described decision making under certain conditions at the Environmental Protection Agency. The model has also been applied to understanding decision making in textbook publishing (Levitt & Nass, 1989), decisions regarding energy conservation efforts (Goitein, 1989), and routine nonconformity in organizations (Vaughan, 1999).

Extraorganization level. Other applications of the garbage can model have involved extraorganizational decisions, including understanding the processes by which broader policy decisions are made. For example, Kalu (2005) explored the Medicare reform efforts of the United States in the 1990s and argued that the dynamics of the reform process could be explained in garbage can terms. Levy (2006) used a garbage can approach to describe decision making during the initial crisis stage in which the European Commission was overloaded by the need for managerial reforms for the European Union. Likewise, Lipson (2007) adopted a garbage can perspective to understand the emergence of peacekeeping as a legitimate role of the United Nations. Arguing that the U.N. represents an organized anarchy in the Cohen et al. (1972) sense, the garbage can model provided an explanation for how peacekeeping came to be seen as a legitimate U.N. function after the end of the Cold War. Similarly, the model has also helped researchers to understand the emergence of issues like school choice in the conversation on educational reform (Dougherty & Sostre, 1992) and which issues capture the attention of policy makers in housing (Tiernan & Burke, 2002). Others have used a garbage can approach in broader contexts to understand decision making in public policy (Albaek, 1995; Mandell, 1989; Teasley & Harrell, 1996) and industrial policy (Atkinson & Powers, 1987), as well as more general applications including relations between intergovernmental organizations like NATO and the United Nations (Keohane, 2002).

Theoretical Integrations of the Garbage Can Model

Individual level. In addition to providing insight into decisions being made in specific contexts, scholars have also been successful integrating the garbage can model with other theoretical perspectives to craft more robust theoretical models that have served a variety of literatures. At the individual level, the garbage can model has been integrated with the literature on cognitive biases to understand better how such biases might influence decision making in garbage can contexts (Das & Teng, 1999).

Organization level. At the organizational level, the garbage can model has been paired with theory from the literature on issue selling to understand better the process of organizational change (Dutton, Ashford, O'Neill, & Lawrence, 2001). Similarly, Padgett (1980) integrated the garbage can model with more traditional notions of classical bureaucracy to understand better the manner in which ambiguity might affect decision making in structured settings.

Extraorganization level. Similar theoretical integrations have occurred at the level of policy formation as well. For example, Mezias and Scarselletta (1994) integrated a garbage can approach with institutional theory to explain the decision process of a public policy task force examining financial reporting standards. Likewise, the garbage can perspective has been linked with theory on political power to describe how power shapes the interaction among individuals and thus influences the outcomes of political activity (McGrath & Moore, 2001).

These efforts to integrate garbage can thinking with other theoretical perspectives have created a rich set of hybrid theories that have closer ties to the specific decision contexts involved, and have expanded our thinking about the capacity of the garbage can approach to speak to a variety of issues. In all, we believe the garbage can model has demonstrated its value in helping to explain a variety of decision phenomena at multiple levels, especially when paired with sound theory from the area to which it is being applied. We suggest similar benefits might accrue to the ethics literature by considering a garbage can application to ethical decision making.

A Garbage Can Model of Ethical Decision Making

A garbage can model of ethical decision making explores the process by which ethical decisions emerge from a vessel filled with chaotic organizational forces. For this model to provide a framework that will enhance our thinking about ethical decision making, it needs to be able to accommodate and synthesize the individual, contextual, and issue-related forces outlined earlier in the chapter.

Note that in discussing the ethical decision models above we have not suggested that the *content* of these frameworks—the constructs themselves—was not accurate. Rather, we have suggested that the linear, rational, way in which the constructs are arranged—the way the decision *process* is portrayed—does not describe the way decisions are actually made in real organizational settings. Therefore, it is not our intent to dispose of the constructs set forth in any of the models we have reviewed. To the contrary, building better theory often consists of taking existing models and reorganizing them to reflect reality more accurately. That is the goal of this final section—to synthesize existing constructs of ethical decision making into a framework that more accurately describes the real ethical decision process.

In applying a garbage can approach to organizational ethics, the first question is whether ethical situations resemble the organized anarchies described by Cohen et al. (1972). In the next sections we consider how ethical situations reflect the three distinguishing characteristics of organized anarchies: problematic preferences, unclear technologies, and fluid participation.

Problematic Preferences

Ethical situations do reflect problematic preferences; individuals' preference sets may be unclear, ill-defined, or inconsistent. For example, consider the moral judgment component of Rest's (1986) four-component model. Moral judgment includes individuals' cognitive moral development (and other developmental approaches to ethical decision making like Gilligan's [1982] ethic of care) and moral evaluation tools like deontological and teleological frameworks (Jones, 1991). These moral judgment characteristics provide the basic building blocks for individuals' ethical reasoning. Because individuals differ in terms of moral cognitions and moral frameworks, we can expect repeated confusion as to whether, say, utilitarian or formalist reasoning should determine what constitutes moral behavior.

Unclear Technologies

Ethical situations also reflect unclear technologies (decision processes) in that individuals often find the decision process itself to be ambiguous for at least two reasons. First, because many ethical dilemmas (and thus, ethical decisions) are by nature secretive, and little shared understanding exists in most organizations about how they are, or should be, addressed. Second, no single ethical decision model has emerged as the acknowledged "best" empirical or theoretical descriptor of the ethical decision-making process. (Consider the variety of decision models outlined above.) In fact, the frequency with which new models appear suggests that as researchers we are not confident that we have found *the* model that accurately describes the process.

Fluid Participation

We may view participation in ethical decisions as fluid on at least three dimensions: presence, individual characteristics, and opportunity. First, consider participants' presence at or near the ethical issue. Turnover, transfers, and promotions are a fact of life in most organizations. Members come and go and with them, their ability to participate in ethical debates. Second, not all participants who do remain in an organizational setting participate in all moral issues that might arise. Three components of Rest's (1986) four-component model suggest specific individual characteristics that may affect the decision to participate: moral sensitivity, motivation, and character.

Moral sensitivity. To participate, one must be sensitive to the existence of an ethical issue. We have seen that an individual's moral sensitivity may be affected by a host of social, economic, organizational, and individual effects (Ferrell et al., 1989; Hunt & Vitell, 1986; Jones, 1991), and individuals with increased awareness of ethical issues are more likely to notice ethical problems when they arise.

Moral motivation. To participate, an individual must also be motivated to act on the ethical issue. Moral motivation largely reflects moral intent. The TRA-based models described above suggest that moral intent flows from moral evaluations, organizational culture and opportunity, the ethics of significant others, and other individual-level factors (Ferrell et al., 1989; Hunt & Vitell, 1986; Jones, 1991). Moral motivation reflects the extent to which an individual places relatively greater importance on ethical values. Therefore, moral issues will be accorded greater weight and scarce resources of time and effort will more likely be channeled to ethical problems and solutions.

Moral character. To participate, an individual must possess the moral character to follow up on that motivation. A number of individual-level factors affect moral character including ego strength, perseverance, and strength of conviction (Rest, 1986), and these characteristics played a role in several of the ethical decision frameworks presented above (e.g., Bommer et al., 1987; Ferrell & Gresham, 1985; Treviño, 1986). In a sense, moral character provides the "glue" that holds together the necessary ingredients long enough for ethical decisions to be made and ethical actions to be taken.

Presence and personal inclination are not enough to guarantee participation. Additionally, an individual must be in an organizational position that provides the opportunity to participate in a moral issue. Although a clerk at the university bookstore might be opposed to some of the hiring policies of the university, he may not be in a position to affect the debate on the issue, though he may possess a surfeit of moral sensitivity, motivation, and character.

Thus, ethical dilemmas in organizational settings seem quite consistent with the Cohen et al. (1972) description of organized anarchies. That is, they reflect problematic preferences, unclear technologies, and fluid participation. Therefore, a garbage can approach may provide a sound basis for exploring how ethical decisions are made in organizations.

Garbage Can Ingredients

Recall that four ingredients—participants, problems, solutions, and choice opportunities—swirl in the garbage can, and that these ingredients sometimes exist in isolation and sometimes link with one or more other ingredients. However, for ethical organizational behavior to happen, all four must join together simultaneously. The question is what each of these represents in terms of ethical decision processes.

Participants. A participant in the ethical garbage can is simply a moral agent, which Jones (1991) identifies as an individual involved in a moral decision (regardless of whether he or she recognizes the issue as an ethical one). As we saw in the individual-based ethical models previously, these participants are complex ethical creatures who vary across a number of dimensions (cf. Hogan, 1973; Forsyth, 1980) including moral judgment, sensitivity, motivation, and character (Rest, 1986). Their participation is fluid, and is enhanced by moral sensitivity, motivation, and character. However, for ethical action to occur, one or more participants must connect with the other three ingredients.

Problems. A problem in the garbage can is a moral issue, which is "present when a person's actions, when freely performed, may harm or benefit others" (Jones 1991, p. 367). Recall from the issue-based ethical models described previously that these issues or problems are endowed with some degree of moral intensity (Jones, 1991). In the garbage can, greater levels of moral intensity increase the chances that these problems will be noticed and acted upon. The moral intensity of an issue is the red flag that attracts participants and solutions, and may lead to choice opportunities.

Solutions. Solutions to moral problems may abound in the garbage can due to the many (and potentially conflicting) ethical preferences of participants. However, they may also be created and poured into the mix without organizational awareness of any specific problem to be solved. For example, many organizations regularly provide ethics training for employees. In most cases these efforts are aimed not only at existing ethical violators, but are also cast more broadly at organizational participants, seeking to prevent ethical violations. They may be solutions without specific, identifiable problems.

Choice opportunities. Opportunities to address and even solve ethical issues may arise either by chance or by design in the garbage can. In either case, they evolve from the organizational setting, and thus are reflected in the situation- or context-based models described previously. That is, ethically "thoughtful" organizations may create more opportunities to solve ethical problems than might exist by chance alone. For example, ethics officers or ethics hotlines may create situations in which organizations face ethical issues and seek action. In a sense, these choice opportunities are the "flypaper" to which the other ingredients—participants, problems, and solutions—may stick long enough to assemble themselves into meaningful clusters that include a participant, facing an ethical problem, armed with potential solutions, and in a context that provides the opportunity to do something to address the ethical issue.

These four forces flow continually through organizations. Sometimes they exist independently, and sometimes two or three of them may join together. In these cases the "rational" ethical decision chain is not completed. That is, we may have opportunities with no willing participants. We may have problems for which there are no solutions. We may have participants with solutions for which no problems currently exist, or participants that do not have the opportunity to apply the solutions. However, once in a while, the four ingredients do connect and hang together long enough to solve meaningful ethical issues. Note that this condition does not necessarily happen in the rational, linear way many current ethical decision models suggest. Rather, the four may—and do—come together in odd, unpredictable, nonlinear ways. To an outside observer, it might appear as if a rational ethical decision process has happened. But in reality, the random action of the garbage can's swirling ingredients did its job in linking the four ingredients.

Implications

The implications of a garbage can model of ethical decision making are many. First, it integrates a number of diverse ethical models and frameworks. One criticism of the field of business ethics as it has recently evolved is that as we continue to explore issues—often from multiple perspectives—we do not do a very good job of integrating past, current, and emerging theory. This framework will accommodate a variety of managerial ethical issues like those in the previous chapters, and beyond.

Second, it may account for some of the instability we see in trying to map individuals' ethical behavior. If the milieu in the garbage can is full of a variety of actors and ethical frameworks, the model suggests that a particular actor does not necessarily always align himself or herself with one particular framework. In one situation, a gender-driven model might dominate while in another gender may play a minor role, while an outcome-based utilitarian framework may emerge as most applicable.

Third, it allows us to explore a host of sticky ethical questions. For example, why do we feel uncomfortable when teaching that some moral dilemmas simply seem to have no good solutions? The garbage can approach allows ethical dilemmas to exist in the absence of acceptable solutions. (Sometimes there are no good solutions, or even if there are, the correct actors have not been able to "link up" with them in the mix.) Another often-troubling topic is the question of why good companies do bad things. Because a garbage can approach allows us to divorce ethical intentions from ethical outcomes, we are able to explore issues like this more meaningfully by making clear that being involved in a situation that resulted in bad outcomes does not imply immoral actors or unethical intentions. These and other complex permutations of the various forces at work in the ethical decision process may be more easily—and accurately—framed using a garbage can approach.

Of course, not all decision contexts lend themselves to the garbage can approach. Not all organizational settings—even those involving ethics—align with the image of the organized anarchy envisioned by Cohen at al. (1972). Further, even in situations in which the Cohen et al. image fits, a garbage can process will not describe all issues within that context. Previous research bears this out. For example, when investigating the choice of reforms undertaken to resolve a political crisis involving management of the European Union, Levy (2006) suggested that the garbage can approach was used only in the initial "crisis" stage, after which other, more rational models were employed. Similarly, in researching the Environmental Protection Agency's decisions regarding hazardous waste site cleanup, Waguespack (2004) found evidence that the perceived importance of the problem determined the mode of decision making employed. Rational decision-making models were used when problems were of low or high importance, and the garbage can model was used under conditions of moderate importance. We believe the garbage can model is capable of providing significant insights with respect to the manner in which ethical dilemmas are confronted and solved in organizational settings. However, we also believe research exploring the boundary conditions under which the garbage can model applies represents an important area for future inquiry.

Before we close, a final note is in order. We have argued here that the ethical decision-making process is often not a rational one. However, that does not imply that organizational members should throw up their hands in surrender. To the contrary, although garbage can decision systems are nonlinear and nonrational, they may be, and in fact *must* be, managed like any other process. As in any recipe, the quality of the ingredients, the "flow rates" at which the ingredients enter the garbage can, the enthusiasm with which the ingredients are stirred, are all under the control of the chef, or in this case, the manager. Much of what we know about ethical decision making suggests managers play an important role in encouraging participation, raising ethical sensitivities, creating better quality moral solutions, and enhancing the chances that effective choice opportunities will arise. The particular order in which the ingredients link to one another may be random, but enhancing the quality and frequency of those links represents an important *management* issue.

References

Ajzen, I., & Fishbein, J. (1980). *Understanding attitudes and predicting social behavior.* Englewood Cliffs, NJ: Prentice Hall.

Ajzen, I. (1991). The theory of planned behavior. *Organizational Behavior and Human Decision Processes, 50,* 179–211.

Albaek, E. (1995). Between knowledge and power: Utilization of social science in public policy making. *Policy Sciences, 28,* 79–100.

Atkinson, M. M., & Powers, R. A. (1987). Inside the industrial policy garbage can: Selective subsidies to business in Canada. *Canadian Public Policy, 13,* 208–217.

Backer, L., & Clark, T. S. (2008). Eco-effective greening decisions and rationalizations: The case of Shell Renewables. *Organization & Environment, 21,* 227–244.

Bartunek, J. M., & Keys, C. B. (1979). Participation in school decision making. *Urban Education, 14,* 52–75.

Bazerman, M. H. (1986). *Judgment in managerial decision making.* New York: John Wiley & Sons.

Bitektine, A. (2009). What makes us faddish? Resource space constraints and the "garbage can" model of social science research. *Scandinavian Journal of Management, 25,* 217–220.

Brady, F. N. (1990). *Ethical managing.* New York: Macmillan.

Bommer, M., Gratto, C., Gravander, J., & Tuttle, M. (1987). A behavioral model of ethical and unethical decision making. *Journal of Business Ethics, 6,* 265–280.

Browning, L. D., Soernes, J. O., Stephens, K., & Saetre, A. S. (2006). A garbage can model of information/communication/technology choice. In A. Schorr & S. Seltmann (Eds.), *Changing media markets in Europe and abroad: New ways of handling information and entertainment content.* Lengerich: Pabst Science Publishers.

Chenhall, R. H. (2003). Management control systems design within its organizational context: Findings from contingency-based research and directions for the future. *Accounting, Organizations and Society, 28,* 127–168.

Cohen, M. D., March, J. G., & Olsen, J. P. (1972). A garbage can model of organizational choice. *Administrative Science Quarterly, 17,* 1–25.

Connelly, S., Helton-Fauth, W., & Mumford, M. D. (2004). A managerial in-basket study of the impact of trait emotions on ethical choice. *Journal of Business Ethics, 51,* 245– 267.

Damasio, A. (1994). *Descartes' error: Emotion, reason, and the human brain.* New York: Penguin Books.

Das, T. K., & Teng, B. S. (1999). Cognitive biases and strategic decision processes: An integrative perspective. *Journal of Management Studies, 36,* 757–778.

Davern, M. J., & Kauffman, R. J. (2000). Discovering potential and realizing value from information technology investments. *Journal of Management Information Systems, 16,* 121–143.

Decrop, A., & Snelders, D. (2005). A grounded typology of vacation decision-making. *Tourism Management, 26,* 121–132.

Dougherty, K. J., & Sostre, L. (1992). Minerva and the market: The sources of the movement for school choice. *Educational Policy, 6,* 160–179.

Dubinsky, A. J., & Loken, B. (1989). Analyzing ethical decision making in marketing. *Journal of Business Research, 19,* 83–107.

Dutton, J. E., Ashford, S. J., O'Neill, R. M., & Lawrence, K., A. (2001). Moves that matter: Issue selling and organizational change. *Academy of Management Journal, 44,* 716–736.

Eisenberg, N. (2000). Emotion, regulation, and moral development. *Annual Review of Psychology, 51,* 665–698.

Eisenhardt, K. M., & Zbaracki, M. J. (1992). Strategic decision making. *Strategic Management Journal, 13,* 17–37.

Etzioni, A. (1988). Normative-affective factors: Toward a new decision-making model. *Journal of Economic Psychology, 9,* 125–150.

Ferrell, O. C., & Gresham, L. G. (1985). A contingency framework for understanding ethical decision making in marketing. *Journal of Marketing, 49,* 87–96.

Ferrell, O. C., & Gresham, L. G., & Fraedrich, J. (1989). A synthesis of ethical decision models for marketing. *Journal of Macromarketing, 9,* 55–64.

Fishbein, J., & Ajzen, I. (1975). *Belief, attitude, intention, and behavior.* Reading, MA: Addison-Wesley.

Fletcher, J. (1966). *Situation ethics.* Philadelphia: Westminster Press.

Forsyth, D. R. (1980). A taxonomy of ethical ideologies. *Journal of Personality and Social Psychology, 39,* 175–184.

Friedman, M. (1957). *A theory of consumption function.* Princeton, NJ: Princeton University Press.

Gaudine, A., & Thorne, L. (2001). Emotion and ethical decision making in organizations. *Journal of Business Ethics, 31,* 175–188.

Gilligan, C. (1982). *In a different voice: Psychological theory and women's development.* Cambridge, MA: Harvard University Press.

Goitein, B. (1989). Organizational decision-making and energy conservation investments. *Evaluation and Program Planning, 12,* 143–151.

Greene, J. D., Sommerville, R. B., Nystrom, L. E., Darley, J. M., & Cohen, J. D. (2001). An fMRI investigation of emotional engagement in moral judgment. *Science, 293,* 2105–2109.

Haidt, J. (2001). The emotional dog and its rational tail: A social intuitionist approach to moral judgement. *Psychological Review, 108,* 814–834.

Hickson, D. J. (1987). Decision-making at the top of organizations. *Annual Review of Sociology, 13,* 165–192.

Hogan, R. (1973). Moral conduct and moral character: A psychological perspective. *Psychological Bulletin, 79,* 217–232.

Hume, D. (1740/1969). *A treatise of human nature.* London: Penguin. (Original work published 1739 & 1740.)

Hunt, S. D., & Vitell, S. (1986). A general theory of marketing ethics. *Journal of Macromarketing, 6,* 5–16.

Janis, I. L., & Mann, L. (1977). *Decision making: A psychological analysis of conflict choice and commitment.* New York: The Free Press.

Jones, T. M. (1991). Ethical decision making by individuals in organizations: An issue-contingent model. *Academy of Management Review, 16,* 366–395.

Kalu, K., N. (2005). Competing ideals and the public agenda in Medicare reform: The "garbage can" model revisited. *Administration and Society, 37,* 23–56.

Kant, I. (1789/1959). *Foundations of the metaphysics of morals* (L. W. Beck, Trans.). Indianapolis, IN: Bobbs-Merrill. (Original work published 1789.)

Keohane, R. (2002). Intergovernmental organizations and garbage can theory. *Journal of Public Administration Research and Theory, 12,* 155–159.

Kohlberg, L. (1981). *The philosophy of moral development.* San Francisco: Harper & Row.

Kurland, N. B. (1995). Ethical intentions and the theories of reasoned action and planned behavior. *Journal of Applied Social Psychology, 25,* 297–313.

Levitt, B., & Nass, C. (1989). The lid on the garbage can: Institutional constraints on decision making in the technical core of college text publishers. *Administrative Science Quarterly, 34,* 190–207.

Levy, R. P. (2006). European commission overload and the pathology of management reform: Garbage cans, rationality and risk aversion. *Public Administration, 84,* 423–439.

Lipson, M. (2007). A "garbage can model" of UN peacekeeping. *Global Governance, 13,* 79–97.

Mandell, M. B. (1989). A simulation-based assessment of the value of enhancing the credibility of policy analysis. *Knowledge in Society, 2,* 39–56.

March, J. G., & Simon, H. A. (1958). *Organizations.* New York: Wiley.

Masuch, M., & LaPotin, P. (1989). Beyond garbage cans: An AI model of organizational choice. *Administrative Science Quarterly, 34,* 38–67.

McDevitt, R., Giapponi, C., & Tromley, C. (2007). A model of ethical decision making: The integration of process and content. *Journal of Business Ethics, 73,* 219–229.

McGrath, G. M., & More, E. (2001). The Greta system: Organizational politics introduced to the garbage can. *Decision Support Systems, 31,* 181–195.

Mezias, S. J., & Scarselletta, M. (1994). Resolving financial reporting problems: An institutional analysis of the process. *Administrative Science Quarterly, 39,* 654–678.

Mingo, J. (1994). *How the Cadillac got its fins.* New York: Harper Business.

Mintzberg, H., Raisinghani, D., & Theoret, A. (1976). The structure of "unstructured" decision processes. *Administrative Science Quarterly, 21*, 246–275.

Moore, A. B., Clark, B. A., & Kane, M. J. (2008). Who shalt not kill? Individual differences in working memory capacity, executive control, and moral judgment. *Psychological Science, 19*, 549–557.

Morton, K. R., Worthley, J. S., Testerman, J. K., & Mahoney, M. L. (2006). Defining features of moral sensitivity and moral motivation: Pathways to moral reasoning in medical students. *Journal of Moral Education, 35*, 387–406.

Padgett, J. F. (1980). Managing garbage can hierarchies. *Administrative Science Quarterly, 25*, 583–604.

Piaget, J. (1932/1948). *The moral judgment of the child.* Glencoe, IL: Free Press.

Pizarro, D. (2000). Nothing more than feelings? The role of emotions in moral judgment. *Journal for the Theory of Social Behaviour, 30*, 355–376.

Rest, J. R. (1986). *Moral development: Advances in theory and research.* New York: Praeger.

Rest, J. R. (1994). Background: Theory and research. In J. R. Rest and D. Narvaez (Eds.), *Moral development in the professions: Psychology and applied ethics.* Hillsdale, NJ: Lawrence Erlbaum & Associates.

Reynolds, S. J. (2006). A neurocognitive model of the ethical decision-making process: Implications for study and practice. *Journal of Applied Psychology, 91*, 737–748.

Rozin, P., Lowery, L., Imada, S., & Haidt, J. (1999). The CAD triad hypothesis: A mapping between three moral emotions (contempt, anger, disgust) and three moral codes (community, autonomy, divinity). *Journal of Personality & Social Psychology, 76*, 574–586.

Sarasvathy, S. (2001). Causation and effectuation: Toward a theoretical shift from economic inevitability to entrepreneurial contingency. *Academy of Management Review, 26*, 243–263.

Schminke, M. (1998). The magic punchbowl: A nonrational model of ethical management. In M. S. Schminke (Ed.), *Managerial ethics: Moral management of people and processes* (pp. 197–214). Mahwah, NJ: Lawrence Erlbaum & Associates.

Sekerka, L. E., & Bagozzi, R. P. (2007). Moral courage in the workplace: Moving to and from the desire and decision to act. *Business Ethics: A European Review, 16*, 132–149.

Simon, H. A. (1957). *Models of man.* New York: Wiley.

Sonenshein, S. (2007). The role of construction, intuition, and justification in responding to ethical issues at work: The sense-making-intution model. *Academy of Management Review, 32*, 1022–1040.

Staw, B. M. (1981). The escalation of commitment to a course of action. *Academy of Management Review, 6*, 577–587.

Teasley, C. E., III, & Harrell, S. W. (1996). A real garbage can decision model: Measuring the costs of politics with a computer assisted decision support software (DSS) program. *Public Administration Quarterly, 19*, 479–492.

Tenbrunsel, A. E., (1998). Misrepresentation and expectations of misrepresentation in an ethical dilemma: The role of incentives and temptation. *Academy of Management Journal, 41*, 330–339.

Tenbrunsel, A. E., & Smith-Crowe, K. (2008). Ethical decision making: Where we've been and where we're going. *Academy of Management Annals, 2*, 545–607.

Tiernan, A., & Burke, T. (2002). A load of old garbage: Applying garbage-can theory to contemporary housing policy. *Australian Journal of Public Administration, 61*, 86–97.

Treviño, L. K. (1986). Ethical decision making in organizations: A person-situation interactionist model. *Academy of Management Review, 11*, 601–617.

Treviño, L. K., & Victor, B. (1992). Peer reporting of unethical behavior: A social context perspective. *Academy of Management Journal, 35*, 38–64.

Treviño, L. K., & Youngblood, S. A. (1990). Bad apples in bad barrels: A causal analysis of ethical decision-making behavior. *Journal of Applied Psychology, 75*, 378–385.

Tversky, A., & Kahneman, D. (1974). Judgment under uncertainty: Heuristics and biases. *Science, 185*, 1124–1131.

Vaughan, D. (1999). The dark side of organizations: Mistake, misconduct, and disaster. *Annual Review of Sociology, 25*, 271–305.

Waguespack, D. M. (2006). Reconciling garbage cans and rational actors: Explaining organizational decisions about environmental hazard management. *Social Science Research, 35*, 40–59.

Weber, J. (1990). Managers' moral reasoning: Assessing their responses to three moral dilemmas. *Human Relations, 43*, 687–702.

Author Index

Subject Index